BUT SHE'S FAMILY

"Susie has done this,"  vid spoke when he heard ders. And when he con had to be involved, his silence:

"Don't say that. You don't know that. . . . She's family."

Susie was on the minds of others that night. For, later when the Newsoms heard about the killings, they telephoned Susie, offering to have someone come over and stay with her. Susie declined, breaking off the conversation by saying, "Well, my dog has run off. I've got to go find him. I'll talk to you later."

A strange reaction to the revelation that her parents and beloved grandmother had been murdered. . . .

"I haven't been gripped so relentlessly by another story in years." —Reynolds Price

"Riveting . . . a first-rate piece of writing!" —Lewis Grizzard, syndicated columnist

JERRY BLEDSOE is a senior writer and columnist at the *Greensboro News & Record*, where his series on the Lynch-Newsom murders first appeared. He is the author of six books, and adds the National Headliner Award to the growing list of professional prizes that have marked his career.

JERRY BLEDSOE

BITTER BLOOD

A True Story of Southern Family
Pride, Madness, and
Multiple Murder

AN ONYX BOOK

ONYX
Published by New American Library, a division of
Penguin Group (USA) Inc., 375 Hudson Street,
New York, New York 10014, USA
Penguin Group (Canada), 90 Eglinton Avenue East, Suite 700, Toronto,
Ontario M4P 2Y3, Canada (a division of Pearson Penguin Canada Inc.)
Penguin Books Ltd., 80 Strand, London WC2R 0RL, England
Penguin Ireland, 25 St. Stephen's Green, Dublin 2,
Ireland (a division of Penguin Books Ltd.)
Penguin Group (Australia), 250 Camberwell Road, Camberwell, Victoria 3124,
Australia (a division of Pearson Australia Group Pty. Ltd.)
Penguin Books India Pvt. Ltd., 11 Community Centre, Panchsheel Park,
New Delhi - 110 017, India
Penguin Group (NZ), 67 Apollo Drive, Rosedale, North Shore 0632,
New Zealand (a division of Pearson New Zealand Ltd.)
Penguin Books (South Africa) (Pty.) Ltd., 24 Sturdee Avenue,
Rosebank, Johannesburg 2196, South Africa

Penguin Books Ltd., Registered Offices:
80 Strand, London WC2R 0RL, England

Published by Onyx, an imprint of New American Library, a division of Penguin
Group (USA) Inc. Previously published in a Dutton edition.

First Onyx Printing, April 1989
40   39

Copyright © Jerry Bledsoe, 1998
All rights reserved

 REGISTERED TRADEMARK—MARCA REGISTRADA

Printed in the United States of America

for Linda,
who loved me and endured,
and for
Erik, who kept the
computer functioning

ACKNOWLEDGMENTS

This book evolved from a series of articles that appeared in the *Greensboro News & Record* in August 1985. Cole Campbell and Van King conceived that series and assigned me to report and write it and I am indebted to them. Campbell is due additional credit for editing it so ably. Ben Bowers and Ned Cline allowed that series to be published at extraordinary length and I admire them for it. I also thank the *News & Record*, a newspaper that I love, for allowing me to use material from the series in this book and for granting me time to work on it.

Special thanks are due Annie Henry, who had faith in this book, and me, from the beginning. Joyce Engelson, my editor, has my lasting gratitude. All of her suggestions were sound. My copy editor, Ravin Korothy, should receive a medal for catching my multitude of mistakes.

I long ago lost track of the number of people—in the hundreds—who gave me their time and supplied me with helpful information, but I am grateful to all. I am most grateful to those who opened their lives to me so that this book could be written. Their names will be obvious in the text. I have changed a few names to protect privacy, but the names of all the major characters in this tragic story are their own.

For friendship and encouragement in time of need, I offer thanks to Sarah Avery, David Boul, Hubert Breeze, Mutt Burton, Penny Craver, Pat Gubbins, Nick Hancock, Karl Hill, Dot Jackson, Jim Jenkins, Maria Johnson, Bill and Harriet Lee, Phil Link, Sara Looman, Susan Luce, Mark McDonald, June Milby, Don Patterson, Buck Paysour, Chip Rabon, Jim Schlosser, Kay and Stan Swofford, Nat Walker, Terri Wackelin, and Ernie Wyatt.

I can never repay Bernard Dekle, who first told me that I could write, then tried to teach me how; Tom Wingate, who first gave me a chance to report and write; Irwin Smallwood, who had faith in me when few others did, and whose support has continued, unflagging, into a third decade; and Greta Tilley, who prodded, pushed and cheered me throughout these long months of work. I love you all.

CONTENTS

"And I stood upon the sand of the sea, and saw a beast rise up out of the sea, having seven heads and ten horns and upon his horns ten crowns, and upon his heads the name of blasphemy."

—REVELATION 13:1

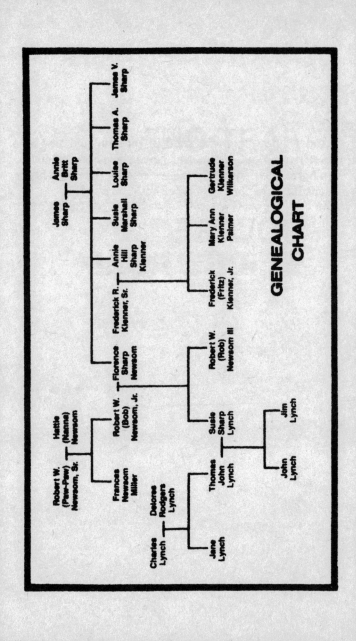

GENEALOGICAL CHART

PART ONE

THE HOUSE ON COVERED BRIDGE ROAD

1

Delores was late. That was unlike her, and Marjorie Chinnock was concerned.

Marjorie and Delores Lynch met every Sunday morning in the parking lot of Grace Episcopal, a small granite church in south Louisville. Usually, Marjorie arrived first and waited for Delores's car to come down the long drive to the back of the church. Delores would park beside her and they would go inside, where Delores always went to the rest room before they entered the sanctuary. After the thirty-minute service, they would join other church members in the parish hall for coffee, a time Delores particularly enjoyed. Unlike Marjorie, Delores was gregarious and often made herself the center of attention at these gatherings. Afterward, she and Marjorie would walk to their cars and chat until Delores said, "Well, I must go. Janie will have our doughnuts."

Delores lived in a country house seventeen miles from the church, and during the three years she and Marjorie had been attending church together, her daughter, Janie, had been a student at the University of Louisville's School of Dentistry, training for her third career. Janie had a student apartment at the downtown campus, but she often spent weekends at home. On those days, while her mother was at church, she would drive to Ehrler's Dairy Store in Prospect and buy yeast doughnuts, only two, and have them ready with coffee when her mother got home. When Janie wasn't home weekends, she often drove out to spend Sunday mornings with her mother, stopping for the doughnuts on the way. Later, Delores and Janie would drive back to Louisville to the House of Hunan for the Sunday lunch special.

For Delores, the day provided a satisfying weekly ritual.

She craved ritual. Indeed, it was the reason she belonged to Grace Episcopal. When the Episcopal church adopted a new prayer book, Grace defied the diocese and refused to accept it, clinging to the more ritualistic liturgy of the 1928 prayer book, a defiance that eventually would cause Grace Episcopal to disaffiliate itself from the diocese. Grace was the first church Delores attended regularly after moving to Louisville in 1967, but she left it in 1969 because she didn't like the priest. He looked "greasy," she complained, and she felt dirty after shaking his hand. That was something that Delores, with her obsession for cleanliness, couldn't abide.

She attended several churches before settling at St. James Episcopal in Pewee Valley, a tiny town northeast of Louisville, much closer to her home. But eventually she would leave that church also—in bitterness. Made a rebel by her conservatism, she had returned to Grace five years earlier, in 1979, because of the maverick stand the church took on the prayer book issue. The "greasy" priest had departed, and she now felt comfortable at Grace.

Marjorie Chinnock met Delores in 1967, when she originally came to Grace. At first, Marjorie didn't understand why Delores sought her friendship. Marjorie was reserved, almost withdrawn. And she was far from being on the same financial footing as Delores, the wife of a top General Electric executive. Delores lived then on stock dividends and a monthly allowance from her husband in an expensive home on the grounds of a prestigious country club. Marjorie, a divorced mother of grown children, lived in a modest apartment in an older section of Louisville and worked at a Kroger supermarket.

This is strange, Marjorie told herself at the beginning of the relationship. Why does she seek me out? I'm a working person. She belongs in a high echelon. Doesn't she know who she is?

But after careful consideration, she began to think: Maybe I'm the snob, and accepted Delores's friendship without question. After Delores left Grace Episcopal, the two friends gradually drifted apart, and Marjorie had been surprised three years earlier to get a call from Delores. Disenchanted, Marjorie had left the church altogether in 1970, and Delores had never questioned why until she called that Sunday afternoon.

"You were always such a devout Episcopalian," Delores said. "Why don't you come back? Meet me in the parking lot next Sunday."

Marjorie did, and their Sunday mornings became ritual.

But on this morning, the fourth Sunday of July 1984, Delores was late. Marjorie kept looking impatiently at her watch as time for the 8 A.M. service neared. Finally, she decided she could wait no longer. She would not be late. She went inside, and just as the service was about to begin, Delores slid into the pew beside her, smiling apologies.

After the service, conducted by a visiting priest from Cincinnati because the regular priest was on vacation, Delores explained that she just had been running behind. She was her usual self at coffee, flitting about, joking and laughing and talking loudly—the usual Sunday morning chitchat that nobody would recall later. Marjorie noticed that Delores's two-piece dress, a wispy thin print of tiny blue and red flowers, didn't match. The top was faded, as if it had been washed more than the bottom. That was nothing unusual, Marjorie knew, for despite her obvious wealth, Delores bought all of her clothes at discount houses and bargain shops and wore them long past their fashionable usefulness.

As always, Delores and Marjorie walked to their cars together and stood between them to chat. Delores was excited about the impending visit of her son, Tom—TJ, she called him—of whom she frequently boasted. He was due to arrive Friday from Albuquerque with his new wife, Kathy, and two sons from a previous marriage, grandchildren Delores rarely got to see. Three days earlier, Janie, fresh from taking her final tests to practice dentistry in Kentucky, had moved her belongings from her university apartment back into the house. The house was a mess, Delores said, and there was much to be done before Tom arrived.

Delores complained constantly about the demands her

house made on her—especially since she'd given up her once-a-week maid—but until recently Marjorie had had no idea of the scope of those demands because she'd never been to the house. But two weeks earlier, as she and Delores were leaving church, Delores had said, "Why don't you come and have breakfast with me at the house?"

Marjorie was delighted to accept, and Delores went back into the church to call Janie and tell her to forget the doughnuts. They rode in the seven-year-old gray Volkswagen Dasher that had belonged to Delores's husband. As they pulled into the long driveway to the house, Marjorie took one look and said, "Delores, what's the name of this hotel?"

The house did bear some resemblance to a Ramada Inn. Set on four and a half acres of wooded hillside, it was a sprawling ranch house of pink brick with white shutters and wrought iron grillwork, two stories, fourteen rooms, four and a half baths—and Delores had been its sole occupant since the death of her husband, Chuck, eight months earlier.

Delores laughed. "I ride the mower four days a week," she said.

Two Sunday mornings later, as Delores stood complaining about the size of the house and her fear of being in it alone, Marjorie said, "Delores, why don't you just get rid of it? You're a prisoner of that house." She knew that Delores had wired her home with elaborate alarms, had outfitted it with strong locks, and was scared to the point of paranoia about somebody breaking in on her.

"No, it's not that house that makes me a prisoner," Delores said. "It's criminals that make me a prisoner."

Later, Marjorie recalled that it must have been about 10 A.M. when Delores uttered her routine line about Janie and the doughnuts and departed with a wave. The next time Marjorie saw her friend, Delores would be on the TV news and Marjorie would recognize her only by the mismatched dress she had worn to church that Sunday.

About 10:30 that morning, Delores pulled up to the gas pumps at the Prospect Chevron station on U.S. 42, only a few miles from her house. She stopped regularly at the station, had minor work done on her cars there, and the station's young employees all knew and liked her.

Delores was sixty-eight, but she acted much younger than her years. A tiny, trim woman whose short hair still showed as much brown as gray, she was lively and entertaining, always talking and joking with the young men at the station, even occasionally offering advice about personal problems. Butch Rice, the station's twenty-two-year-old assistant manager, a thin man with a mustache, always looked forward to Delores's visits—"She was like a mother to me," he said—and he hurried out to wait on her.

Delores got out of the car as usual and commented about what a pleasant day it was now that clouds had moved in and the scorching heat of previous days had dissipated. The weatherman had said the temperature would climb only to 80 this day, and with little sun it would be a good day for working outside. Delores wanted Butch to put some gas for her riding mower into a red can in the back of the car. She gave him the keys and went inside to say hello to the other guys working that morning. She paid with her Chevron credit card, and as she started to pull away, Butch leaned down and said, "Have a nice day, Mrs. Lynch."

She smiled. "You too."

Delores drove south from the station to the intersection of State Road 329, known locally as Covered Bridge Road but not marked so by signs. It is a picturesque country lane: narrow, curvy, hilly, with no shoulders. From its first mile at U.S. 42, trees, many of them huge sycamores, grow fast by the pavement, their branches overhanging the road from both sides, giving it a tunnel effect, cool and soothing on a hot summer day. Soon after the road passes out of Jefferson County with its urban sprawl into rustic Oldham County, it opens onto big horse and cattle farms, the rolling green hills patterned by dark wooden fences. It passes an expensive new subdivision before dipping around a sharp curve and crossing Harrod's Creek, where once stood the covered bridge that gave the road its name. The bridge was replaced long ago by a dangerous, one-lane bridge with an overhead framework. (Called the Old Iron Bridge, it, too, was about to be relieved by a wide, modern concrete bridge then under construction.)

Just beyond the bridge is the entrance to the Boy Scout camp where a week earlier Delores's 1977 Oldsmobile had broken down, leading to an angry dispute with the camp's caretaker that had left her ranting and threatening to call the police and sue for damages. (The caretaker had used a tractor to push the abandoned car a few feet to keep it from blocking the camp entrance.)

From the creek, the road continues alongside a small, lazy stream that meanders to the creek, passing over several miniature waterfalls as it goes. The creek winds through Delores's front yard, and she followed it the last mile home, stopping at the top of the driveway to fetch the fat Sunday edition of the *Courier-Journal* from her roadside box.

The asphalt driveway went downhill, across the small stream over a wooden bridge, then uphill to the house, where it formed a loop at the front entrance with its iron-barred double doors. A branch of the drive continued up the hill to a wide parking area adjoining the house. The first level of the house on that end was a two-car garage, which never housed cars. Delores kept its concrete floor waxed and used it only for storage—everything neatly boxed, labeled, and stacked, although it was in some disorder then from Janie's belongings, which the movers had deposited there three days earlier. Between the double, roll-up garage doors was a white wooden door that Delores and family members used as the main entrance to the house. Anybody inserting a key into that door had twenty seconds to walk across the garage and flick a switch to keep the alarm from sounding.

Delores pulled the Volkswagen between her recently repaired green Oldsmobile Cutlass and Janie's 1970 gold Chevrolet Nova. She got out carrying her beige purse, a yellow-bound Bible, the Sunday paper, the gas receipt, the white sweater she'd carried against the morning coolness, and her keys on two rings held together by a safety pin. She was about to insert one of those keys into the center garage door when a shot rang out, splattering the door with her blood. The shot was followed quickly by another, and a few seconds later by a third.

2

When Delores Lynch moved into the big house on Covered Bridge Road late in 1970, she vowed that this was the last move she would make. She was fifty-four, her children were grown, and every time she had begun to establish roots, she had been yanked up and moved. She resented it. Needing order and stability, she felt haunted by change.

Not since her early childhood in Pittsburgh's east end had she had security of place. Her father, John Rodgers, a machinist at Union Switch and Signal Company, had died in 1932 when Delores was fifteen, leaving his wife, Lilie, and two teenage children to fend for themselves in the depths of the Depression. Delores's brother, Elmer, three years older, took upon himself the responsibility of seeing that the family had a roof over their heads and food on the table—and that his younger sister would be able to stay in Westinghouse High School and eventually achieve her dream of becoming a nurse. But work was scarce, pay short, and as the family's situation steadily deteriorated, they were forced to move several times. The hardships of those years would have a lifelong effect on Delores, who decades later still proclaimed that nobody ever lived poorer than she. "I know the value of a dollar," she enjoyed telling people. "I lived through the Depression."

Delores didn't get along with her mother and seldom talked about her childhood in later years. If anybody asked about it, even her children, she changed the subject. When her mother died in 1974, she mentioned it to none of her friends.

Near the Depression's end, Delores's brother became a Sealtest milk routeman, a job he would keep until his retirement, and he was able to help his sister complete her nursing training at Pittsburgh's Mercy Hospital. Soon after she started to work as a nurse at the hospital, a friend invited her on a blind date, and she met the man she would marry.

Charles R. Lynch, Jr., grew up in the steel mill town of Vandergrift, thirty miles northeast of Pittsburgh. His father was a chemist in the mill laboratory. The second of seven children, Chuck, as he was to be called throughout his life, grew up loving sports. Although he was a wiry five-foot-three, his pugnacious nature allowed him to claim a spot as a starting guard on the basketball team at Vandergrift High and to become a bantamweight Golden Gloves boxer. But it was in academics that he really excelled, and he was rewarded with a scholarship at the University of Pittsburgh, where he became a business major.

After his graduation, Chuck went to work as an accountant at the General Electric plant in Pittsburgh, but the coming of World War II prompted quick decisions. He enlisted in the navy and asked Delores to marry him. The wedding took place on January 11, 1942, at his family's Evangelical and Reformed Church in Vandergrift. Chuck spent most of the next three years at sea guarding Atlantic convoys and rising to the rank of chief petty officer, while Delores lived near his home port in New Jersey, working as a nurse until the birth of her first child, Jane Alda, on October 28, 1944. At the war's end, Chuck returned to his new family and his old job at GE.

Before his son, Thomas John, was born on August 16, 1947, Chuck was already a young man on the rise at GE. After taking the company's business training course, he was assigned to GE's staff of traveling auditors at the huge plant in Schenectady, New York, where Thomas Edison had started the company in 1886. This was a plum assignment for promising would-be executives, and Chuck was proud to get it. The traveling auditors were dispatched to GE plants all over the world and often were away from home for months at a time. Delores resented being left alone with two small children and grew bitter about it.

Ater three years as an auditor, Chuck got a quick succession of assignments in New York and New Jersey. He moved his family four times in three years, living for the longest stretch—two years—in Livingston, New Jersey, before he got his first management job at a GE distribution center in Washington, D.C. The family settled in Springfield, Maryland, for the next three years. The constant moving didn't bother Chuck. It was a price he expected to pay for his ambition. He was the quintessential company man, willing to give whatever the company asked. "He lived for GE," a friend said of him after his death. "GE was his life."

Chuck's dedication paid off with a promotion and a transfer to Chicago, where he was to become distribution manager for GE's Hotpoint appliance division. The family settled into a comfortable, two-story older house with a lawn and trees on Hoyne Drive in south Chicago, and Chuck, a golfer, joined the nearby prestigious Midlothian Country Club. Janie and Tom had attended private schools in Washington, and in Chicago both were enrolled at Morgan Park Academy, only a few blocks from their home. Here the family was to achieve its longest period of stability, nearly six years.

Chuck's work, as usual, was consuming. He was one of a handful of executives who made the Hotpoint division highly profitable, and he was handsomely rewarded with bonuses and stock options. With her husband devoted to his job, her daughter away at college and her son in high school, Delores decided to return to work. For three years she was a nurse at her son's school. "When she was school nurse, all of the kids, the troubled kids, would go over and talk to her," Tom later recalled, "and she was very much in tune with everything."

Delores quit work after Tom's graduation, and while going off to college in North Carolina, she and Chuck were moving into a new waterfront home they had built at 259 Lake Shore Drive in Barrington, an upper-crust bedroom community northwest of Chicago. But they hadn't even finished the landscaping before GE merged its appliance divisions, and, much to Delores's chagrin, Chuck was transferred once again, this time to Louisville and the world's largest appliance factory.

GE's sprawling Appliance Park covers one thousand acres in Buechel on Louisville's southern edge and is Kentucky's largest employer. It produces all of GE's major appliances—washers, ranges, refrigerators, air conditioners—and at its peak in 1973, it employed 22,000 people, a figure that was to drop drastically in the early eighties. Chuck became one of the plant's top executives. As manager of product distribution, he oversaw warehousing and shipping and was responsible for getting every appliance to its eventual destination. Several thousand employees answered to him.

The Lynches bought a two-story gray Cape Cod house near the tenth hole of the golf course at Hunting Creek, an exclusive country club in the green hills of the Ohio River bluff north of Louisville, off U.S. 42, but Delores could find no happiness in that plush and tranquil setting. She liked Chicago—with the exception of its blustery winters—had friends there, and didn't want to leave. She was disgruntled with the very idea of being in Louisville. While Chuck was engrossed in his new job, Delores was fighting with her new neighbors. She resented intrusions onto her property and confronted golfers who came into her yard to retrieve stray balls. She had a dense line of pines planted across her back property line to shield the yard from the golf course.

Although she mothered some neighborhood children, she often bickered with others who wandered into her yard. She had a particular animosity for the six Dougherty children who lived across the street. She hated their Great Dane, Rebel, and threatened to shoot him if he came into her yard. She toted a BB rifle when she went to the streetside mailbox, claiming she needed it for protection from the dog. One day she shot Rebel at close range, sending him home yelping with a tiny hole in his haunch. After one of the Dougherty children confronted her about it, Delores called the child's church school and reported her for impudence.

Carolyn Kraft, who lived next door to Delores, was friendly with her at first. Delores called her "good buddy" and frequently popped in or telephoned. But Carolyn found her strange and her problems with the neighbors self-created and unnecessary.

"Everything irritated her," she recalled years later from her retirement home in Florida. "The world is full of people like that. They look for problems. One day I told her, 'Delores, you should live on an island. You should live where no other people are around, because other people aren't always going to do what you want.' She said, 'I would if I could find one.' "

By 1969, after a dispute with the Krafts about drainage from their swimming pool, during which Delores hid in bushes and snapped pictures of her neighbors, she had found her refuge—four and a half acres on Covered Bridge Road, about five miles from Hunting Creek. There, far back from the road, she started building the dream house in which she vowed to live out her days. The land wasn't exactly an island, but it was isolated, set among the trees on the hillside, and the nearest neighbors, the Cables, were out of sight.

When Delores finally moved into her new house, her neighbors at Hunting Creek breathed a collective sigh of relief and remarked how happy they were that she and her strident paranoia were gone. Delores was just as happy to leave. The people at Hunting Creek, she told her friend Marjorie Chinnock—her only friend in Louisville at the time—were just a bunch of snobs.

Delores had no sense for decorating, and her new house was an incongruous mingling of elegance and gaudiness—expensive Persian carpets were offset by sturdy and plebian furniture that sometimes had been picked up at auction sales or on other bargain hunts; sterling silver serving sets clashed with art from cheap department stores. Delores admired the beautiful and tastefully decorated white-columned brick home of her neighbors, Howard and Katy Cable, and often remarked to Katy how much she wished her own house could look the same. Later she sometimes brought friends to see the Cables' house.

Whatever talent Delores lacked in decorating was more than made up for by her obsession for cleanliness and order. She spent hours every day cleaning, dusting, polishing, spraying with deodorants and disinfectants. The house was immaculate, and Delores's determination to keep it so often made visitors uncomfortable. She kept shoe racks by entrances and expected guests to deposit their footwear so they would not scuff her highly polished hardwood floors. Overnight guests would laughingly tell, with only slight exaggeration, of drying every drop of water from the shower stall after bathing, searching bed linens for lost hairs, and scouring lavatories for stray drops of toothpaste so they wouldn't risk upsetting Delores.

She kept her yard as immaculate as her house, and during warm weather, neighbors frequently saw her wearing bib overalls and riding her big red lawn mower. Fallen tree limbs barely hit the ground before they were burning in a big barrel. Leaves were raked several times each fall. Every dropping left by her tiny dogs in the fenced backyard was picked up in tissue paper and disposed of properly.

After settling in her new house, Delores began building a new life for herself. Her children were again nearby. Janie had received a degree in education from Bradley University in Peoria, Illinois, and moved to Kentucky, where she first taught in Scott County schools, then in Fayette County schools, before enrolling as a graduate student in special education at the University of Kentucky in Lexington, only seventy-five miles away. Tom had been graduated from Wake Forest University in Winston-Salem, North Carolina, and newly married, had enrolled at the University of Kentucky School of Dentistry. Delores kept close contact with both.

By 1975, however, Janie had moved away to California, and Tom had finished dental school, joined the navy, and was beginning his practice repairing the teeth of Marine Corps recruits at Parris Island, South Carolina. Delores began looking for new interests—and a new church.

After leaving Grace Episcopal Church in 1969, Delores joined St. James Episcopal Church in the picturesque village of Pewee Valley, only about ten miles east of her home. St. James was a beautiful church, built of granite, set on a broad lawn shaded with spreading maples and festooned each spring with dogwood and azalea blossoms. Delores loved the priest there, Father R. C. Board, a traditionalist, and became very active in the church, even serving as a member of the vestry. She disdained the new priest who came after Father Board retired in 1975, led a faction of the congregation that sought to oust him, and eventually left the church in anger because of the bitterness that ensued. For several years, she had no church and often traveled many miles to attend services where Father Board was filling in for absent priests. After trying several churches, she finally returned to Grace.

Delores began spending a lot of time in Pewee Valley when she joined the church there. The town, once a thriving grape-growing area and early resort for wealthy people from Louisville, was the place where Annie Fellows Johnston, a local resident, wrote early in the century a series of popular books about a little girl who befriended an old plantation colonel. In 1934, *The Little Colonel* stories were made into a movie starring Shirley Temple, providing the later inspiration for an amateur theater group in Pewee Valley.

The Little Colonel Players, one of Kentucky's oldest community theater groups, presented four plays each year, plus a special summer production featuring only high school and college students. The group had converted an old grocery store next to the town hall into the Little Colonel Playhouse, with a tiny stage and seating for ninety on folding metal chairs.

Delores began attending Little Colonel productions, then joined the group and tried out for a part. Her first appearance was in "My Three Angels" in December 1975, and she was widely congratulated for her skill. She had a knack for acting, the others told her, and she thrived on the attention. She became one of the company's most enthusiastic members. In coming years, she would appear in eight more productions, always playing "little old lady parts," as she laughingly called them. She liked the other members of the company, formed several friendships within the group, and particularly enjoyed the regular covered-dish social gatherings, where her Strawberry Delight dessert was always praised—and always the first to disappear.

Delores usually came to theater functions alone. Only a couple of times did Chuck ever come, and then he seemed uncomfortable. Louise Mahin, who, with her husband, Frank, was a founder of the theater, became friends with Delores and directed her in four plays. She thought Delores bright, curious, outgoing, funny, an excellent actress, "a sweet kid." She did not like Chuck. On the few occasions she had been around him, she found him rude, belligerent, demanding, all words that could have come straight from Delores's mouth. Delores filled her ears with complaints about Chuck, and Louise offered solace.

The entire theater company was aware that Delores was unhappy at home. She broadcast her discontent to anybody who would listen. One night at a party at the theater, Delores was complaining about her husband to a group in the kitchen.

"I wish he'd die," she said.

Her friend Eddie Logsdon, who knew Chuck and liked him, stepped into the awkward silence that followed.

"Now, Delores, you don't mean that," he said.

"Oh, yes, I do too," she replied.

Nobody knew the truth of that better than Delores's maid, Helen Stewart, who started working for her shortly before she moved into her new house on Covered Bridge Road and had become a close friend. Hundreds of times she had heard Delores declare her wish for Chuck's death. "He never walked out the door that she didn't wish him dead," Helen recalled.

The animosity between Delores and Chuck was of long standing. Neighbors at Hunting Creek knew that they lived separately—Chuck in the basement, Delores upstairs—an arrangement that continued in the house on Covered Bridge Road. The main living area of the house, the upper floor, was ruled by Delores, and Chuck was allowed to venture there only when Tom visited. The rest of the time he was remanded to the downstairs den, where he holed up with his business awards, his son's athletic trophies, and the color TV on which he watched sporting events alone. Delores still cooked his meals, sometimes delivering them to the den, other times leaving them on the staircase in the foyer for him to retrieve. Two copies of the *Courier-Journal* came to the house because Delores refused to touch a newspaper that her husband had handled.

Chuck wasn't secretive about his situation. "She lives upstairs in the farthest corner and I live downstairs in the farthest corner and we communicate by CB radio," he joked to fellow jurors once when he found himself on jury duty.

Although he rarely talked about his private life at work, his colleagues were aware of the conflict at home. They knew that when Chuck came to GE social affairs he usually came alone and that the few times Delores had come with him she had done her best to embarrass him with outspoken opinions and put-downs. Delores's friends knew in no uncertain terms how she felt about GE people: she detested them and wanted nothing to do with them.

At work, Chuck was an authoritative figure, widely respected and promptly obeyed. But at home he shrank before Delores's unrelenting scorn and rarely stood up to her. He had learned that there was no winning against Delores, and he retreated to the comforts available in alcohol.

"A worthless drunk," Delores called him.

Whatever drinking Chuck did, it never affected his performance at work, where he was greatly admired. But the pressures of his job were great, and combined with the conflict at home, they had taken a toll. In Chicago in 1965 Chuck had suffered a heart attack that kept him out of work for several months, and more recently he had been treated for ulcers. His boss of many years had retired, and a friend with whom he'd risen through the GE ranks was about to step down as well. Sales had slumped drastically, and automation was bringing great change. GE was about to lop 6,500 workers from its payroll at Appliance Park, some with as much as fourteen years seniority. Tired and feeling less than well, Chuck didn't think he could muster the energy to deal with the coming new problems, and, in 1980, at sixty-three, he announced his retirement.

Delores was livid about his decision. She told friends that he was retiring only to keep her from doing what she wanted to do. "He just wants to cramp my style," she insisted. She had been taking courses in music at Bellarmine College, a Catholic school in south Louisville, as well as studying piano. She often banged away on her piano, sometimes taping her efforts, but when Chuck retired, she stopped her lessons in protest, draped the piano in black muslin, and topped it with white lilies to symbolize her martyrdom and the murder of her musical dreams.

Chuck discovered that the pressures of retirement weren't so easy for him to deal with, either. He tried doing things around the house, but nothing that he did pleased Delores. He couldn't even mow the grass to suit her, he complained to friends. Delores didn't want him at home expecting meals at certain hours, creating messes in his downstairs quarters, and fouling the air with smoke from the Pall Malls on which he puffed addictively.

Of all the things that irritated Delores about her husband, his smoking might have bothered her most. She once had smoked heavily herself, so much so, she joked, that she couldn't even shower without a cigarette. But after she quit, she became a fanatical antismoker. She reprimanded people who smoked near her in restaurants, elevators, and supermarket lines. She posted a big NO SMOKING sign beside the door leading from the garage into the house and had smaller signs in the house and in her car. Helen Stewart, the maid, had to go into the backyard to smoke. But no amount of harping could stop Delores's husband from smoking in the house. She even tried physically wresting cigarettes from him when he brought them home from the store, but he always smuggled in more. Delores refused to deal with the butts and ashes that he scattered throughout his quarters, leaving them for Helen to clean up.

GE had been too big a part of Chuck's life for too long, and he was lost without the company. Retirement, he realized, was not for him, and he sought escape in volunteer work. He served on a mayor's committee in Louisville, reorganized the transportation system of the Red Cross, advised small business operators at the Chamber of Commerce. He left home almost every morning and didn't return until evening, just as he had done when working.

Delores became convinced that he was having an affair. Moist Pearl, she derisively called the woman, without the slightest proof that she even existed.

Janie had returned home from California to attend dental school by the time Chuck retired, and Delores enlisted her as an ally in her battles with Chuck. Delores did not use only Janie to try to catch Chuck in his affair, she even called on friends and one of Janie's old boyfriends for assistance.

This former boyfriend, John Trent, a lawyer in Lexington, wasn't surprised when Delores tried to get him to assist in her scheming, but he wanted nothing to do with it. He only hoped her suspicions were true. He liked Chuck and well knew the humiliations and turmoil he'd suffered because of Delores. Trent had once spent Christmas at the house on Covered Bridge Road, and on Christmas Eve, when Janie and her mother went to church, he had stayed home with Chuck.

Chuck began to talk about Delores, almost as if in apology, as though he needed to try to explain why she was the way she was. "She's a good woman," he kept saying. He accepted much of the responsibility for her actions. The demands of his job, his inattention, the many moves had affected her, he said. What seemed clear to Trent was that he loved her and forgave her the abuses he endured. "He seemed like a moral guy," Trent recalled. "I think he considered this was his payback for the suffering he had inflicted on Delores."

Joyce Rose was one friend Delores asked to help trap Chuck in his supposed dalliances. Joyce and her husband, Paul, open and friendly country people, felt close to both Delores and Chuck. Paul first met the Lynches when he was running a garage and they began bringing in their cars and lawn mowers to be repaired. Paul particularly liked Chuck, who he considered to be a man of great character and breadth, and enjoyed talking with him about business and sports. Paul knew that Chuck was a man of integrity the day he brought a car to him that he was about to sell. A part was wearing but not yet defective. Paul told him that it would be a while before the part produced a problem, and since he was going to sell the car, he could get by without replacing it. Chuck told him to replace it. He didn't think it right to sell the car knowing that a problem would soon surface.

Delores and Joyce became close friends. In the summertime, the Roses often drove to the house on Covered Bridge Road carrying dishpans filled with fresh vegetables from their big garden. Delores popped in frequently at the Roses' old oak-shaded white house in Pewee Valley to sit at Joyce's kitchen table, drinking coffee and talking. "You've got the warmest kitchen in the county," Delores said.

Joyce shied from Delores's efforts to recruit her into exposing Chuck's supposed affair. But one day Delores called and said she'd discovered that Chuck was taking his paramour to the Sleepy Hollow Golf Club not far from the Lynch house, and Joyce drove to the club and questioned the manager to satisfy her curiosity.

"That poor man comes out here and sits for hours just looking at the golf course," she remembered the manager telling her. He figured that Chuck was either lonely or disturbed and didn't bother him. Joyce decided that Chuck was deeply depressed. She felt sorry for him and ashamed for spying on him.

Delores's friends didn't understand why she didn't just divorce Chuck and let him have somebody else if she thought that was what he wanted, but she made it known that she wasn't about to meekly walk away and let somebody else waltz in and take half of what she had earned with "years of misery." Her friends were only reconfirmed in their suspicions that Delores's misery was her greatest pleasure.

Chuck's drinking worsened. "He wasn't a mean drunk," said a friend. "He would get sad and lonely and sentimental when he was drinking." Delores complained constantly about the empty bottles downstairs, bottles left for Helen Stewart to cart out. With Chuck's increase in drinking came deterioration in his health, but when he grew sick and too weak to get to the doctor, neither Delores nor Janie would take him. He was forced to call Helen to come for him. He bought her lunch and gave her twenty-five dollars for her trouble.

In June 1983, Delores and Janie were getting ready to fly to Albuquerque for Tom's second wedding, to his former dental assistant. Chuck was going, too (Delores dared not displease Tom by opposing his presence), but a few days before their departure, Helen got a disgusted call from Delores telling her she had better come and attend to Chuck.

Helen found him in the throes of delirium tremens. He was hallucinating that he was hosting a big gathering of GE people and was distraught that he couldn't find their cars outside. Helen talked him gently to his car and drove him to the doctor, who admitted him to the hospital. Delores and Janie flew to Albuquerque without him.

Chuck was still hospitalized when Delores and Janie returned, but neither visited him. When Delores's closest friend, Susan Reid, asked what was wrong with Chuck, Delores said, "I don't know. I don't care. I don't bother to find out."

Helen took Chuck home from the hospital. Drinking was killing him, the doctors had told him. He heeded their advice to stop, but he returned to a hostile home and a future made even bleaker without alcohol.

Less than five months after Chuck's release from the hospital, on Saturday, November 5, Delores called Susan Reid about 4:30 in the afternoon. Susan had listened for years to Delores's diatribes about Chuck (Delores called him the Poobah to Susan), had heard over and over her wishes for his death. Susan knew that whatever love Delores might once have had for him long ago had been overwhelmed by hatred and contempt, but she never really understood the reason for it. Like all of Delores's friends, she was a little weary of hearing about it and dreaded that inevitable part of Delores's conversations. But on this afternoon, to Susan's relief, Delores chatted about other things.

"Well, I've got to go," Delores said after a while. "I've got to cook the Poobah's dinner."

"What are you fixing?" Susan asked.

"Green beans and scrambled eggs."

"Oh, Delores, that's a terrible combination."

"He doesn't even deserve that."

Two hours later, Susan got another call from an excited Delores.

"I think Chuck's dead," Delores said.

"*What?*"

"He's lying on the floor in front of the TV and I can't find a pulse."

"Have you called the rescue squad?"

"No."

"For God's sake, Delores, call the rescue squad! Don't call me!"

Susan drove the eight miles to Delores's house, arriving before the rescue squad. The emergency technicians tried without success to resuscitate Chuck. The county police came, as did the county coroner, Harold "Skippy" Corum, an insurance agent. The coroner viewed the body, talked with emergency technicians and police, conferred with Chuck's doctor by telephone, and ruled the death of natural causes, an apparent heart attack. Delores displayed no emotion, and neither did Janie when she arrived later. Other things seemed to be on Delores's mind.

"I don't know whether I'm going to be a princess or a pauper," she remarked to Susan.

A pauper she was not.

"I had no idea that man had that much money," she later told Eddie Logsdon, a friend from the playhouse.

Chuck had been wise with his investments, and unbeknownst to Delores he had set up trusts for every member of his family. Not only was Delores the recipient of a handsome annual return from her trust, but by scrimping on her household allowance, she had secretly accumulated a tidy nest egg of her own. She could afford to live out her life in ease and comfort, free of the strictures of the monthly allowance Chuck had imposed upon her, the parsimonious nature of which she had complained about frequently while stashing a good part of it away. But lavish living and unnecessary spending were not her style. She had, after all, lived through the Depression. Her habits were too deeply ingrained to change.

She spent hours each week clipping and redeeming newspaper and magazine savings coupons and rarely let a rebate offer pass. She drove miles out of her way to pick up sale items. She packed her lunch on trips to keep from spending money in restaurants. She rarely threw away anything deemed usable. She wore the same pair of shoes to both of Tom's weddings, thirteen years apart, dyeing them from their original lime green to match her outfit the second time. She even kept scraps of soap and molded them into new bars.

Helen Stewart knew those frugal habits as well as anybody. That was the reason she delayed telling Delores that she'd had to raise rates for her customers by five dollars a day. For fourteen years, Helen had been cleaning Delores's big house every Tuesday. She put in a long day, and Delores's passion for cleanliness made it a hard day. Helen polished floors on her hands and knees, washed windows, painted, burned trash. For this, her fee was twenty-five dollars. From her five customers, she eked out a bare subsistence. She, better than Delores, knew the value of a dollar.

But three months after Chuck's death, when Helen told Delores about the increase, Delores balked, saying she couldn't afford it. Despite Delores's constant cries of poverty, Helen knew better. If Delores didn't pay, she wouldn't be able to come anymore, she said. Fine, said Delores.

Helen had traveled with Delores, shopped with her, gone out to eat with her. On many Tuesday afternoons, they had sat together after work, drinking beer, talking, and laughing. She thought of Delores as friend, confidante, and adviser. Delores had helped her with her children's problems, stood up for her boyfriend when he killed her uncle in a drunken argument. But Helen wasn't going to let Delores bully her into accepting a lower rate than she got from her other customers. She left and didn't return.

On Friday, July 20, five months after Helen quit, Delores called just to chat. "TJ's coming to visit next week," she said with delight, adding that he was bringing the kids. She thought Helen would want to know. Helen had taken care of the boys several times and traveled with Delores to visit them.

"Who's cleaning your house now?" Helen found herself asking.

Delores said that she was doing it herself, that she hadn't been able to find anybody who suited her, and she had a lot to do before Tom arrived.

"You want me to come back?" Helen asked.

Delores was exultant. She called several friends that day to report that Helen was coming back—and at the same rate.

3

The phone at Delores's house rang all afternoon and into the evening of Sunday, July 22, 1984. Strange. Her callers knew that Delores always left the phone off the hook when she was away, one of her many ways of foiling robbers, who, she was convinced, always called to see if anybody was home before breaking in. Besides, the phone's ringing upset her dogs, and she would never allow that.

Fern Morgan started calling about 1 P.M. and kept at it until after 4. Fern had met Delores at the monthly meetings of the Prospect Homemakers Club, where Delores had learned to cook new dishes and make dolls from old copies of *Reader's Digest*. Fern owned a moving company that had been started by her husband, and three days earlier she'd sent a truck and one of her crews to move Janie's belongings from her university apartment. She hadn't heard from Delores and wondered if everything had gone to suit her. Delores had talked about going swimming with Fern sometime when Fern was visiting in nearby Prospect with her daughter, who had a pool, and Fern wanted to invite Delores to bring her swimsuit and come over this afternoon.

"That's funny, Denise," Fern said to her daughter after several attempts to reach her friend. "Delores never leaves her phone on the hook if she goes out."

Susan Reid started calling shortly after Fern quit trying. She hadn't talked to Delores since Friday, when Delores called to tell her about Helen coming back and to ask if she was going to church Sunday. Susan sometimes went to church with Delores and Marjorie Chinnock. She had done so the Sunday before, and Delores had invited her home for breakfast afterward, but Susan declined. She had to have a cigarette with her coffee, and she didn't want to go into the backyard to do it.

Delores sometimes nagged her about going to church, and Susan told her that if she decided to go, she'd meet her there. But she hadn't felt well that morning and had decided to stay home.

That Delores would become such a close friend had at first seemed highly unlikely to Susan. They had met in 1970, when Susan was working at the real estate agency that Chuck and Delores contracted to sell their house in Hunting Creek. Delores either called or dropped in at the agency almost every day complaining because the house hadn't been sold. "She'd just raise hell," Susan remembered. All the agents dreaded hearing from her and maneuvered to avoid her, Susan included.

Susan got to know Delores better when Delores joined St. James Church, where Susan was a member. They sided together in the dispute that split the congregation. But it wasn't until after the death of Susan's husband, Carroll, in 1975, that they became close. Delores was wonderfully supportive. After going through the church fight and the loss of Susan's husband together, they began to see each other or talk by telephone several times a week.

When the phone rang without an answer Sunday afternoon, Susan knew something was wrong. She figured Delores's phone was out of order again, as it had been a month or so earlier, when a caller would hear a ring, although the phone was dead at Delores's house.

Susan tried calling a few more times Sunday night with the same result. Surely the phone would be fixed tomorrow, she thought. She waited for Delores to call Monday with her can-you-believe-it? complaints about the phone company. When she didn't, Susan tried calling again. The phone rang and rang. Boy, Delores would be hot, Susan thought. She pitied the phone company employees who would have to make the repairs.

Susan tried calling again Tuesday morning without result and decided that she would just drop by to see Delores later in the day. She had to work until 1 P.M. at

Clore and Duncan Real Estate Company. The office was at Interstate 71 on State Road 329, the road on which Delores lived just four miles away. But when Susan got off work, she decided to first drive to her sylvan red cottage in Pewee Valley, four miles away, to change clothes and pick up Abbi, her Shih Tzu. She knew that Delores would want to see Abbi. Their dogs had helped bind their friendship.

Susan was well aware that, with the exception of her children, Delores's dogs were the most important things in her life. They were pampered Yorkshire terriers. Pooky was twelve, Poppy eleven. Delores not only lavished them with attention, but, more significantly, had no qualms about spending opulently on them. She had special covers made for their beds and pillows. She bathed them with expensive soaps and perfumed and powdered them with Estée Lauder. She gave them birthday parties with decorated cakes and took them to the vet to have their teeth cleaned. While picking up store-brand canned goods for her husband's meals, she sometimes bought steak for her dogs.

Delores was convinced that Pooky wanted to talk, and she spent hours on end training him to say "mama," sometimes preserving his howling efforts on cassette tapes. Unsurprisingly to those who knew Delores and her dogs, Pooky was diagnosed as neurotic and required daily tranquilizers. Because he couldn't control his bladder, he spent most of his time in a wire pen in the kitchen, where the floor was covered with big sheets of plain newsprint that Delores bought especially for their absorbant qualities.

Abbi looked expectantly out the car window as Susan turned into Delores's driveway and headed for the house. As she neared the parking area, Susan saw the three familiar cars side by side—Delores's Olds, Chuck's VW, Janie's Nova—but she didn't see the rivulet of blood that had trickled more than thirty feet down the driveway and dried in the hot July sun. Not until she topped the hill did she see the body lying at the garage door.

Horrified, Susan jerked her car into reverse and backed quickly to the front of the house. Later, she wouldn't remember the drive back to her office, but her fellow employees never would forget the look on her face when she burst through the door. She was shaking so hard that her teeth chattered. She had to sit before she could say anything.

"Call the police," she finally stammered. "Delores is dead at the garage door. Janie's probably in the house. There's two dogs in there, too."

Steve Nobles was heading home in his police cruiser on State Road 329 near Crestwood, only a short distance from the real estate office where Susan Reid was trying to get control of herself, when he heard a call on his car radio for one of his officers to check a report of a woman down at 10420 Covered Bridge Road, the road on which he was traveling. The call was meant for Detective Tom Swinney, who was home at the time, away from his radio. Nobles picked up his mike and told the dispatcher that he was not far from the address and would check it.

At thirty-two, Nobles had been chief of the Oldham County Police for four years. A lean man with military bearing, he wore his formfitting khaki uniform starched and creased, gold eagles flashing at the collars.

Nobles arrived at Delores's house only minutes after the call came at 2:55. He pulled into the driveway, stopped, looked around, saw nothing amiss, then drove slowly to the loop in front of the house and blew his horn. No reaction. He got out for a look around. He started up the drive to the side of the house when an unusual odor hit him and he spotted the body beside the garage. Suddenly, he realized he was in an exposed position. He drew his revolver, and, crouching, retreated quickly to the cover of his car.

Tom Swinney had received a telephone call from the dispatcher and was on his way to the scene, only a few miles away on Covered Bridge Road.

"Three-o-five, step it up," Nobles called to him from his portable radio. "We've got trouble here. Run code three."

Nobles also notified the dispatcher to get car 315, Officer Steve Sparrow, to the scene.

Nobles's first thought was that the daughter the dispatcher had mentioned might have gone crazy, killed her mother, and was still holed up in the house. He kept a close watch on windows and doors until Swinney arrived.

"We've got a body up here beside the garage and according to the lady who called in, there's supposed to be a daughter somewhere," Nobles told Swinney when his cruiser pulled up behind the chief's. "We've got to go inside."

"I know the house," Swinney said.

He also knew Delores and Janie. He was the officer who had investigated Chuck's death eight months earlier.

With revolvers and portable radios in hand, the two officers advanced cautiously upon the house.

4

Tiny, sweet Janie. That was how family and friends thought of Janie Lynch, framed in their minds by her stature and disposition. In many ways, she was like her mother. She had inherited her mother's size, for one thing, a petite five-foot-two, and, as she approached forty, still wore a size three dress. Her mother's outgoing nature was hers as well. *Perky, bubbly,* and *vivacious* were words frequently used to describe Janie, although she also harbored a certain reserve that sometimes made her seem cool and distant, hard to get to know. Once that reserve was breached, she was witty and charming, fun to be around, just as her mother frequently was. In one crucial aspect, though, Janie was very much unlike her mother. She was without her mother's abrasiveness and guile. Underlying Janie's character was a sincere sweetness that endeared her to all.

For the past year, however, Janie had not been her usual self. She was in the clutches of a malaise she couldn't escape. She tired easily, became quickly irritated, was plagued with vague aches. She complained of having no energy and feeling bad all the time.

Anemia, the doctors told her, and she had been to several. They seemed to think that her complaints were related to the stress of her final year in dental school. They gave her thyroid medicine and vitamin shots and sent her on her way. Stress from school no doubt was part of the problem, but those who knew Janie best suspected something deeper. Once again, she was approaching one of those points in her life that she dreaded and sought to avoid: a time for decision making, for setting a course.

Janie never had been able to figure out what she wanted from life, and now, after four years of striving for her latest degree, her third, and only a few months from turning forty, she again was questioning. She had talked of moving to Albuquerque and joining her brother in his dental practice, of starting a practice near Louisville, of moving to some other state and making a whole new start, but she had seen drawbacks in all of these options and wasn't really drawn to any one of them.

Her mother told her not to worry. Just move in with her, rest, recover her health, then decide. That was the course Janie chose, the course of delayed decision, a nondecision that would be the most decisive of her life. Delores couldn't have been happier about it. Her friends knew that she had Janie exactly where she wanted her.

Delores had flabbergasted Janie's fellow students at dental school with her hovering presence in her daughter's life. Janie lived at home when she began classes, but when she moved into the university's apartment building for dental and medical students, it was Delores who came with her maid to clean and paint, fix and decorate. And when Janie moved from the second floor to a larger apartment on the seventh floor, Delores repeated the performance. Delores had a key to the apartment and came almost daily to clean and straighten and bring food. She cooked all of Janie's meals at home and brought them to her in heat-and-eat containers. She left fresh milk in Janie's refrigerator and took home for herself the still unspoiled milk she'd left earlier. Janie was expected to call her mother every night at 11, and if she was late by a few minutes, the phone rang and Delores wanted to know what was wrong. If Janie was to be out late, she had to call her mother before leaving and again upon returning, no matter the hour.

Janie seemed unbothered by such smothering and laughed it off, telling friends, "She's just a Jewish mother who isn't Jewish."

Her mother, friends figured, was the reason Janie never married. They thought that Delores's constant harping against her husband had helped sour Janie on the idea of marriage. But more important, they believed that Janie simply was afraid that she never could find anybody who would please her mother. Four times, Janie seriously contemplated marriage, three times to lawyers (her mother not only boasted that Janie dated lawyers but she also kept in touch with two of her daughter's old boyfriends after the relationships ended in case she needed their services), but as the moment of commitment neared, Janie inevitably stepped back.

"Every time somebody asks me to marry him, I go get another degree," she laughingly told Denise Payne, a friend from the dental school who was about to marry.

That wasn't exactly true. Janie's first serious romance was over by the time she got her degree in education at Bradley University in Peoria, Illinois, in 1966. Encouraged by her mother, she followed her parents to Kentucky to begin teaching and got an elementary school job in Cobb County, some eighty miles from Louisville. After two years, she enrolled at the University of Kentucky in Lexington to get her master's degree in special education.

Janie shared her mother's paranoia about crime, and to protect herself, she began taking karate lessons, a skill in which she eventually won a brown belt. She attempted to teach karate to her mother in weekend classes in her parents' front yard at Hunting Creek, much to the amusement of neighbors, who speculated about which of them Delores was planning to use it on. Janie's instructor was a lean, muscular young man, a native of Lexington enrolled at a prestigious out-of-state college. John Trent was nineteen, Janie twenty-five. Their relationship would last five years, during three of which John was away at school. In the beginning, their romance was one of holiday visits, summer vacations, letters, and long-distance calls, but it grew deeper when John returned to Lexington to attend law school.

Once, when it seemed that marriage might be in the offing, John was visiting at the big house on Covered Bridge Road into which Janie's parents had moved, and Janie's father pulled him aside and said, "You know, Janie is a lot like her mother."

John took it as a warning, and later Chuck made it

clear that that was how he had intended it. "You might want to read this," he said, offering John a gift of a book, *The Manipulated Man* by Esther Vilar.

After getting her master's degree in 1970, Janie became a speech pathologist in the Fayette County schools, then went to work at the Clinic for Communicative Disorders at the University of Kentucky in Lexington. By 1975 she was restless and unhappy, troubled at work by an older man whose sexual advances she'd refused, uncertain about her feelings for John, a vegetarian she described as being "into weeds and seeds."

After a trip to Los Angeles to visit a sorority sister from Bradley, she became enthralled with the idea of California. Suddenly, she seemed to know exactly what she wanted—and it lay beside the Pacific. She sent out applications and was accepted as a speech pathologist in the Santa Monica schools.

She needed time to think, she told John, and although he never understood exactly what she needed to think about, he drove her to California to allow her the opportunity.

Friends thought that in moving to California and fleeing commitment with John, Janie might be fleeing her mother as well. Delores was upset about the move. Her son was in South Carolina, her daughter in California, and she was left in a big house in Kentucky with only her dogs and a husband she detested.

Janie settled into an apartment only a few blocks from the beach in Santa Monica and wrote to friends that her life was more free and open than it ever had been—and she was loving every minute of it.

Romance blossomed anew for Janie in California, again with a lawyer, but that relationship, like the others before it, would pass without commitment.

By 1977 she was again enrolled in school, this time in Santa Monica College, taking courses that would allow her to enter dental school. In her work as a speech pathologist, she had encountered a doctor who corrected speech problems with dental changes, and he had inspired her to seek her own degree in dentistry. Delores was quick to seize on her daughter's new ambition. She checked out the University of Louisville's School of Dentistry and began pitching it to Janie. She could live at home, Delores pointed out, and her father would foot the bills.

So it was that four years after she left for California, fleeing commitment, Janie returned to Kentucky, fleeing not only another romantic involvement but her one fling at freedom from her mother.

In the fall of 1980, Janie was back in school in a class that was only one-fourth female and far younger than she. If her age concerned her, she never showed it. Anyway, she looked so much younger than her years—by at least a decade—that few of her classmates ever realized she was their oldest member.

By her second year, Janie's grades were at the top of the class, and, as usual, she was finding no shortage of attentive males. Her beauty was intact: her slim, shapely figure; her long, auburn curls; her dark, expressive eyes; and her quick, engaging smile still had their effect. She restricted her dating to classmates, and although she dated many and forged strong friendships with several others, she didn't dabble with serious romance again until her final year at school.

Her father's death in November 1983 was the catalyst for that. Janie was in her apartment when her mother called to tell her about it. She went looking for Ron King, her closest friend at the school, but he wasn't in his room. Her search took her to Phil Pandolfi's dorm room.

Phil was surprised to see her. He was a first-year student, and he had met Janie on his first day at school. He had been seeking advice from Ron King when Janie came in and gave him a big smile. "Who's this, Ron?" she'd asked. "He's kinda cute."

Phil paid little attention to her remark, but later he realized that Janie was always flashing smiles at him, that she made a point to say hello, to stop him to chat about classes and how he was doing. He knew flirting when he saw it, but because she was a final-year student, he had been reluctant to respond.

On the night she came to his room, he invited her in and offered something to drink before he realized she was upset and hadn't come to visit.

"Have you seen Ron?" she asked.

"No, is something wrong?"

"My father died," she said, and broke into tears.

"I'm sorry," Phil said, moving to comfort her.

"He was an alcoholic," she whispered as he put an arm around her and let her cry on his chest.

"If you need somebody to talk to, I'm here," he told her. "I just want you to know that."

After that night, Janie and Phil were together often. Because of her fear of crime, Janie never walked anywhere on campus without an escort, and Phil took on the job full-time. He walked her to class every morning and back to her apartment in the evening. They had lunch together and chatted in lab. He started taking her out for pizza on Friday nights and dropping by her apartment on weeknights to watch TV. After Christmas, Janie took him home to meet her mother, and on Valentine's Day she sent him a big card with two funny frogs on it with hearts bubbling over their heads.

"You probably think you're getting this valentine because you're special . . ." it said.

"You're right," was inside.

It was signed, "Love, Janie. P.S. Hope you did well on your exams. I'm sure you did!"

In March, Phil told her that he'd fallen in love. She cried and said she felt the same way. Shortly afterward, she took him to spend a weekend at the big house on Covered Bridge Road. He cooked a spaghetti dinner for Janie and her mother. Pooky barked at him, but Delores made much ado over him.

An unusual thing happened that weekend. Phil was sleeping downstairs—in the room where Janie's father had slept—when he was awakened by a strange feeling that left him bathed in sweat and gripped by fear. It was as if he had found himself in the very presence of evil, had been enveloped by it, as if the house itself was evil.

At first he tried to rationalize it away. He had been a tough, street-smart kid in the Palisades of New Jersey, an athlete, a bodybuilder, an army officer in an airborne rapid deployment force. He'd faced all kinds of danger and never been afraid of anything. He couldn't be scared of a house. Impossible.

But he had to admit that he was.

"You've got to get out of here," an inner voice kept telling him. "Get out of here and take Janie with you."

In the dark, he fumbled for his rosary, and by clinging to it and praying he made it through the night.

He was embarrassed to mention this to Janie, and even tried to deny to himself the feelings that had overcome him that night, but when he returned to the house a couple of weeks later, he experienced the same presence.

"I didn't want to be near that house," he recalled later. "It scared hell out of me."

Yet he kept the fears to himself, unwilling to mention them to Janie out of concern that she might think him crazy. He would come to torture himself over that decision.

The approach of graduation was a busy time for Janie. She studied long hours for her state board tests and had little time for other activities. But she and Phil did go to see her mother play the part of Daphine Drimmond in "There Goes the Bride" at the Little Colonel Theater, and Phil took Janie to the graduation dance, he in a three-piece corduroy suit, she in a dress of pink chiffon with a lace bodice to which Phil pinned the pink carnation corsage he bought her.

On graduation day, May 13, Delores came with cheese and wine for Janie's friends; on the next day, Phil left for New Jersey and a job teaching high school biology in summer school.

"I'll be back before you know it," he assured Janie, then made her promise that when her work at school was finished she would come to New York to visit. He wanted her to meet his family. He would get tickets to see the Mets play the Cubs, her favorite team. They would take in all the sights and eat fantastic pizzas and have a wonderful time.

Phil was thoroughly in love, but one thing bothered him about the relationship: the age difference.

"No way!" he said, when Janie told him soon after they began getting close that she was thirty-nine, fourteen years older than he. He couldn't believe it. There seemed no gap at all. He told her that age was unimportant, but he knew that in one big respect it did matter. He was Italian. He wanted a big, raucous family. Lots of kids. Her childbearing years were limited.

As soon as he got home, Phil sat down to talk about this with his mother. Her acceptance was important.

"If you feel that way about this girl," she told him, "don't let her go."

That decided it.

Janie, too, was thinking about their relationship. "But, Jesus, he's so *young,*" she told a friend. He was also passionate and exciting, and she loved his dark good looks, was flattered by his attentions.

Delores had taken note. "I don't know what I'm going to do," she told her friend Joyce Rose one day that spring. "Janie has dragged home a New York street Italian." She mentioned him to Susan Reid as well. She didn't like him. He was clearly rabble—a Kennedy lover. Besides, he'd made a terrible mess of her kitchen cooking spaghetti that wasn't very good.

From the day he left, Janie wrote to Phil every few days. She had remained at school, completing her lab work, and her letters were chatty, filled with news of classmates and school and everyday affairs, never romantic or gushy—that wasn't Janie. But she signed them with love and an occasional "I miss you."

On the first of June, Jackie and Mario Timpone, old friends from Chicago and the parents of one of Janie's early loves, came to visit Delores and Janie, bringing eight quarts of homecooked spaghetti sauce and a boxful of pastries from Naples Bakery in Chicago. Janie took a day off from school to be with them. In mid-June, Janie and her mother went to a picnic with the Little Colonel Players. By the end of the month, Janie was making final adjustments on her patients' teeth at the school clinic and the university was pressuring her to leave her apartment. She tried for an extension through July but won a reprieve only until the eighteenth.

By the Fourth of July, she'd finished her work at school, received her diploma, and moved out all of her equipment. But she remained in her apartment and seemed reluctant to leave.

"I went back to the Dr. on Mon.," she wrote Phil. "He said the same old thing—I'm anemic and continue taking my thyroid med.—also I'd gained 4 lbs since Dec. I know I'll not be able to hold down a job in dentistry feeling this bad—so I'll probably try another Dr. for a 2nd opinion or just go into hibernation."

The following weekend, Janie went to Lexington to visit an old friend, Vicky Graff. Janie had gotten to know Vicky at the University of Kentucky in 1969, when Vicky was an undergraduate student. Vicky later went to graduate school at Vanderbilt University in Nashville, and Janie visited her there several times. Vicky married a doctor, a pathologist, and in 1979 they settled in Lexington. Now Vicky was pregnant with her third child, and she and her family were temporarily living in an apartment while their new house was being completed.

More than two years had passed since Vicky had seen Janie, and she was surprised at the changes. Janie was still perky, all smiles, but worn and older, with a harder edge. "She seemed a little more cynical, a little more sarcastic," Vicky later recalled. A little more like her mother, Vicky thought.

As Janie played with Vicky's children, reading stories to William well past his bedtime, Vicky sensed remorse in Janie that she hadn't yet found her place, settled down, married, and had children. But that possibility seemed far away. Janie gave Vicky the distinct impression that she had no intention of pursuing her romance with her young friend in New Jersey. "Maybe with Janie," Vicky said later, "the harder you pushed the more she ran."

Later, Vicky took Janie to see her new house, and as they stood in the unfinished living room, Vicky said, "The next time you come, we're going to be in here having a gin and tonic."

Vicky wanted Janie to stay for a few days, but when they got back to the apartment, Delores called. Her car had broken down. She'd had a big fight with the man at the Boy Scout camp, who'd pushed the car out of the entrance. She was alone and upset and didn't know what to do. Vicky saw that Delores was pulling the old guilt trip, and it worked, as always. Shortly afterward, Janie left to return to her mother and the big house on Covered Bridge Road.

Three days later, on Wednesday, Janie wrote to Phil for the first time in two weeks. When she had told him earlier that she wouldn't be coming to New York after all, Phil, sensitive to any perceived slight, had hurt feelings. He didn't write or call for a week. When he did write, it was only a short, meaningless note that he signed "Thank you, Phil."

His hope was that she would realize his pain and, if not change her mind about the trip, at least rush to comfort him with affection.

"Dear Phil," she wrote. "Hope your summer has been a good one. It has gone really fast and will soon be over.

"Thought you might be interested in your fall semester book list—each year the book list, fortunately, gets smaller and smaller.

"Have a good rest of the summer. Sincerely, Janie."

It was the only letter she wrote to him that she didn't sign with love—and it was the last letter she would ever write.

After removing all of her belongings from her apartment on Thursday, Janie returned to the dental school on Friday to say her good-byes. Denise Payne ran into her and got the impression that Janie was having a hard time separating herself from this place that had consumed so much of her energies for the past four years.

The next day, Saturday, July 21, Delores and Janie remained home all morning. That afternoon they drove into Crestwood to drop off some small appliances to be repaired at Stoess Hardware. Delores looked at holsters. She wanted one for her revolver, she said, a .32, but she put off the purchase until Monday. That night, Janie went with her mother to the Little Colonel Theater to see the summer student production "Aunt Abby Answers an Ad."

Delores went backstage after the show to congratulate the cast and director Bill Aiken, to whom she gave a big hug, but Janie lingered in the background, as she usually did in her mother's presence, smiling but saying little.

The next morning, while her mother was at church, Janie did not go out for doughnuts as usual. Nobody would ever know why.

5

Delores was sprawled on her left side by the garage, her knees sticking up, legs apart. The top of her head and the left side of her face were gone. The hot sun had blackened the remains of her head, which squirmed with maggots and was swarmed by flies and ants, the most grotesque sight Police Chief Steve Nobles and Detective Tom Swinney had ever seen.

The officers moved past the body, holding their breath against the stench, and headed toward the back of the house, where a stone wall rose to the backyard. The second floor of the house was on the same level as the backyard, and stone steps at the back of the house led to it.

As Nobles and Swinney were climbing the steps, Officer Steve Sparrow announced by radio his arrival at the front of the house.

"Don't let anybody come up here," Nobles told him over his hand radio.

But Sparrow misunderstood him to say "Come up here," and he got out of his car and started for the back of the house.

He called to Nobles and Swinney as he topped the steps and saw them on a small concrete patio checking a locked sliding glass door. Both jittery officers whirled on him with their revolvers drawn.

Sparrow returned to secure the front of the house, and Swinney made his way to another door near the far end. He saw that the glass storm door was closed, but the inner door stood open. As he was about to open the storm door, he noticed what appeared to be a bullet hole in the gutter drain at the end of the house and silently pointed it out to Nobles.

Both officers were anxious about what they might find inside. Nobles's first thought—that the daughter who was supposed to be in the house might have gone berserk, killed her mother, and still be holed up inside—had been joined by other possibilities. Perhaps the daughter, too, was dead, the victim of murder or suicide. Maybe she had killed her mother and fled. Or perhaps she had been kidnapped by the killer. Maybe she had been taken hostage and her mother's killer was at this moment waiting for a policeman to stick his head inside the house so he could blow it off, too.

The storm door was unlocked, and Swinney pulled it open gingerly, to be greeted not by gunblast but by the barking of two small, skittish dogs weakened by hunger. The smell of dog feces and urine assaulted his nose. The door opened into the kitchen, and as the two officers stepped into the air-conditioned coolness, crouching, seeking cover from a counter jutting out to their left that enclosed the electric stove, they saw two drops of dried blood on the floor beside the counter, just inside the door, near a telephone on the wall.

From the kitchen, the officers could see into the family room at the back of the house and the dining room at the front. Swinney checked the dining room and adjoining living room, stepping over a folding dog gate as he went. He noticed that expensive Oriental carpets on the floors and a silver tea service in the dining room were undisturbed. Nobles stepped over another dog gate into the family room, where he saw nothing out of the ordinary. A cheap, plastic-webbed chaise longue sat in the middle of the floor near the sliding door, as if somebody recently had brought it inside from sunning on the patio. Nobles peeked into the hallway at the foyer, where he again was joined by Swinney.

Neither officer spoke as they clung to the walls, creeping down the hallway, pushing open doors to peer into a bathroom and seldom-used bedroom. The door to the linen closet in the hallway stood open, revealing a tiny red light aglow on a control box, indicating that the burglar alarm was off.

As Swinney poked his head around Janie's open bedroom door on the front side of the house at the end of the hallway, he saw the contents of her purse scattered on her bed and a jewelry box dumped upside down. Boxes filled with items moved from Janie's apartment occupied one side of the room. An open suitcase lay on the floor. Swinney started to call to Nobles, who'd just stepped into Delores's bedroom at the back of the house, but Nobles called first.

"Tom, she's in here. I found her."

Janie lay facedown on a small rug in a sun room with jalousie windows that reached nearly to the floor on two sides. The room adjoined Delores's bedroom at the end of the house. The sun rarely penetrated the room because Delores kept the beige draperies drawn most of the time. Visitors who pulled into the parking area at the side of the house often saw her peering through those draperies to see who was outside. The room was called the French room because of the double doors that opened into it from Delores's bedroom, the only access. The French doors always stood open, and bead curtains had been hung there. The French room was filled with wicker furniture and a few plants. On one wall hung a bamboo scroll bearing the reassuring rules for serenity of the *Desiderata*, some of them incongruous considering the present setting: "Go placidly amid the noise and haste and remember what peace there may be in silence. As far as possible without surrender be on good terms with all persons. Speak your truth quietly and clearly; and listen to others, even the dull and ignorant; they too have their story. Avoid loud and aggressive persons, they are vexations to the spirit . . . Nurture strength and spirit to shield you in sudden misfortune. But do not distress yourself with imaginings. Many fears are born of fatigue and loneliness. You are a child of the universe, no less than the trees and the stars; you have a right to be here. And whether or not it is clear to you, no doubt the universe is unfolding as it should . . . With all its sham, drudgery and broken dreams, it is still a beautiful world."

On another wall, a wide-eyed owl stared down from a calendar onto a scene of horror.

Janie was barefoot. Her slim, sun-browned legs protruded from black nylon jogging shorts. The black-and-white-striped jersey that she wore had been torn by a bullet that struck her in the back near the right shoulder blade. Her hair was in white plastic curlers, one of which had been driven into her brain by a second bullet, which caught her at the base of her skull and exited from the left side of her neck, leaving a gaping hole. Her left eye stared blankly. Definitely no suicide.

Nobles and Swinney continued their search of the house, moving on downstairs, even checking closets to make sure that nobody else was present, before going back outside through the kitchen door. Both knew they'd have to call a mobile evidence lab.

"Let's call Jefferson," Nobles said, meaning the Jefferson County Police in Louisville, "and I'm going to go ahead and call the state."

Nobles's cursory inspection had told him that this was going to be a difficult case—two women murdered in a big house in a wealthy area with no weapon in sight and few clues evident. His entire department amounted to nine officers, only two of them detectives, one of whom—his brother, Lennie—only recently had been elevated to the job. He had neither the manpower nor the money to conduct a big murder investigation. He would need the Kentucky State Police and their far greater resources. Besides, he didn't want to shoulder full responsibility for the case. If it weren't solved—and from the looks of things, it might well not be—he wanted to share the blame.

Nobles told his dispatcher to call an evidence unit and inform the state police that he had a double murder. "And get Dennis out here," he said.

Sergeant Dennis Clark was the department's public information officer. Nobles knew that reporters soon would be swarming on Covered Bridge Road, and he wanted Clark there to hold them at bay.

The previous weekend had been a busy one for Katy and Howard Cable, Delores's next-door neighbors. They'd driven to Akron, Ohio, so that Howard, a retired engineer, could play in a golf tournament with their son, who lived there. As always when they were to be away, Katy called Delores to tell her how long they'd be gone. The two neighbors looked out for one another's houses when either was away. The Cables felt confident with Delores looking after their place. She was quick to call the police at the slightest hint of suspicion.

Whenever the Cables traveled, Katy usually brought a small gift back for Delores—a book, a whatnot, a household gadget—and delivered it to her on their return in appreciation of her watchful eye. But this had been a rushed trip, the Cables hurrying back on Sunday because their daughter from Virginia was to arrive with her family for a visit. The Cables got home Sunday to find their daughter already there, and in the excitement of the visit, Katy forgot to deliver her present to Delores, or even to call and let her know of their return.

Two days later, Howard walked into his house and said, "Honey, the police are next door. There's something wrong."

Katy drove over only to be stopped at the top of Delores's driveway by Officer Steve Sparrow. She explained who she was and that she had a key to the house.

"What's wrong?" she asked.

"Something's happened to Mrs. Lynch," Sparrow said.

"Oh, for goodness sakes," Katy said. "Whatever you do, be sure you don't let her daughter, Janie, come in and just walk into something like this. She and her mother are really close."

Sparrow thanked her and told her that somebody would be over to talk with her later.

Susan Reid soon returned to the house on Covered Bridge Road. Still trembling from shock, she was driven by a co-worker, Terry Barrickman. Susan also had keys to Delores's house. Sparrow let her car into the driveway and called Swinney to talk to her. Swinney confirmed what she'd feared—that Janie, too, was dead. She told him that Delores had a son in Albuquerque, a dentist, TJ, Tom; somebody would have to let him know. Swinney assured her that they'd take care of it.

"What about the dogs?" Susan asked.

"They're all right."

"Can I have them? Can I take them to the vet? They were like Delores's children."

Maybe later, Swinney told her. Meanwhile, he'd feed and water them. "You go on home and try to rest, Mrs. Reid," he told her, "and we'll call you after a while."

Not until six hours later, when Susan called, would she be allowed to come with her vet and pick up Pooky and Poppy.

Lieutenant Dan Davidson was working on reports at his desk at Kentucky State Police Post Five on State Highway 146 near La Grange, the county seat, about ten miles from Delores's house, when his telephone rang and the post dispatcher told him about the murders. He pulled a plaid sport coat over his white short-sleeve shirt and the .357 Magnum on his hip and went out the back door to his white 1982 Ford cruiser. Officers from Post Five, uniformed troopers and detectives, were responsible for six counties along the Ohio River—Oldham, Henry, Trimble, Carroll, Gallatin and Owen—reaching to within thirty-five miles of Cincinnati. It was a big territory, and the criminal division, of which Davidson was in charge, had only a handful of men to cover it. Four detectives, a detective sergeant, and an arson investigator answered to Davidson.

On his radio, Davidson asked the dispatcher to call one of those detectives, Sherman Childers, and have Childers meet him at the house on Covered Bridge Road.

Most of Oldham County's police department was at Delores's house when Davidson arrived and parked his cruiser at the top of the driveway. A yellow police line already had been stretched around the house. The afternoon was sweltering, the temperature near 90, and Davidson took off his coat and laid it on the front seat as he got out of the car. Sergeant Clark, the Oldham County public information officer, spotted him and came over.

"Hey, Dan."

"What's happenin', Dennis?"

"We got a rough one here."

Dan Davidson was an imposing figure, a man who would stand out in any crowd. Wide-shouldered, broad-chested, with narrow hips, he stood six-foot-three and weighed 215 pounds. His hair, swept back on the sides in a fifties cut, dipped low onto the forehead of his forlorn face. He wore a huge turquoise belt buckle, heavy turquoise rings, and a broad silver watchband swathed in the same blue stone. Buckled, low-cut dress boots protruded beneath his tapered slacks. On his right arm was a tattoo that almost kept him out of the state police, which has a rule against visible tattoos. His was just above the sleeve line of a short-sleeve shirt. WARRIOR, it said in neat letters put there by playmates with a straight pin and school ink when he was eight. He was forty-five now, only two and a half months away from forty-six, and not only was he one of the best horseshoe pitchers and bass fishermen in the state of Kentucky, he was one of the most respected detectives. As a bass fisherman, Davidson eschewed the razzle-dazzle and high-tech gimmickry that had turned that once simple leisure activity into a big-time commercial sport. Using only instinct, cunning, and patience, he could compete with the best of the pros. He applied the same techniques to his work. A taciturn man, Davidson moved slowly and deliberately, and when he spoke it was with a mountain drawl that caused some young, big-city reporters in Louisville to make the mistake of thinking him less than bright.

Davidson succinctly greeted the officers at the side of the house and went over to look at Delores's body.

"We've got another one in the house," Steve Nobles told him.

Davidson waited a few minutes for Childers to arrive before going in to look at Janie. While he and the other officers were inspecting her body, Swinney noticed a hole in the draperies. He pulled back the curtain to reveal the remains of a copper jacketed bullet imbedded in the aluminum frame of the jalousie windows, one panel of which had been shattered into an intricate but intact web of tiny cracks. It was the bullet that had passed through Janie's head.

Davidson saw immediately that this would indeed be a tough case, and he assumed it would be his. Still, it belonged to Oldham County, and formalities had to be observed.

"How do you want to handle this, Steve?" he asked Nobles.

"Well, Dan, why don't you take charge of it, and I'll assign Lennie to work with you on it."

Davidson nodded, and without changing expression went outside and set to work. Later, he admitted to a certain excitement that day.

"I'd be lying if I said I didn't get charged up on a homicide. Yeah, it was a challenge to me. Any homicide investigator who sees a body laying there and no perpetrator in sight, it's a challenge.

"A lot of homicides I went to, a man's standing there with a gun saying, 'I did it and I'm glad.' But you get a body that's been there a couple of days, that's a challenge, a real one.

"You've also got an uneasy feeling. What if you don't solve it? What if you don't solve it? That's there every day. Every minute. That uneasy feeling gets worse, too, as the case drags on."

6

Daniel Davidson, Jr., was introduced to homicide at age fifteen by his father, the sheriff of Clay County in the Appalachian Mountains of eastern Kentucky. His father took him to a cabin where an old man, an old woman, and their two grown but feebleminded children had been slaughtered over a boundary dispute at their crude supper table while eating corn bread and soup beans (the Kentucky mountain term for pinto beans). Davidson never would forget the sight of the old man's brains mingled on the plate with his soup beans, but it wouldn't affect his taste for the beans, one of his favorite foods.

In the thirty years that had passed since, Davidson had been witness to the effects of more murders than he could remember, so many that he needed something to remind him of individual cases. Under his living room coffee table he kept a grisly scrapbook, fat with photographs of victims of murders he had investigated. In it were people who had been shot, stabbed, garroted, hung, scalded, clubbed, hacked, choked, smothered, left out to freeze, run down by vehicles, and otherwise dispatched, often for trivial or inexplicable reasons. He had investigated cases in which a four-year-old girl shot her three-year-old brother, in which neighbor shot neighbor in an argument over a twenty-nine-cent toy, in which brother killed brother over a slice of watermelon. One young couple doused their four-year-old child with boiling water because he cried too much.

Of the scores of murders Davidson had investigated in twenty-seven years with the state police, only two had gone unsolved—and they still nagged him. He'd worked ten years on one of those cases: the asphyxiation of an old mountain storekeeper in a robbery. He knew who did it but couldn't get proof that would hold up in court. "I did everything, by God, except use voodoo on them sons-a-bitches," he told colleagues in exasperation.

Solving murders, busting moonshine stills, putting outlaws in jail—all the things his father had done—was the only career Davidson ever considered. In the hills and hollows where he grew up, he knew he'd never face a shortage of work.

Davidson was born on Bullskin Creek near the tiny coal-mining town of Oneida on the South Fork Kentucky River, delivered by frontier nurses, who took medical care to isolated mountain people by Jeep and horseback. His parents divorced when he was five, leaving him to live temporarily with his grandfather, a storyteller of such repute that people came from all over the hills to hear his tall tales (a noted columnist from Louisville, Joe Creason, even came to record some of them for city folk). After his father remarried and settled into a small white house in Oneida, a settlement built around the Oneida Baptist Institute, a school established for mountain children who had no other place to go, Davidson went to live with him. His father had married a teacher, a proper woman named Ima Jean, who not only had a master's degree but knew the value of etiquette as well as education. She set about transforming the free-spirited mountain boy who loved fishing and frog gigging into a young gentleman who could make his way outside the hills. She honed his table manners, required daily readings of Emily Post, made sure that he did his school lessons, and even, over his protests, taught him such skills as crocheting.

By the time Davidson was in high school, playing forward on Oneida Institute's basketball team and winning a state marksmanship contest, his daddy was sheriff, and Davidson already knew that he, too, wanted to be a lawman. As a small child he had been impressed by the uniform his father wore during the year he was a highway patrolman, before the state police agency was formed in 1948. He enjoyed the company of lawmen who were his father's friends, and by age thirteen he and his own friends had started a weekend game of cops and robbers that would continue for years and range for miles over the mountains. Even then, Davidson took pride in his ability to catch the bad guys.

Later, he tried to explain why he was sure of what he wanted to do with his life long before he got out of school. "Every movie you saw, every book you read, had something to do with a lawman. It just seemed interesting to me. I thought it would be prestigious."

After his graduation from high school in 1956, Davidson was staying with his mother in Cincinnati when his father called to tell him about an opening for a state police dispatcher at London in adjoining Laurel County. He came home, took the required test, and got the job. He lived at the post; worked eight hours a day, six days a week, on the radio; and when he wasn't sleeping, he was riding with troopers, getting experience for the day when he would become one himself.

After four years as a dispatcher, he was admitted to the State Police Academy in Frankfort in September 1960. By then he had married a nurse, and two days before his graduation, he drove nine hours round-trip over snow-covered mountain roads to be present for the birth of his first child, a daughter, Deanna Lynn. He made it back to Frankfort in time to complete his training, and returned proudly to the mountains wearing a trooper's uniform, his youthful ambitions fulfilled. His first assignment was Post Ten in Harlan, the seat of Harlan County, where he had worked his last year as dispatcher.

Harlan County is a testing ground for many new troopers. The most rugged of Kentucky's mountain counties, it clings to the Virginia border in the southeastern corner of the state, its mountains underlain with five seams of bituminous coal, one atop another, in one of the world's richest deposits. Bloody Harlan, it was called, because of the battles fought between the coal companies and the miners for half a century, battles waged by night riders with tommy guns and dynamite, battles that on several occasions had brought the National Guard to occupy the county.

When Davidson came to it as a trooper, Harlan was a

county of rickety coal camps, poverty-ravaged hollows, and grimy little towns, its streams sluggish with silt from slag heaps, their banks laden with the stripped carcasses of abandoned cars and appliances, its tortuous roads clogged on weekdays by monstrous, gear-grinding coal trucks and on weekend nights by wild young men sloshed with bad whiskey in overpowered cars. It was a county of independent-minded people, where the first possession a boy longed for was a gun, and where guns were the first things reached for when disputes arose. "That's just the way they settle their problems, using their guns," Davidson recalled matter-of-factly. "They don't spend a whole lot of time trying to talk these things over."

Some young troopers are quickly broken by the violence, the long hours, the tensions of duty in Harlan County, but Davidson thrived on it, and heeding lessons learned from his father, he began building a reputation as tough but fair.

Troopers in Harlan spend much of their time working traffic, and Davidson had long been accustomed to the carnage that is common on mountain roads. As a teenager, when his father was sheriff, three boys he knew died when their car ran under a logging truck, leaving their bodies so mutilated that they were carried away in parts. Only after the bodies were reassembled at a hospital was it realized that a part was missing. Davidson was present when somebody brought his friend's head into the sheriff's department in a bushel basket.

In the eight years he spent as a trooper, Davidson investigated so many bloody accidents that only the worst remained seared in his memory: the bodies of five teenage boys crumpled in a creek after their car left the road at high speed and overturned; a head-on crash on a blind curve that killed nine people, leaving only the crying of a single bloodied little girl to break the eerie silence of the aftermath.

Troopers also worked criminal cases—thefts, robberies, fights, murders—and that was what appealed to Davidson. By his second year on the job he had become the most famous trooper in the district to at least one segment of the population—the moonshiners and bootleggers. He loved catching moonshiners at their stills and stopping bootleggers' cars heavy with their illicit loads. His father, too, had been a big still hunter, credited with busting 290 stills in his four years as sheriff. "I kinda picked that up, actually, from him," Davidson admitted, acknowledging that he attempted to break his father's record.

"I was really on a tear. I was on a crusade. Those guys were smart. It really presented a challenge to catch 'em, just like catching a big bass."

His fervor was such that the bootleggers organized and put a $15,000 bounty on his head, but a plan to kill him by calling him to a fake accident was foiled when officers got a tip about the setup. Davidson didn't let the threat stop him.

"I don't guess I had enough damn sense to worry that much about it," he said.

The bootlegging and moonshining had much to do with the violence with which Davidson had to deal. "Friday and Saturday night, Sunday afternoons, especially in summertime, it'd get up in the nineties, and they'd go to drinkin' that moonshine and it started workin' on 'em. Everybody'd get mad at everybody else. You could just about predict when you'd get a killing. It'd be hot and muggy. You'd be riding around saying 'Well it won't be long and we'll get a call' and sure enough . . ."

Most of the killings came in moments of passion brought on by love triangles or disputes of one kind or another—"Harlan County justice"—and were no challenge to investigative skills. Occasionally, a case of another type cropped up—such as the librarian found stabbed sixty-eight times. She had one butcher knife protruding from an eye, another from her throat. Davidson spent nearly a year tracing that to a mental patient who once lived in the victim's neighborhood. The killer claimed that the Lord had directed her to send the librarian home to heaven. And there was the case of the storekeeper on Jones Creek, near Verda, who had been bound, wrapped in a curtain, and left to suffocate after a robbery in 1961—the case on which Davidson had spent the most effort of his career, earning for him only frustration.

By 1969 Davidson had given up his trooper's uniform to devote himself completely to criminal cases as a detective. Two years later, in January 1971, he was promoted to detective sergeant and transferred across the state to Post Five at La Grange in Oldham County. By then he was separated from his wife and two children (a son, Daniel Keith, was born in 1962), and he looked at the move as a chance to start anew. In September of that year, as soon as his divorce was final, he married a receptionist he'd met at Harlan Hospital. He and his new wife, Karen, moved into a trailer on the Oldham County Fairgrounds, next to the state police post, and Davidson built horseshoe pits in one of the exhibition buildings. Karen worked for a while at the women's prison, then took the job of clerk-receptionist at the police post. Later, Dan and Karen moved into a small brick house on Highway 53 overlooking ninety-acre Crystal Lake, where he could fish for bass whenever he pleased. He put covered horseshoe pits in his backyard, set aside one room for his pitching trophies, and hung over his bed a large painting of Jesus holding a protective hand over a state trooper's car.

The change from Harlan County was dramatic. Oldham was a prosperous rural county with almost no poverty and little violence. "For a long time, I kinda felt like I didn't have anything to do," Davidson remembered.

By 1982, Davidson had attended the FBI National Academy, where local law enforcement agencies send their elite for training, had served as president of the National Academy's graduates in Kentucky, and had risen to the rank of lieutenant. After his promotion, he was sent to another post on temporary duty to help solve some difficult homicide cases, then was offered a chance to move to headquarters in Frankfort as head of intelligence. He tried the headquarters job for six weeks and requested a return to Oldham County. He chafed at desk work. His heart lay in catching outlaws, not in administration. As deputy post commander and head of criminal investigation, administrative duties took up most of his time, but he still could be a detective, still could get his juices stirred by an intriguing case.

But by July 1984, when he got the call about the murders on Covered Bridge Road, Davidson had begun entertaining notions of retirement. Being so often in the presence of death, violence, and evil bothered him more now than it had in his days of youthful exuberance. Under his tough veneer, he was a gentle and sensitive man who soon would miss a day's work while grieving over the death of his dog, Sarge. Unlike most men who grew up in the mountains—and many of his friends— Davidson didn't like the sport of hunting. Tracking the animals was fine, but he'd never been able to bring himself to shoot a rabbit or deer. He often dreamed of being in shootouts in which he was wounded, or in which he had to shoot somebody, a prospect he dreaded. Only once had he fired at a human being. That was in his second year as a trooper, when he had to stop a fleeing kidnapper who had hit him in the head and escaped. Davidson fired two warning shots before aiming low to stop the man and hitting him in the foot. "A lucky shot," said the onetime state marksmanship champion, whose eye was so keen that he could throw ringers in horse-shoes 80 percent of the time. Davidson even resisted using his nightstick in scuffles—and he had been in many. He took a lot of ribbing from other officers when, while trying to subdue a marauding, drug-berserk motorcycle gang member who'd attacked several people, he chose to stop him with an uppercut instead of his nightstick, and broke his little finger for his humanitarian effort, keeping him from the horseshoe pits for weeks.

Other things, too, had set Davidson to thinking about retirement. He wasn't sure he liked the direction police work was taking. He saw too much interagency rivalry, too much demand for credit. "They forget the objective is to put the outlaws in jail," he said. "When I first started in law enforcement, we just tried to put the goddamn outlaws away and it didn't matter who shut the door."

He also feared that the day of the old-time detective who followed his intuitions, using legwork to chase leads wherever they led until he solved the case, was past. He foresaw a day when detectives would spend most of their time at computer terminals following the directions of bureaucrats. He resented the by-the-book, no-common-sense, bureaucratic young officers who seemed to be seizing command without really knowing how to work a difficult case.

"Homicides, you've got to live 'em," he said. "You can read all the books in the world and that won't help you in a homicide."

With more than twenty-seven years in the state police, Davidson already had more service than many retired officers. He knew he could get a nice pension. And he could envision himself enjoying a life where no outlaws or murderers intruded, chasing after nothing more elusive than lunker bass, sitting back employing his droll sense of humor in the service of tall tales, as his grandpa had done.

Friends told him that he was crazy. He wouldn't know what to do if he retired, they said. The first time a big murder broke, he'd be champing at the bit to find the killer. And as soon as he got to the house on Covered Bridge Road, saw the bodies of Delores and Janie, realized what a tough case this was apt to be, and felt the juices of challenge beginning to flow again, Davidson knew that his friends were right.

7

Some things were evident quickly. The decomposition of Delores's body, the Sunday newspaper beneath it, the Bible nearby told Dan Davidson and the other officers that the murders had not taken place in recent hours and most likely occurred two days earlier, probably as Delores was returning from church. That meant a cold trail.

The position of the body, the wounds, the keys near the door indicated that she had been taken by surprise from behind, hit with high-speed bullets, probably from close range. The angle of the wounds, the blood splatters on the entrance and garage doors said that she had been hit first in the back, again in the head as she was falling, most likely by somebody lying in wait behind one of the cars. The frame of her glasses was found twelve feet away, a lens thirteen feet beyond that. Bits of skull and flesh were scattered for thirty feet.

Delores had been killed first, Davidson surmised. The bullet hole in the storm drain at the end of the house indicated that Janie had taken the first shot in the back as she was trying to get inside the kitchen door. In her left hand was a tissue filled with dog dung. Later, when Davidson learned that Delores and Janie always picked up the dog droppings from the yard, he concluded that Janie definitely had been outside when the killer accosted her. Either she was already dead when her mother arrived, or she was in the backyard, or returning inside, heard the shots that killed her mother, went to investigate, and surprised the killer, who might not have been aware of her presence.

Whichever, it appeared certain that she had been chased through the house before receiving the fatal shot to the base of her skull. Blood drops on the kitchen floor just inside the door indicated that she paused there, probably trying to grab the telephone. She apparently had run around the counter in panic, through the kitchen, jumped a two-foot-high dog gate with bullet holes in her right lung, passed through the family room, and continued down the hallway, perhaps pausing again at the linen closet in an attempt to set off the alarm. She left another blood smear on the corner of her mother's bedspread as she raced around it into the bedroom, only to find herself trapped in the French room. The angle of the killing shot indicated that she was crouching when the second bullet struck her. Unlike her mother's death, hers came with terror.

Guesses about the small bullet lodged in the window frame centered on a .223, used in military assault rifles. A grease smudge on Delores's white chenille bedspread outlined the impression of such a weapon, laid there, no doubt, while the killer rummaged through the inexpensive contents of Delores's jewelry box.

Was robbery the motive for these brutal slayings? Steve Nobles, the Oldham County police chief, thought so. His department had answered several calls to the Lynch house in recent years, usually to investigate prowler reports from Delores, or because an alarm went off when nobody was home. In November 1977, somebody broke out a window and set off the alarm before fleeing. In September 1980, somebody stole Delores's big red riding mower. It later was recovered by state police, and the thief, an escaped prisoner, was sentenced to serve more time.

The house, however, had not been ransacked. Items that an ordinary thief might take—TVs, tape recorders, the police scanner (illegal in Kentucky) beside Delores's bed, the silver service in the dining room—were left untouched. The most valuable items in the house—the Oriental rugs in the living room, dining room, and foyer (estimated value, $50,000)—were still on the floor. Only Delores's and Janie's jewelry boxes had been dumped onto their beds. Still, Nobles thought perhaps the thief had been surprised in his work, had killed Janie in panic, then had to kill Delores to make good his escape. Perhaps he'd killed both women, then been frightened off before he could make his haul. Or maybe he'd come to steal a specific item and had found it without having to ransack the house.

Sherman Childers, the detective who'd worked for thirteen years with Davidson, had another theory.

"This was a hit," he said, after examining both bodies. "A pro took these people out."

Davidson tended to side with Childers, whose instincts he trusted implicitly. But he didn't rule out the possibility of robbery. His experience taught him never to rule out anything without evidence.

Daylight was waning and much had to be done. Davidson put out calls for Dr. George Nichols, the state medical examiner, who would perform the autopsies—Dr. Death, the officers called him—and for commonwealth attorney Bruce Hamilton, who would prosecute the case if it came to court. Both were colorful men with forceful opinions and no reluctance to offer theories, which Davidson knew he would have to suffer. His quest now was for fact, though, not theory. He called for more uniformed troopers, sent some to canvass nearby roads looking for abandoned vehicles or anything else suspicious, others to question neighbors. The Jefferson County evidence team arrived, but left after learning that a state police mobile crime lab was on the way from Frankfort. After the crime lab arrived and the technicians set to work dusting for fingerprints, collecting fibers, hairs, bullet fragments, blood samples, and other possible evidence, Davidson organized a group of officers for a thorough search of the yard and nearby woods. Spreading out arm-to-arm, the officers moved across the yard on hands and knees.

Within forty-five minutes of Davidson's arrival, reporters and photographers began showing up. Kept on the road by officers assigned to guard the perimeter of the property, the reporters sought comments from all who would offer them. Photographers trained their cameras on the house and the comings and goings of police. Powerful lenses picked up Delores's body, barely visible from the road.

Davidson believed in keeping good relations with the press, which, he knew, could be helpful. "I believe in letting the public know as much as you can," he explained later. "There's very few crimes, if any, where somebody doesn't know something about it. They may not know it's important, but it may be just the one little thing that we need. If you let the reporters know all you can and keep 'em up with what you're doing, somebody will come forward eventually." Like all homicide detectives, however, Davidson held back key bits of information, things only the murderer could know. Those bits would help eliminate attention seekers who might confess to the crime, and could prove crucial in tripping up suspects in interviews.

In this case, though, there was little to give out other than barest details—the identities and ages of the victims, that they had been shot, Delores found outside and Janie inside. As for motive, Sergeant Dennis Clark, the Oldham County information officer, hedged "A possible motive is robbery" he told reporters. "There are a few things in disarray that makes that a possibility."

The reporters wandered off to talk to neighbors and later questioned Dr. Nichols, who told them about the wounds, speculated that they had been caused by small-caliber, high-velocity bullets, and reported no signs of sexual molestation.

At 6 P.M., news of the murders was on every TV station in Louisville. By 8 P.M., crime lab technicians had finished their work around Delores's body, and men wearing surgical masks lifted it into a black plastic body bag and carried it to a hearse that would take it to the morgue at Humana Hospital in Louisville. Janie's body would remain in place two hours more.

When thorough searches of the parking lot and house turned up no empty shell casings, Sherman Childers's belief that a hit man had done this job was reinforced. The average thief wouldn't use a shell catcher on his weapon and likely wouldn't have the presence of mind, or take the time, to collect empty shells—especially a thief who was frightened off before he could make his haul.

Childers knew, too, that he and Lennie Nobles, the

Oldham County detective assigned to the case by his brother, would be doing most of the legwork in the investigation.

"We've got problems here," he told Lennie, who'd been a detective only five weeks and had never worked a murder. "It's just too neat. No evidence. No nothing."

Like his boss and close friend Davidson, Childers was a man of few words, a native of the Kentucky mountains and the son of a lawman. At forty-three, twice married and twice a father, his hair was graying; and at 210 pounds, he carried a little more weight on his six-foot frame than he liked. He had been a detective for fourteen years.

Lynn (Lennie) Nobles had just turned twenty-nine. He was short, lean, and freckled, with orange-tinged hair that lay in curls. The son of a career military man, he had spent most of his early years in California but had finished high school in Louisville. He had followed two of his brothers into police work seven years earlier. Rarely at a loss for words, he was cocky and eager to get on with finding out who killed Delores and Janie. That the murders might not be solved never entered his mind. Davidson smiled at the brashness of this new detective, knowing that this case likely would temper his confidence.

There was no supper break for Davidson, Childers, and Lennie Nobles that night. They drank Cokes from Delores's refrigerator and ate bananas from her kitchen as they began a thorough search of the house, looking for things that would tell them about Delores and Janie—and lead them, they hoped, to the killer. They found address books, letters, a few tape recordings, bank records, Delores's will. They made note of several large disbursements by Delores to her son, Tom, in Albuquerque. They also noticed that in her will Delores left the house and cars to Janie, the remainder to be divided by Janie and Tom. Was that an indication of favoritism that could have led to resentment?

As the evening wore on, information began accumulating. A neighbor thought he heard shots Saturday night. Another saw a suspicious black trucklike vehicle turning around in his driveway after midnight Sunday morning. And Davidson had discovered in Delores's records that

Helen Stewart had been Delores's maid. He'd investigated the killing of Helen's uncle by her boyfriend, whom Delores had supported in jail and court, a man who'd done odd jobs around her house. Davidson also had had dealings with members of Helen's family who'd been in scrapes with the law. His suspicions were aroused.

But detective work is often a process of elimination, and he knew the first person he'd have to eliminate was Tom Lynch, the one person who would gain financially from the deaths of his mother and sister.

It was 1:30 A.M. before the weary officers decided to quit for the day. Davidson assigned a trooper, Tom Kelly, to guard the house through the night, and suggested that he stay inside and watch TV. Kelly, who had a reputation for fearlessness, declined. There was something he didn't like about that house, he said. He didn't want to be in it alone. He'd watch it from his cruiser.

8

An hour after the news of the Lynch murders appeared on TV in Louisville, a volunteer minister who served one day a month as chaplain of the Albuquerque Police Department approached Tom Lynch's Spanish-style dental office on Montgomery Boulevard. It was a little before 5 P.M., and Tom was rushing to get away. His wife, Kathy, was waiting for him at the Hiland Theater. His young sons from his first marriage were in Albuquerque on their court-ordered summer visit, and he was trying to spend as much time with them as possible. This evening, they were going to see *Conan, the Destroyer*. Kathy had called earlier to say that she and the boys would meet him at the theater for the five o'clock showing. He'd have to hurry, she said, because she had only two dollars, hardly enough for tickets, and the boys didn't want to miss any of the movie.

Tom was on his way out when the chaplain stopped him and introduced himself.

"I've got some real bad news," Tom later remembered him saying, filling Tom instantly with fear that something had happened to his wife and children.

"There's been an accident," the chaplain said. "Your mother and sister have been killed."

Mother and Janie dead? An accident? A car wreck, no doubt. That treacherous road his mother lived on. He'd warned her it was dangerous. He'd been especially worried about her driving after her recent cataract surgery.

Actually, it was worse than an accident, the chaplain was saying. Tom's mother and sister had been murdered in a robbery at home.

How could that be? His mother took so many precautions. She had alarms and backup alarms. She had phones in almost every room, even bathrooms. She had a battery-powered CB radio in case the phones and power failed.

Stunned, Tom went out into the dry New Mexico heat and drove to the theater. Kathy knew that something was terribly wrong as soon as she saw him get out of the car across the street. "He looked dazed," she recalled later.

"We have to go," he said, pulling her out of line. "Let's go."

"Why?"

"No, Daddy!" the boys protested. "The movie's about to start."

"I've gotten some bad news," Tom said. "Something's happened to Mother and Janie."

"What?"

"They've been killed."

"No!" cried Kathy.

"Well, Daddy, who shot 'em?" asked Jim, the youngest son, startling his father. Why would a child of eight ask such a question? All the violence on TV?

"That's right, Jim," his father said. "Somebody shot them, but they don't know who."

Kathy gathered up the bewildered boys and followed Tom home, crying all the way.

Next-door neighbors Henry and Irene Eichel took in the boys and sent out for pizza while Kathy and Tom went home and began calling friends and family with the news.

Later that evening, Tom got a call from Helen Stewart, his mother's former maid. She couldn't believe what had happened, she said. She filled him in on details she'd heard on TV and told him she was there to help.

Marjorie Chinnock worked until 9 P.M. at the Kroger store on Brownsville Road in Louisville and came home weary. She turned on the TV and went about some household chores. She paid no attention when she heard a newsbreak about a murder in Oldham County. When a second newsbreak mentioned a mother and daughter being killed, Delores and Janie flitted through her mind, but she dismissed the thought as silly.

The thought struck again when she heard about the murders on a lead-in to the eleven o'clock news. She was turning the dial to another channel when an announcer said the name Lynch. Then she saw Delores's house flash across her screen. She watched with disbelief as the camera zeroed in on the partly obscured body lying by the garage and she recognized the faded dress Delores had worn to church that Sunday.

"It was just paralyzing," she recalled later.

Alone, she had an overpowering need for human contact, and in distress called her sister. That was not enough. Later, she realized what she needed. She got her prayer book, the 1928 book that Delores had fought the church to keep, and read the Requiem. Not until morning, though, did she realize that she might have information that would interest the police.

After his summer school class that Tuesday, Phil Pandolfi got together with boyhood friends. They played football for a while late in the afternoon, lifted weights afterward, then hung out on the street that night, drinking beer and talking about old times. It was after 11 P.M. when Phil got home.

"Ron King called for you," his mother, Rosalie, told him.

"Did he say what he wanted?"

"No, he said he'd call back."

"I hope Janie's not sick," he said.

He'd been thinking a lot about Janie in recent days. Just that morning he'd received her curt note signed "sincerely." It bothered him, and he answered it immediately, trying to smooth things without sounding alarmed, but he couldn't resist trying to make her a little jealous.

"Thanks for the book list," he wrote. "Hope you are feeling better. It's too bad you can not come up. I am going to get tickets for the Mets game this Sunday at Shea. I'll go with my friends. Two more weeks of teaching and I will be done. I will then have four days until I return. I think I might go down to the shore for the last weekend. This girl I went to high school with called me and said she had an extra ticket for Air Supply at the Arts Center so I said I would go. Well, take care of yourself and try not to worry about things. I keep you in my prayers daily. I hope you say yours too."

He signed it with love and enclosed a cartoon he'd enjoyed. He'd mailed the letter only hours earlier.

Phil had just stepped out of the shower when Ron King called again. Reeling from the news, Phil went into his parents' bedroom, where his father, Everett, was watching TV.

"What's the matter?" his father asked.

"He said that Janie and her mother were murdered."

Later, he remembered his mother trying to console him as he kept repeating, "She's not dead."

"I'm not going to Kentucky," he suddenly announced. "This is some nasty trick to get me down there. I'm not going."

In bed later, fighting to sleep, he had a vision of Janie that he recalled vividly. "Janie's mad. She's mad. She's pointing her finger in my face. 'What do you mean you're not coming to the funeral?' she's saying. 'You *better* be there.' Her mother was there just smiling and Janie's shaking her finger at me. 'All right, all right,' I'm saying. 'I'll come, I'll come.' "

When sleep finally came, he found himself jolted awake by a dream. Janie was in a vortex. She was crying out for help. He was struggling to save her, but she was sucked away, leaving him reaching helplessly. Never before had he felt such anger and frustration.

Oldham County was unaccustomed to murder, and by Wednesday, July 25, the county was abuzz with talk of the deaths of Delores and Janie. The *Louisville Courier-Journal* carried a picture of the hearse bearing Delores's body away from her house. The story quoted a neighbor, Zelma Jones, saying of Delores, "She was as plain as an old shoe."

"Nothing like this has ever happened around here," said another neighbor, Anthony Parrish, a young man who had done yard work for Delores. "It's a pretty quiet community. It makes me feel insecure."

No neighbors were feeling quite as insecure as Katy and Howard Cable. Police hadn't found the key to their house that Delores kept. The Cables called a locksmith to change all their locks.

Insecurity wasn't confined to Delores's immediate neighbors. Much of Oldham County's population had come there to escape fear of crime, and now it had reached out to them.

"There was a lot of 'Oh, it couldn't happen here, this is Oldham County,' " recalled Kit Wolfe, the young editor of the county's only newspaper, the *Oldham Era*, a weekly.

For generations, Oldham had been a sparsely populated rural county of large dairy farms and horse farms and only one major employer, which, ironically, was dependent on crime—the state prison system. But the population had burgeoned in the early seventies as affluent people filtered in from Louisville to escape big-city woes. Court-ordered school busing to achieve racial integration brought another wave of middle-class white flight in the late seventies. In little more than a decade, the county's population more than doubled to nearly thirty thousand. Most of the newcomers were in the western half of the county, which bounded the Ohio River, and a rivalry between the newcomers and the old-time residents was reflected in heated sporting events between the county's two middle schools. A rich county, ranked first in the state in percentage of high-income households, Oldham had few blacks and poor people and only one area that could qualify as a slum—Lake Louisvilla, a one-time resort that now resembled a poverty-stricken hollow in the mountains of eastern Kentucky. Lake Louisvilla was familiar to all of the county's law enforcement officers, who often traced minor criminal problems there.

While most of Oldham's residents were pondering the possibility of murder and robbery in their serene midst, some who knew Delores were wondering if robbery had indeed been the cause of the killings.

Paul Rose heard the news and said to his wife, Joyce, "Has Delores offended somebody so much that they've shot her?"

Knowing Delores's abrasiveness and stridency, the Roses considered it possible.

Delores's friends knew that she muscled her way into others' lives and tried to control them.

"Delores put into things that were none of her damn business," Susan Reid said. "She could push you into responding. She could nag the living hell out of you. She never let anybody alone."

"She tried to control me and my kids, and I just told her it was my damn life," said Helen Stewart.

Friends knew, too, that Delores's temper and her feelings of being put upon had caused her to offend many people.

"She could be just as pleasant and nice as anybody," said Susan Reid, "but she could turn just as quick."

Helen Stewart had been witness to many of these incidents. She had slunk away in embarrassment as Delores angrily chastised hapless clerks and waitresses when things didn't please her. She had been present in even touchier situations. Delores didn't like horseback riders passing along the road in front of her house, where the horses occasionally left unsightly plops. She had Paul Rose plant a hedgerow to keep them off her property. When the riders persisted in passing along the road's shoulder, she hid in the shrubs and jumped out with a camera to confront one woman. An argument ensued, and Delores claimed the woman tried to run her down with the horse.

But if somebody was going to kill Delores over such a thing, her friends wondered, wouldn't it be in a moment of passion, not a calculated murder also claiming innocent Janie?

"Delores was a pain in the ass," said Janie's former boyfriend, John Trent. "She was the kind of person you'd invite to leave, then take an aspirin and sit down to rest for an hour or two. But, you know, shooting her in the head is a bit extreme."

9

The Kentucky State Reformatory rises from the open hills of Oldham County like a medieval castle, its twelve-story granite tower an imposing presence on the countryside. Set in the middle of three thousand acres of farmland near La Grange, the prison is Kentucky's largest. At the edge of one of the prison's bean fields, close by State Highway 146, is a modest red-brick structure that is Kentucky State Police Post Five. At the eastern end of the building, in the bedroom-size, institutionally furnished office of the post's two lieutenants, Dan Davidson, the criminal division commander, and Ray Herman, the patrol commander, was a chair upholstered in dull green fabric where guests were received. On Thursday, July 26, two days after the discovery of the bodies on Covered Bridge Road, Davidson was waiting for that chair to be filled by Tom Lynch. So far Davidson was feeling good about the progress being made in case 5-84-543.

"We have gathered an enormous amount of evidence," he had told a *Louisville Times* reporter that morning. "I feel very optimistic."

He and his detectives had indeed collected a lot of information. First thing Wednesday morning, Childers and Nobles had gone to Lake Louisvilla to question Helen Stewart. She claimed to know nothing about the killings, and both detectives believed her. They asked her to go to the house to see if anything was missing. She noticed nothing gone but remembered that Delores had had a gun, a revolver, which the officers hadn't found. She also recalled that Delores usually wore a turquoise cross on a silver chain around her neck. That wasn't on her body, and the detectives couldn't find it in the house. If that was all the killer took, the officers noted, it was small bounty for two lives.

Later that morning, Childers and Nobles had gone to Louisville to watch the autopsies, which had turned up something curious. Delores's blood contained .06 alcohol, only .04 away from legal intoxication. That meant she'd probably had the equivalent of at least two drinks in the hour before her death. The detectives had found two empty beer cans in her bedroom waste baskets, but if she had drunk those before leaving for church, her body would have burned up the alcohol before she got home. Marjorie Chinnock had seen no sign of drinking by Delores, except for the sip of wine at communion, and neither had Butch Rice at the gas station where Delores stopped on her way home. Had she gone somewhere for drinks with someone after leaving church? She hardly had time. Had she been drinking in the car on the way home? If so, she'd left no evidence. The information was puzzling and would remain a mystery.

Davidson had requested an intelligence check on the only surviving family member, Tom, but it had produced nothing of consequence. He also had called airlines to see if Tom had made reservations into or out of Louisville in the past week. He found only the reservation Tom had made for himself, Kathy, and his sons for their planned trip to see his mother on the coming weekend.

Shortly before noon on Thursday, a day ahead of his planned arrival for his visit with his mother, Tom landed at Standiford Field in Louisville with a friend from Albuquerque, Steve Mahieu. He was met by an Oldham County police officer and the department's chaplain, a volunteer Methodist minister, who drove Tom and his friend the twenty-five miles to Post Five. Awaiting them were the four detectives: Davidson, Childers, Nobles, and Swinney.

Tom Lynch was thirty-six, but he still had the rangy, muscular build that had enabled him to become a high school basketball star. At six feet, he towered nearly a foot over all other members of his family. ("Isn't he tall and handsome?" his mother liked to boast when she showed him off to friends. "It's because I kept him so well nourished and gave him so many vitamins.") His long arms, slightly sloped shoulders, and loping gait still gave him the appearance of the point guard whose moves can't be anticipated. His boyish good looks lurked behind a Vandyke beard, and his short brown hair, parted on the right, was combed over his forehead to disguise a slightly receding hairline. His blue eyes were rimmed with red from lack of sleep.

Escorted into Davidson's office, Tom shook hands with the detectives as they offered condolences. "Have a seat," Davidson said, taking a moment to study Tom's face. He saw such a devastated man that he was almost hesitant to question him. He began by asking if Tom had any idea why the murders occurred.

"I've just laid awake two nights thinking how it could happen," Tom said in a voice heavy with pain.

But he had no idea why. He couldn't understand how somebody could have foiled the alarm. His mother always had it on.

"What we need from you is to know if anything is missing," Davidson said.

Tom replied that he wasn't that familiar with his mother's belongings. He knew she had TVs, radios, tape recorders. Not much jewelry. She usually wore plastic jewelry. "My mom's kinda cheap. She didn't want to spend a lot of money."

"I notice she was right meticulous, kept good records," Davidson said.

"She wasn't one to carry a lot of cash."

Davidson wanted to know when Tom last talked with his mother.

"I think it was last week sometime."

She usually called two or three times a week, he explained, but he'd spent the past weekend with his kids and some friends fishing on a lake in Colorado and didn't return home until late Sunday.

"We kind of thought it was strange that she didn't call us Sunday or Monday of this week."

Had his mother expressed any fears?

"No. Other than she's paranoid about the alarm system. I don't know why the alarm didn't go off. I've set it off a million times taking the garbage out."

Tom asked for details of the killings, but Davidson was cautious in reply, not wanting to give away too much.

"This doesn't happen to me," Tom said of the murders, his voice filled with despair.

Davidson changed the subject to Janie.

She was sweet and attractive, Tom said. No serious relationships that he knew about. He mentioned John Trent, the lawyer in Lexington of years ago.

How about friends of his mother?

There was Helen Stewart. "When I got divorced, Mom and Helen came out and cleaned house and cooked for me."

Others?

"I don't remember names too good. I met Susan Reid."

What was Delores like?

"My mom was kind of a character. She's a little bit eccentric, but she had a heart of gold."

Had Tom given any thought to who might have done it?

He figured it was somebody who knew his mother, knew the layout, or knew somebody who did. "My first inclination was that it was somebody who knew Helen."

After some questions about the contents of the house, including Delores's revolver, an H&R .32, Davidson decided that the time had come to get to touchier business.

"Doctor, to be quite candid with you, I don't know whether you realize this or not . . ."

"I think I know what you're going to say," Tom said. "I'm the sole heir. I think you'd be negligent if you didn't look at that possibility, too."

"What's your opinion about a polygraph?" Davidson asked.

"I don't know anything about a polygraph test. I certainly couldn't have done it myself. I was fishing on a lake in Colorado. That's a possibility that didn't occur to me until yesterday."

"Everything there is yours," Davidson said. "There's also a possibility, whoever did this, you could be next. Could be a possibility somebody else wants to inherit it."

"I don't even know who could possibly be in line for it. My whole family is gone."

"This issue here of your inheritance is hard to address.

If you're innocent, which I hope you are—it's very difficult to talk to a feller who's had a tragedy like this."

"This is a nightmare on top of a nightmare, Lieutenant."

"What is your financial condition, Doctor?"

"Well, let's see. I've been in practice about eight years, and I've got a few bills, and I make about a hundred and twenty thousand a year, and I live in a nice house. I've got two cars, I've got an IRA and a little money in the bank. That's it."

As an afterthought, he added that he paid five hundred dollars a month in child support.

Davidson made a note and again brought up the polygraph test.

"If you take care of it and deal with it at the outset, if anybody says what about this guy who got this inheritance, we can say he took a polygraph, he's clean, he's innocent."

"This is elimination," Childers added.

"What I'm trying to get at as tactfully as I can is before you go back to Albuquerque, we'd like to have a polygraph test," Davidson said.

"Well, obviously, that's the only thing to do. I can't refuse to take it."

"Well, you could."

"Obviously, that would be the worst thing to do. I don't know how it works. I've got a little high blood pressure. Obviously, I'm a little upset."

"All of that is taken into consideration."

"I can't imagine anybody killing my mother. I never met anybody who knew them and didn't like them."

"We've got some leads on this case," Davidson said.

"I hope so. I can't imagine somebody getting away with it."

"I hope they don't."

"I'm really concerned," Tom said. "I didn't know if this was a cracker outfit out here in the country, to be honest with you. I felt maybe we had some big ol' Jackie Gleason type of a sheriff and it would just be . . . You guys seem to be working real hard at it. I'd like to be the guy who'd come out here and demand everything be done and stuff, but I realize you guys are pros and you have to do things your way. I mean, I want something done now, but I realize if you don't catch the guy right there, you have to go step by step. I'll try to be patient, too."

"I can assure you, you've got three of the finest investigators in the country on this case," Davidson said of the detectives before him.

Tom agreed to take a polygraph test, and Davidson arranged for it to be administered immediately in Louisville. Childers and Nobles would take him.

Not long into the interview, Davidson's intuition had told him that this mild and emotionally wounded man was not capable of murdering his mother and sister. He wanted to know if he was alone in that feeling.

"I don't think he did it," he said to Childers after Tom had left his office.

"I don't either," said Childers.

But at 5:20 that afternoon, when Sergeant Ron Howard of the Jefferson County Police finished the polygraph test, he reported to Childers that it had proved inconclusive. Tom was too tense and upset, he thought, to get an accurate reading.

Tom was tired, but the detectives wanted him to do one more thing before they took him to his room at the Melrose Inn in Prospect—go by the house and see if he could spot anything missing or out of the ordinary.

When Tom walked into the house and saw the disarray, the scuff marks on the floors left by the officers who'd been trooping in and out, the black fingerprint dust everywhere, his first thought was that his mother was really going to be upset about this mess.

10

The funeral for Delores and Janie, whose bodies had been cremated, was at 10:30 Friday morning at Stoess Funeral Home, a remodeled frame house in Crestwood, next door to the hardware store where, on the day before her death, Delores had gone to see about a holster for her revolver. The chapel was filled with Delores's friends from the Little Colonel Theater and Janie's friends from dental school. Delores's favorite priest, the retired Father R. C. Board, presided, reading the Requiem from the 1928 *Book of Common Prayer*.

Phil Pandolfi thought the service cold and impersonal. Nobody said anything about how sweet and wonderful Janie was. To come to the funeral, Phil used the money he had intended to spend when Janie came to New York—the trip she would have been on the weekend she was killed, if she hadn't changed her mind—and he was feeling lost, left out, and helpless. He thought himself the closest person to Janie present, yet he had no say in anything and nobody knew how he was hurting. "I had so much to share," he said, "and nobody even knew."

During the service, Tom Swinney and a lieutenant from his department, Jim Roberts, took license plate numbers in the parking lot, and afterward they scanned the crowd for suspicious faces.

The ashes of Delores and Janie were taken to Harrod's Creek Cemetery beside Brownsboro Christian Church, a small country church on Covered Bridge Road only a couple of miles from the Lynch home, and buried on a maple-shaded rise.

Saturday morning at 9, Tom arrived again at the Jefferson County Police Department in Louisville with Detectives Swinney and Childers to face his second round of questioning from Ron Howard, the polygraph operator. The session lasted until 12:40, and Tom emerged emotionally drained and agitated. "I was terrified," he recalled later. "I could feel I wasn't doing well. I had a lot of pressure on me, self-imposed pressure. I was worried that somebody would think I did it. I could just see the headlines, 'Son Fails Lie Detector Test.' That would be great, and here I am knowing I'm perfectly innocent. I was so afraid I would respond that I did respond."

Once more, Childers had to report to Davidson that the results were inconclusive, causing his normally placid lieutenant to explode with curses. Tom was leaving the next day for Albuquerque and wouldn't return to deal with family matters for another month—a month of not knowing whether he had something to do with the killings.

The second week of the investigation began with a break that gave Davidson a better idea of what happened on the day of the murders as well as a new clue that might prove valuable.

A citizen called to say he was a sport bicyclist who rode regularly past the Lynch house. His route was marked for distance, and he timed himself as he rode. On Sunday morning, July 22, he passed the house without noticing anything unusual. A short time later, as he reached the entrance to Sleepy Hollow Golf Course, only a mile away, he heard two distant shots in rapid succession, followed a few seconds later by a third. The golf course entrance was one of his distance marks and he was looking at his watch. It was 10:47.

The man hadn't connected the shots with the murders at first, because he thought the killings had occurred on Monday. He also remembered something else that might be significant. About a quarter mile from the Lynch house, he had seen an empty, battered car—yellow with a dark top, maybe an Oldsmobile, 1960s model—parked by a road sign.

A trooper sent to the spot found a wrapper from a Budweiser twelve-pack and several empty cans. Had somebody parked there drinking beer and plotting murder?

The new information not only gave Davidson the exact time of the shootings, it told him that Janie had been alive when her mother arrived. The first two shots had been for Delores, the third, delayed, shot no doubt had been aimed at Janie when she came to investigate and the killer discovered her in the backyard. The fourth shot, fired inside the house, would have been too muffled for the bicyclist to hear.

Next morning, Tuesday, July 31, Davidson held a meeting of detectives in his office. He reviewed everything they had learned, including a new wrinkle—rumors that Tom was a heavy gambler. Assignments were divided. Davidson wanted all of Delores's friends and acquaintances questioned, as well as people who had worked at the Lynch house. He also wanted all of Janie's friends interviewed, particularly anybody she had dated. Even though Delores seemed the primary target, an angry suitor rejected by Janie couldn't be discounted as the killer. Weeks of work lay ahead.

The detectives had been back to the house on Covered Bridge Road every day checking for specific items or clues they might have overlooked. Davidson had spent hours there alone, poking around and contemplating, as if he hoped the house itself might tell him something about the evil it had seen. He didn't like the house. It gave him a strange feeling. "It was a lonely damn place," he recalled later. But he was not ready for the radio call he got from Childers on Wednesday morning, August 1.

"What are these crosses doing down here?" Childers asked, his voice agitated.

"What are you talking about?" Davidson said.

"These damn crosses on the floor."

"Are you guys going crazy?"

Davidson thought it a joke, but Childers made clear it wasn't. He and Nobles had entered the house through the garage and spotted six small crosses fashioned of palm leaves arrayed on the hallway floor, as if some kind of hex. Frightened, they retreated hastily. If Davidson wasn't playing a practical joke, as his detectives knew he was prone to do, somebody had been in the house—or other forces were at work.

Neither Davidson nor Childers believed in ghosts, and both had paid little attention when Helen Stewart mentioned strange experiences she had had in the house. Helen thought the house haunted and didn't like to be in it alone. She'd heard footsteps when no one else was there, she said, had answered voices that never responded. After Chuck Lynch's death, she'd spotted faint impressions of male footprints in the Persian rugs where Delores allowed no feet to tread. "That house was spooky," she adamantly insisted.

Joyce Rose, Delores's friend, who had been to the house many times, didn't think it haunted, but she didn't like the house and had mentioned having strange sensations there. "You could feel the tension and misery in that house," she said.

Childers and Nobles returned with weapons drawn and made a cautious and thorough search. The only explanation they could offer for the crosses was that they had been tucked into the back of a picture on the hallway wall and had fallen when a departing officer slammed a door, but that wasn't a satisfactory explanation, and the mystery of the crosses would forever perplex them.

During his search that day, Childers opened the lavatory cabinet in the bathroom off Delores's bedroom and spotted a revolver and a box of shells. It was Delores's .32 that had been thought stolen. The find was a disappointment. A recovered stolen weapon could be the piece of evidence linking a killer to the scene. Now that possibility was out.

Later that day, Davidson got a call from Albuquerque police asking if he had Tom Lynch under surveillance. Tom had reported strange cars in his neighborhood and was frightened. No, Davidson said, he had no officers in New Mexico. Perhaps the killer was stalking Tom, as Davidson had warned. He told about the rumors of Tom's gambling and asked for help in looking into that.

On August 5, Davidson got his best lead in the case to date. A woman called to report her suspicions that her daughter's boyfriend might be the killer. The boyfriend, José Peralta, was a Cuban refugee who had drifted into Kentucky with another refugee, Felipe Alonzo, to work in the stables of horse farms. After arguing with his girlfriend, he hit her with his fist and threatened her with a gun. The girlfriend's mother said that on the weekend of the Lynch murders, Peralta and Alonzo had stolen riding apparel from a horse farm near the Lynch house, and Peralta had come in with blood on his clothing. Friends of Peralta had told her that he pulled a robbery in another Kentucky town, that he carried a derringer in his boot, and that he bragged of killing people in Cuba.

The detectives grew excited when they learned that Janie had been to the stables a couple of times while Peralta worked there. They got even more excited when they discovered that his friend, Alonzo, drove a beat-up yellow car.

Peralta sold goods at a flea market in Louisville, and the detectives went there, bought riding paraphernalia from him, and took it straight to the horse farm, where it was identified as stolen. Davidson thought his men were closing in on the killers.

Suspicions about the Cubans were buoyed on August 24, with the discovery of two pairs of black riding gloves, similar to those stolen at the stables, in a field behind the Lynch house, an indication that the thieves might have been at the house.

Two days later, Davidson was ready to move against Peralta. Warrants in hand, a group of officers raided his house and arrested him for burglary.

Alonzo was brought in the next day and questioned by Childers and Nobles. He denied knowing anything about the murders and agreed to a polygraph test, which he passed the following day.

"We can write 'em off," said Childers.

On August 29, the detectives confronted Peralta, who insisted he knew nothing about any murders. He agreed to a polygraph test with the stipulation that the questions not stray into burglary.

"After Peralta passed the polygraph," Nobles later recalled, "me and Sherman hit the Patio Lounge in Louisville and got drunk."

That same day, two weeks after his thirty-seventh birthday, Tom returned to Louisville to begin removing his family's belongings from the house on Covered Bridge Road, the house his mother had intended Janie to have. Now it was his, and he wanted to sell it as quickly as possible. Two days after his arrival, Nobles drove him seventy miles to Covington to take his third polygraph examination. Disappointed at the results of the first two tests, Davidson wanted to try another operator this time.

The operator, Louis Mathias, Jr. asked five relevant questions.

1. Regarding the shooting of your sister and mother, do you intend to answer truthfully each question about that?

"Yes," said Tom.

2. Did you yourself shoot your sister and mother?

"No."

3. Did you have someone shoot your sister and mother?

"No."

4. Did you know your sister and mother were going to be killed before it happened?

"No."

5. Do you know for sure who shot your sister and mother?

"No."

Mathias noted reactions to question four, but Tom had explained that he felt something was wrong that weekend when his mother didn't call, and Mathias thought that could have been the reason for the reactions. After studying the polygrams, Mathias reported his opinion: Tom had answered all questions truthfully.

Less than six weeks after the murders, Dan Davidson already had eliminated all suspects. One question was bothering him: Where do we go from here?

When Davidson's mind was troubled, the one spot that offered serenity was the big lake on the grounds of the Kentucky State Reformatory, just over a hill from his office. There he had landed many a lunker bass and gigged many a fat bullfrog while cleansing his mind of tribulation and restoring order to his thinking. The lake had offered him such comfort and pleasure that he told his wife he wanted his ashes scattered over it from the Kentucky State Police plane when he died. As the fall of 1984 approached, Davidson found himself going to the lake with increasing frequency as he fretted about the Lynch murders, a lonely figure hunkered in his tiny boat, rod and reel in hand, rehashing details of the case over and over, searching for answers.

After the Cuban refugees had been eliminated, his detectives, left without primary suspects, had plodded doggedly on, tracing and questioning friends of Delores and Janie, tracking down many of Janie's former dental school classmates, some of whom had moved as far away as Florida. They were searching for anything that might provide new clues but were having little luck.

Many of Janie's friends, they found, were suspicious of Tom. Janie frequently had expressed displeasure about her brother's turning to his parents for financial help to get him out of his first marriage. She blamed him for causing their mother distress with his problems.

Most suspicious of all was Phil Pandolfi, who had been in love with Janie. He had returned to the dental school in such a dazed state over Janie's death that he had trouble concentrating on his studies. Frequently, he drove to Harrod's Creek Cemetery and sat by Janie's grave for hours. He planted geraniums and marigolds, the only marker.

Once Phil even forced himself to face again the house where he'd felt such fear and sensed such evil. He sat on the steps where the killer had clambered to fire the first shot at Janie, and he condemned himself for not paying heed to his fears and doing something to get her away from there. If only she'd come to New York to see him as she'd promised . . . Several times, Phil had been troubled by a dream about Janie. He was sitting with all their friends in the cafeteria at the dental school and she strolled in. "She was so beautiful, dressed in white, her skin and hair aglow. I said, 'Janie, why did you have to die?' She just smiled. 'I'm not dead.' "

*   *   *

On October 18, Albuquerque police called with the results of an extensive background check on Tom. They'd found no evidence of heavy gambling or wrongdoing. Four days later, Davidson called Tom to report on developments and asked if he gambled. Nothing more than losing a few dollars at the track now and then, Tom said.

On October 26, Phil Pandolfi wrote to Tom.

> *I'm sorry it has taken me so long to contact you, but I just did not know the right time. Janie was very special to me and I loved her very much.*
>
> *Janie and your mother were wonderful people. Your mother always made me feel at home when I went out to the house.*
>
> *I really do not know what to say but I want you to know how I felt about them. A day does not go by that I don't think about her or miss her. It just does not seem fair because everything seemed so perfect.*
>
> *If there is anything that you need or want to know don't hesitate to contact me. Is it possible for me to have something of Janie's to remember her by? I think it would help a little.*

He made a handwritten copy of the letter, and on the back he wrote: "This is a copy of the letter I sent to Janie's brother. I might have indicated to him that I know something so if anything should happen to me this letter may (most likely) have been the cause. My past history does not suggest that anyone else would be out to get me."

His suspicions of Tom grew deeper when he received no reply.

The strain of having half its detective force assigned to a single case began to show on the Oldham County Police Department, and Lennie Nobles had to be pulled off the Lynch investigation from time to time to ease the burden. By November, he was heavily involved in a pressing child abuse case, but at night he occasionally was troubled by dreams of Delores's face crying out to him, "Lennie, find my killer."

At one point, Nobles went to Louisville and talked with a long-time homicide detective about the case. "That family has a dark cloud in it somewhere," the detective said. "Find that cloud and you've found your killer." Nobles eagerly repeated the quote to Davidson.

Faced with no new leads, Davidson called Tom and asked him to increase by $5,000 the $10,000 reward he'd already offered. Tom agreed, and Davidson began running ads in Louisville newspapers.

The new reward provoked only a couple of crank calls. One man insisted that TV evangelists Jerry Falwell and Jimmy Swaggart were behind the murders. A woman said that Delores's dogs should identify any suspects, and Davidson tried to picture himself going to court with two neurotic Yorkshire terriers as his chief witnesses, only one capable of talking and it with a grand vocabulary of one word—*mama*.

By early December, Davidson was seeking help from the press. DOUBLE MURDER LEAVES POLICE FRUSTRATED, read the headline in the *Courier-Journal* on December 5.

"Our biggest problem in solving this case is that there is no definite motive," Davidson was quoted. "I feel that there's someone out there who can help us. I believe there is someone who can give us enough information to lead us in the right direction that just hasn't come forward yet."

He concluded with this: "We never forget a murder case. We never shelve it. It's always there, especially this one, where we've got two people. We're going to find out who did this if it takes forever."

The story brought no new information, and Davidson began looking to other sources. He prepared a synopsis for a nationwide bulletin over the police information network to see if similar cases had occurred elsewhere. He checked into a case in Illinois in which a woman had been shot dead at her garage door.

Six days before Christmas, Nobles and Childers put the whole case together and delivered it to the FBI in the hope that a psychological profile of the killer could be compiled. But that, too, proved futile, because their information was insufficient.

Christmas passed with no new developments, and the new year brought only more frustration.

"It's disgusting," Childers told a *Louisville Times* reporter in late January.

"About the only thing we haven't done in this case is recruit the efforts of some psychics," Davidson said. He had little faith in psychics, but he had done some research and was ready with records and recommendations if Tom or higher officials wanted one.

Davidson was more than frustrated. His preoccupation with the Lynch murders bordered on obsession. The case had grown to two fat books, each nearly a foot thick, and he spent hours poring through them, reading and rereading reports. At night as he lay in bed, scenarios marched through his brain, preventing sleep. When he did sleep, he was frequently jolted awake by a forgotten theory, a new possibility, and he would climb from bed, careful not to awaken his wife, and go to the living room to make notes. His stomach was in such advanced rebellion that the antacid and Tagamet tablets he regularly gobbled no longer could quell it.

February brought another blow to the case. Childers slipped on ice, broke his ankle, and was out of work for three months. He felt that he was letting Davidson down, especially now that Nobles was regularly being pulled away to work burglaries and other cases for his hard-pressed department.

Davidson was desperate for new leads. His detectives had spent many fruitless hours checking reports from prisoners hoping to curry favor by implicating other inmates or ex-inmates in the killings, but Davidson thought a former prisoner might have done it, and he requested a computer printout of all inmates released from Kentucky prisons for two years preceding the murders and began studying it for suspects. He also assigned an ambitious young trooper, Rick Yetter, to a month of special duty interviewing service people who had been to the Lynch house, as well as Janie's dental school patients.

He even entertained a theory that he thought outlandish. Knowing how much Delores hated her husband and all the humiliations she had heaped upon him, could Chuck have executed a postdeath contract on her, perhaps with a Chicago hit man, so that she wouldn't be able to enjoy the fruits of his long and productive labors?

The last day of February brought a new break from an anonymous caller. Jason King either killed the Lynch women or knew who did, the caller said. Lennie Nobles recognized the name immediately. A week after the murders, a Louisville detective had called Oldham County police to say that King should be checked, but Nobles dismissed the tip after learning King was in custody on other charges.

Now Nobles discovered that King had escaped from a juvenile detention center on Friday, July 20, two days before the murders, and hadn't been returned to custody until July 24, the day the bodies were discovered. Moreover, Delores's friends from the Little Colonel Players remembered that she spoke of trying to help a troubled young man named Jason, whom she'd met at the Actors Theater in Louisville.

Troubled was hardly the word for Jason King. He had an above-average IQ, a hatred of women and authority figures, and a fascination with cruelty and violence. He had been in trouble with police since childhood. "A worthless little terror," Nobles called him.

By the time he was in high school, King and his closest friend, Calvin Richards, had formed a gang of twelve boys and two girls, all from affluent families, Nobles was told. The gang met for occult rituals involving alcohol and drugs, including LSD, as well as animal sacrifices. They boasted of slitting a cow's throat and holding an orgy in its blood.

The gang played a game called Invasion. They broke into upper-class homes and rearranged the furniture without taking anything, leaving the gang's symbol spray-painted on a wall as a reminder of vulnerability. The group also occasionally rounded up neighborhood pets and buried them alive with their heads protruding so that King and Richards could run power lawn mowers over them.

Nobles discovered that King had several weapons at different times, including an M16 assault rifle, the same type of weapon used in the Lynch murders, as well as Ping-Pong ball explosives and diagrams for more elaborate bombs. King had also boasted to friends of earlier killings, although they had not believed him.

On March 16, Nobles found one of the gang's hide-outs, a cavelike rock overhang just off Interstate Highway 71 north of Louisville, only six miles from the Lynch house. Jason King's name and the gang's symbol were scratched into the rock. Nobles had hoped to find evidence there, perhaps a spent bullet that could be matched to the one that killed Janie, but he turned up only the remains of a fire, some garbage, and a couple of soft drink cans riddled with bullet holes.

Nonetheless, Nobles was confident that he was on the way to fulfilling Delores's demand that haunted his dreams. Even Davidson was warily optimistic.

When King refused to be interviewed, Nobles and Davidson supoenaed his juvenile and psychiatric records. With the help of Detective Les Simpson, Nobles questioned people who had interrogated King, as well as his friends and gang members.

King, the detectives learned, had escaped with the idea of freeing his friend Richards from a detention center in Louisville, but after being picked up by police following the attempt, he had written a letter saying he couldn't tell what happened that weekend because it could get him in big trouble.

The center from which King escaped was in south-central Kentucky, and King didn't make his way back to Louisville until late Saturday. He'd spent that night at the home of a female friend. She told Nobles that he'd left about 10 Sunday morning—less than an hour before the murders—unarmed and on foot, with plans to meet a friend. The friend said he'd picked up Jason at a subdivision on U.S. Highway 42 between 11 and 11:30, and had taken him to the Central Kentucky Treatment Center northeast of Louisville, where they had failed to make contact with Richards. King was neither armed nor bloodied, nor was he acting as if he'd just killed somebody, when he was picked up, the friend said.

The spot where the friend had picked up King was 7.6 miles from Delores's house. Nobles drove the route over and over, timing himself. The fastest he made it was ten minutes, thirty-three seconds. The first shots at the Lynch house came at 10:47. King couldn't have gotten there and back on foot. He barely could have done it with a car. Did he hitchhike? If so, where did he get the weapon? Who would give him a ride carrying an M16? And what had he done with the gun afterward? Did he have an accomplice? If so, King's friends had no idea who it might be, and Nobles couldn't find any such person.

Beyond that, King had mentioned nothing about the Lynch killings to anybody. If he had done it, Nobles thought he would have bragged. Reluctantly, after a month of hard work, Nobles concluded that King and his gang were not involved. It was the lowest point in the investigation not only for him but for Dan Davidson. Then, on March 28, something happened that took them even lower.

When Ruby Bickers, the city clerk of Carrollton, failed to show up for work, and telephone calls to her house went unanswered, the town's police chief went to see what was wrong. He found the front door of the middle-class brick house open, and stepped inside to a startling scene. Blood was everywhere—on the walls, the floors, the ceilings—and Ruby Bickers was lying in the hallway, her body hacked repeatedly with a hatchet. In a utility room at the back of the house lay her husband, Roy, also hacked to death.

Carrollton, an Ohio River town about thirty miles north of State Police Post Five at La Grange, is within the post's jurisdiction, and when state police were called into the investigation, responsibility fell to Dan Davidson. Never before had he had two double murders at one time, and he called Steve Nobles, chief of the Oldham County police, and told him that the new case would have to take priority.

Davidson suspected no link between the cases. The Lynch murders were cool and professional, but the Bickerses had been slaughtered in a savage frenzy, perhaps by somebody on drugs, Davidson thought. Many items were missing from the Bickers house.

Davidson felt no stirring of juices over these new homicides, only depression.

"I thought, goddamn, I'm going to wind up going out of the state police with two double murders not solved," he recalled.

"After that, nobody had to ask was he retiring," said his wife, Karen. "They knew he wouldn't until those two cases were solved."

As the new investigation stretched on, Davidson couldn't shake his obsession with the Lynch case. So frustrated was he with his inability to penetrate its mysteries that not even the trusted and dependable waters of Kentucky State Reformatory Lake, still drawing him irresistably, offered much comfort and hope. In early May 1985, he assembled the reports from the case along with Delores's private files and took them home to go through again at night. Surely, somewhere in that huge mound of material was something he had overlooked, something that would give him a new direction, and he intended to find it.

PART TWO

MURDER IN THE FAMILY

11

The tobacco cycle dominates life in Reidsville, a town of 13,000 near the Virginia border in north-central North Carolina.

In late winter, fabric-covered plant beds sprout in the red-dirt countryside, nurturing tobacco seeds to an early start. After last frost, the fragile plants are set in the hilly fields, and by midsummer they are head high and richly green, and the farmers and their families can barely be seen as they prowl the rows, snapping off the white blossoms to encourage new growth. Late summer brings the harvest. The heavy leaves are stripped from the stalks a few at a time from the bottom up—"priming," the farmers call this—and taken to barns for curing. Early fall sees the golden leaves hauled into town in huge, burlap-wrapped bundles on the back of tail-drooping pick-up trucks. For weeks, the pungent, dusty air of the cavernous warehouses rings with the traditional singsong chants of the auctioneers as the overall-clad farmers anxiously wait to see if their labors were profitable.

The aroma of tobacco—the smell of money, the towns-people call it—clings to Reidsville year-round, wafting from the old red-brick buildings of the American Tobacco Company with its huge smokestacks proclaiming the town the home of Lucky Strike cigarettes. Lucky City, Reidsville once called itself.

Reidsville grew from a settlement around a tobacco plantation on Little Troublesome Creek in Rockingham County. The first tobacco factory opened in 1858, fifteen years before the town was incorporated. By the end of the century, the number of tobacco factories had burgeoned to eleven, and Reidsville's production of smoking tobacco was second highest in the state. One of those factories was opened by F. R. Penn, who came from Patrick County, Virginia, in 1874. The Penn factory soon grew to be the biggest in town. In 1911, it was bought by James Buchanan "Buck" Duke, who created a tobacco monopoly with his American Tobacco Trust. That same year, the federal government forced the dissolution of Duke's monopoly, but the Penn Company remained part of American Tobacco under the direction of C. R. Penn—Mr. Charlie, he was called around town—the founder's eldest son. Two years later, Mr. Charlie was made a vice president of American Tobacco and assigned to company headquarters in New York, where he was said to have perfected the blend for a new cigarette. That cigarette was given the name of one of the earliest commercial chewing tobaccos, Lucky Strike, a throwback to the gold rush days and an apt description for the prosperity it would bring Reidsville for decades to come.

By 1914, two years before the appearance of Lucky Strikes, four thousand people called Reidsville home. It was not only a prosperous town but a lively one. Saloons were said to outnumber churches, and on the southern edge of town was the only mile-long harness racing track between Atlanta and Washington. That year, the year he turned thirty-seven, James Merritt Sharp drove into town in a Model-T Ford. With him were his wife and four small children, behind him a string of failures and bad luck that he hoped Reidsville would change.

James Sharp was born in New Bethel Township west of Reidsville, the sixth of nine children. His father, James Marshall Sharp, who bore a striking resemblance to Robert E. Lee, was a Civil War veteran who'd returned home from Gettysburg with rifle balls in his chest and jaw. A farmer and orchardist, James Marshall Sharp was an erudite man, the only person in his community who subscribed to the *Atlanta Journal*. His wife, Eliza Garrett Sharp, a severe-looking woman who wore her long hair in a tight bun, was a fierce, foot-stomping Primitive Baptist with strong ideas about heaven and hell.

As boy and young man, James Merritt Sharp labored in his father's fields, but he had a keen mind and craved education. For several years he attended a one-room log school near his home. Later, he used money saved from raising tobacco to attend Whitsett Institute near Greensboro, twenty-five miles away. He longed for college, but lacked money, and at eighteen, he began teaching children in a one-room school in the Madison Township. Within five years he had organized and built his own boarding school, Sharp's Institute, not far from his father's farm. He even won a post office for the community, and when postal authorities demanded that the community have a name, he thought its informal name, Bald Hill, inappropriate and called it Intelligence.

Sharp's Institute, a two-story, white frame building with a big front porch and a bell tower with a railed lookout on top, opened in October of 1900 with 50 students. When Professor Sharp was not teaching, he was riding a bicycle over dusty and muddy wagon roads in the northern part of the state drumming up students. By 1906 enrollment had grown to 225, and progressive Governor Charles B. Aycock not only had visited Sharp's Institute but had proclaimed it the best preparatory school in its area. Professor Sharp even had time to field and coach a team in his favorite sport, baseball. And he considered himself prosperous enough to wed.

On July 3, he married Annie Britt Blackwell. He had met her when her sister, who taught at his school, invited him to stay at her father's home, a two-story farmhouse in Vance County, while he was bicycling on one of his recruiting trips. In an earlier day Annie Britt would have been a belle of the genteel Old South. Her grandfather had owned a huge tobacco and cotton plantation with many slaves, and although the family fortunes had been dissipated by the war, and the family members reduced to hardship and hard work, they clung to the refinement and social graces that their earlier wealth had granted them. Annie Britt didn't like the rough-edged young country professor at first. He angered her when he jerked her horse. But later, when he invited her to join her sister as a teacher in his school, she accepted and was surprised to find herself attracted to him. Their plans to marry were already set when her father fell ill with Bright's disease (a kidney disorder), and she left her job to attend him. Her father died shortly before the wedding, and she wore mourning clothes on her honeymoon to Baltimore and Washington.

Disaster struck the following year, when fire destroyed Sharp's Institute. Unable to get financing to rebuild, a dejected James Sharp moved his bride to Rocky Mount in the eastern part of the state, where their first child, a daughter, was born on July 7. They named her Susie Marshall for Annie Britt's adored younger sister and James's admired father, continuing family traditions of naming children for other family members. Misfortune continued to plague James Sharp, however. He went bankrupt trying to sell insurance, causing his wife to lose her heirloom furniture.

Even before the fire, James Sharp had been reading law, and afterward he continued with greater purpose. For a few weeks he went to Wake Forest College north of Raleigh, where he took a law school review course under Dean N. Y. Gulley. At that time, North Carolina law required no formal education to take the state bar exam. James Sharp passed the bar and was granted his license on January 27, 1908. He moved his family back to Rockingham County and opened an office in Stoneville, not far from his family home. Later, he moved to the larger town of Madison, where his wife gave birth to two more children—a son, James Merritt, Jr., born on November 13, 1910; and a daughter, Sallie Blackwell, born four days before Christmas in 1911.

Finding his practice slow in building, James Sharp thought he saw greater opportunity in the land. He bought a farm on Turkey Cock Mountain near Martinsville, Virginia, just over the state line, and moved his family there. Like his father, he grew fruit and tobacco, but he intended his main source of income to be the trees on his land, and to this end he set up a sawmill. Again disaster struck, this time in the form of a forest fire that destroyed his timber, forcing him into his second bankruptcy, a hard blow to a man so proud.

A lawyer acquaintance in Reidsville, Ira R. Humphrey, heard of James Sharp's plight and invited Sharp to join his growing practice. By this time there was a fourth child, Annie Hill, born at the mountain farm on February 19, 1914. James Sharp moved his family into a house on Piedmont Street in Reidsville and worked long hours to support them. But the tribulations that had plagued the family continued. Shortly after the move to Reidsville, James, Jr., called Man Boy by the family because of his stocky build and mature bearing, was discovered to have a brain tumor. James Sharp insisted that his son have the best care, despite cost, and took him to Richmond, where surgeons performed a craniotomy. Man Boy underwent two more operations and wore a constant skull dressing to contain his bulging brain lining before his death on September 29, 1916, six weeks short of his sixth birthday.

Annie Britt Sharp was devastated by her son's death. She stood weeping by the grave, unwilling to leave, as the dirt was shoveled onto the small coffin. "Come on, we've got to go," her husband said, taking her gently by the arm. "We've done all we can for the dead, now we've got to look after the living."

By then the family had moved into a bigger house, on Maple Avenue, and another son, Thomas Adolphus, had been born (on July 24, 1915). Another daughter, Louise Wortham, was born in the house on Maple Avenue on August 29, 1917, but two months after her birth, James Sharp bought a two-story, white frame house with a low-hipped tin roof at 629 Lindsey Street, only a few blocks from his downtown office. The house stood beside the abandoned Reidsville Graded School, for which it had served as a teacherage. It was shaded in front by big oaks—a white oak on one side, a post oak on the other—and in back by black walnut trees. The sloping backyard provided plenty of room for a large garden, a few pigs, and a cow. This was the last move for James Sharp's family. This house would become the family home for generations to come.

In this house four more children were to be born. Florence Abigail came on April 14, 1919. Twins James Blackwell and John Pomfret arrived on August 9, 1921. The coming of the twins was a joyous occasion. The whole family doted on them. James Sharp built a double carriage so that the older children could push them through the neighborhood. He also had a wide, wraparound front porch added to the house so they'd have a place to crawl and play. Later, he built a low rock wall topped with an iron picket fence across the small, grassless front yard to keep all the younger children from wandering into the busy street.

Until the arrival of the twins, all the Sharp children had drunk raw milk from the family's Jersey cow, but Annie Britt worried about that and switched to dairy milk. The decision proved fatal. The twins and their older sister, Florence, all weakened by earlier bouts with whooping cough, fell desperately ill with colitis from tainted milk. James was first to die, on June 17, 1923. John followed on July 4, less than a month from his second birthday. Florence, then four, recovered from the brink of death but had to be taught to walk again.

A pall fell over the family. The life went out of Annie Britt Sharp. She sank into deep depression, ignoring all about her. She wore black and sat staring vacantly and wringing her hands. Her children, tended by their eldest sister, Susie, then sixteen, tiptoed around her, fearful of the stranger she had become. As weeks dragged on, her husband worried that she might never recover. But Matilda Purcell, a black farmer's wife who normally came once a week to help with the washing, ended the problem.

Matildy, as she was called, had been hired to cook for the family while Annie Britt was incapacitated. "Miz' Sharp, it's not right for you to set here and grieve like this," Matildy told her one day. "And if you don't stop it, the Lord's goina punish you for it. He's goina take another one of your chil'ren." From that moment, Annie Britt began to rejoin her family. When she was her old self again, she signified her complete return by buying a new hat with pink flowers on it, an extravagance such as she rarely permitted.

A year later, on July 17, 1924, Annie Britt gave birth to her tenth and final child, another son. She named him James Vance. She'd lost both sons named James and she was determined to have a child named for his father. Her mother-in-law told her that the Lord never intended for her to have a son by that name and her defiance would bring down His wrath. But this son proved healthy, strong, and smart, and Annie Britt had the satisfaction of proving her mother-in-law wrong.

Yet, two generations hence, brothers born into the Sharp family, great-grandchildren Annie Britt Sharp would never know, and ironically bearing the same names as her lost twins, John and James, would meet tragedy unfathomable to the family.

The recovery of Mother, as James Sharp had taken to calling his wife, signaled the beginning of a long, happy period for the Sharps. In Reidsville, James Sharp had found the success that long had eluded him. His hard work and pugnacious nature in the courtroom earned him respect and affection and caused the townspeople to defer to him and call him Mr. Jim.

"Mr. Jim was what they called a fighting lawyer," his friend, W. C. "Mutt" Burton wrote of him in the *Greensboro Daily News*. "He gave his all to every case he took, thousand-dollar retainer or two-dollar fee, it didn't matter. The pits of perdition could stir no blacker scowl than which darkened Mr. Jim's brow at the merest suggestion that his client might be guilty as charged."

"He makes the fur fly when wrought up," the *Reidsville Review* said more succinctly.

Without question, Mr. Jim had a theatrical flair. A dapper man of medium height and build, he wore starched collars, bow ties, and wire-rimmed glasses. He was never without a hat outdoors—straw bowlers and Panamas in summer, fedoras in winter. Every morning as he left for work, his wife pinned a fresh flower in his lapel. His appearance, his conviction of the innocence of all his clients ("He just assumed that anybody who showed the good judgment to engage him as a lawyer had to be of good character, explained Mutt Burton), his booming voice and emphatic way of speaking had their effects on juries. Many responded favorably to his familiar denunciation of the state's case: "There is not one eye-oh-ta of evidence . . ."

Mr. Jim's natural inclinations and talent for oratory led him to politics, and in 1925 and again in 1927 he served in the state Senate. But the pay was short and the time away from his practice costly, and after he lost his new Nash touring car in a garage fire in Raleigh, he decided there must be less expensive ways to serve his community. Later, he ran for the office of solicitor and for the position for which he hungered most, superior court judge, only to find defeat. He won the rural vote but lost in Reidsville, where his independent spirit had not found favor with the paternalistic American Tobacco Company, which dominated the town. He took his defeats without bitterness, however, and remained a strong force in the county's Democratic Party.

Denied elective positions, he sought others, serving as county attorney, president of the Chamber of Commerce, and president of the county Farm Bureau ("He gets all the honors that don't pay anything," his practical mother observed). He was a Mason and a dedicated member of the fraternal Junior Order of United American Mechanics. For a while, because he loved the game, he even volunteered as treasurer of the local minor league baseball team, the Luckies, paying the players and going to every home game to retrieve the receipts. His wife had no taste for baseball, but she always went with him because she worried about him coming home alone with all that money.

Despite all of his duties, Mr. Jim still longed for the land, and several times, over his wife's objections, he mortgaged his house to buy farms, which he usually allowed tenants to farm on shares. Often, though, afternoon found him slipping away from the office to putter in his fields.

Over all else, Mr. Jim treasured family. To his family he was utterly dedicated, and his wife and children worshiped him. But in the big house on Lindsey Street it was Annie Britt Sharp who reigned over the family's daily life.

A short, thin woman with long, dark hair that she loved for her daughters to comb before she wrapped it atop her head, Annie Britt Sharp was blessed with a gentle, sweet disposition and complete devotion to her family. She loved birds and flowers ("I'm an outdoor girl," she'd say) and books and music, and she worked, as the family put it, "like a Turk" for her brood. Heralded for her cooking, she prepared three big meals a day on a wood range in a poorly ventilated kitchen, baking bread and cakes and pies between, and on summer days she often emerged for a breath of fresh air, glistening with sweat, her clothes clinging to her. She worked in the garden, canned its bounty, churned butter, and made all of her own and her children's clothing and all of the family's sheets, pillow cases, and curtains, often embroidering them with fancy designs. She was the first up in the morning to stir the fires, the last to bed at night. The family often went to sleep to the hum of her sewing machine.

She looked constantly for ways to cut costs, reminding her children to stop dripping faucets, flick off lights, close doors to retain heat. "We can't help Daddy make a living," she said. "The only way we can help is by saving."

She had little social life outside the home except for attending meetings with her husband and school activities for her children. She was grade mother for all of her children's classes and an active member of the PTA. "I had so many in school at one time that at PTA meetings I stood so much at room count that I became a laughingstock," she told an interviewer on being named Reidsville's Mother of the Year.

To avoid conflict with Grandma Sharp, the family belonged to no church. Grandma Sharp believed there was only one way to Heaven and that was the Primitive Baptist way, which did not condone frills such as Sunday school. Her daughter-in-law, reared a Methodist, wouldn't accept that. She wanted her children to attend Sunday school and took them every week to Main Street Methodist Church. The children knew to make no mention of it when they went on regular Sunday afternoon visits to Grandma's house in the country. James Sharp raised no objections and even sometimes attended services at the Methodist church with his wife, although he usually picked apart the sermons at the Sunday dinner table. He couldn't completely accept the Primitive Baptist doctrine, but he faithfully attended the monthly meetings of Reidsville's small Primitive Baptist church and, ever the devoted son, regularly took his mother to her overnight associational meetings. "Your grandma would just curl up and die if she didn't get to go to association," Annie Britt told her children.

It was Mama who taught the children social graces, saw that they attended to their chores and studies, insisted that they get musical training, read to them from such works as Uncle Remus and the poetry of Edgar Guest, her favorite (when he came to lecture in nearby Greensboro, her husband took her to hear him, creating great excitement in the family). It was Mama who sang to them in the porch swing on summer afternoons, songs such as "Jimmy Crack Corn," and "Froggy Went a Courtin'," sometimes sad love songs that always made Louise run into the house in tears. It was Mama, too, who was the disciplinarian, a firm believer in "Dr. Switch." James Sharp never raised a hand to any of his children. A simple inflection of his voice was all he needed to instill quiet and obedience.

Quiet was not a customary condition in the big house with its echo-producing, high-ceilinged rooms. "Chatterbox," Mama called the house, because it was always alive with children's voices, not only those of her own but of their friends as well. The house was a community gathering spot for ice-cream churnings and watermelon cuttings, candy pullings and popcorn poppings.

The Sharp children were taught honesty above all virtues. Industry and family pride were close behind. They knew that much was expected of them, and all became achievers and such proud defenders of integrity and family that some would consider them haughty. There was never any question that they would attend college. Both parents were determined that all of their children would get the higher education they had been denied, and that all, male and female, would go forth trained for careers, prepared to make their own ways.

Susie, the eldest child, ever diligent and responsible Susie, the substitute mother, the one to whom the other children always turned for decisions, was perhaps most studious of all. Scrap, she was called in her younger days, because of her love for brightly colored bits of cloth. Susie-Boosie-Stix-Stax-Stoosie, her sisters called her when Susie turned her scathing sarcasm on them. She wanted to be her father's stenographer long before she could pronounce the word. In high school she tried out for the girl's basketball team, failed, and turned to the debating team, which was coached by Judge Allen Gwyn, who had won the judgeship her father coveted. "He praised me to the skies, and I worked like a dog," Susie remembered. She became a star on the debating team, and her father often drove her and the other team members to their matches in his second Nash touring car. So great were her skills that many people told her she should become a lawyer, like her father. "After a while," she recalled, "I just went along with it." She graduated as salutatorian of the Reidsville High School Class of 1924 and entered the Woman's College of North Carolina, twenty-five miles away in Greensboro, taking courses designed to lead her to law school. At that time, no undergraduate degree was required to enter law school, and her plan was to spend two years at WC, as Woman's College was called, before transferring to law school at the University of North Carolina in Chapel Hill. The next child, Sallie, was five years behind her, and Susie knew that her parents couldn't afford to have more than one child in college at a time. Susie was the only female in her law school class of sixty, only the fourth in the history of the school. An honor student, an editor of the *Law Review,* she passed the bar exam and was granted her license to practice a year before she got her degree in 1929. She joined her father in his work, becoming the first female lawyer in the history of Rockingham County. Her reception by the townspeople was wary. For years, the family would tell the story of the old black man who came to James Sharp's office shortly after Susie joined his practice. "Are you that lady lawyer?" he asked. "Indeed, I am," she said, thinking he might be a client. "What can I do for you?" "Nothing, ma'am," he replied. "I just wanted to see what you looked like."

Sallie, the musical one, the prettiest of all the Sharp girls, entered WC in the fall of 1929 with dreams of becoming a professional violinist. In June 1934, she became the first of the Sharp brood to marry, wedding Lawrence A. Taylor, who had come to Reidsville to manage the Montgomery Ward store. Soon the young couple moved away to Michigan.

Annie Hill, called Higgy by her family, the one who most resembled her mother, became a guard on the Reidsville High girl's basketball team, and, like her sister Susie, was salutatorian of her graduating class. She would fulfill one of her mother's dreams. Annie Britt had wanted to be a nurse, but her father said no. She had spoken often of her failed dream, spoken highly of nursing as a profession, and Annie Hill became the first of her children to be influenced by it. She went off to Durham to study nursing at the Duke University Medical School, and became only the second female to receive a bachelor of science degree there. While working on the wards, she met a tall, young medical student named Frederick Klenner, who had fallen ill. She helped nurse him back to health, and romance blossomed. Her family was aghast when they learned about it. Not only was this young man from the state where bluecoats had permanently implanted rifle balls in Grandpa Sharp, he also was Catholic, and in the rural and small-town South of that time, Catholics were regarded with even more fear and suspicion than Yankees. Annie Britt was distraught to discover that her daughter had secretly joined the Catholic Church. Grandma Sharp would have an absolute fit, certain that her granddaughter had bought a spot in hell. Both mother and eldest sister tried desperately to talk Annie Hill out of marrying the young man, but she was strong-headed and in love and nothing could deter her. The young couple settled in Winston-Salem, where Dr. Klenner was completing his residency at the North Carolina Tuberculosis Sanitarium, and there Annie Hill joined the nursing staff.

While Annie Hill was graduating from Duke, her younger brother, Thomas, perhaps the most brilliant of the Sharp children, was receiving a degree in chemical engineering at the University of North Carolina. He moved to New Jersey to take a job with Du Pont.

Like two of her sisters before her, Louise—Pokey to the family, because of the deliberate pace at which she moved—went to WC in Greensboro. Like her sisters Susie and Annie Hill and her brother Tommy, she, too, was salutatorian of her graduating class at Reidsville High. She majored in elementary education, received her degree in 1939, and began her teaching career with a seventh grade class at Caesar Cone School in Greensboro.

Two years after Louise entered WC, she was joined by her sister Florence, who had been nicknamed Punkin, Pandy Poo, and finally, Flukie, a name she carried into college. Bright, but the least academic of all the Sharp children, Florence was the gay one, the carefree one, one of the most popular girls at Reidsville High. Laughter followed wherever she went. She would receive her degree in secretarial administration in 1941 and embark on a teaching career.

By 1939, only one Sharp child remained at Reidsville High School. That was James Vance, the baby, called Kits. Only Jimmy and his eldest sister, Susie, now a distinguished lawyer, still lived in the big family house on Lindsey Street. The Sharps were proud of all of their children and proud that they had been able to educate them in the midst of the Great Depression.

Reidsville had not suffered as much from the Depression as had many other areas. United Bank and Trust Company had closed in 1931, reopened, then failed in 1933. The new Annie Penn Memorial Hospital, named for the wife of the founder of F. R. Penn Tobacco Company, opened in 1930, was forced to close after a year, then reopened in 1932. But the American Tobacco Company not only kept operating but increased its business, protecting the town, and Reidsville was emerging from the Depression relatively unscathed.

The Sharp family suffered only minor setbacks. Mr. Jim and Miss Susie, as the father-daughter partnership came to be known around town, lost clients early in the Depression, forcing Susie to take a temporary job in Chapel Hill as secretary to the dean of the law school. Mr. Jim had to accept some fees in chickens and farm produce and allow other clients to work out law bills on his farm in the years ahead, but by 1939 better days seemed on the way.

Only one problem nagged the family—Annie Hill's marriage. Although the family had been hurt by Annie Hill's decision, and acceptance was difficult, once she had made it, the family tried to heal the rift—blood, after all, was binding—and went out of their way to make her husband feel welcome. The strain, however, was evident to all.

In the summer of 1939, Dr. Klenner finished his internship at the sanitarium and decided to begin his practice in his wife's hometown. Anticipating that patients would be slow in coming, Annie Hill took a job at Duke Hospital until her husband could get established. Her family invited their son-in-law to live with them, and Mr. Jim even helped him set up an office on the same floor as his in the Whitsett Building.

In the weeks ahead, though, the Sharps would become more troubled over what they learned about this young doctor their daughter had brought home. For one thing, he suffered frequent and severe migraine headaches that caused him to act, as Annie Britt said, "as crazy as a moon-eyed horse." Even when he wasn't under the influence of pain, they found his actions more alien and unacceptable than they had imagined, and they were relieved when his practice burgeoned quicker than expected, allowing Annie Hill to return from Durham and the two of them to move into a small house of their own.

12

In the spring of 1985, the ring of children's voices was but a distant memory in the big house at 529 Lindsey Street that Annie Britt Sharp once dubbed the Chatterbox. Little about the house itself had changed in the six decades that had passed since the Sharp children were growing up in it. The front porch was much as it had been when Mr. Jim took his ease there on warm evenings, his feet propped on the rail, his hat tilted over his eyes. The big wood range, never used anymore, still stood in the kitchen, a monument to Annie Britt's revered cooking. Grass grew now in the tiny front yard, no longer kept bare by the batterings of children's feet, and the iron picket fence that Mr. Jim had built to keep his children out of the street now guarded the yard from intrusion. The post oak that once had shaded half the yard had died and been cut down, but the white oak on the other side survived, a marvel of gargantuanism. The holly sprigs that Annie Britt planted on both sides of the sidewalk near the gate had grown into handsome trees, offering shade of their own.

The house was home now to only one Sharp, the fourth daughter, Louise, who never married, but it remained a shrine to family. Family photographs decorated walls and furniture in almost every room, and the house was a repository for cherished photo albums, family heirlooms, and the big family Bible with its carefully kept records of every family member.

Annie Britt Sharp had been the keeper of that Bible. In it, she had entered the marriages of her children, the births of grandchildren and great-grandchildren. Deaths had been added, too. In August of 1952, in sorrowful hand, Annie Britt wrote the last entry on her husband, James Merritt Sharp, who died from uremic poisoning at age seventy-two. He practiced law and farmed until he fell ill three weeks before his death. The following year, she recorded the sudden death from an embolism of her second daughter, Sallie, the violinist, mother of two sons, dead at forty-one. The two losses, within thirteen months of each other, were almost more than Annie Britt could bear.

"I hope I'm the next person to die in this family," she said in her grief.

The words were prophecy, though not for nearly two decades. For several years, Annie Britt lived alone in the big house, checked regularly by family members and others. "I'm fine," she inevitably replied to anybody who inquired of her well-being, prompting her daughter Florence to write a poem about her by that title. But in 1968 she got pneumonia, and although she recovered, she was never quite herself again. She lived with Florence until Louise could return home to care for her and eventually to record in the Bible her mother's death from heart congestion at age eighty-seven on April 9, 1971. Louise became the keeper of the family Bible and the family home, touchstones for the entire family and symbols of their unity.

The pride in family instilled by James and Annie Britt Sharp remained intense, and rightfully so, for the Sharps had become a family of great achievement and of high reputation that was zealously guarded.

The parlor of the house on Lindsey Street was dominated by an oil portrait of the family's greatest achiever, the eldest daughter, Susie, a matriarch who never bore children or married, beaming regally in judicial robe. Susie had achieved her father's dreams and more. Like her father, she had become involved in Democratic politics, working in campaigns for two governors and one congressman. "I was doing it largely for Daddy," she recalled years later. "He was the politician." She did it without expectation of reward, but in 1949, after serving as county campaign manager for Governor Kerr Scott, a dairy farmer from nearby Alamance County, she was offered a superior court judgeship. She knew the appointment would be controversial. No woman ever had held such a position in North Carolina. Knowing that she likely would face great difficulties, she was reluctant to accept. She overcame her reservations only when she spoke them to her father. "Certainly you'll take it," he said.

On the day she left home for her first session of court, her father offered his only advice. "Sue," he called to her from the porch, "plow a straight furrow. And remember, you're the boss."

Judge Sharp gained a reputation for being fair and stern, and in 1962, Governor Terry Sanford, later to be a presidential candidate and U.S. Senator, appointed her to the North Carolina Supreme Court, the first woman in the state to hold that position. As an appeals judge, she was conservative but never shied from controversial decisions, a stickler for detail and truth, a perfectionist in her opinions who labored into the late hours almost every night on her old Royal typewriter at her stand-up desk. She might have been the first woman appointed to the U.S. Supreme Court if her friend, Senator Sam Ervin, who gained fame in the Watergate hearings, had had his way, but she was born ahead of her time and had to settle for being the first woman elected chief justice of a state supreme court in the nation's history. That was in 1974.

Hailed as one of the finest and most astute chief justices in the state's history, she was forced by mandatory retirement laws to step down after her seventy-second birthday in 1979. She still owned the family home in Reidsville with her sister, Louise, and retained her old bedroom there, where she occasionally spent nights, but Judge Susie, as her friends now called her, chose to remain in her apartment in Raleigh.

Although overshadowed by their eldest sister, the rest of the Sharp children had distinguished themselves as well.

Thomas, the chemist, married into a New York Social Register family, then went into defense research. He worked on the team that developed radar housing and invented new lacquers and fabrics before retiring from Sperry-Rand and moving to Florida.

Annie Hill, whose marriage had troubled the family, returned to Duke to teach student nurses during World War II. The mother of three children, she later worked with her husband, whose controversial vitamin treatments gained him international attention before his death in 1984. Annie Hill lived only a short distance from the family home, and in the spring of 1985 went there regularly to have dinner with Louise.

After three years of teaching, two of them in Reidsville, Louise had been stirred by patriotic fervor during World War II to answer a call for more nurses. She went back to school at Duke University, got a degree in nursing, and joined the Cadet Nurse Corps as a teacher. In 1947, she enlisted in the navy and rose to the rank of lieutenant commander before she retired in 1968 and returned home to care for her ailing mother.

Florence was a high school teacher before marrying Robert W. Newsom, who became an executive with the R. J. Reynolds and P. Lorillard tobacco companies, then started his own consulting firm in nearby Greensboro. She had returned to teaching at a business college in recent years, and had retired only a few months earlier. She was mother of two, grandmother of five.

James, the baby of the family, still called Kits, had become a surgeon, joined the U.S. Marines, and risen to the rank of captain. Now stationed at the U.S. Naval Hospital at Charleston, he, too, was nearing retirement and soon would move to Lake City, Florida, to become chief of surgery at a veterans hospital.

The sense of family pride and honor that bound and nurtured the Sharps extended beyond brothers and sisters, children and grandchildren, nieces and nephews, to aunts and uncles, cousins and distant cousins, and, less than two years earlier, it had been pierced by the shock of violent, scandalous tragedy.

Annie Britt Sharp's younger sister, Susie, married James Sharp's first cousin, Early Garrett, who was in the tobacco business in Danville, just across the state line in Virginia. Uncle Early and Aunt Susie and their children were always welcome visitors at the Sharp house, especially at Christmas, when they would gather everybody around the piano to sing carols. Uncle Early and Aunt Susie's daughter, Alice Marie, married her high school sweetheart, George Anderson, who became a lawyer, a civic leader in Danville, and a member of the Virginia House of Delegates. The Andersons' marriage of thirty-two years ended in divorce on December 2, 1982, and George Anderson, fifty-six years old, began dating his young secretary, Gayle Richeson, and spoke of plans for marriage. In the summer of 1983, Anderson and his secretary slipped away from the office one afternoon, picked up her son, who was twelve, and drove into North Carolina to a cabin he owned on Lake Wildwood in Caswell County, not far from Reidsville. The three were on the boat dock, preparing for an outing on the lake, when a yellow convertible pulled up and Alice Marie Anderson got out. She opened fire with a .22 pistol, killing her former husband and wounding his secretary before putting the pistol to her own head and pulling the trigger.

Although news reports of the incident made no mention that Alice Marie was a double cousin of the Sharps, the Sharps were nonetheless horrified and embarrassed that such a thing could happen in their family.

They could not have believed that before the spring of 1985 was out, far greater carnage and scandal, indeed beyond their imaginings, would shake the family to its foundations.

13

Trepidation filled the young man, but he was determined not to show it. He did not want the older man to think him a coward, but as the black Chevrolet Blazer pulled away from the campground onto the Blue Ridge Parkway, he still wasn't sure that he could go through with it, no matter its importance to his future. He hadn't thought he would be so anxious. He had pictured himself cool and deliberate, like the older man, prepared for whatever might happen. But he was scared and worried about how he might react under pressure. And he knew that the older man sensed it.

"Don't worry, everybody is nervous on his first mission," the older man said, assuring him that even he had been a little anxious.

The young man knew that he was more than a little nervous, but he was thankful that he would not have to take part in the killing itself. His role was one of support only. And if he pulled himself together and did it well, he knew that a favorable report would be on its way to the Central Intelligence Agency in Langley, Virginia, only two hundred miles from this campground in the Virginia mountains.

The young man considered himself a patriot. He was strongly conservative, an enemy of communism, and he had dreamed of the intrigue, adventure, and excitement of serving his country on clandestine operations as an agent of the CIA. He had a great-uncle who was involved in intelligence work in Europe. He had sought career advice from him, and his uncle had supplied him with the name of a friend who could assist him through the CIA screening process once he had completed college, but that was still more than a year away. The young man could not believe his good fortune in discovering opportunity much sooner and much closer to home. When he had spoken of his dream to the older man, a neighbor he had known all of his life but with whom he'd become close only in the past year, the older man had suggested that he might be able to help. The young man had long wondered about his neighbor's mysterious comings and goings and the exotic weaponry he possessed, and although the older man had hinted that he was involved in important secret activities, he had not been specific until a couple of months earlier.

That was in late March. The older man had come to visit him at Lexington, a historic town in the mountains of western Virginia, where the young man was a junior at prestigious Washington and Lee University, a chemical engineering major who had found the going tough and switched to philosophy. He had taken his guest on a tour of the campus, ending at Lee Chapel, where Edward Valentine's famous statue of a recumbent Robert E. Lee dominates the altar, and where, in the basement, Lee himself is entombed.

Afterward, they had sat under a tree on the greensward near the chapel, not far from the grave of General Lee's horse, Traveller, and in low and cautious tones, the older man confided that he was a contract agent for the CIA—"the Company," he called it. He spoke of years of covert activities, including several missions on which he nearly had been killed, incidents that had caused him to become very close with God. Now he was about to undertake another mission, he said, this one in Texas. Weapons, he explained, were being stolen from armories in the Midwest and shipped to insurgents in Central and South America in exchange for drugs to be sold in this country at huge profit. Not only were the guns expanding Communist domination in this hemisphere, the drugs were undermining our nation. The older man hinted at involvement by the Russian KGB. As he talked, a gray-uniformed cadet from the adjoining campus of Virginia Military Institute strolled close by with his girlfriend, and the older man paused and gave them hard looks, as if they might be eavesdroppers. His mission, he went on, when the couple had passed from hearing range, would be to stop one of these despicable and traitorous weapons dealers. A "touch," he called it. On this one, he said, he needed help. Somebody he could trust. Would the young man be interested? He would serve only in support capacity, drive, provide cover. It would be a short operation. A long weekend. And he would be paid for his time. Most important, it would be a chance for him to prove himself with the Company, a foot in the door toward a career in covert service to his country.

The young man knew that a "touch" was a killing, but he understood that killing was often necessary in defense of one's country and moral principles. He had no qualms about that. He was impressed that the older man had such faith in him, excited at the opportunity, and without hesitation he answered yes.

When the young man went home for spring break, his neighbor presented him with a government-issue .45-caliber pistol. The young man worried that his mother or another family member might discover the weapon and question him about it, so he concealed it and carried it back to Lexington. As mid-April, time for the scheduled mission, neared, the older man returned to Lexington. He brought another .45 to replace the pistol he had given the young man earlier.

"I got it from somebody who won't need it anymore," he said, and the young man asked no questions. Instead, he watched the older man deftly replace all the springs in the weapon and put a new Accurizer barrel on it.

The mission, he said, had been postponed. He needed time for more surveillance.

May arrived with no further word, and on May 10, the young man's twenty-first birthday, he went home to North Carolina. Two days later, on Mother's Day, the older man came for him. They went to the country and practiced with their .45s and a .22 Ruger semiautomatic pistol, and the older man told him that their mission would be disguised as a camping trip and that it would be soon. That night, the young man returned to the room he rented in a private home in Lexington, and the following day the older man called to say the plan was on for

Wednesday, two days away. Could he still go? A pang of fear struck the young man as he answered yes.

But on Wednesday the older man called again. Another postponement. He was having problems with his vehicle. A bearing would have to be replaced. Hang loose. He called again Thursday to say he would call on Friday. At three o'clock on Friday afternoon he called. Everything was go. He would bring the gear. Meet him at the Blue Ridge Parkway overlook on Roanoke Mountain, sixty miles southwest of Lexington, at six o'clock.

The young man went to the mountain, and there, at an overlook where hang gliders embark on daring and spectacular flights, he waited for hours, watching the sun set and the lights of Roanoke Valley twinkle on below, leaving briefly only once to drive down the mountain for a Coke and a candy bar, but the older man did not appear—no surprise, really; the older man rarely showed up when he said he would—and as ten o'clock neared, a ranger came to say the overlook was closing. The young man didn't know what to do and returned to his room in Lexington. He was upstairs watching TV when the telephone rang downstairs and his landlady answered. The older man was calling, but the landlady thought the young man had left for the weekend and didn't know he had returned, and before he could get downstairs, she had told the older man that he wasn't there and hung up. The young man feared that he might have blown his opportunity, damaged the mission by not remaining in place (could that have been part of his test?). He called the older man's mother, a family friend. If her son called would she tell him that he was back in Lexington? An hour later, the older man called back. He was at Roanoke Mountain. He would come to Lexington.

The Blazer was cluttered, as usual, with military field gear and weapons, including, the young man noticed, the Uzi machine gun in a camouflage bag that he'd seen on several occasions when they'd gone shooting in the country. The older man asked for his pistol and zipped it into a black canvas bag with another .45, his favorite. It was well after midnight when they headed for the Blue Ridge Parkway to acquire proof that they had spent this weekend camping. They stopped at Otter Creek Campground, but found it unsatisfactory and drove on to the south-west. Peaks of Otter would be better, the older man said. On the way, he mentioned a change of plan. A "situation" in North Carolina connected to the Texas mission had to be taken care of first. It required that touches be made in two cities, Winston-Salem and Charlotte, but the young man was not to worry. He would not have to put himself in danger, and he would be back in Lexington in plenty of time to pick up his take-home final exam in his medical ethics class.

"I'll help you with it," the older man said with a reassuring smile, pleasing the young man, who knew that his companion was a physician.

They arrived before dawn at Peaks of Otter, a National Park Service recreation area, and drove into the self-check-in campground near the base of Sharp Top, a cone-shaped mountain, 3,875 feet high at its stony peak. They selected campsite B-3, because none of the campsites near it was occupied. The campsite, which rose from a paved parking spot, was set into the mountainside behind a large granite boulder. A steel grill and fireplace had been built into the back of the boulder, near the concrete slab table. A stone wall made a level spot for the tent site. The fallen trunk of a huge tree separated the site from the one adjoining it. Through the trees down the mountainside, lights from the popular Peaks of Otter Lodge reflected off the surface of Abbott Lake, twenty-four acres of cold, clear water behind a grassy dam.

By the time the men got their camp set up, dawn was breaking pink behind Flat Top, a 4,000-foot mountain rising from the lodge, but both men were tired and they fell asleep quickly as the sparsely occupied campground stirred around them. The young man got up well after noon. His friend was seated at the picnic table with a black briefcase open before him. In the case, the young man saw a large scabbarded knife, perhaps a bayonet, a stainless steel .22-caliber semiautomatic pistol, a .45, several ammunition magazines, and a rechargeable electric razor. Lying nearby were a soft hat, a gray windbreaker, a pair of dark canvas sneakers. The older man pulled a surgical glove onto his right hand and began removing the standard .22-caliber long rifle bullets from the magazines and replacing them with subsonic shells, better for a job such as this, he said, because the sound would not carry so far. The glove was necessary, he explained, so that he would leave no fingerprints in case he didn't recover all the brass.

When that job was finished, the older man produced a packet of hundred-dollar bills, peeled off three and handed them to the young man. "That's yours," he said. "I'm getting nine hundred for this operation. That's a third. If I have to make it look like a robbery, we'll split the take fifty-fifty."

After the job was done, the older man said, he would dispose of the clothes he wore, even the hat and shoes. Thoroughness was essential in every mission, he emphasized. No detail should be overlooked. "That's the reason the average criminal gets caught," he said. "He doesn't think about all of these things."

The young man had heard him speak of thoroughness before. A shot to the body to bring a man down, the older man said, another shot to the head to finish him. Thoroughness.

Both men went down the hill to the small, cedar-shingled rest room, where the young man shaved and his companion nipped off the bristly hairs on his neck below his full, dark beard. Afterward, they gathered firewood and placed light sticks around the campsite to make it look "lived in." The older man was hungry and they drove around the lake to the elegant waterside restaurant with its chic gift shop before returning briefly to the campground. They stopped at the gate, and the older man wrote his name and address on a registration envelope, folded the six-dollar fee into it, and dropped the envelope into the padlocked honor box, proof of their alibi if it should be needed. At a little after 5 P.M., they pulled onto the parkway, heading for North Carolina.

After a few miles, the Blazer left the parkway and wound down curvy and dangerous Highway 43 into the small, flood-ravaged town of Buchanan on the James River, then turned onto Highway 11 for the short connection to Interstate 81. Even on the interstate, the older man drove slowly, following his custom, rarely getting above forty-five miles per hour. Normally, the trip to Winston-Salem took three and a half hours; at his deliberate pace it took more than five.

On the way, they discussed the mission. Many things the young man would not be told. That's the way it was in the Company. Information was closely controlled and released only on a "need-to-know" basis. The young man understood. This was the plan: In Winston-Salem, the young man would drop off his partner near the site of the touch, then go to a prearranged spot to wait—they'd decide exactly where when they got there. After the older man completed the job, he'd take a car from the site and drive to the meeting spot. The young man would follow him to U.S. 52, then give him a fifteen-minute head start and drive south to Interstate 85 and west to Charlotte. The young man was to note the last rest area before reaching Charlotte, then double back to it and wait. They would meet there after the second touch. On the way to Charlotte, the older man would stop and shave his beard, leaving a Fu Manchu for the second leg of the mission. On the return to Virginia, he would shave off the mustache—and dispose of his clothing along the way.

West of Pulaski, the older man turned south onto Interstate 77, and as darkness descended, he crossed the North Carolina line and pulled into the welcome center. He went into the rest room carrying a canvas bag and emerged in different clothing—dark slacks, a mesh T-shirt, and the gray windbreaker and canvas shoes that he had displayed earlier. Under the T-shirt was a bullet-proof vest.

"You want to drive?" he asked, and the young man agreed, thinking it might take his mind off his fears. But he had driven only a short distance, turning east on North Carolina 89 and south on U.S. 52 in Mount Airy, skirting the Mayberry Mall—a reminder that this was Andy Griffith's hometown—before the older man decided he should be driving because he knew where they were going.

"Stop at a Neighbors station," he said. "We need to get gas anyway."

But the young man missed the first Neighbors station

on the edge of Mount Airy, and his companion told him to drive on to another some distance ahead. When the young man missed that one, too, he turned around and went back. The station was a garish spectacle—red, orange and yellow, flag-bedecked, and brightly lighted, set at the base of one of North Carolina's most beautiful and famous landmarks, Pilot Mountain, with its distinctive tree-topped granite knob, a lone sentinel hunkering in the reflected lights of Winston-Salem, only twenty-five miles away. The young man was worried that he was growing noticeably more frightened. He went to the rest room to check himself, then bought a caffeine-free Coke to calm his troubled stomach.

As he drove on to Winston-Salem, sipping a Tab, the older man showed no signs of fear or anxiety. Calmly, he went over the alibi. If anybody ever asked about this night, they had been on a hike up Flat Top Mountain. Near the summit, they had been caught in a shower, stopped and built a fire to dry themselves, then hiked back down, returning to the campground early in the morning. This bothered the young man. The honor code at Washington and Lee, introduced by General Lee himself, was simple and explicit: a student should not lie, cheat, or steal, and should conduct himself as a gentleman at all times. He knew that the honor code was the foundation of the university and that lying could disgrace him and get him thrown out of school. But in this case, he was assured, deception was a matter of national security, overriding any honor code.

Soon both saw the skyline of Winston-Salem, with its distinctive Reynolds Building, a smaller version of the Empire State Building. It was nearly 10:45 when the older man turned west onto Interstate 40, then exited into downtown with its tobacco-perfumed air. As he drove northwest, he talked through their plan again. They passed shopping centers, a McDonald's, a Burger King, and the young man saw a sign that said they were on Reynolda Road. It was a busy road, four lanes wide. A funeral home loomed on the right, Vogler's, soon to profit from their mission, although the young man could not know that. The road swung to the right and curved downhill into open country. At the foot of the hill was a stoplight and another shopping center, Loehmann's Plaza. The older man turned left at the stoplight and asked, "Where do you want to wait?"

The young man had seen a Hardee's across from the shopping center near the stoplight. He'd wait there, unless it closed. If not there, he'd be at the Burger King they'd just passed. Or McDonald's as a last resort. If he couldn't stay at any of those places, he'd come back to Loehmann's Plaza and park in front of the Food Lion.

The older man turned left at an old tile-roofed gas station that had been turned into a rental shop. The area was dark, the street a narrow concrete lane. No other cars were in sight. A few hundred feet past the turn, the Blazer stopped in a red-dirt lot beside a tiny concrete bridge. The lot was filled with dump trucks and construction equipment. Fetching his briefcase from behind the seat, the older man opened it for a final check, snapped it shut, pulled on a pair of leather driving gloves, got out, and disappeared into the night. The young man climbed behind the wheel and pulled cautiously away.

Eleven o'clock had just passed and Hardee's had closed. The young man drove to Burger King. He parked near the road so the Blazer would be easily visible, locked up, and went inside, trying to appear nonchalant but fearful that his guilt and anxiety were showing. He got a cup of coffee and sat by the window, smoking cigarettes and watching the comings and goings of late-night hamburger eaters. He got up once for a refill, and after forty-five minutes he began worrying that the store employees were becoming suspicious. He went out to the Blazer and sat for several minutes fiddling with a Bach tape. His friend always carried classical music and often played it as he drove. Why didn't he come back? Had something gone wrong? If so, how would the younger man know? What was he to do?

He didn't want to go to McDonald's, so he drove back to the small shopping center and waited in the empty parking lot. Fifteen minutes later, he saw a small gold car approaching slowly and recognized his partner at the wheel.

Relieved, he cranked up the Blazer and pulled into traffic behind the gold car, headed south on Reynolda, back toward downtown. He expected to follow it to Highway 52, as planned, but after a short distance, the older man turned onto a side street and stopped at a small vacant building, where he sat for a minute as if uncertain what to do. The young man waited, thinking his friend might get out with a change of instruction. Instead, he suddenly turned around and drove back to Reynolda Road. The young man followed as he turned right, heading south again. At a stoplight near Burger King, the young man pulled alongside the gold car, hoping for a signal. Ignored, he dutifully followed when the light changed. At Coliseum Drive, the older man turned left, eastward. At University Parkway, another major thoroughfare, he turned left again, northward, past the coliseum. Caught by the light, the young man hurried to catch up when it changed. He made the turn and saw his friend some distance ahead, still driving slowly. Suddenly a police car appeared behind the Blazer, as if from nowhere. It passed in a rush and fell in behind the gold car ahead. Fear shot through the young man. Had somebody already put out a bulletin on the stolen car? Was his friend about to be arrested? Would he allow himself to be taken? What should he do if the policeman stopped the car? They hadn't planned for this eventuality.

The young man slowed and switched lanes. As he did, the older man did the same thing, the police car following. The young man slowed even more, holding back, watching. The brightly lighted business district fell away, and a grassy median now separated the parkway. The lighted steeple of Wake Forest University's Wait Chapel appeared over the treetops to the west. Another police car came up quickly, falling in behind the first one, frightening the young man even more. At an intersection, the second police car turned left and sped off—just as blue lights began flashing atop the first car. The older man stopped in the left lane. The young man was panic-stricken as he drove slowly past the two cars, straining to see. He topped a hill and at the bottom saw the welcoming glow of another Burger King sign. He pulled in and parked so his friend could spot the Blazer—if he came. His heart was racing, and he took deep breaths trying to calm himself. He needed desperately to go to the toilet, but he wasn't sure his legs would carry him inside.

He emerged from the rest room and went to the counter to get another cup of coffee. Standing in line, he noticed a policeman dozing in a nearby booth. The policeman stirred, got up, and walked to the front, stopping only a few feet from the young man, who turned away, staring straight ahead, struggling to control his fear and nervousness. He was certain the policeman could see his guilt, and he got his coffee and left quickly, expecting to hear the click of the officer's heels behind him, a voice calling, "Just a minute there, young man!"

He hurried to the Blazer, still not knowing what to do, but before he got in, he was startled to see his friend approaching the door of the restaurant. The older man saw him, turned abruptly, got back into the gold car, and drove away. Relieved, the young man jumped into the Blazer and followed.

They went back the way they had come, and the young man realized they were returning to the area of the mission. They turned at Loehmann's Plaza, as they had upon arriving, but continued past the rental place where they previously had turned. Around the bend from a stoplight, the older man pulled onto the shoulder and stopped. Uncertain, the young man drove by him and stopped a couple of hundred feet ahead. He looked back to see his friend get out and walk toward him, carrying the briefcase.

"We've got a change of plan," the older man said, thrusting the briefcase through the window. "The car won't make it to Charlotte. I've got to dump it. We'll have to scratch the Charlotte operation. Pick me up where you let me out in twenty minutes."

The young man followed back to Reynolda Road. His friend turned right. He went left, driving aimlessly for several miles. He remembered a convenience store across from the Burger King where he first had waited, and drove there, used the rest room, bought another caffeine-free Coke, and sat in the parking lot, smoking a cigarette before returning to the construction lot. He parked and waited, smoking compulsively, listening to the night sounds of creatures from the nearby creek. The night had turned chilly, the temperature barely in the fifties, and his cough was getting worse. Were the cool night air and the tension activating his allergies, or was he coming down with a cold? This was a new moon night, especially dark, but the glow of a single bare light bulb from the old store building across the street that now served as the construction company office made the Blazer visible. He worried that somebody might come by and question what he was doing there at nearly one o'clock in the morning. Perhaps somebody at one of the small houses just up the street would notice him and call the police. How could he explain his presence? He kept looking back over his shoulder, hoping to see his friend emerging from the darkness. After what seemed an eternity, the older man finally appeared and climbed into the seat beside him.

Driving away, the young man was eager to know what had happened but uncertain whether he should ask. He told the older man that he had been frightened when the policeman appeared. The cop only wanted to see if he'd been drinking because he was driving so slowly, his friend said. He'd told him he was having trouble with a wheel bearing and was just trying to nurse the car home.

"I don't think he radioed in the license number," he said.

"Did you give him your real license or a fake?" the young man asked.

"I've got a fake, but I didn't want to dig around for it, so I just gave him mine. I can have a new one made later without the beard, report the old one lost. It's a good thing he didn't ask me to get out of the car. I had my forty-five under my jacket and I'd have had to blast him. He had on a vest, minimum protection, not as good as mine. I'd have shot him in the head anyway."

The young man reached Interstate 40 without knowing how he had done it, and soon was on Highway 52, heading northward again, back to the mountains. He was hungry for details of the touch, but his friend was sparing with them, telling him that the less he knew the better it would be for him and the Company. He said only that the mission was successful, that he'd had to kill three people, two of them guards.

"Did you have to use the knife?"

He nodded grimly. "On the guards."

The older man was thirsty, and they stopped for soft drinks about twenty miles north of the city. They stopped again on the edge of Mount Airy and used the toilet at a convenience mart. The older man removed the surgical glove, some pieces of blue foam rubber, and the hat from the briefcase, shredded them with the bayonet, and tossed them into a dumpster. After changing shoes, he took over driving, stopping a short time later at the Virginia Welcome Center on Interstate 77. He took a bag into the rest room, changed clothes, and removed his bullet-proof vest. Standing before the mirror at one of the five sinks set in red Formica, he began shaving his beard with his rechargeable razor, reverting to medical snips when the charge ran down, finishing with a straight razor. He handed the bullet-proof vest and T-shirt to the young man and told him to stash them in the Blazer. As the young man was secreting them under camouflage netting in the back of the truck, he saw a young man in a Washington and Lee T-shirt getting out of a car. He assumed him to be a fellow student, although he did not recognize him, but he studiously attempted to avoid him in case the student had seen him around campus. Soon, the older man appeared, clean shaven, and before they left, he tossed the shoes he'd worn on the mission into a garbage can.

By the time the Blazer reached Interstate 81, the young man was drowsy. His friend stopped for more soft drinks, and soon after they were back on the highway the young man fell asleep. He awoke when the Blazer pulled into a truck stop north of Roanoke for gas. Dawn had broken, and the young man rousted himself to go to the rest room. The next stop was at a trash dump in the mountains above Buchanan. The older man dug a hole and buried the ammunition from the briefcase, then ripped apart the briefcase and returned it to the Blazer.

They reached the campground at about 7 A.M. and began a fire for coffee. The older man got a handful of tablets from his medical bag and instructed the young man to take several. "They'll cut down the coughing," he said, swallowing a handful himself.

He removed a roll of money from his pocket and

handed the young man thirty-five dollars. "That's for your gas Friday," he said.

"Forget it," said the young man, declining the money.

"No, I promised you half if I had to make it look like a robbery. That's what this is."

The young man pocketed the money and turned his attention to the fire, which was barely smoking. He blew it alive, put water on to boil, and fetched military field meals from the Blazer. His friend went downhill to the rest room three times before they ate, returning the final time with a grinning explanation. "I always get the runs about twelve hours after a job, probably a nervous reaction." The young man soon found himself in the same fix.

After eating, both got back into the Blazer and went looking for places to dispose of remaining evidence. They stopped at a picnic area, and the older man shredded the gray jacket and threw the remains into a dumpster along with the mangled briefcase. They drove around the lake and stopped at an access path opposite the campground. The young man stayed in the Blazer while the older man scrambled down the steep path to the water, carrying the barrel from his .45 and the sheathed bayonet. He was gone for fifteen minutes and returned with the bayonet to report that he'd thrown the pistol barrel into the lake. He drove to the parkway, turned northeastward past the lodge, and shortly made a U-turn, stopping on the shoulder. Carrying the bayonet, he disappeared into the woods and was gone again for long minutes. The young man saw him emerge near the edge of the woods carrying only the sheath, which he used to dig a shallow trench. He rammed the sheath into the trench, then stamped it down with his boot before scraping loose dirt back over it.

Back at the campground, they packed their gear and left, stopping at the nearby ranger station and museum to get maps of the area. The young man went across the road to the camp store for cigarettes. On the way back to Lexington, he was instructed to familiarize himself with the maps. It was important that he be able to knowledgeably verify the story of the camping weekend and night hike up Flat Top Mountain. His prospects with the Company could depend on it.

He had done well despite his fear, the older man told him, and he had begun to feel good about his weekend's work and his prospects for the future. But he was curious about one thing. Would a career with the Company preclude marriage and a family?

"It could," the older man said, going on to tell of his own failed marriage. When he'd proposed, he told his wife everything, he said, and she said that she could handle it. But after a couple of years, she tired of it.

"She threatened to go public if I didn't get out and settle down. I had to tell her that if she did that, an *accident* would be arranged. Some poor soul would die in my Blazer and that would be the end of me." He smiled. "I don't have any dental records. I told her that she would have an accident, too, but it would be a real one."

The message was clear to the young man. The secret of this weekend always would be safe. He wanted no "accidents" to happen to him.

14

The afternoon had slipped up on Rob Newsom. Shortly after four, his wife, Alice, asked what could be keeping his parents. They should have been home by now, bringing Rob and Alice's daughter, Page, with them.

For more than two years, Rob and Alice and their three children had lived with his parents in their two-story brick and frame house on Fairgreen Drive in Hamilton Forest, an upper-class subdivision in northwest Greensboro. Soon, Rob and Alice would have the house for themselves, because his parents, Bob and Florence, were planning to move back to Bob's family home near Winston-Salem, thirty miles away, so that they could keep a closer watch on Bob's mother, Hattie—Nanna to the family. Nanna was eighty-five, and her family had decided that she should no longer live alone. This was May 19, and since Thanksgiving, when extensive renovations had begun on Nanna's big house, Bob and Florence had spent nearly every weekend with her. The renovations were only a couple of weeks away from completion, and Bob and Florence already had been carrying things over in anticipation of their move. After a troubled Friday morning, they had left for Nanna's at about 2 P.M, hoping to use the weekend to accomplish some cleanup work. They were due back Sunday afternoon, and they were to bring Page with them. Page was eleven, the eldest of Rob and Alice's children. She had spent the weekend in Winston-Salem with her mother's parents, Fred and Page Hill, so that she could take part in a cousin's wedding on Saturday. Bob had said he would pick her up at midafternoon because he needed to get back to Greensboro and attend to some business.

At 5 P.M., Alice's mother called. The Newsoms hadn't picked up Page yet. Was something wrong? Should they feed her?

Yes, feed her, Alice said. She'd try to find out what was wrong and call back. She called Nanna's house but got no answer. That was puzzling. Could Bob and Florence have gone out with Nanna? Wouldn't they have let somebody know? Could Nanna have fallen ill and Bob and Florence be now at the hospital with her?

Perhaps Nanna was at church, Rob thought, and his father, preoccupied, had just forgotten to pick up Page and driven straight to his office in downtown Greensboro to do his work. Knowing his father was not apt to answer the phone at the office, Rob drove there to check but found nobody.

For the next two hours, Rob and Alice kept trying Nanna's number without success. Maybe they all were out in the yard working, as they frequently were. Maybe they had gone to a church supper. Maybe the phone was out of order.

Alice called her parents and arranged to pick up Page. Her parents would drive Page to Suzie's Diner, just off Interstate 40 at Kernersville, halfway between Greensboro and Winston-Salem, and Rob and Alice would meet them there. They left for Kernersville about eight o'clock, and after returning home, they kept trying Nanna's number. Worry had replaced concern by the time they settled in front of the TV to watch a miniseries about Christopher Columbus. Neither could concentrate.

At ten o'clock, Rob stood up abruptly. "I'm going over there," he said.

"Let me call mother," Alice said.

Her mother suggested calling the Suttons, Newsom family friends, who lived not far from Nanna's. Maybe they could check.

Homer Sutton had been the Newsom family doctor for more than thirty years. He'd seen Nanna only a few days earlier, when he'd sent her to a cardiology clinic for a test. She had an irregular heartbeat, and he liked to keep close watch on it. He was lying in bed reading when Rob called. Rob knew him well. They had been neighbors when Rob was growing up in Green Meadows, a small, private development on two small ponds, only two and a half miles from his grandmother's house, and the Suttons still lived there. Dr. Sutton had heard nothing from Bob or Nanna. He was sure he would have if any of the Newsoms had fallen ill or been injured. He'd be glad to drive over and see what he could find out, he said.

Dr. Sutton and his wife, Katy, arrived at Nanna's house at 3239 Valley Road, near Old Town, at about 10:20. They both loved the old two-story brick house with black shutters, even had considered buying it at one time, when Nanna's late husband, Robert, claimed to be tired of yardwork and threatened to sell it. It sat well back from the road under huge oaks and was as elegant and homey as Nanna herself. A low chain-link fence separated the yard from the road. A walkway that led from the road to the front door had been overtaken by huge boxwoods that lined it. An asphalt driveway with a gate at the road led to a parking area at the northwest side of the house and looped back on itself.

As Dr. Sutton drove slowly up the dark drive, the headlights of his car fell on three cars. One he recognized as Bob Newsom's new Buick. The blue Plymouth Fury and gold Plymouth Voláre, he knew, were Nanna's. Like her, they were getting on in years. If all three cars were here, surely so were the Newsoms. Perhaps they'd been out and had just returned. Lights were on inside.

The Suttons got out and started for the back door, behind the garage, the door the family always used. The house was quiet. They could hear a dog barking across the street. As they stepped onto the flagstone patio, they saw that the upper glass in the storm door had been broken, the step littered with shards. That was odd. Nanna wasn't one to leave broken glass lying around.

"Something bad has happened here," Dr. Sutton said suddenly.

He peeked in through the living room window. A lamp was on in a far corner, and he could hear the TV playing softly just under the window. Through the sheer curtains, he saw Nanna. She was in a beige nightgown, lying on a walnut-frame antique sofa upholstered in beige with tiny pink roses. A plaid afghan in autumnal colors that she normally kept on the back of the sofa covered her nearly to her chin. She seemed asleep. On the floor lay Florence. She was on her right side, wearing a white skirt and knit top, no shoes. At first glance, Dr. Sutton thought she might be lying there watching TV, but he knew her dignity wouldn't allow that. He looked closer.

"There's blood on the floor," he said. "Something has happened to them."

He tapped the window. No response. Nanna and Florence, he realized, were dead. Where was Bob? He couldn't see him. Had Bob gone berserk and killed his wife and mother? Was he dead in another room? Was a murderer still lurking inside? The immensity of his discovery sent a shudder through him.

"Let's get out of here," his wife said, and they hurried back to their car, shaken by dread and fear.

15

"There was forever in that town a smell of raw tobacco, biting the nostrils with its acrid pungency. It smote the stranger coming from the train."
—THOMAS WOLFE, writing about Winston-Salem in *Look Homeward, Angel*

Winston-Salem is a city of two histories, two major influences, that melded in the marriage of Robert W. Newsom and Hattie Carter as they did in the merging of their two towns. He was Winston, she Salem. He was tobacco, she Moravian.

The Moravians came first to this hilly, forested land in the North Carolina Piedmont. The Brethren, they called themselves. A pacifist Protestant sect, they had been driven from their homes in Bohemia, later to become Czechoslovakia, by persecution from the Catholic Church. They settled first in Austria, then sent emissaries to find a place in the New World. An attempted settlement in Georgia failed, but in 1740 a permanent settlement was established in Pennsylvania at a place the group called Bethlehem. Twelve years later, Lord Granville offered the Brethren land in North Carolina, and Bishop August Gottlieb Spangenburg chose 100,000 acres in what was to become Forsyth County. He called the tract Wachovia, in honor of the Austrian family who had offered protection to the early Moravians. In 1753, fifteen single men arrived from Bethlehem to hack a settlement out of the wilderness, and two years later, seven married couples came to join them. They called their commune Bethabara, and as it grew, some found it too restrictive and moved three miles away to begin another settlement called Bethania. Both towns thrived as more members moved south from Pennsylvania, and in 1765, the elders chose a site on a hillside five miles southeast of Bethabara, which by then was generally called Old Town, for a third, central town designed for tradesmen. Soon the new town of Salem began to rise, growing beyond expectations until it surpassed both early settlements to become the state's major frontier town.

In 1849, when Forsyth County was organized, the chaste Moravians refused to allow Salem to become the county seat, fearing the rowdy court days that move would bring. Instead, the elders sold to the county fifty-one acres north of Salem for a new town. It was named Winston, in honor of a Revolutionary War hero from nearby Stokes County.

By fall of 1874, when a tall, dark-haired tobacco trader named Richard Joshua Reynolds arrived from Virginia, Winston was a town of four hundred people on a newly built railroad, and Reynolds saw opportunity in it. He bought a lot on Depot Street, later to become Patterson Avenue, and there, on an area smaller than a tennis court, he erected a two-story brick building—"the little red factory," he called it. He lived on the second floor and made chewing tobacco below, using brand names such as Red Meat, Fat Back, Frog, and Brown's Mule. By 1890, when he incorporated R. J. Reynolds Tobacco Company with himself as president and his brother Will as vice president, he was talking of building the biggest tobacco factory in the South, and within sixteen years, with buyouts and expansions, he had done it. In 1907, he introduced Prince Albert Smoking Tobacco, and six years later he brought out a cigarette that was to become the world's most popular. He named it Camel because it was a blend of Turkish and domestic tobaccos, and to him the camel represented the exotic Middle East from whence the tobacco came. In 1917, after years of construction, Reynolds finished Reynolda Manor, his self-sufficient, 1,000-acre estate with its sixty-room "bungalow" near Bethabara. He didn't get to enjoy it long, for in 1918, five years after the growth he brought to Winston had caused it to overtake Salem, resulting in the merger of the two towns into a single city, he died at the age of sixty-eight. He left an immense fortune and a company in Winston-Salem with 10,000 employees and 121 buildings that would grow into one of the world's major corporations and remain the basis of the city's economy for generations to come.

Robert Newsom and Hattie Carter were married the same year that R. J. Reynolds died. He was nineteen, she eighteen. Both had been born in adjoining Surry County, but their families had migrated to the city for the available jobs. Hattie's family settled in Salem, where her father worked in a furniture factory; Robert's family moved first to Reidsville, then to Winston, where his father became a tobacco auctioneer. Hattie, a slim, dark-eyed beauty, barely five-foot-two, who wore her long hair pinned atop her head, completed only seven grades of school. She was working in the office of a textile company when she met Robert. He was ruggedly handsome, standing only a couple of inches taller than she, but he had broad, muscular shoulders and enjoyed hard work. He'd quit school in the sixth grade and gone to work delivering groceries when he was barely in his teens. He soon found a factory job at R. J. Reynolds. A proud man, he was adamant in his view that a man did not allow his wife to perform "public work," and Hattie quit her job after their marriage.

The young couple bought a four-room frame house on 25th Street, northeast of downtown, and there, on February 4, 1920, their first child, Robert, Jr., was born. A daughter, Frances, arrived on July 21, 1921. Hattie fell ill with Bright's disease after Frances's birth, was sick for months, and doctors advised her against having more children. When Frances was two, R. J. Reynolds built a new plant in Jersey City, New Jersey, and Robert, a mechanical whiz, was sent to set up and run the cigarette machines. His young family lived in Jersey City for two years, homesick and miserable much of the time.

An ambitious man, Robert realized that he was limited by lack of education and had gone as far as he could with Reynolds. He left the company and returned to Winston-Salem to become a tobacco auctioneer like his father, Colonel John Abe.

Robert had spent his early years hanging around tobacco warehouses, watching his father and other auctioneers, men revered in the tobacco business, learning their techniques. With his quick mind and deep, resonant voice, he was a natural. He began at Brown's Warehouse, where his father worked, and soon was competing with the best, traveling to markets in Florida, Georgia, South Carolina, and eastern North Carolina.

He had settled his family happily into a six-room, story-and-a-half house with dormer windows and a big front porch at 2422 Glenn Avenue, just around the corner from their previous home and only a few blocks from his parents' house. But in 1933, he announced that they would be moving. He'd spent his early years on a tobacco farm and he loved rural life. He wanted a place convenient to town where he could have a big garden and see wild creatures. And he'd found it: a plain, two-story, tin-roofed farmhouse two miles beyond the Reynolds estate near Old Town, halfway between the Moravian settlements of Bethabara and Bethania. The house was on Valley Road at a place once called Valley View. It sat on nearly seven acres, which had been part of the first tract of three thousand acres that the Moravians sold to an outsider. The land had been bought by Jacob Kapp, a millwright, who in about 1770 built a log cabin on the site where the house now stood. The history of the house itself was lost, but it had belonged to Colonel E. S. Reed, a Civil War veteran, and was thought to have been constructed before the war.

Corn grew in front of the house, and behind it a steep slope slipped into heavy woods. Nearby was the Strangers' Graveyard, where the early Moravians buried outsiders, a spot of mystery and intrigue to children. Everybody in the family but Frances, called Frankie, who was then twelve, liked the country house. She was devastated. She missed her friends, her neighborhood, the easy comings and goings of town life. She felt isolated, and moped around, heartsick, until her father could stand it no longer. He had rented the house on Glenn Avenue, but he asked the tenants to vacate so his family could reclaim their home and happiness. Not until both of his children were safely in college during the early 1940s did Robert finally sell the Glenn Avenue house and move to the country house to stay.

Hardworking, honest and frugal, Robert saved or invested every extra dollar. He bought shares in Brown's Warehouse, where both he and his father worked as auctioneers. By 1942, he was helping operate the warehouse with his friend Bill Simpson, whose father, John, ran it when Colonel John Abe was auctioneering. Four years later, Robert and Bill built another warehouse on Trade Street and named it Star.

By 1950, Robert was doing well enough to quit auctioneering. Only occasionally in the future would he grin and launch into his familiar chant when some of the fellows at the warehouse would say, "Come on, Mr. Bob, sell this pile." Indeed, he was doing so well that he started a major renovation of his house on Valley Road. He bricked the outside, affixed shutters to the broad windows, put on a new roof, added a wing on the back, and tore away the front porch, leaving an uncovered stone veranda in its place. He built a garage with a connecting breezeway on one end, and installed a new kitchen, new bathrooms, and large cedar-lined closets. On the back of the house, he put a big covered porch where he could sit and watch squirrels, rabbits, birds, and chipmunks as they frolicked in his yard. When he was finished, the house was a showplace, dominating the area. And when Robert wasn't at his warehouses, or out visiting farmers and seeking business, he usually could be found puttering around the house. He constructed a barbecue pit out back with a picnic shelter for family gatherings. He built himself a shop where he made sturdy furniture from maple, cherry, and walnut, which he frequently offered as gifts to family members. He loved working in the yard and garden, and he created a small nursery where he grew boxwoods, other shrubbery, and fruit trees. Whenever he worked outside, Hattie usually was beside him. She loved to garden, believed in organic methods, and always produced a bounty of vegetables and flowers.

Robert and Hattie were different in almost every respect, perfect counterbalance to each other. He was gruff with a terrible temper (he once took a shotgun to a bumblebee that got after him). She was gentle and calming. ("Now, Rob," she'd say when he erupted with profanities.) He was quiet, she talkative. He was serious, she lighthearted and funny. She enjoyed socializing. He preferred staying home. She was a joiner. He belonged to nothing but the Presbyterian Church and the Republican Party. They disagreed on religion and politics, as well. Every Sunday he went to Lee Memorial Presbyterian Church in their old neighborhood, where he was a deacon. She went to nearby Bethabara Moravian, one of the oldest churches in the state, where she was one of the staunchest and most dependable members. She was a moderate Democrat. He was a strongly conservative Republican. They always went together to vote, each canceling the other's ballot and joking about it.

The arrival of grandchildren, two by Bob, three by Frances, brought changes in identity. In the family, Robert ever after was called Paw-Paw; Hattie was Nanna. Bob lived close by while his children, Susie and Rob, were growing up, and they were regularly at the big house with their grandparents. Frances's brood—Nancy, David, and Debbie—lived in Raleigh, but they came often, were there on all holidays and for extended visits in the summer. Paw-Paw and Nanna doted on their grandchildren. Paw-Paw was mischievous with them, regularly gave them money and taught them to play penny poker. Nanna, a gifted storyteller, not only loved to read to her grandchildren, she also made up stories to tell them, using a character called Little Abraham that she created to teach the lessons of life.

As they entered their sixties, Nanna convinced Paw-Paw, a tight man with a dollar, that they should use some of the money they'd accumulated to enjoy themselves a little, and each year, after the tobacco season, they traveled, touring Europe, North Africa, Hawaii, the Caribbean, and many other exotic spots. Every summer, Paw-Paw rented a big cottage at the beach, and the whole family spent a week together.

Age seemed to slow neither Paw-Paw nor Nanna. Both stayed strong, fit, and working right into their seventies. In November 1971, however, Robert's partner of thirty years, Bill Simpson, suffered a heart attack. Paw-Paw went to the hospital to see him.

"Doctor told me to get the hell out," Bill said when his partner inquired when he might return to work.

Robert pondered that a few moments. "Well," he said. "We'll just quit."

Paw-Paw hadn't wanted to retire, and he was lost without his work. During the tobacco season, he went to one of the warehouses every day and sat with his old cronies. At other times, he joined them at W. G. White's old-time grocery nearby. He spent many hours puttering in his yard or his backyard shop.

In the summer of 1979, Paw-Paw suffered a series of small strokes that took the spirit out of him. No longer could he do the hard work that he loved; he couldn't even drive himself to see his cronies at the warehouse. Nanna regularly took him downtown and left him at White's store, where he often sat alone on a rickety metal stool by the seed bins under the country hams hanging by wires from the ceiling. But he continued to deteriorate, and on March 21, 1980, seven weeks past his eighty-second birthday, he died of congestive heart failure.

Everybody worried about how Nanna would get along after Paw-Paw's death, but she assured them they shouldn't. She didn't want to leave her big house. Taking care of it wouldn't be too much. She would do just fine. She had no financial worries. Paw-Paw had left half of his nearly $2 million fortune of stocks, property, and savings in trust to his son and daughter, the other half to his wife. Nanna had her church, her friends, plenty to keep her busy. She never was one to complain or feel sorry for herself anyway, always positive, always looking on the bright side. She went right on teaching Sunday school, as she had for thirty-five years, right on baking chicken pies for the church's monthly sales, right on trimming and finishing the beeswax candles for the Moravian Service League to sell at Old Salem, the restored tourist village downtown. She still attended her Bible study group, still taught the younger women in the church to bake the thin, traditional Moravian Christmas cookies. She contin-ued her gardening and canning, kept on with her quilting, basketmaking, embroidery, and decoupage, making gifts for family and friends.

She had many friends, some far younger than she, and she always sought to make new ones. She visited often with friends and neighbors, belonged to a neighborhood book club, helped organize an annual neighborhood Christmas party.

"She made you feel good," said her neighbor and close friend, Mary Brownlee, who was less than half her age. "Just to drive down the street and see her out there with her lawn tractor or little wheelbarrow and her ridiculous outfits was reassuring. She was a wise person, always willing to share. No matter what happened to me, I knew I could go up there and tell her and she would understand. She was a woman at ease with the world. She didn't have any false pride. I always said I wanted to be just like her."

Nanna was generous with her neighbors and friends and particularly so with her church and family. All who found themselves troubled, financially or otherwise, knew they could turn to Nanna for help. She was beloved by family, church, and community, so much so that in 1984, her church, where she was commonly called Miz Hattie, staged Hattie Newsom Day to pay tribute to her.

When Nanna began having heart problems, her family became concerned, but not Nanna. She didn't let it interfere with her life. She made it known that she would not indulge self-pity or embrace fear. She trusted the Lord and humanity to the point that she rarely locked her doors when she went to bed, which almost always was after midnight.

As her family's concern for her health grew, her son, Bob, began spending more and more weekends with her. He asked Mary and Fam Brownlee down the street to keep a watch on her during the week, asked other friends to call regularly and keep check on her when he couldn't be there. After Nanna slipped on an acorn and broke her foot in the autumn of 1984, Bob and Florence decided that she shouldn't be alone any longer and made plans to move in. Nanna laughed about the accident and went on with her yardwork wearing a cast, but she welcomed the decision by her son and daughter-in-law and even suggested remodeling the house to suit them.

Although the house had changed little since Paw-Paw first remodeled it, things around it had changed greatly. The city had surrounded it. New houses lined Valley Road, and new subdivisions jutted from it. Two acres had been chopped off the back of the Newsom land to make Reynolda Road into an expressway, where traffic zipped by day and night. Still, the house remained a serene oasis, guarded by huge oaks.

Bob wanted to make many changes. For one thing, he thought the house should have a circular drive in front, and Nanna encouraged him to rip out the huge boxwoods that she and Paw-Paw had planted and install one. When a friend asked how she could stand to see the boxwoods go, Nanna smiled and said, "I've had my forty years here. Now he can have his time."

The renovation, which began at Thanksgiving, took far longer than anticipated. The whole back wing was being redone, with a new kitchen and dining room and a new bath upstairs for the refurbished guest room. Paw-Paw's back porch was being enclosed with floor-to-ceiling sliding windows, creating a spacious new sun room. Nanna had grown a little impatient as the work dragged on. Her house was a mess. Furniture was piled in different rooms. Dust covered everything. Workers tramped in and out—when they showed up.

Nanna had moved her refrigerator into the breezeway connecting the living room to the garage, where she also put a hot plate on which she prepared her meals. It was a troublesome arrangement, and her family worried that she was foregoing cooking because of it and not getting proper nutrition. She suffered from diabetes, and proper diet was essential. As Nanna began to appear more drawn and stooped, her family became convinced that she wasn't taking care of herself.

That made completing the house imperative, and by May of 1985, much to everybody's relief, Nanna had been assured that the end was in sight. Painters and flooring people were at work. Soon order would be restored and Bob and Florence would be living with her.

Mother's Day fell on one of those rare weekends when

Bob and Florence weren't at Nanna's. Bob had arranged to take Florence to visit friends in Maryland while he attended to business in Washington. He knew that his sister, Frances, and her husband, Bing, would be with his mother that weekend.

Frances and her mother always had been close. From the time she was a child, Frances knew what she wanted to be in life: a newspaper reporter. Her mother encouraged her, even drove her to the *Winston-Salem Journal* when Frances was twelve so that she could submit a story for publication. Frances had gone on to become the first female news reporter for the *Raleigh News & Observer*, covering the legislature and writing the popular "Under the Dome" column on the front page until she gave it up to marry Bing Miller, a former professional baseball player who became a professor at North Carolina State University. She later returned to work in public relations and was now, as she had been for many years, director of the North Carolina Nurses Association. Frances and her mother were much alike in temperament. They always found something to laugh about, if nothing more than going shopping and trying on outrageous hats just to giggle about them.

Nanna didn't feel well that Sunday. She'd stayed home from church because she knew Frances and Bing were coming. She was fretting about her messy house. Over the years, she and Paw-Paw had filled the house to overflowing with antiques and bric-a-brac, and with the renovation it was even more cluttered than usual.

Frances was helping her mother look for something in one of her big closets when she spotted an awful-looking old dress and pulled it out.

"Why in the world are you keeping this?" she asked.

"I don't know," Nanna said, shaking her head. "You know, I sure hope, honey, that you don't have to come in here and take care of all this stuff if something happens to me."

"I hope I don't either," Frances said. "I've never seen so much stuff that you don't need." And they both began to giggle.

16

Fam Brownlee was playing with his new computer in the book-lined study of his antebellum home, a two-story, white farmhouse with teetering chimneys that looked out of place amid the modern city subdivision that had enveloped it. A writer who had published a history of Winston-Salem, Fam was now in public relations, and the computer was to be a boon to his work. This was the second night he had sat up late in the downstairs front room exploring its many facets.

He was interrupted by his wife, Mary, who had come from upstairs, already dressed for bed. Their two sons were upstairs watching "Christopher Columbus" on TV.

"There's a car in the driveway," Mary said.

It was late for visitors, nearly 10:30, and Fam couldn't imagine who might be calling. The driveway was at the back of the house, and while his wife went to pull on some clothes, Fam walked through the kitchen, put on the outside lights, and stepped onto the porch to see who was there. His back steps were collapsing and he didn't want anybody to get hurt on them. He saw a man and a woman with fear and panic in their faces.

Both started talking at once, and they were so excited that Fam couldn't discern what they were saying. He had to calm them before learning that they were the Suttons, friends of the Newsoms. They'd just been to the Newsom house. Something was terribly wrong.

"We looked in through the windows and the TV was on and they were in there," Homer Sutton said, the words tumbling out. "We tapped on the window and we couldn't wake them up. We've got to call the police and an ambulance."

He said nothing of murder, and Fam thought maybe there'd been a gas leak or some other accident. He helped the Suttons onto the porch and invited them into the kitchen, where there was a telephone. Mary had returned downstairs and was waiting with a look of anxiety.

"Something has happened at the Newsoms'," Fam told her. "Call 911 and get somebody out here."

While Mary was dialing the emergency number, Fam suggested that he and Dr. Sutton go to the Newsom house, which wasn't visible from the Brownlees'. It was across the street and a couple of hundred feet to the southeast, and unlike the Brownlee house, with its narrow front yard, it was set well back from the road. Fam and Dr. Sutton left by the front door and walked quickly up the dark street, but at the foot of the Newsom driveway, Dr. Sutton hesitated, and Fam got the distinct impression that he didn't want to go back to the house.

"You want to go up and see if we can find out what's going on?" Fam asked.

"The police will be here in just a minute. Why don't we just wait here?"

At the Brownlee house, Katy had pulled herself together and called her son, Steve. She told him what they'd seen and asked him to call Rob Newsom in Greensboro and tell him that something had happened and that he should come immediately.

Rob was waiting nervously for the call he knew would soon be coming, and something told him that it was not likely to be a happy one. Soon after calling Dr. Sutton to ask him to check on his parents and grandmother, Rob had called his aunt in Raleigh.

"Aunt Frances," he said, "there's something wrong at the house in Winston."

"What is it?" she asked.

"I don't know. I've not been able to get the phone to answer. I just think there's something bad wrong. I've sent somebody to find out and I'll call you as soon as I hear something."

Rob sprang to the phone at first ring and listened

somberly as Steve Sutton repeated what his mother had told him.

"Okay," he said. "I'll be there as soon as I can."

His wife, Alice, knew from his expression that the news was bad, and as soon as Rob hung up and explained the situation, they both were seized with fear. There had been trouble in the family and suddenly they were afraid for their own lives and those of their three children. They turned on every light, inside and out, checked the locks on all the doors and windows, and began calling friends and neighbors to come over. While Rob got out his shotgun and loaded it, Alice called the police and asked for a patrol on their street.

The night was growing chilly, but neither Fam Brownlee nor Homer Sutton noticed it as they waited in the darkness at the foot of the Newsom driveway. They noticed only the quietness. They had expected to hear approaching sirens, but they heard only the sounds of traffic on nearby Reynolda Road. Fam realized that fifteen minutes had passed.

"Homer, you wait here," he said. "I'm going to run back and tell Mary to call again."

Mary called 911 again, and Katy told Fam that she'd called Hattie Newsom's minister, the Reverend John Giesler, to find out if she had been at church that day. No, he reported, she hadn't been for the past two Sundays, and he was worried about her, thought perhaps she was sick. He was shocked to hear what Katy told him.

Fam returned to the foot of the driveway, where he and Dr. Sutton continued to wait. Shortly, they saw the headlights of an approaching car. It stopped, and John Giesler, who lived only a mile and a half away, got out.

The three men briefly discussed the situation and decided that they should go to the house for a look. As they walked up the driveway, Fam broke off and went to the living room window at the front of the house. Through it he could see across the room to the window Dr. Sutton had first looked in. He saw Hattie on the sofa just a few feet away. He could see only Florence's back where she was curled on the floor in front of the TV.

"They look like they're sleeping," he reported to the others.

"They're not sleeping," Dr. Sutton said.

They went on to the back of the house and saw the broken storm door. Fam and John Giesler peered through the window on this side. From this viewpoint, there was no question that Dr. Sutton was right. Fam had seen enough corpses in Vietnam to know death when he saw it. He noticed bullet holes, big ones, in the plaster wall above Hattie's head.

"Well, they're dead," Fam said.

All three had the same thought. "Surely Bob didn't do this," Giesler said.

"He must be dead, too," said Fam. "He must be in there somewhere."

"Maybe somebody's still in there with a gun," Dr. Sutton suggested.

All three thought it prudent to retreat down the driveway to wait, but Fam was losing patience. More than half an hour had passed since Dr. Sutton had come to his back door.

"Where are the police?" he asked angrily.

He ran back to his house, where his wife, who had come outside to see what was happening, met him on the front porch.

"Mary, get in there and call again!" he said. "Tell them we've got at least two people dead and probably three. Shot to death!"

Mary was shocked to disbelief. "No," she said. "I can't tell the police that. You know they're not dead."

"Call them!" Fam said. He was shaking with anger. "Tell them to GET OUT HERE!"

He rejoined the other men at the driveway, where they stood contemplating the possibilities of what had happened, shaking their heads with disbelief that no help had come yet. Another fifteen minutes passed before a Winston-Salem police car pulled up, without blue lights or siren, and a lone patrolman got out.

The three men quickly explained the situation, especially their concern about Bob, and all four walked to the house. The officer peeked in the front window, then went around the back for another look.

"I'm going to have to go inside," he said, drawing his revolver.

The officer was still taking a cautious look through the house when four more police cars arrived, one behind the other, in answer to Mary's latest frantic call. The officers in the cars jumped out and ran toward the house with weapons drawn.

"They came up there like the marines storming a beach in the Pacific," recalled Fam, who rushed to meet them, saying, "Please be careful. There's a police officer in the house. Don't shoot him."

Before the other officers reached the house, the first officer stepped out the door he had entered, holstering his gun.

"There's a man on the floor right inside the door," he said. "He's dead, too."

Fam Brownlee, Homer Sutton, and John Giesler all looked at one another. Nobody had to say anything. They all knew it was Bob.

Frances Miller was growing more and more anxious as she waited for her nephew to call back.

"It's been nearly an hour," she said to her husband. "What should we do?"

No sooner had she said that than the phone rang. She was surprised to find Steve Sutton calling from Winston-Salem.

"Mother says you must come here," Steve said.

"Steve, what's happened?" Frances asked.

"She asked me not to tell you anything, just that you need to come."

At that moment Frances saw everything clearly, a phenomenon she later would not be able to comprehend, but she knew that her mother, brother, and sister-in-law were dead—and not by accident. Murdered. She felt it in the deepest reaches of her soul.

"Steve," she said firmly, "are my folks gone?"

He paused for long moments before answering in a near whisper. "Yes."

Frances handed the phone to her husband, who began quizzing Steve for details as his wife sank weakly into a chair.

* * *

Other calls were being made. Alice Newsom called her parents in Winston-Salem, and they, in turn, called their minister, the Reverend Dudley Colhoun, rector of St. Paul's Episcopal Church in downtown Winston-Salem, the church Bob and Florence Newsom had joined soon after their marriage and to which they recently had returned. Reverend Colhoun made plans to pick up Fred Hill, Alice's father, and drive to the Newsom house. They knew that Rob would be arriving soon and would need their support.

Neighbors began calling Mary Brownlee to find out what was going on. But she had not heard from her friend Maya Angelou, who lived two doors away, directly across the street from the Newsom house, so she called to make sure that she was all right. Maya's house was often a gathering spot for literary, political, and show business celebrities. A professor at nearby Wake Forest University, Maya was also an internationally known singer, dancer, actress, director, screenwriter, composer, civil rights leader, and author whose series of books about her life had been highly acclaimed. Maya had been unaware of the commotion in the neighborhood until Mary told her what had happened. Soon afterward, Maya called back in disbelief.

"Mary, did you just tell me that Hattie was *murdered?*"

More police had arrived. Fam Brownlee now counted nine cars, with more on the way. Officers were milling around, going in and out of the house. One asked Fam if he could identify the three cars beside the garage, and as Fam stepped between Bob's Buick and Hattie's gold Plymouth, he nearly stepped on a ring of keys.

"There's some keys," he said, and the officer stooped to pick them up, stopping only when Fam said, "They could be evidence."

Still upset that the police had taken nearly an hour to respond to his wife's calls, Fam became even more agitated as he watched their actions. Nobody seemed to be in charge or to know what to do. Officers kept going into the house to look at the bodies, drawn, Fam was certain, by nothing more than morbid curiosity. He thought he heard things being moved inside. Was evidence being destroyed inadvertently?

"Don't you think you should get those people out of the house?" he asked one officer.

"We'll take care of this," she responded snappishly.

Fam went back to the foot of the driveway, convinced that the police were in a state of confusion.

On at least one count, he was right, for some officers had realized that the Newsom house might not fall within the newly annexed area of the city, that this might not be their case after all, and twenty-eight minutes after the first policeman arrived, a call went to the Forsyth County Sheriff's Department.

17

The phone rang just before midnight at Allen Gentry's modest brick home in Pfafftown, a village less than five miles from the Newsom house.

"County's calling," said his wife, Lu Ann, nudging him awake.

The young couple had been asleep for less than two hours after spending a tiring day at the sports car races at Charlotte Motor Speedway. They had, in fact, spent the weekend at the racetrack, driving the eighty miles back and forth each day. Allen Gentry never could get his fill of sleek, fast cars in close competition.

The call didn't surprise Gentry. In the nearly two and a half years since he had been promoted to sergeant in the Criminal Investigation Division of the Forsyth County Sheriff's Department, he had become accustomed to middle-of-the-night calls. He usually got two or three a week, almost always about minor matters that required a supervisor's attention. He would make a decision, roll over, and go back to sleep.

But this time as he uttered his groggy hello into the receiver, the dispatcher began rattling on about a triple murder. His mind was too sleep-stilled to grasp that.

"I'm saying, 'Huh?' " he recalled later. "You just don't have triple homicides in Winston-Salem. You have those in California or somewhere else, not here."

The news brought him awake quickly, and he jotted down the details on a side-table pad. "I'll be right there," he said.

"What is it?" asked his wife.

"A triple homicide," he said incredulously.

He hurriedly pulled on jeans, a gray slipover shirt, and sneakers, and left by the carport door, passing his gleaming, black, T-top 280Z Datsun with its MY1VICE license tag as he made his way to the unmarked Dodge cruiser he detested.

For as long as he could remember, Gentry, a native of mountainous Wilkes County, had been drawn between two loves, the glamour of fast cars and the excitement of police work, and he never could reconcile the two.

After graduation from Elkin High School, he was torn about which course to follow: cars or law enforcement. He enrolled in a community college auto mechanics course but soon switched to a criminal justice program at another community college. He wanted to be a highway patrolman, but he weighed too little and his eyesight was too poor, so he dropped out of college and began selling cars in Winston-Salem.

On an outside chance, he submitted an application to the Winston-Salem Police Department and was surprised three months later to be offered a job in the communications division. He took it and a year later moved on to become a deputy with the sheriff's department. A week before he was to start patrol duty, on September 1, 1973, he married Lu Ann Crump, whom he'd met in Spanish class in high school.

In five years as a patrol deputy, Gentry clung to his dream of becoming a highway patrolman. He gained weight, though not enough, and corrected his vision with contact lenses. But his repeated appeals were denied, and instead he became a juvenile officer for the sheriff's department for a year before stepping up to criminal investigations.

As a detective, Gentry thought he had found his calling. Bright and quick to learn, he was methodical and thorough, scrupulously honest and fair. He didn't worry and was rarely rattled. He was a diplomat, never a bully, able to talk his way through almost any situation and achieve his objective. His even disposition, shy, soft-spoken approach, and boyish smile infused confidence, and made people trust him and want to talk to him. In good-guy, bad-guy situations, he was always the good guy.

Always eager to learn, Gentry sought whatever training was available. In addition to graduating from the FBI National Academy, he'd learned such varied skills as Breathalyzer operation and hypnosis. With his promotion to sergeant in January 1983, he clearly was on the rise in law enforcement.

Gentry was indeed almost too good to be true, the epitome of the all-American boy. He was always polite, rarely swore, still used expressions such as "gosh" and "neat," didn't smoke or drink, regularly attended the Baptist church. A sharp dresser, he was always meticulously groomed and had a standing weekly appointment with his barber, who kept his wavy, dark hair trimmed close.

At thirty-two, Gentry could finally meet the weight requirements of the highway patrol. He'd gained more than forty pounds since joining the sheriff's department, although he was still trim. But he was glad now that he hadn't won his battles to get into the patrol. In the years that he had kept that dream, he and Lu Ann had lived in apartments, knowing that if he got accepted they would be moved to some desolate part of the state. When the dream died, they bought the ranch-style house in Pfafftown and furnished it tastefully in vogueish country style. On their walls were prints by Bob Timberlake, a fashionable North Carolina artist whose simple rural scenes fetched handsome prices. Although they had no children, that void was partly filled by a twelve-year-old gray miniature poodle named Duffy, who stirred to see what was happening as Gentry hurried from his house in answer to the homicide call.

Gentry was happy with his life. He loved his work. But in his secret heart, he wished the flashy Datsun in his carport was a Porsche 911 convertible, and he couldn't give up the idea that instead of going off to work each day in a business suit to investigate mundane burglaries, he should be wearing fireproof coveralls gaudy with patches and pulling on driving gloves and helmet to take to the track at Sebring or Riverside.

But that was not on his mind as he nudged his sluggish

Dodge up the narrow, broken concrete lane that is Valley Road. *Three people killed.* Surely, Gentry thought, it must be a murder-suicide, a case that would be quickly cleared with a medical examiner's ruling.

He didn't have to search for the house. He topped the hill and saw police cars everywhere. Rarely had he seen so many at a crime scene. He parked on the opposite side of the street a short distance from the house and walked to the driveway. The confusion that had reigned earlier had subsided, and the house had been sealed off by Winston-Salem police. Two patrolmen were guarding the foot of the driveway, where rescue squad members and several bystanders also had gathered. Gentry saw his lieutenant, Earl B. Hiatt, usually called EB, arriving and waited for him. The two walked up the driveway, where they were greeted by Larry Gordon, the first deputy to reach the scene. Any thought Gentry had of a case easily cleared was dispelled when Gordon told them that three bodies were in the house, two women and a man, all shot several times, and no weapon in sight. He read the names of the victims from a pad, but neither Gentry nor Hiatt had heard of the Newsoms. Gordon explained that jurisdiction was in question, and Hiatt and Gentry agreed they should proceed on the assumption that this was their case. More specifically, Gentry knew, the responsibility likely would fall on him.

Big changes had taken place in the Forsyth County Sheriff's Department in the previous six months. In November 1984, when longtime sheriff Manley Lancaster was forced by failing health to step down, county commissioners had chosen as sheriff Preston Oldham, the hard-eyed commander of the criminal investigation division, who had built a legendary reputation for his undercover narcotics work. Less than three weeks earlier, Oldham had realigned his department. Ronald Barker was appointed new captain of detectives. A former public school teacher who had spent years as crime prevention officer, holding rape clinics for women, teaching bank tellers how to respond to holdups and homeowners how to discourage burglaries, Barker had expected to be appointed sheriff himself. Indeed, news reports had proclaimed him the leading candidate, and he had been asked to be present at the commission meeting at which Oldham's appointment was announced. Disappointed, he had nonetheless sworn his allegiance to the new sheriff.

Barker had formed the department's first homicide division with one other detective following a spate of murders in 1976, but he had worked at it for less than two years, never had a case of this magnitude, and had been away from it for a long time. Gentry, who was aware of the politics involved in his department but tried to distance himself from them, had only restricted homicide experience himself. The handful of cases on which he had worked all had been quickly solved by confessions. He realized, however, that he was the department's most experienced investigator on the scene, and although he knew that a difficult case—and this one had all the earmarks of being just that—would require hard work by almost every detective in the department, he knew, too, that the case had to have a lead officer, somebody to take charge, and in his unobtrusive way he quietly assumed command.

"Well, let's see what we've got," he said, heading for the back door of the Newsom house.

To the right, just inside the back door, a short hallway with rose-adorned wallpaper led to the living room, foyer, and staircase. There Bob Newsom's tall, slender body lay on its right side in a near-fetal position. He was wearing blue jeans; a green, blue, and lavender plaid flannel shirt with long sleeves; and black corduroy house slippers with no socks. He had been shot three times in the abdomen, once in the right forearm (the only close shot), and once in the back of the head. He was just outside the arched entrance to the living room, and it appeared that he had been trying to flee when fatally wounded.

On the drop-leaf cherry table in front of which Bob's body lay was a large antique hurricane lamp with a rose-colored globe that was a particular treasure of his mother. Once the lamp had had a twin, but Debbie Miller, Nanna and Paw-Paw's youngest grandchild, kicked and broke it while sliding down the bannister as a child, a memorable experience to the family because it marked the only time anybody ever saw Nanna angry at one of her grandchildren. A tall grandfather clock, one of Paw-Paw's most prized possessions, stood near Bob's head, and on the floor beside the clock, where it had been placed to wait out the renovation of the house, was a wood-framed table clock with a .45-caliber bullet casing on top. Only six inches from Bob's feet, in front of a small table with its single drawer pulled out, another orphan of the re-modeling, a hole thirty inches in diameter had burned through the olive green carpet, charring the floorboards underneath. Inside the circle were ashes and odd bits of scorched paper, some from an organic gardening maga-zine that apparently had supplied fuel for the fire. Flor-ence's pocketbook lay beside Bob's body, its contents dumped onto the carpet.

In the living room, a large mirror over the fireplace at the end of the room opposite the archway reflected a macabre scene of disorder. A wooden rocking chair lay on its side between the flickering console TV, tuned to a High Point station, and the door to the breezeway where Nanna had set up her temporary kitchen. A set of fire-place tools had been overturned. A green recliner near the fireplace was in the full rest position, and beside it, neatly aligned, were Florence's shoes. A bunch of red grapes lay on a *Fortune* magazine by a Winston-Salem telephone directory on a marble-topped table next to the chair. On the telephone directory was a green plastic supermarket vegetable tray with raw cut cauliflower on it. A full can of spray starch stood on the coffee table.

Florence's thin body lay in a grotesque sprawl in front of the TV in a pool of dried blood. She was wearing a white skirt and a light blue-and-white striped knit top. Although investigators would not notice it immediately, her throat had been slit, a deep, two-inch gash just above the glasses that hung around her neck on a decorative chain. She had two shallow stab wounds in the right side of her neck, a third in her right shoulder. More promi-nent were three deep stab wounds that penetrated her back. One, it later was discovered, had severed her aorta. A single shot in the right side of her chest had penetrated her liver, heart, and both lungs. She also had been shot in her left temple as she lay on the floor, the bullet passing through and lodging beneath her. Her wedding band was bent, the finger under the ring cut and broken, as if somebody had tried unsuccessfully to remove the ring. Her engagement ring, with its three-quarter-carat diamond, was gone.

Nanna, who had grown a bit plump in her later years, had been shot three times. One bullet, apparently a wild shot, had grazed the left side of her head. A second hit her in the lower right side. The fatal shot struck her right temple, passed through her head, and lodged in her shoulder. She lay on the sofa with hands clasped beneath her chin, and many police officers who saw her were convinced that she had been praying when she was shot, although later evidence showed that she had been placed in that position after being shot. On the wall above her head, near two bullet holes in the plaster, was a framed antique needlepoint quote from Joshua: "As for me and my house, we will serve the Lord."

A floral-patterned blue-and-green easy chair near the archway had been pierced by a bullet that also went through one corner of an ornate étagère and ended up in the wall. Another bullet passed through the archway, struck a piece of molding on the far side of the staircase, and plopped back onto the steps. From the angle of the shots, most appeared to have been fired from near the breezeway door.

In a clear glass dish on the étagère, easily visible, was a small wad of currency—four one-hundred-dollar bills, a fifty, four twenties, a ten, and a one. Propped next to the dish was a North Carolina Department of Revenue income tax refund check for $661.26. In Nanna's bedroom, on the other side of the hallway, drawers had been pulled from a chest and stacked on the floor. A heavy gold-and-pearl bracelet worth thousands of dollars lay on the floor near the foot of the bed. More drawers were stacked in an upstairs bedroom that Nanna once had used, a bedroom decorated with photographs of important events in the lives of her two children and five grandchildren. In another upstairs bedroom, the one Bob and Florence used every weekend, Bob's briefcase lay open on the floor by an antique washstand. On the stand was a china urn handpainted with roses. Paw-Paw had brought the urn home one day wrapped as a gift for Nanna.

"What in the world am I supposed to do with that?" she had asked on opening it.

"Well, I don't know," he'd replied with a grin, "but I'll bet you've got the prettiest chamber pot of any woman in Forsyth County."

The briefcase was empty except for a calculator and some pens.

His walk-through of the house convinced Allen Gentry that this was not going to be an easily solved case. For one thing, the trail was cold. The murders obviously had occurred hours earlier, maybe a day or more. And what was the motive? Clearly, this was no typical robbery. What robber would leave behind plainly visible cash and expensive jewelry? The murders looked like executions to him.

Several things about the scene were puzzling to Gentry. Why was the storm door broken, while a key was left in the back door lock? Had one of the victims been surprised by the murderer while entering the house? Why was another set of keys found between two of the cars? Was that footprint in the sand by one of the new windows at the back of the house significant? Why had Florence Newsom been so savaged, a blatant example of overkill? Why had the fire been set in the hallway? Was it an attempt to burn down the house and cover the murders? If so, why hadn't it been fueled by the paint thinner and other volatile substances so handily available in the part of the house that was being remodeled? Had the purpose of the fire been only to burn a specific item or items? Had the killer or killers come only to find and destroy such items? Had they been found in Bob Newsom's briefcase? Why was the briefcase empty? Gentry realized that he would have to find the answers to many hard questions before he could put this case behind him.

Shortly after Gentry and Hiatt left the house, their new captain, Ron Barker, arrived with his son Mike, a Winston-Salem police detective who had come along out of curiosity. Gentry and Hiatt filled in Barker, and the three decided to call for the State Bureau of Investigation mobile crime lab. They wanted investigative help from the SBI, too. Little could be done until the lab crew had completed its work and morning had arrived. Men couldn't be sent to ask questions of neighbors and family acquaintances after midnight, but Gentry did want to talk with those who found the bodies and any other witnesses who might still be about.

"The son and grandson just arrived," one officer told him, motioning down the driveway.

Rob Newsom had arrived from Greensboro, driven by his friend Tom Maher, while Gentry was inside the house. Gentry walked to the foot of the driveway and was told that Rob had been taken to Fam Brownlee's house down the street, so Gentry went to his car, got one of the legal pads on which he preferred to take his meticulous notes, and walked the short distance to the old farmhouse.

Rob was in the living room with his father-in-law, Fred Hill, and his parents' pastor, Dudley Colhoun, who had come to comfort him. He looked to be in shock. At times he sat with his head in his hands. "I can't believe this has happened," he kept repeating.

Gentry introduced himself and offered condolences. He had a few questions. Basic things. Ages, address, occupations of Rob's parents. When was the last time he'd seen them? How had he learned of their deaths?

Rob told about his parents spending weekends with his grandmother, their plans to move in, the remodeling that had been under way. Briefly, he went through the events of the day, his futile attempts to reach his parents, the call to the Suttons.

Did Rob know why anybody might want to kill his parents and grandmother?

He didn't.

Had there been any problems, any unusual events in the family?

"Well, last summer," Rob answered, "my sister's former mother-in-law and sister-in-law were murdered in Kentucky."

PART THREE

FAMILY UNIONS

18

Music built the framework for Robert Newsom, Jr.'s life. His mother, Hattie, insisted on musical training for her two children. Frances, his younger sister, took quickly to the piano, but Bobby, as Robert was called in the family, screeched badly on violin. Not until his mother sent him for voice lessons did he find the true joys of music and begin to build his dreams around them.

By the time he was in high school, his heart was set on becoming a professional singer. The passing of his adolescence brought him a rich baritone voice and he had developed it well. Not only was he a soloist with his church choir as well as with the glee club and chorus at Hanes High School, he also was frequently invited to sing, accompanied on piano by his sister, at other churches and clubs. His high school music teacher, Flavella Stockton, encouraged him greatly, and because of her he began planning a career in music.

This concerned his practical, traditionalist father, the tobacco auctioneer. He had taught his son manly skills: how to fix machinery, how to build things with his hands, how to make plants grow from the earth. Was music an apt trade for a man? Could a decent living be made at it? Would it satisfy his bright mind?

His mother, who had instilled in him his love of music and literature, was secretly pleased with his choice. Her concerns about her son were others. All of his life, she had worried about his health. He was a puny child, a finicky eater. "He likes beans and apples and not much of anything else," she said in exasperation. She took him to doctors. She wheedled him to try different foods.

"Mother, if you'll hold my nose, I'll try to swallow it," he'd say.

Sometimes he pretended to eat his vegetables, but they would be found under the edge of his plate when the table was cleared.

He grew tall and precariously thin, almost pretty, with his dark good looks and bright brown eyes. Even one of his closest friends, Jesse Mock, thought him a bit sissy, but Bob was competitive and didn't allow his size to hinder him from doing what he wanted to do. He was a Boy Scout. He played tennis. He even went out for his high school football team and became a gangly line-backer, although he spent most of his time on the bench. At almost everything but football, he excelled. He was an honor student, as gifted in math and science as in music and literature. Quiet by nature, he commanded respect and was extremely popular, elected class pres-ident every year and student council president in his final year of high school. As a senior, his classmates chose him best-looking, most intellectual, and best all-around.

After his graduation in 1938, Bob attended special summer classes in voice at Salem College, an all-female school, before enrolling in the music program at the University of North Carolina in Chapel Hill. By the end of the first semester, his dreams were wrestling with his father's practicality. Some of his friends thought he had been encouraged in music beyond his ability.

"You can sing pretty well," his longtime friend Charlie Clarke told him bluntly, "but you'll never be able to make a living at it."

Charlie was an engineering student at North Carolina State College in Raleigh, and he encouraged Bob to consider the industrial engineering program there. Indus-trial engineering is businessman's engineering, Charlie explained. Industrial engineers work closely with people. They do time and motion studies, long-range planning. They determine what has to be done to produce certain amounts of products in certain amounts of time. They make things work.

"You've got a good analytical mind and you handle people really well," Charlie said. "You'd be great at it."

Besides, he pointed out, if Bob came to State, they could room together. They'd have a fine time.

Robert Newsom, Sr., was more than happy to write the check for tuition when his son announced his intentions to study industrial engineering.

As usual, Bob excelled in his studies, but in his final years in college he often was tempted away. Something even more significant than music and achievement had befallen him. He was in love for the first time. He'd had a girlfriend in high school, but that wasn't serious. Mostly, they'd gone together to group affairs or on double dates with his sister. This was serious. She was from the eastern part of the state, a student at nearby Peace College. Bob's friend Charlie didn't like the girl, thought she treated Bob badly, but Bob could see no faults. As he neared graduation, he told his family of his engagement.

Graduation in the spring of 1943 was a time of bittersweet excitement. Most of Bob's classmates were going off to fight World War II. He didn't have to. He was so underweight that the draft board had declared him 4-F. A patriot like his father, he yearned to serve his country. Turned down by the military, he joined the Merchant Marines and shipped out as an assistant engineer on a freighter of the American–South African Line. Over the next three years, he made trips to Italy, Africa, even across the North Sea to Russia. Numerous times his ship dodged bombs and torpedoes. Years later, he would tell his only son that he didn't mind being shot at for his country, but he was glad he never had to shoot at anyone.

Bob returned from one of his trips to learn that his fiancée had found someone else. Although his family knew that he was deeply hurt, he never talked about it and seemed to shrug it off.

Late in 1944, music again stepped in, indirectly, to fashion his life. He came home on leave and went to Hanes High School to visit his music teacher, Flavella Stockton. She had somebody she wanted him to meet, a new teacher at the school, about his age, very pretty, with long wavy hair, dark eyes, and a bright smile.

"Bob," she said, "this is Florence Sharp."

Some people who knew the Sharp family well called Florence the dumb one. Not that she wasn't plenty smart, for she was. But in a family of brilliant achievers, somebody had to be at the bottom of the list academically, and that was Florence. It never seemed to bother her, but some of her brothers and sisters bristled to her defense if anybody even hinted that she might be less than brilliant.

Florence, they pointed out, had had some bad breaks. For one thing, she was "double spoiled." As the baby girl in the family, she was doted over as an infant. Her close brush with death at age four, when her younger twin brothers died of an illness all three contracted from tainted milk and she was left having to relearn to walk and talk, had caused her to be spoiled a second time. "She got over it mostly," her sister Louise later recalled. "Let's say she improved. There was a time when she was a mess."

Florence also got a bad start in school. The method of teaching reading changed the year that she began, and many children had difficulty with the new method. Florence fell behind, and her mother began to worry. By the time she was in the fourth grade, Florence was doing so poorly that her mother decided to hold her back a year and let her catch up. That seemed to work, but the simple truth was that Florence never shared her brothers' and sisters' interest in academic achievement. She'd rather have fun than study. She had an outgoing nature, a keen sense of humor, a zest for life and adventure. She made friends easily and was by far the most popular of all the Sharp children. Laughter and joy were always around her.

As a teenager, Florence developed a talent for cosmetology. She fixed the hair of her mother, sisters, and friends, but she never seriously considered making a career of it, for she knew that higher callings were expected of Sharps. She had trouble choosing her course after high school, but from the limited choices available to women at the time, she finally picked teaching and followed her sisters to Woman's College in Greensboro. She chose business administration as her major and made spending money giving home permanents to her dormmates. No less fun-loving than ever, Florence did buckle down at college, not only achieving respectable grades but taking part in many outside activities. She belonged to the Adelphian Literary Society, Gamma Alpha Sorority, the Education Club, and the Young Democrats. She was an ardent and outspoken supporter of Franklin D. Roosevelt. One of her classmates at WC was Frances Newsom, who, by skipping more than a year of grade school, had finished high school at the same time as her older brother, but Florence didn't get to know Frances well and didn't even realize that she had a brother.

After her graduation, Florence took a job teaching typing and business English at Kings Mountain, forty miles west of Charlotte, but she didn't like it because it was so far from home. She had no car and took the bus home on weekends. After a year, she moved to Walkertown, near Winston-Salem, where she taught for two years before moving on to Hanes High School, where she became a friend of Flavella Stockton.

Bob was immediately taken with Florence. He invited her out, and they had such a good time that he asked her out again. On the second date he proposed marriage and she accepted. Family and friends were stunned. Some blamed the war. Bob's family thought he was reacting on the rebound from his failed engagement. Surely, the marriage wouldn't come about.

Bob's leave ended all too soon, and he returned to sea filled with romance. Some months later, when his ship docked in New York, Florence took the train to visit him. They planned their wedding for his next leave.

It took place on August 25, 1945, at First Methodist Church in Reidsville. Florence wore a dress made by her mother. Bob was resplendent in dress uniform. After the ceremony, they settled briefly in Gray Court Apartments on Fifth Street in Winston-Salem. When Bob returned to sea for the final nine months of his enlistment, Florence's younger brother, Kits, then a student at Bowman Gray School of Medicine, moved in to await Bob's return.

Bob was released from his tour in May of 1946 and applied for work at R. J. Reynolds, where his father had begun his career. The company was wary. Robert Newsom, Sr., had been a successful warehouseman, widely known in the tobacco business. Reynolds officials were sure that Bob soon would leave them to join his father. Bob argued that he had no interest in the warehouse business. His field was industrial engineering. The company countered that it had no industrial engineering department. "Let me prove you need one," Bob said.

He was hired as a machinist in the engineering department and later worked in personnel. Within four years, Reynolds decided that it did indeed need an industrial engineering department, and Bob, at age thirty, was named chief industrial engineer of what was then the world's largest tobacco company and was fast becoming one of the world's largest multicompany corporations, a job he would hold for many satisfying years before giving it up in disappointment.

19

Despite the suddenness of their marriage, Bob Newsom and Florence Sharp proved a proper match. Each found quick acceptance with the other's family.

Bob was just the sort of man the Sharps hoped their daughters would marry: solid, dependable, intelligent, a man of great promise. Best of all, he was from good stock, a true gentleman, kind, generous, thoughtful, attentive, wryly humorous.

The Newsoms took immediately to Florence and she to them. They thought her the perfect wife for their quiet son, one who would bring out his best qualities. Florence quickly became a devoted and loving daughter-in-law. Robert Newsom particularly liked his new daughter-in-law's sense of humor and the feistiness with which she spoke her mind. He thought the Sharp family a bit aristocratic—"highfalutin," he called it—but he saw no pretentiousness in Florence. Still, he enjoyed teasing her about her family.

"Those Sharps keep their pedigrees on the wall, don't they?" he'd say.

Florence laughed off his good-natured jibes.

Both families were pleased when, soon after Bob returned from the Merchant Marines, Florence announced that she was expecting a baby, a first grandchild for the Newsoms.

The baby came as a Christmas gift, born on Christmas Eve 1946, at Annie Penn Memorial Hospital in Reidsville, a lively girl with her father's bright brown eyes, delivered by her uncle, Dr. Fred Klenner. She was named Susie

Sharp, for Florence's beloved eldest sister, by then a popular lawyer working with their father in Reidsville.

The happiness of their daughter's birth soon turned to fear for Florence and Bob. A mentally unstable young woman, A.W.O.L. from the Women's Army Corps, was being held at the hospital awaiting military authorities. She wandered from her room and made her way to the nursery, where she stood admiring the babies. When a nurse left the babies momentarily unsupervised, the young woman darted in, picked up Susie, and fled. She was stopped before she got out of the hospital, the baby returned unharmed, but when a nurse told Florence about the incident, Florence became distraught. For the remainder of his family's stay at the hospital, Bob sat outside the nursery, keeping a close watch on his newly born daughter.

As if that weren't enough, a new worry soon arose. After examining Susie before her departure from the hospital, Dr. Klenner announced that the baby had a heart murmur. He advised that Susie not be allowed to cry, lest it trigger an irregular heartbeat, perhaps a stoppage. For the first year of their daughter's life, her parents' efforts to keep her quiet were often frantic, sometimes heroic.

Soon after settling in their Winston-Salem apartment, Bob and Florence had gone searching for a church. Bob had grown up attending Lee Memorial Presbyterian Church with his father; Florence had gone to Reidsville's First Methodist with her mother. But denomination didn't decide their choice. Music still drove Bob. He wanted to find the best choir in Winston-Salem and join it. He picked the choir at St. Paul's Episcopal Church, an imposing granite structure near downtown. There he soon became a soloist and popular choir member. There, too, Susie was christened. Her Aunt Susie, for whom she was named, commemorated the occasion by presenting her with a small cross on a silver chain that had been given to her by her own mother's sister, Susie Blackwell, for whom she was named, a tangible symbol of the binds of family over generations. Susie later lost the cross, but nobody saw that as portent of the terrible break she eventually would make from family.

Susie's arrival brought the need for more living space, and Bob rented a small house on Jarvis Street. Five days before Susie was to celebrate her third birthday, a baby brother arrived. He was named Robert W. Newsom III, to be called Robby by the family, later Rob.

Susie had been smothered with affection, particularly from her father, and she resented the baby, pouting when he received attention.

Within months of his son's birth, Bob had a second reason for joy. He was given a big raise and promoted to chief industrial engineer at R. J. Reynolds. New status and a new child sent him looking for a new place to live. He bought ten wooded acres atop a steep hill between the old Moravian settlements of Bethabara and Bethania, just a few miles from his parents' big house, and there he built a small, neat, three-bedroom, brick-and-frame house. But before his family could move, fear struck again.

Bob's sister, Frances, had given birth to her first child, a daughter, Nancy, in Raleigh in June of 1948. Soon after Nancy's second birthday, she fell ill with polio. Her left arm, legs, and body trunk were paralyzed, and she languished with high fever. Robert Newsom, then called Paw-Paw by his two granddaughters, rushed home from South Carolina, where he had been auctioning tobacco. "Find the best place in the United States and let's take her there," he said, but the doctors said there was little anybody could do.

Florence called Frances to tell her differently. "Fred Klenner has done a lot of work with polio patients," she said. "I'd like him to see Nancy."

The work Dr. Klenner had done was experimental. He believed that massive doses of vitamin C, administered intravenously, could stop polio. Frances talked it over with her pediatrician. He didn't believe the treatment would help, but he wouldn't stand in her way if she wanted to try it. Frances and her husband, Bing, desperate, agreed to the treatment.

Dr. Klenner arrived in Raleigh, driven there by his sister-in-law Susie, who a year earlier had been appointed North Carolina's first female superior court judge. He gave Nancy vitamin C equivalent to what he said would be found in five gallons of orange juice. He returned several more times to give her injections. Her temperature dropped and the paralysis began to recede. Later, Frances put Nancy through intensive physical rehabilitation, which left her with only the barest signs that she had suffered polio.

Bob and Florence were frantic with worry because Susie had played with Nancy at Nancy's second birthday party. When Susie became listless soon after Nancy's condition improved, her parents rushed her to Dr. Klenner in Reidsville. He confirmed their fears. She did indeed have polio, he said, but he thought they had caught it soon enough. He began the vitamin treatment, and Susie soon regained her liveliness. Although Florence blamed a painful chronic lump that later formed at the base of Susie's spine on the disease, she credited her brother-in-law with saving her daughter's life and preventing her from being crippled.

Susie had developed into an active and precocious child. She was called Susie Q to distinguish her from her aunt. Susie Q couldn't understand how two Susies could be in one family, so she called her aunt Su-Su, a nickname the entire family picked up and one that would cling to the distinquished jurist for the rest of her life. Susie was especially fond of Su-Su and anticipated with great excitement the times when her aunt would stop by while going and coming from court assignments around the state, because Su-Su always brought presents. Susie also looked forward to the regular family gatherings in the big Sharp house in Reidsville, when Su-Su would take her to the depot to see the trains, one of her favorite activities.

Susie came to one family gathering clinging to a small doll. When her uncle Tommy, visiting from the North, asked if he could take her picture, she refused. No amount of cajoling could get her to agree.

"How about if I take a picture of your doll, then?" her uncle asked.

"Okay," she said, and posed holding the doll while her uncle snapped her picture, creating a story that would be laughed about and retold in the family every time the picture was shown.

Susie was not often so easily fooled, however. When

she was four, her mother came home from her job at Old Town School to find her housekeeper, Neely Davis, so upset about Susie's misbehavior that she was ready to quit. "That child is just too much to handle," Neely said.

Florence took Susie aside for a talk.

"I'm trying to be so bad that she'll quit and you'll stay home with me," Susie said.

"I can't do that," her mother explained. "I've signed a contract. I can't quit."

"Oh, I didn't know you'd signed a contract," Susie said, as if that changed everything.

The problems Susie caused Neely subsided somewhat the following year, when Susie entered Meadowbrook Kindergarten, where she was chosen Queen of the May and posed regally in a long gown on her high-backed throne, attended by her court, while a professional photographer took her picture.

Her proud father worshiped her, and she in turn was a daddy's girl. Early on she had learned to charm him to get what she wanted, but when charm failed she resorted to other tactics. Her relationship with her mother, who was not so easily manipulated, was often tense. If her mother told her no, or her will was otherwise thwarted, Susie often threw tantrums. At first, her mother dealt with them by closing her in her room. But they grew so intense and violent that she later tried quelling them with cold showers.

"Susie held that against Florence all of her life," her aunt Su-Su said later.

Florence's attempts to alter Susie's behavior created a simmering rift between mother and daughter. Florence was so concerned about it that she took a course in child psychology, hoping to learn to deal better with Susie's problems. When Susie started biting other children, Florence decided that the time had come to take her daughter for counseling.

"On the whole, Susie was a sweet child," her aunt Louise recalled, "but she had a mean streak. She used to torment her brother."

"Rob was a gentle little boy who didn't throw tantrums," his aunt Frances remembered. "Susie was overbearing to him. Bossy. He didn't fight back a whole lot."

At five, Robby was diagnosed as having an ulcer.

High-strung was a phrase that popped quickly to mind when relatives attempted to describe Susie's nature. "Not your placid, happy-go-lucky person," said Frances. "Nobody else uses this word, but I always had a feeling of her being brittle. She could not allow anybody else's will to overwhelm hers."

"She was an adorable little girl," her adoring aunt Su-Su recalled, "but she was rather willful. She wanted her way."

When Susie got her way, everything was fine, and at times life was almost idyllic on the Newsoms' beautiful hilltop, with its commanding view through the trees. Florence loved the place. Rob-Su Acres, she called it; "living on the hill." A creek ran at the base of the hill behind the house, and Paw-Paw had a pond built on it for the family's Christmas one year. Bob got a small rowboat for the pond, and the children used it to play pirates. He later built a baseball diamond for Rob and bought a big mare pony that Susie named Flicka and over whom she alone could exercise her will, for Flicka would allow no one else to ride her.

Susie and Rob were close with their cousins Nancy and David. They regularly visited back and forth, spent time together each summer at the beach and at Nanna and Paw-Paw's. Nancy was tomboyish and loved playing outside with the boys. Susie took part, but usually on the fringe of activities. She was more prim and preferred dressing in lacy things and playing inside to getting rowdy and dirty in blue jeans. She had much of her mother's fastidiousness.

Florence was fanatic about cleanliness and germs. Her house was immaculate. She allowed no pets to enter it. She made her children wash their hands numerous times daily. A piece of candy dropped on the floor could not be eaten, even if the floor had just been scrubbed and sanitized. Susie and Rob could not drink from the same cup nor take a bite from the same sandwich. Food couldn't be taken outside because of flies.

Florence taught her children social graces and was emphatic about their value. She emphasized the importance of family, social position, and socially acceptable behavior, and Bob joined in full support.

"He wanted his children always to be circumspect," his sister, Frances, recalled. "It was important to him that they not deviate from the norm, from what was expected."

The Newsom children grew up in an atmosphere of cordial and genteel formality, a throwback to Old South aristocracy, their lives structured to family, St. Paul's Episcopal Church (where Susie later taught a children's Sunday school class), and the Forsyth Country Club. They were keenly aware of the differences between themselves and their less affluent rural neighbors, and each reacted differently. Rob took on a swaggering redneck pose before his peers, but Susie withdrew, and in her isolation began to think herself and her family special.

Susie spent much time reading and studying, especially about her favorite topics: history and anthropology. She developed an avid interest in the royal family of Great Britain, collected books about them, and decorated her bedroom walls with their photographs. Once, when Nancy came to visit, she found Susie in a party dress and her room decorated. "What's the occasion?" Nancy asked. "Why, it's the queen's birthday," Susie replied, as if everybody should be celebrating. Her interest in royalty continued through high school, leading some classmates to suspect she thought herself a princess.

Susie worked hard at her studies, but no matter how hard she tried, she never was the academic and intellectual equal of her younger brother and she resented it. Rob's mind retained almost everything that entered it, and he could summon what he needed in an instant. He made top grades with minimal effort and eventually would have his choice of prestigious academic scholarships. Susie complained to friends about her brother, whom she nicknamed Three for the numerals that followed his name. He was given too much, she said, had things too easy. She thought her parents should be harder on him.

"There was a lot of sibling dislike directed toward me," Rob later acknowledged. "I don't recall and I don't think there ever was any physical cruelty, but I think there was a lot of envy and that sort of thing."

Susie developed into a strikingly beautiful young woman

with a slim, well-proportioned figure. She wore her dark hair in a short pageboy cut with curls in the front. Family members thought she looked exactly like Nanna as a young woman, and they displayed pictures of the two side by side as proof. Susie dressed demurely and tastefully, choosing expensive and fashionable clothes. She had an outgoing, bubbly personality, but little concern, it seemed, for the things that interested most girls her age.

Florence had been strict, not allowing Susie to use makeup, shave her legs, or wear nylons until long after other girls her age were doing so. Florence also had imparted her narrow view of sex to her daughter. Nancy was astounded at Susie's naïveté about boys and sex when she brought up those subjects during their teenage years.

At Northwest High School, a sprawling country school several miles from her home that Susie entered in the ninth grade, she showed little interest in boys and made few close friends. She kept her grades high and avoided most school activities, especially sports, which she disdained. During the spring of her sophomore year, she received a lot of attention from teachers when her namesake aunt became the first woman to be appointed to the North Carolina Supreme Court. Her teachers thought of her as sweet, bright, a hard worker with great promise, obviously from a good family.

Some of her classmates didn't hold such a high opinion of her. They thought her aloof, haughty. Her interests were not theirs. She preferred classical music to rock and roll, theater to drive-in movies, reading to cruising.

"She was not a frivolous person," said Linda Crutchfield, Susie's best friend in high school. "She set high standards for herself. She was very self-assured and responsible. I think Susie's goals and aspirations were far beyond some of her classmates', therefore they didn't have a common ground. I think it may have been viewed as snobbishness by some."

Linda thought that Susie was perhaps more comfortable with adults than with her peers, but she saw no snobbishness or haughtiness in her. She found instead a lightness of spirit, a deep caring for others. Linda's family was not on the same economic plane as Susie's. Her father was a foreman at R. J. Reynolds, a volunteer special deputy sheriff. Yet Susie loved and respected Linda's parents. She even accompanied Linda's father when he made rounds delivering firewood and food to poor families.

Susie was reserved, Linda knew, shy, slow to warm to people, but once she did she was a devoted friend. Perhaps a little too devoted. At times, Linda felt that Susie was almost possessive of her friendship.

They had a lot of fun together. They talked about boys, although later Linda couldn't remember Susie ever dating. They went to movies, played badminton, the only competitive sport that seemed to interest Susie. They swam at nearby Crystal Lake, hiked, canoed, and rode horses at Tanglewood Park (Susie had a gentling touch with animals, especially horses). Susie loved hunting Indian artifacts and attending antique auctions, and they regularly pursued those passions. They also frequently spent nights at one another's houses.

Linda enjoyed staying with the Newsoms. She thought them warm, gracious, welcoming, and she liked the sense of openness she found there, the constant exchange of ideas that seemed so much a part of their family life.

Susie had been a bit shielded by her parents, Linda thought, but not overprotected. Nor had she been overindulged or pampered. Linda knew that Susie's upbringing had been strict, but she detected no resentment about it. She knew, too, that both Susie and her mother were strong-willed, but she was never aware of any conflict between them. Although occasionally she saw Susie flash anger toward her mother, she never saw it returned by Florence. The Newsoms, she knew, were not the type to indulge emotional displays in front of others.

Susie had a direct manner, tended to view things as black or white, harbored a strong sense of right and wrong, and was quick to form an opinion and was unbending in her views. But even when her mother disagreed with her in Linda's presence, she encouraged Susie to express herself.

"I never saw her mother trying to dominate or control Susie," Linda said. "I always saw her encouraging her daughter to develop herself. The Newsoms were a very reasoned, logical family. They talked about things. There was no 'This is the way it is and that's it.' "

Chris Severn, who became close to Susie a few years later and spent time at the Newsom house, saw the situation between Susie and her mother a little differently.

"I always perceived there to be a cautiously respectful relationship," she said. "Her mother hesitated to maybe be critical of Susie because of the reaction she would get."

Family members knew that to be the case, for they were well aware of Susie's propensity to anger quickly—and her unwillingness to forgive. They knew that the least thing might set her off, and she would retain resentment about it forever. They remembered a family friend who angered Susie by teasing that she was too pretty to be her father's daughter. She stalked from his presence and never spoke to him again.

While Susie was in high school, Bob decided that his family needed more space. Florence's mother, Annie Britt, was staying with them frequently, and the house offered little privacy. Bob bought a new, much larger house in a small, private subdivision called Green Meadows, two and a half miles west of his parents' home. The ranch-style brick house, with a stone entranceway, looked to be single-story from the front, but because of the steep lot on which it was built, it was actually on two levels. The glassed back of the house looked onto a small pond at the edge of the lot. Florence moved reluctantly. She loved Rob-Su Acres and later said that some of the best years of her life had been spent there.

At the beginning of Susie's senior year of high school, in the fall of 1963, she suffered the trauma of having to attend a new school filled with strangers. A consolidated high school, North Forsyth had been built near Winston-Salem to accommodate students from three other schools, including Northwest. There Susie took part in but one extracurricular activity, the Anchor Club, a community service club for girls of strong character who displayed evidence of leadership—*the* club for girls at the school. That Christmas, when the club president drew up her traditional list of Christmas wishes for members, she made this one for Susie: "Biographies of royal families

Susie would never dodge. Make her a history teacher somewhat like Mrs. Hodge." Susie didn't know what she wanted to do with her life, but teaching, her mother's profession, was an option she was considering.

When the 422 seniors who made up the first graduating class of North Forsyth High walked to the front of Wait Chapel at Wake Forest College to receive their diplomas on June 4, 1964, Susie was among them, but she was not among the 32 honor graduates. When many of the graduates left on chartered buses the next day for a traditional class trip to New York and the World's Fair, Susie was making ready for an outing at White Lake with friends. Riding a crowded, rowdy bus to New York was not her idea of fun.

Appropriately, Susie chose Queens College, a small, expensive, private school for young women in a wealthy area of Charlotte. She had been taken with the place when she visited with other family members to see her aunt Su-Su receive an honorary degree.

She liked Queens at first, joined her classmates in talking about the boys at nearby Davidson College, but eventually she began to feel uncomfortable and restricted. Too many of her classmates were frivolous, she complained, too concerned with clothes and cars and hairdos. She called them butterflies. Although many were from wealthy families, they clearly weren't from "good families," and good families didn't necessarily have to be wealthy. "She never felt that was something you based on money," her brother later explained. "She felt there was such a thing as genteel poverty." As the family of her grandmother, Annie Britt Sharp, no doubt would attest. Susie said that she wanted a more serious, academic atmosphere for her studies, and after her sophomore year, she returned to Winston-Salem and enrolled as a history major at Wake Forest College, just a few miles from her home.

For 122 years, Wake Forest had been a small college supported by Southern Baptists in the village of Wake Forest, sixteen miles north of Raleigh. But in 1946, the Z. Smith Reynolds Foundation offered the college a perpetual endowment to move to Winston-Salem. Members of the Reynolds family donated six hundred acres of the huge Reynolds estate for the campus, which was built over the next ten years at a cost of $20 million. The college moved to its new home in 1956, and ten years later, when Susie enrolled, it was growing fast in size and prestige and was just a year from changing its name to Wake Forest University.

That fall, shortly after Susie began classes, she went to the library to study and struck up a conversation with a basketball player, a quiet freshman, new to the state. His name, he told her, was Tommy Lynch.

20

Tom Lynch had a toothy smile, sun-bleached hair, and a quiet, easygoing nature. Except in stature, he was much like his father. At an inch under six feet, he stood eight inches taller than his father and weighed 175 pounds. But he shared his father's love of sports and possessed the self-confidence of the natural athlete. He realized early in childhood that he was better at physical activities than most other kids.

At Morgan Park Academy, his prep school in Chicago, he played football, baseball, basketball, and was a member of the swim team, but it was basketball at which he excelled. In his senior year, he averaged thirty points a game and was named one of the top twenty high school players in Chicago. With college scouts sitting in the stands, he scored fifty-three points one night, buoying his dreams of being recruited by major universities.

Those dreams did not pan out, but Duke University and Davidson College, both prestigious institutions, both in North Carolina, expressed interest in him, and in the spring of his senior year his mother went with him to visit those campuses and talk to coaches. His grades kept both schools from offering encouragement. Since he was in the area, Tom wanted to stop at Wake Forest College in Winston-Salem, where Horace "Bones" McKinney had built a winning basketball program with an assistant named Billy Packer.

Wake Forest had a new coach and a losing season in 1966, but Tom showed his newspaper clippings to Packer and came away feeling good about the possibilities. Wake Forest might find a spot for him, Packer told him, but he would have to play his way into a scholarship. First he must prove himself on the freshman team.

Tom enrolled as a pre-med student. Encouraged by his mother, he had long talked of becoming a doctor. Although his grades were not so good in his first year, he ensured his scholarship by averaging six points a game on the freshman team, and in 1967, the year Wake Forest became a university and got yet another new basketball coach, he became a substitute guard on the varsity team. To his disappointment, he never would rise above substitute, averaging less than a point a game for his college career.

His athletic abilities were not what attracted Susie Newsom. She was drawn by his wholesome good looks and medical ambitions. She always had been impressed by doctors, and some of her friends predicted she would marry one. She and Tom began seeing each other frequently on campus. She was always vivacious and happy to see him. She had a car, too, and offered rides to him and his friends. Soon they were attending campus events together.

Susie was two years older than Tom, from a prominent family, one of the most beautiful women on campus, and he was flattered by her attentions. He was teased by his fellow players when Susie was featured in a photo page of fraternity sweethearts in a campus publication, posing by a fountain in a striped minidress, looking demurely over her shoulder from beneath her long bangs.

By her senior year, Susie and Tom were dating regularly, and she wore his fraternity pin. Her friends were seeing little of her anymore. Linda Crutchfield, Susie's best friend in high school, was a day student at Wake Forest, but she was attending her dying mother, was engaged and soon to be married, and had little time for Susie. She had met Tom and wasn't impressed. She knew that Susie never had been attracted to jocks and wondered at his appeal to her. She knew, too, that Susie had dated little and never had a serious love affair, and that worried her.

"In this area she was inexperienced," Linda said years later, "so she had no basis for comparison."

Susie's family had similar concerns. They didn't quite

know what to make of this quiet young man who was two years their daughter's junior. He appeared to be a nice, stable boy, but his drive and ambition seemed no match for Susie's, and his disposition seemed just the opposite of her effervescent, sometimes almost frantic boisterousness.

"He's a lot like Gary Cooper," Paw-Paw observed after Susie brought Tom to meet him and Nanna. "Don't have much to say, does he?"

The family hoped the relationship a passing fancy, but Susie clearly was in love, and nobody was willing to caution her about it.

Chris Severn became one of Susie's closest friends that year. She roomed next door in Bostwick Hall and they attended the same church, St. Paul's. Chris, whom Susie nicknamed Christabel, couldn't understand Susie's attraction to Tom.

"Tom just was not a real dynamo," Chris said. "I never thought Tom amounted to much."

She knew that Susie didn't like any of the fraternity brothers who were Tom's friends and that she loathed Bob Brenner, his close friend, who was on the football team.

"She had her heart, mind, and soul set on marrying Tom," Chris said. "I never thought that was a match made in heaven. I don't think anybody ever tried to convince her otherwise."

In the spring of 1968, only a few weeks after a curfew had been clamped on Winston-Salem, the city's streets patrolled by National Guard troops because of rioting in the wake of Martin Luther King's assassination, Susie received her degree in history. Shortly thereafter, on June 4, she wrote to her aunt Susie Sharp to thank her for a cash graduation gift.

> *Dear Su-Su,*
> *This afternoon while I was lying in the sun, I thought over the exciting things I remembered in the last 19 or so years. My conclusion was quickly drawn: the sole unifying factor was you. My first walking doll, my turquoise bracelet, my first pair of pierced earrings, which are still*

my best, and all the countless little things (trips to the train station and getting to go to a grown-up restaurant on my birthday) which made my childhood exciting. And now you have given that special graduation present— special because without it, I could never have bought the pearl necklace I've wanted for so long. But more especially I want to thank you for being a constant guiding force, for being someone I could always trust and depend on, for being that one person whom I knew no matter what happened I could always turn to. I am and will always be proud to be your niece and namesake.

Love, Susie

Big changes lay in store for Susie's family that summer. R. J. Reynolds Tobacco Company had been growing rapidly, diversifying, buying up other companies, particularly food companies. New management had begun shifting executives, lest they become stale and complacent in their positions. Bob Newsom, who'd been the company's chief industrial engineer for eighteen years, was targeted for a move. He was asked to become chief industrial engineer for R. J. Reynolds Foods in New York.

Bob was not particularly pleased at the prospect. He liked the tobacco business and didn't want to leave it. Neither did he want to leave Winston-Salem, where he and Florence were deeply rooted. They loved St. Paul's Church, where Bob not only was bass soloist in the choir but a member of the vestry. They loved Forsyth Country Club, where they had many friends and belonged to bridge groups. They loved the madrigal group they had formed that met regularly at their house. Both had involved themselves deeply in community activities that they didn't want to abandon. Bob had been chairman of a committee studying what needed to be done to improve Winston-Salem's schools. He worked with the Boy Scouts, served on the board of the North Carolina School of the Arts, headed the city's Goodwill Rehabilitation program, and was three times elected president of the Singers' Guild, the choral arm of the Winston-Salem Symphony. He worked for the local Republican Party. Florence, who had given up teaching before Rob entered junior high, was a member of the Library Commission, active in

Scouting and PTA. She served on several committees at church and delivered hot meals every day to sick and elderly people in the poor, black areas of East Winston where many volunteers feared to venture. Neither relished the idea of leaving their families. Bob's parents were getting on in years, and Florence's mother, now living back at the big Sharp house in Reidsville with Louise, who had retired from the navy to look after her, was in poor health.

Bob's loyalty to the company was strong, however, and he reluctantly accepted the new assignment. That summer, he sold the house at Green Meadows and he and Florence settled, far from children, family, and friends, into a big house in Silver Mine, Connecticut, where they began to try to adapt to a new life-style, with Bob joining the daily hordes of executives commuting to the city by train.

Susie stayed behind to enter graduate school at Wake Forest that fall, living at first with Nanna and Paw-Paw, later moving into an apartment of her own. In an era of war protests, flower children, easy sex, and drugs, Wake Forest, with its conservative Southern Baptist traditions, was an island of middle-American values and stability. Susie scorned hippies, war protesters, and civil rights activists, strongly supported the war in Vietnam (she later said she didn't know why Nixon didn't just end the war by dropping "the bomb" on Hanoi), and she was comfortable in the sedate, conservative atmosphere at Wake. Her main reason for remaining there, however, was Tom.

That year, their relationship became so close that he took her home to meet his parents. Delores and Chuck Lynch had moved to Louisville a year after Tom started at Wake Forest, and Delores had grown progressively unhappier. The weekend visit did not go well. Later, some who knew the strong wills of both women suspected that each recognized herself in the other. Susie, the daughter of privilege and "good family," and Delores, the hardscrabble child of the Depression, disliked each other instantly, instinctively.

"My mother was a little sensitive about her origins,"

Tom said later. "She would get upset if she thought somebody was looking down at her. She always thought that people should earn what they got, that that was much more noble than being born to it. She never felt family name means anything. It's what you make on your own that counts."

Tom was unaware of any conflict between his mother and Susie that weekend, but on the flight home, when he asked Susie what she thought of his mother and she was noncommittal, he realized that no bonds of affection had formed.

Soon after the visit, Susie told family members that Delores was overbearing and domineering. Delores told her friend Marjorie Chinnock that Susie was snooty and pretentious.

Susie had no intentions of letting her feelings about Delores interfere in her relationship with Tom. By then she had made clear to her family that she and Tom would marry, and after a year of graduate school, she got a job as a research assistant at R. J. Reynolds and settled in to wait for Tom to finish his final year of college.

In 1969, Tom gave Susie a diamond engagement ring he had ordered from a catalog, and the wedding date was set to follow his graduation in June of 1970.

Delores was distressed. Susie had resisted all of her efforts to get close to her, she told her friend Marjorie.

"I just have a gut feeling about that girl," Delores said. "I've talked to Tom until I'm blue in the face, and he won't listen."

As Delores went on and on about Susie and Tom, one message emerged to Marjorie: as far as Delores was concerned, no woman would ever be good enough for Tom.

Delores had, indeed, made her feelings known to Tom. "She kept asking me if I really wanted to do this," he recalled. "I knew she didn't think it was a good idea. I thought at the time it was just a matter of, you know, mothers don't want their sons to go off with somebody else. And maybe I was too young or something. She thought people shouldn't get married until they were older."

Susie wanted a big wedding, and that spring she was giddy with plans for it. She was overjoyed that her mother was back to help her with it.

Bob had been very unhappy with his work in New York. From the beginning, his relationship with the chief operating officer of Reynolds Foods was not a good one. He felt thwarted at every turn and undermined by company headquarters in Winston-Salem. He longed for the old days in the tobacco business. Florence didn't like his having to travel so much, leaving her alone. Although they liked their house in Connecticut and had made friends, they still were homesick for North Carolina, their families, and old friends.

One day, Bob came home from work and announced, "I have had it."

"I thought he meant me," Florence later laughingly told a friend.

Bob went to see his friend Curtis Judge, who had been a vice president at R. J. Reynolds. Judge had just moved to New York as president of P. Lorillard Tobacco Company and was looking for new executives. He hired Bob to be director of material and engineering services, assigned to Lorillard's big plant in Greensboro, North Carolina. Both Bob and Florence were overjoyed to be returning home. They bought a new two-story house with a big screened back porch on Fairgreen Drive in Hamilton Forest, an expensive subdivision just beginning to develop in northwest Greensboro, and moved in shortly before their daughter's marriage.

Susie's wedding was set for June 6, 1970, at St. Paul's Church, the reception at Forsyth Country Club. Tom's sister, Janie, was to be a bridesmaid, Susie's brother, Rob, then a philosophy student at the University of the South in Sewanee, Tennessee, an usher.

Tom's parents and sister arrived in Winston-Salem, checked into a motel room arranged by Florence, and a minor uproar soon ensued. Delores thought Susie's family was not paying proper attention to the Lynches. Florence told friends that Delores expected more of her than she could deliver. Susie was furious at Delores, claiming

Delores embarrassed her by drinking too much at the rehearsal dinner.

The wedding was formal. The men wore morning clothes, the women lime-green chiffon dresses. Shortly before the ceremony, Susie found fault with Janie's dress. It was wrinkled.

"We don't have time to get it pressed now," Delores said.

"Well, she just won't be in the wedding then," Susie said sharply, before others stepped in to soothe matters.

The wedding proceeded under great tension. Right to the end, Delores hoped Tom might not go through with it.

"She was saying things like, 'It's still not too late to change your mind,' " Tom recalled later. "She was sort of joking but she was semiserious. If I'd said, 'Yeah, you're right, let's go,' she'd have gone."

Despite their earlier flare-up, after the reception, Susie tossed her bouquet to Janie.

There was no time for a honeymoon. Tom had given up on becoming a physician and chosen dental school instead. His father was paying his way, and his mother had urged him to study in Kentucky, where he was entitled to lower resident tuition rates. He had been accepted at the University of Kentucky in Lexington, and Delores had found and furnished an apartment for him and Susie at Creekside Apartments, where Janie lived, only a few miles from the campus. Tom also had taken a summer job with the Kentucky Department of Health and had to leave soon after the wedding to begin work. He went ahead without Susie, who packed up the wedding gifts and followed a week later. Susie soon found a job at Spindletop Research Company near the campus.

Tom started classes that fall. With his parents paying his school expenses, he and Susie were able to live modestly well on her salary. They saw little of each other, however. Tom was in school all day and studied into the night. In his few free hours, he ran and played intramural basketball and tag football. Susie enjoyed her work, liked Lexington well enough, and was happy with Tom, but she missed home and made trips back to North Carolina whenever she could.

What she didn't like were Delores's calls and drop-in visits. Delores rarely stayed long when she stopped by while also visiting Janie. She told friends that Susie never made her feel welcome and not once offered to cook her a meal. Susie saw the visits and regular calls as interference in her and Tom's lives.

When Susie went home for Rob's wedding in June of 1972, Delores was greatly on her mind.

"She'd be talking about her when it was not the time or place to talk about the woman," Susie's cousin Nancy recalled.

Rob's wedding, like his sister's, was at St. Paul's Church, where his bride, Alice, also was a member. The reception was held at Forsyth Country Club, where her parents belonged. The same fountain of champagne that had flowed for Susie's wedding flowed for Rob's. After the ceremony, Susie rode from the church to the country club with Nancy and her husband, Steve Dunn.

"All she talked about was what a witch Delores was, how awful she was," Nancy said. " 'She's mean and evil,' she said. She just went on and on and on about how much she hated the woman."

"I never had any hint that she hated her," Tom said later. "I knew she didn't want to be around my mother."

Although Tom's parents lived only eighty miles away, Susie refused to visit them. Only once, on Thanksgiving, at Tom's insistence, did she go to the big house on Covered Bridge Road, and then she complained of a headache and stayed in bed. Delores made a tray and took it to her, but Susie didn't touch the food.

"I slaved all day in the kitchen and set this wonderful table and wanted to make everything so special, and she went to her room and stayed the whole time and wouldn't even eat," Delores complained after the visit.

Tom tried to get Susie to visit on other occasions, but without success. "She made it clear that she wasn't interested in doing that," he recalled. "She put up such a fuss that she didn't want to go that after a while you just don't ask anymore. It didn't bother me that much to not go home very often. I was never much of a homebody."

"He's married now. It's his life. This is what he's chosen," Chuck kept reminding Delores, but it didn't decrease her anger and pain.

"That girl's got him wrapped around her little finger," Delores said.

In his senior year, Tom decided to follow in his father's footsteps and join the navy. By enlisting in the reserves, he could be commissioned an officer and would have to serve only two years active duty. It would give him time to decide what he wanted to do and allow him to save money to start a practice. It also would let the U.S. government pay for him and Susie to start a family. They had planned on children from the beginning, at least two, and now with Tom's graduation looming, the time seemed right. Soon after the new year 1974 began, Susie happily called home with the news that she was pregnant.

Commissioned immediately after his graduation, Tom was assigned to the U.S. Marine Training Center at Parris Island. Susie, nearly seven months pregnant, was happy to leave Lexington and its close proximity to her detested mother-in-law. She and Tom settled into an apartment in historic Beaufort, only a few miles from the base, and while Tom went to work repairing the teeth of skinned-head recruits, she began seeing base doctors and making preparations for the arrival of her baby. The child, a boy, was born August 30 at the base hospital. He was named John Wesley for the middle names of his father and his grandfather Newsom.

Tom called his mother with the news, and she said that she and Janie would come to see the baby. They drove to Beaufort soon afterward and arrived while Tom was at work. Delores stopped and called the apartment to let Susie know they were in town. Delores never tired of retelling that conversation later.

"Can we bring something for dinner?" Delores asked.

"Tom's not here," Susie said. "We have plans tonight. You'll have to come tomorrow."

And she hung up.

Delores was furiously offended. "This is ridiculous," she said. "Why should we subject ourselves to this treatment?"

But rather than risk hurting Tom, she and Janie checked into a motel, got up the next morning, picked up some doughnuts, and went to the apartment.

Susie was abrupt and said little. "It was very obvious that she didn't want us there," Delores said. "The tension was *so* thick."

Delores and Janie stayed only a couple of hours, most of it outside with Tom and the baby, before leaving for home. Janie later said that her mother cried most of the way.

Susie was happy in Beaufort, where old hierarchies reigned and family names and traditions mattered. She loved its gray-bearded trees, its centuries-old houses and gracious, Old South atmosphere. She made friends with other officers' wives and attended some social functions, but John, a fretful child, took most of her time.

On trips back to North Carolina, Susie discovered that things were not well at home. Both of her parents were under great stress. Sixteen months after he joined P. Lorillard in 1970, Bob Newsom was promoted to vice president of operations and put in charge of the company's plants in Greensboro and Louisville. He also threw himself back into civic work, serving on the committee that planned the state's bicentennial celebration, the North Carolina University Advisory Council, the board of visitors of Greensboro College, and the board of directors of United Day Care Services, and heading Greensboro's United Way campaign. He was highly regarded by those who worked for him.

"He was a real, real nice person," his secretary, Joyce Jarrett, recalled. "They just didn't make them any finer than he was. He was just genuine, very genuine. He had a lot of compassion for people. He cared about the people he worked for, the people who worked for him. I used to always tell him he was too good for his own good."

That, indeed, was the case. Bob was finding himself more and more often in conflict with his old friend from Reynolds, Curtis Judge, the Lorillard president. Judge thought Bob "sincere, honest, hardworking, intelligent, very capable, a good engineer," but with a serious flaw.

"Bob was too nice a man to be able to handle the real

dirty business of being a top executive," he said more than a decade later. "He was almost congenitally unable to fire anybody. I'd call Bob and say, 'Look, we brought in all of this new machinery. We've got to get rid of some of these people.' It was just beyond him. I don't believe Bob could ever have fired anybody. His days at Reynolds were glory days. It was growing like mad. He didn't have to fire anybody. He was a good man. The only fault Bob had was that he was too good a man in terms of business. You know, in business you sometimes have to be a bastard, and he couldn't do it."

Early in 1975, Bob became embroiled in a dispute about union activities. He had a theory about unions. "He said that unions existed because of bad management attitudes," his son recalled. "Anybody who didn't want them didn't have to have them. All they had to do was treat their employees like humans." When he came out at the losing end of the dispute, Bob felt honor-bound to resign.

He was fifty-five, hurt and disappointed. He had a house, but his few modest investments were far from enough to provide an adequate income. He was uncertain what he would do. Florence was bitter and became deeply depressed. Worried about finances, she returned to teaching at a business school in Greensboro. Bob went into partnership with a friend in a metal-plating business, but it proved profitable enough only for one, and he sold out to his friend and became a private consultant. For two years in the early seventies he had been president of the American Institute of Industrial Engineers, a group with more than 20,000 members. He also belonged to several other professional societies, which he had served in various capacities. Using contacts he had made in those groups, he began landing jobs as a consultant, often with the federal government.

By the spring of 1976, things were looking brighter, and a new grandchild had arrived.

Susie gave birth to her second child, another boy, on March 26, 1976. He was named James Thomas for his great-grandfather Sharp and his father. Florence drove to

Beaufort to see the baby, but Delores did not. Jim would be more than two years old before she ever saw him.

Tom was soon to be discharged from the navy and he was making plans. He was thinking of moving out west to start his practice. Susie confided to family members that it was because he wanted to get as far away as he could from his mother—"that old witch." Tom said he thought it would help his sinus problems. But more than anything, the idea of the West always had appealed to him. He liked the outdoors and open spaces. In dental school he had friends from New Mexico who extolled their home state. He thought he might like to live there. One of his friends gave him the names of two dentists in Albuquerque who could help if he decided to go there.

Tom flew to Albuquerque to check it out soon after Jim's birth. Albuquerque is in the center of New Mexico, on the Rio Grande River, at the base of the bare and imposing Sandia Mountains, a city surrounded by desert. Founded by Spaniards in 1706, it is one of the nation's oldest inland communities, a mile-high city of cool, crisp nights and warm, sunny days. Ernie Pyle, who traveled the country writing columns before he became the nation's most famous war correspondent, picked Albuquerque as the most desirable place to live in America and bought a small white house there before going off to chronicle World War II. When Tom came to look it over, Albuquerque was a burgeoning blend of old and new, a city on the make, with a rising crime rate, growing opportunities, and a metropolitan-area population nearing half a million. It was home of the University of New Mexico and Kirtland Air Force Base, and buried under nearby mountains was a large part of America's nuclear weapons stockpile. Albuquerque seemed to have everything that Tom wanted, including quick access to rugged territory for hunting, fishing, skiing, and other outdoor activities. He loved it immediately.

He also liked the dentists he had come to meet, Armand and Robert Giannini, brothers. They invited him to join them as a partner. He returned to Beaufort excited about the possibilities and later took Susie to see Albuquerque. She wasn't enthusiastic about the place, but Tom thought that would change once she had been there a while.

After his discharge in June, Tom took Susie and the boys to Greensboro to stay with her parents while he flew to New Mexico to get established. He got a bank loan, bought equipment, set up his office, and found an apartment in the Heights, the Sandia foothills that look down on the city. He returned to Greensboro, loaded up his family and possessions, and drove to their new home.

Susie disliked Albuquerque from the beginning. It was too rawboned for her tastes, too informal. There were too many roughlooking people, she complained, too many Mexicans and Indians. She tried to help Tom get his new practice going, but the babies took most of her time.

Soon after Tom and Susie settled in Albuquerque, Jerry and Joy Montgomery came to visit. Susie was happy to see familiar faces. Jerry had been Tom's best friend in college, the star guard that Tom had longed to be on the basketball team, the best man at Tom and Susie's wedding. He was John's godfather. Joy had visited with Tom and Susie while she was attending the University of Kentucky and dating Jerry. They once had gone camping together in West Virginia, Jerry and Joy's home state. Jerry had gone to Bowman Gray School of Medicine at Wake Forest, had just finished his residency, and was looking for a place to settle. Tom talked him into trying Albuquerque, and Jerry soon found a job at St. Joseph's Hospital.

Six months after arriving in Albuquerque, Tom and Susie bought a new house in Thomas Village at 3121 La Mancha Drive in the valley, only a few hundred yards from the Rio Grande and not far from Old Town, the city's historic district. It was a pueblo house, a style popular in the city, fake adobe, stucco over frame, with three bedrooms, a fireplace in the den, and tall cottonwood trees in the backyard. They paid $5,000 down and took out a mortgage for $47,000.

Henry and Irene Eichel, who lived next door, came calling the day after Tom and Susie moved in. Henry was a retired air force colonel, an engineer, then working as an executive at TRW Inc. Irene was from a prominent family in Texas. Susie took an immediate liking to them.

"We had entertained senators and company presidents," Irene said. "That made an impression on Susie." Soon Susie was visiting every day. Irene began thinking of her almost as a daughter. She loved John and Jimbo, as the baby was called, and frequently tended to them while Susie ran errands. John started calling her Granny Goose. He called Hank Opa. Jim would, too, when he was old enough to talk.

Within six months after moving into her new house, a year after her arrival in Albuquerque, Susie began confiding her unhappiness to Irene. She wanted Tom to go back to North Carolina to practice. Albuquerque had no culture, she said. The museums were pathetic. The university was second-rate. Where was the chamber music? She had to go all the way to Santa Fe, sixty-two miles, to see an opera.

Irene suspected that Susie really was unhappy because she had no social identity in Albuquerque. Her family name didn't count. Susie talked frequently about her family back in North Carolina, about her uncle, Fred Klenner, who was, she said, a world-famous doctor, but mostly about her aunt, Susie, the chief justice. She regularly dropped into conversation that *Time* magazine had named her aunt one of the twelve most important women in America. Irene got the idea that Susie Sharp must run North Carolina.

Tom was keenly aware that Susie didn't like Albuquerque. "She wasn't happy here from day one," he said years later. "She didn't have anybody out here who was impressed with her name. Out here, people rely on themselves rather than their family. People tried to like her at first, but after a while they quit trying. It didn't matter to them if she was a Sharp or anything else.

"All her life she was not accepted as herself. She never was. She was accepted as a Sharp or a Newsom. Out here she had to be accepted as herself, and she couldn't adjust or didn't want to adjust or didn't feel like she needed to adjust because she was some kind of special person or something."

Joy and Jerry Montgomery had heard all of the family talk from Susie, too. They concluded that she thought she and her family were a cut above everybody else and therefore deserved special privilege. "She had very rigid ideas," Joy said. "She hadn't learned some of the normal give and take that is necessary in life. She thought she could do things no matter how rude or whatever and there would be no consequences."

Joy and Jerry had a short and simple word to describe Susie: *snob.*

"Susie never really had an identity of her own," recalled Joy. "She had this family and that was all. I always felt like she was just spoiled."

"Susie was very much social-order conscious," Jerry said. "She was always interested in associating with people she perceived to be in some elevated position."

In Albuquerque she found few people worthy of her association.

Turkey was one of Susie's favorite words during that period, *lower class* a favorite phrase. Everything in Albuquerque was lower class. Most of the people were turkeys.

Tom was a turkey, too, Susie told Irene. She wanted to go to the opera; he wouldn't take her. She loved the classics; he had no comprehension of them. He loved to put on boots and go camping, hunting, fishing; she abhorred all of that. Tom bought a Toyota Landcruiser to prowl the desert; she wouldn't set foot in it. He took up running again and began training for a marathon. People who run for miles are crazy, she said, and refused to take the boys to watch him race. Tom loved sports. "Athletes," Susie announced, "are nothing but a bunch of sweaty, overrated turkeys."

"She didn't like anything he liked," Irene recalled later. "She didn't like anything *anybody* liked."

The biggest turkey of all was Susie's mother-in-law, Delores. Susie complained at length about her. She boasted to Irene that she threw away packages Delores mailed to the boys. She spoke proudly of turning Delores away in Beaufort.

"She loathed Delores," Irene said. "She was not paranoid but very close to it about Tom's parents. She absolutely refused to let Chuck and Delores see the boys."

Irene could see trouble ahead next door.

By Tom and Susie's third year in Albuquerque, the trouble had surfaced. Joy and Jerry no longer felt welcome in Susie's house, and neither did other friends of Tom. Susie said cutting, double-edged things about Tom and his friends in front of them. Her only humor took the form of sarcasm. To Joy and Jerry, Susie seemed manipulative and domineering, traits she claimed to despise in her mother-in-law. She was that way not only with Tom and the children, but with everybody, Jerry and Joy thought. When she didn't get her way, she stormed around in a cold fury.

"It was what Susie wanted and that was flat it," Irene said. "I could hear her. We lived next door. I don't think Tom ever had a chance to argue. She would state the absolute facts and then go slam the door. Tom was in absolute misery. He remained silent so there would be no disagreement. Tom got to where if he said two words it was a miracle. She made him miserable in a fiendish manner.

To Irene, Tom seemed to be shrinking inside himself. He was not the type to stand up and confront, she knew, and she noticed that he seemed to be finding more reasons to stay away from home.

The problems between Tom and Susie were marked more with sullen silences than with arguments and screaming matches. Tom had learned early that arguing was futile. "She was a strong character," he said later. "There was no really winning an argument with her. She was right and that was it."

After they first moved to Albuquerque, Tom said, he tried to encourage Susie to do things. When he suggested going Jeep riding in the desert, or visiting Indian reservations or the Grand Canyon, she showed no interest. When he asked her to go to office parties and dental society functions he thought he should attend, she refused and he didn't go. When he wanted to go hunting, she said she didn't want to be left alone with the boys and he stayed home. Eventually, Tom started doing things alone.

"Of course, you felt guilty," he said later, "because she made you feel guilty. That was part of the plan to manipulate you. But I started going anyway, because there was no reason why I shouldn't go."

The more Tom did things alone, the more isolated Susie felt.

"She had no friends," Irene said. "Nobody would come around her. Nobody ever came to see her, and she didn't go to see anyone else."

Financial problems didn't help matters. Tom and Susie had large debts, and with Tom's practice slow in building, they had trouble managing their affairs. Susie partly blamed Tom's family for their situation.

"She felt they had more money than they would ever spend and yet Tom had to borrow money to open his practice," Irene said.

In the spring of 1978, Susie decided to go back to work. She took a job with Competitive Edge, a company that produced TV commercials. She started as a receptionist but quickly rose to be production coordinator, scheduling studio time for ten different offices around the country. Her bosses found her to be pleasant, charming, and highly capable.

Not only was the extra money a help, but Tom hoped the job would make Susie happier and their marriage better.

Susie also found another activity to occupy her time, reviving a longtime interest in Far Eastern culture. She had come to enjoy the subject at Wake Forest because of an Indian professor she admired, Balkrishna Gokhale. In graduate school she studied Far Eastern history, taking a special interest in China, reading everything Pearl Buck ever wrote. With China opening to the West, she got the idea that somebody who could speak Chinese would have a bright future. She found a Taiwanese student at the University of New Mexico to tutor her and began studying Mandarin. She bought books and tapes and diligently spent evenings practicing words and drawing Chinese characters.

Despite Susie's work and new interest, things didn't improve at home.

"We just weren't communicating much with each other," Tom said later. "I don't think we ever really talked. We just didn't have much in common to talk about. I liked outdoor things, hunting and sports and stuff, and I guess she wanted white gloves and teatime in the afternoon."

A constant air of tension permeated the brown stucco house at 3121 La Mancha Drive.

Susie was not relaying her troubles back to North Carolina. Nanna and Paw-Paw came to visit that summer and returned to report to Bob and Florence that all did not seem well between Tom and Susie. Susie brought the boys home for Christmas 1978, leaving Tom behind and offering no explanation for it. Everybody noticed that something was wrong. She was tense, uncommunicative, didn't speak at all to some people. To her cousin Nancy, she talked about her mother-in-law. Delores wouldn't leave them alone, she said. She called all the time, trying to control her, trying to tell Tom and the children how to live. "She's evil," Susie said.

Soon after returning from her Christmas visit, Susie told Tom that the way things were going it might be better if she just took the boys and went back home for good.

"It never occurred to me to get divorced," Tom said later. "It just wasn't part of life's plan. I was a twenty-year-old kid when I got married. The only thing I'd ever known was school and basketball. I thought you went to school, got your career, got married, had kids, and lived happily ever after. Divorce just wasn't part of the picture."

That prospect disturbed Tom. "I told her, 'Why don't you just think about it?' My main concern was for the boys. I didn't want the boys to go. I thought things would get better. They didn't."

Matters grew particularly worse for the boys, especially John. He didn't want his mother to go to work, and when she left him he stood screaming at the window, throwing temper tantrums to rival those of Susie as a child.

Laura Gilliam experienced more of these fits than anybody. Soon after Susie went to work, Laura answered a newspaper ad for a baby-sitter and began tending to John and Jim. Laura had two young children of her own and lived not far from Tom and Susie. On some days she kept all four children at her house, on other days at the Lynch house. Laura was not impressed with Susie as a mother.

"I found that she wasn't concerned over things that she should've been concerned about," she said.

Susie was concerned enough about John's actions to

begin taking him to Dr. Harold Paine, a grandfatherly child psychologist, who later would not talk about John's problems. But Susie's friend Joy, who later became a psychologist herself, thought that Susie was the source of John's troubles.

"She was a person who needed to control every situation," Joy said. "I thought she was inflexible the way she dealt with the children. You got the impression that they had a pretty insulated life. They didn't have the normal freedom that little children want and need."

John wanted to do things on his own, assert his independence. "He would resist," Joy said. "Any time he tried to assert himself as a person, they really got into struggles."

Clearly, Susie cared more for Jim than for John.

"Susie favored Jim," Jerry said, "because she thought that Jim was more like her and John was more like Tom. In fact, it was really the opposite. John did look like Tom, but he was high-strung like Susie. Jim was more docile and relaxed like Tom."

Joy thought that John was deeply frustrated and emotionally wounded by his mother.

"He didn't look like a happy child," she said. "He just seemed like a sort of sad, withdrawn, defeated little boy."

Laura Gilliam would sometimes arrive at the Lynch house to look after the boys and be told by Susie that John was to remain in his room all day.

"She would say he had done something to the other one and he was to be punished," she recalled. "I was not to let him out except to go to the bathroom and for lunch."

On these occasions, John would sometimes rage in his room for hours. Susie instructed Laura to leave him alone until he wore himself down. "He would yell and scream until he got tired of it," Laura said.

Sometimes he did more than yell and scream. He ripped apart his books, damaged his toys, and a few times smeared bowel movements on his walls.

To Laura, Susie seemed less concerned than she should be about such behavior.

By the spring of 1979, Jim, who'd just turned three,

also began displaying behaviorial problems. He kept putting objects into his eyes, and his eyes were constantly red and tearing. After one such incident, Susie got into an argument with the ophthalmologist and created a scene in his office.

"She was becoming a lot more frustrated with parenting," Joy recalled. "The boys were resisting her control, and it was becoming more difficult for her to manage them. It was tense to be around her with the kids. She would be yelling, John would be crying."

Her frustrations began to take physical form. In Jerry's presence, Susie beat Princess, the family dog, with a plastic baseball bat, sending her yelping in pain. Irene could hear other slaps and howls. One day she saw marks on John's face and asked him what happened.

"I fell down," he said.

"He didn't fall down," Susie said. "I slapped him."

"My god," Irene said, "you must have slapped him hard."

"I did," Susie said with no hint of remorse. "I knocked him across the room."

Irene was flabbergasted and told Hank what Susie had said. They debated whether to tell Tom about it, but decided they shouldn't meddle.

One day that spring, Tom came home from work to find John holding his arm in an unusual manner. As soon as he took John's shirt off, he realized the arm was broken.

"What happened?" he asked.

"I was doing trampolines on the bed at the babysitter's and I fell off," John said.

Tom took John to the hospital and had the arm set. He didn't question the baby-sitter. If he had, she would have told him that the boys never got near beds at her house. Her husband worked nights and slept all day, and she kept the bedrooms closed. Because both boys had bedwetting problems, she didn't even let them sleep on the couch at her house. She had pallets fixed for them on the dining room floor. John had suffered no accident at her house, and when he left the day before with his mother, his arm was fine. When Susie brought him the next morning, John was in a cast.

"She said something about a fall and he landed on his arm," Laura recalled.

Laura was not unaccustomed to seeing injuries in the boys, especially John. He frequently had bruises on his legs and traces of blood in his nose. Susie told her that John often had nosebleeds in the night.

"She always had some excuse when she'd bring them to me and they had these things," Laura said, "and they always sounded legitimate to me."

One day, while John's arm was still in the cast, Susie brought the boys to Laura's house and left them without mentioning any injuries. Laura noticed that Jim's eyes were red, but that was not unusual. Not until a few hours later, when she felt Jim's head and he winced, did she realize something was wrong. Under the hair on the side of his head was a big lump.

"It was mushy," Laura said. "If you can picture an overripe tomato, that's what it felt like. I got scared."

She called Susie at work, but Susie didn't seem concerned. Susie said that John and Jim had been jumping on the bed the night before and Jim had fallen off. Laura said she thought Jim should see a doctor and offered to take him to the hospital. But Susie instructed her to bring the boys to her office and she would take care of it.

Instead of taking Jim to a doctor, Susie drove the boys to Irene's house and asked if she would look after them for a few hours because the baby-sitter couldn't keep them. Irene didn't notice Jim's injury.

Tom saw the lump on Jim's head when he got home from work, and expressed concern. One of Jim's eyes was beginning to blacken. Susie told him that John had pulled Jim off the bed at the baby-sitter's while Jim was sleeping. Worried, Tom called his friend Jerry, who told him that he should have Jim checked. Susie went with Tom when he took Jim to Presbyterian Hospital.

"I could tell that the doctors suspected something was not right," Tom recalled later. "You could kind of feel that they were looking at you weird."

Jim had suffered a mild concussion and facial bruises, and the doctors wanted to keep him overnight for observation. Susie didn't want that and argued with the doctors. When the doctors and nurses strongly suggested that this might not have been an accident, Susie got even more upset.

"I got kind of upset, too," Tom said, "because I couldn't believe that. I can't imagine anybody hitting a kid hard enough to hurt them. I said, 'No, this is just an accident.' "

Jerry came and looked at Jim, and he didn't think it was an accident. The injuries didn't seem compatible with a fall. They were compatible, he thought, with blows from a fist. He suspected they had come from Susie's hand, but he didn't press the matter with Tom.

"It was hard for me to believe," Tom said. "I'd never seen her act that way, never saw her even spank the kids very much, never saw that kind of violence. If I'd seen that, I'd have sent her packing immediately."

Irene didn't hear until the next day that Jim had been at the hospital. Susie told her that John had knocked Jim over in his high chair. Later, when she learned from Tom that Susie told him that Jim had been hurt at the baby-sitter's, she was furious because she knew the boys had been with her that afternoon.

"I was extremely indignant," Irene said.

When she asked Susie about it, Susie said the doctors suspected child abuse and indicated that the baby-sitter might have done it. "She said, 'There's not anything I can do.' I said, 'The hell there isn't.' She *wouldn't* do anything about it."

Irene's suspicions about Susie were provoked. "I started watching her," she said. "I know damn well that she did it."

But not until later did she admit that to Tom.

Soon after Jim was hurt, Susie did something that astonished everybody.

In the nearly nine years that Tom and Susie had been married, Delores had never spent a night in her son's house. Several months earlier, Delores had flown to California to drive back to Kentucky with Janie so that Janie could begin preparing for dental school. They planned their trip through Albuquerque, and they arrived to find that Susie had booked a room for them at the Sheraton. Even Janie was offended. "We weren't even offered the floor," she said.

During that visit, Delores realized that things were not

going well between Tom and Susie, and through her regular telephone calls since that time, she knew that the situation had deteriorated.

After Jim was hurt, Delores called Tom and suggested that Susie and the boys come to Kentucky to visit until things calmed down. Chuck would pay the plane fares. Tom said she would have to talk to Susie. Surprisingly, Susie accepted.

"I think she just wanted to get out of town," Tom said later.

Delores told all of her friends that Susie was coming.

"They're having problems and she's going to come with the boys and stay a few days," Delores said to Joyce Rose.

During Susie's stay, Delores took her and the boys to visit in Joyce's homey kitchen. After all the derogatory things that Joyce had heard Delores say about Susie, she couldn't believe how friendly they acted to one another. "This was a person Delores hated more than anybody in the whole wide world," Joyce recalled. "She said Susie thought she came from royalty because her family had so much political power. 'She's got more power than I've got money,' Delores said. She felt like she was a wealthy spoiled brat, but she had to tolerate her."

Helen Stewart, Delores's maid, was equally surprised at the visit. "She said Susie stole her son but she had to put up with it until TJ could get out of the mess," Helen said.

Helen and Chuck kept the boys while Delores and Janie took Susie to the spring production at the Little Colonel Theater.

Later, Delores reported that Susie had acted very strange during the visit. She hardly let Jim out of her sight. She insisted on sleeping with him and wouldn't even let him go out to play. When Delores suggested that Susie take the Lynches' car and spend the day shopping, Susie chose to stay at the house with the children.

On the second day of her visit, Tom called.

"How are things going?" he asked.

"Well, not too good," Susie said.

She and the boys flew home the next day.

Soon after her return, Tom and Susie were called in

for consultation by the doctors who had treated Jim. They said they believed Jim's injury was more than an accident.

"I just couldn't bring myself to believe it," Tom said. "I told them, 'I don't think what you guys are thinking is right.' "

Tom and Susie heard no more about the matter, and not until much later did Tom learn that they had been reported to authorities as suspected child abusers, although he was never aware of an investigation.

Matters did not improve between Tom and Susie, and that summer, when Paw-Paw suffered a series of small strokes and was hospitalized in Winston-Salem, Susie decided to take the boys home to see him. She told Irene and Joy that they would be gone a couple of weeks. Joy volunteered to drive them to the airport, and on the morning of July 16, when she came to pick them up, she realized that something was wrong.

"It was tense," she recalled later. "Susie was sort of strung out. She was really nervous. She didn't talk much. I felt bad for the boys. John was worried. He kept asking, 'Mommy, are we coming back?' "

Joy suspected that Susie might be planning to not return, and she was right. It had not been spoken between Tom and Susie, but they both understood that she probably was leaving for good, and before he left for work that morning, Tom took snapshots of the boys.

A week after she got back to North Carolina, Susie called to confirm what Tom already knew. She and the boys would not be coming back.

21

Word spread quickly through the Sharp and Newsom families that Susie had returned to stay, her marriage at an end. As Susie told it, Tom asked her to leave and take the children. He simply didn't want to be married anymore, she said.

Tom had undergone a personality change, Susie told her friend Annette Hunt. She thought it might be related to medicine he had been taking. He'd been diagnosed as having high blood pressure soon after their move to Albuquerque and had been taking pills for it since. The medicine wasn't supposed to be taken over a long period, Susie said, and she wondered if it could be responsible for the changes she perceived in Tom.

"He just wasn't the same person I married," Susie said.

"She blamed everything on that," said Annette, who thought Susie was seizing it as an excuse.

Susie's aunt Su-Su, who, due to mandatory age restrictions, stepped down as chief justice of the North Carolina Supreme Court only two weeks after Susie returned home, suggested that she hire an attorney. She recommended a young lawyer in Reidsville, Alexander P. Sands III, called Sandy. Sands was a Sharp family friend. He'd grown up in Reidsville, where his father operated tobacco warehouses. After his graduation from Duke University, he went to law school at the University of North Carolina and worked a year for a corporate firm in Winston-Salem before returning home to join a group of Reidsville lawyers. One member of that group was Norwood Robinson, who as a young lawyer had practiced with Susie's grandfather, Jim Sharp. Sands was Susie's age, and he and his wife, Ginny, had two children, a son, Andy, who was three, and a daughter, Anna, just a year old.

Sands drew up a separation agreement that gave full custody of the children to Susie, with Tom to pay $200 a month for support of each. Tom also was to pay Susie $100 a month in permanent alimony, plus full expenses to attend graduate school for four years. Additionally, he was to pay her for half the equity in their house, plus $1,500 for home furnishings Susie had left behind and half of their accumulated interest in forty acres of desert land Tom had bought, sight unseen, for $5,000 at $49 down and $49 a month. She would relinquish any claim to his dental practice.

Susie didn't send the separation agreement to Tom immediately. Her friend Annette Hunt was convinced that she secretly hoped for reconciliation. Some family members, too, thought that Susie still loved Tom and that leaving him was just a dramatic gesture to get his attention. Her real dream, they thought, was to work things out and reunite her family, perhaps even to convince Tom to move back to North Carolina, where she could be happier. But her mother had no illusions about that possibility. She thought that Susie was too bitter toward Tom, that she wouldn't accept any of the blame for the failure of the marriage, and that reconciliation was impossible as long as Susie maintained that attitude. She had argued with Susie about it.

Susie planned a trip back to Albuquerque early in September, ostensibly to retrieve her car and other possessions, but Annette thought that she clearly was excited about seeing Tom again.

"It was like the night before the prom," Annette recalled. "She'd have gone right back out there with him if he'd just asked."

But Tom had no intention of asking, and he made that clear with a cold reception upon Susie's arrival. Scorned, hurt, and angry, Susie spent the night next door with her former neighbors, Hank and Irene.

Next morning, Tom told Susie to take what she wanted from the house, but he expected her to be gone before he returned from work. Irene said later that she couldn't remember seeing Susie so furious as she was when she went through the house piling up stuff to take with her. She cursed Tom and threw things at the walls. But before Tom got home, she had struck out for North Carolina in her blue 1974 Audi Fox, the car jammed with clothing, toys, household items, and personal treasures.

Tom followed the next day in his four-wheel-drive vehicle, pulling a U-Haul trailer loaded with furniture Susie's family had given them, much of it made by Paw-Paw. He received a cordial welcome from Bob and Florence and spent two nights at their house visiting with his sons while Susie stayed away, avoiding further confrontation.

Soon after Tom returned to Albuquerque, Susie signed the separation agreement and forwarded it to him. He suggested a few minor changes and signed a final draft a few weeks later without consulting a lawyer.

Delores was pleased about these developments, and that fall, unannounced, she set out driving cross-country with Helen Stewart to visit her son. Few things suited her on the trip, and she complained most of the way. She talked a lot about Susie, about what a cold and cruel person she was and how lucky Tom was to finally be rid of her. From a motel in Oklahoma, after complaining to the manager that her room was not clean, she called Tom to tell him that she and Helen were on the way.

"We'll be there tomorrow," she said happily.

Helen was listening, and she realized that Tom must have asked where they were planning to stay, because Delores looked startled and said, "Why we're staying with you!"

When they arrived for Delores to spend her first night ever under her son's roof, Helen saw the reason for Tom's question. Delores was startled to find another person at the house—Tom's tall, long-haired, attractive, young dental assistant, Kathy Anderson, who'd come to Albuquerque from Nebraska and had gone to work for him in the spring of 1978. Tom and Kathy had become close friends as Tom talked about his problems at home. After Susie left, they began dating, and Kathy soon was spending a lot of time at Tom's house.

Delores didn't like that. She had thought that she was

regaining her son, not simply losing him to another woman. She didn't like the state of his house or his life-style, and after making her feelings known, she set about trying to straighten out his life while Helen cleaned house. On leaving, she hugged Kathy and told Tom she thought Kathy was good for him. But that was not what Helen heard on the way back.

Susie, too, had heard that her husband's leggy dental assistant was spending a lot of time with him at what was still her house. She learned about it in a call to Irene, and she was outraged. She bitterly profaned Tom's name to relatives and claimed he'd been fooling around all along. She vowed that she never would allow her children to go back and witness such shameful behavior.

After Susie accepted that her separation was permanent, she began trying to decide what to do with her life. "I was faced with a decision most women in my situation must be faced with: how to provide for my family," she later wrote. "For me the answer would have to be either graduate school or another job in advertising or television production."

She chose graduate school, but it would come later. First, she wanted to expand her knowledge of Chinese. If she knew Chinese culture and could speak the language, she figured that she could parlay a graduate degree in business or political science into a career in diplomatic service or with one of the corporations trying to cash in on the big new market in China. At Guilford College, not far from her parents' house, she found a young student from Taiwan, Bie Ju, who agreed to tutor her in Mandarin. Susie soon became convinced that if she went to Taiwan to study she could learn the language much faster because she would be forced to use it regularly. Bie suggested the Mandarin Training Center of Taiwan Normal University in Taipei, where non-Chinese study the language as well as Chinese history and culture. Susie applied in the fall of 1979, was quickly accepted, and began making plans to spend a year in Taiwan.

"I realized that I had chosen a very competitive field and that I was going to be playing 'catch up' for the next four years, or more," she later wrote. "I had a limited budget and no time to waste. I knew that I could also do primary research while I was in Taiwan that would be the kind of firsthand information other graduate students would not have. This was no time to do things the tried and true way. It was a one-shot chance to have a better future for the three of us, and I was obsessed with taking it."

She dreaded telling her parents. John and Jimbo had settled happily with them, and Bob and Florence were enjoying their company. Her parents didn't like the idea of her going to live in a strange country with two small children. They tried to talk her into leaving the children with them. Tom was upset, too. She had mentioned to him in September that she was thinking of going to Taiwan, but he never dreamed that she would go through with it. When he called Susie to see about having the boys visit for Christmas, Susie told him that they couldn't because she and the boys were leaving for Taiwan. He tried to talk her into leaving the boys with her parents or dropping them off in New Mexico with him. This was a Third World country, he reminded her; she'd never been out of the Carolinas or New Mexico; she had no idea what it could be like. But Susie was determined that she was going and taking the boys. When Delores found out, she was flabbergasted. Why on earth would Susie want to do such a thing? And why would Tom allow it? It was the craziest thing she'd ever heard, she told friends. But Susie's parents and Tom realized that Susie had made up her mind and that no amount of reasoned argument would change it. Stopping her would be all but impossible.

"I was firmly advised that I could not do it (not true)," Susie later wrote, "that I did not have enough money (almost true), and that if I were more experienced I would know better than to try (true)."

Susie wrote to another friend from Taiwan, Gwen Kao, whom she had met in Albuquerque, to tell of her plans. Gwen was visiting her family in Taipei and wrote to say that she would still be there when Susie arrived. She also mentioned that her sister-in-law owned an apartment that Susie could rent for eighty dollars a month. Susie called Gwen in Taiwan and accepted. Things were falling into place perfectly, she thought. She even had received a favorable response from one of several institutions in

Taipei she had written to in hopes of finding a part-time job teaching English during her stay. And Bie had called her brother, Henry, and asked him to meet Susie at the airport on her arrival.

Susie was more excited and ebullient that Christmas than her family could remember seeing her in a long time, and three days later, she said happy good-byes and departed with six suitcases, $1,800, and a bagful of Star Wars toys.

"It was to be for all of us the journey of a lifetime," she later wrote.

Her plane was late leaving Los Angeles, and twenty-six hours later, after several stops, it landed in Taipei at 2 A.M. Susie and the boys were exhausted, and Susie was nervously uncertain about what lay ahead. She was irritated to learn that her luggage had been left in Los Angeles. She had only two carry-on bags, one containing a single change of clothes for the boys, the other filled with toys. She was buoyed, however, when she walked into the reception area and saw a big banner, held aloft by Bie's smiling brother and his wife, Marie, saying WELCOME SUSIE LYNCH.

The Jus took Susie and the boys to their apartment and put them to bed. Susie remained with them three days while she got established in Taipei and waited for her lost luggage. Gwen came and helped her enroll at the Mandarin Center and find a childcare center for John and Jim where the director spoke a little English and the fee for both was only eighty-five dollars a month. Then she took Susie to see the apartment she had rented. It was new, just six months old, but small and cheaply constructed, a fourth-floor walk-up on a narrow alley in Yuan Ho City (city of eternal harmony, Susie later translated in a letter home), a working-class area, a sharp contrast to the luxury Susie had known all of her life.

Susie would have to share the apartment with her landlady, who did not live there but retained the largest bedroom and came three or four nights weekly to cook for and entertain friends, occasionally sleeping over. Susie and the boys had two small bedrooms. They shared the bath, kitchen (two gas burners, a tiny refrigerator, and a sink), and living area, which included a TV, with their landlady. Susie decided to sleep in the same room the boys slept in and turn one of her rooms into a study. Not until she moved in did she realize that she had no closets and much of her precious room would be consumed by stand-up dress racks that she had to buy.

Originally, Susie had planned to spend the first month getting to know the city, but her classes were to begin only five days after her arrival, long before she had learned streets, bus schedules, shopping techniques, and other things she needed to know to attend to their daily needs. By her second week, she knew that she was in trouble.

"I had come to realize how out of control the situation was," she wrote. "I found myself being too demanding of myself and of John and Jim. I was expecting all of us to be 'super heroes' and developed a 'Lone Ranger Complex.' I felt (guilty?) I was being especially unfair to John and Jim since this trip was for my career and to their advantage in that respect but it was not something to which they felt a real commitment. I knew only too well that this trip had been my decision and mine alone. I felt total responsibility for success or failure for the first time, and it was frightening."

She systematically began to organize her life, studying maps, exploring, learning bus routes and shops, making lists of contacts she might need, finding a church to attend, and within two weeks, although her performance in class suffered, she felt that she was beginning to get control. With the strain, as well as the novelty and excitement, of being in a new place beginning to dissipate, she also began discovering many things she did not like.

The pollution that constantly clouded the city annoyed her, as did the constant noise and crowds. The buses were so packed that she felt like a sardine riding them, she wrote. And everywhere she seemed to encounter filth. She was wary of eating in restaurants because of the poor hygienic practices she observed, and the only public rest rooms she would use were at the Hilton Hotel. All others she found abominable. She carried packets of sanitized towelettes wherever she went.

In her apartment, she discovered hordes of roaches and set about killing them with noxious sprays. She blamed the roaches on her landlady's poor housekeeping, which she resented. "I found many frustrations and aggravations from sharing a bathroom and kitchen with Chinese," she wrote. "My standards were simply not theirs. I ended up doing a ridiculous amount of cleaning just to stay even. For example: the refrigerator was never cleaned by anyone else; in six months the floor was mopped twice. In the bathroom the standard method of cleaning was to rinse everything with water—no soap or disinfectant. However, the most difficult thing for me to handle was the occasional guest of my landlady who deposited his or her toilet paper in the trash can instead of the toilet. I was totally shocked the first time it happened and had to instantly create a new rule that the children were not to ever use that trash can.

"This place is wonderful for germs and not so wonderful for people," she wrote Aunt Su-Su.

Few foreigners ever had lived in the area of her apartment, and she and the boys attracted attention every time they went anywhere. Some people reached out to touch the pale, fair-haired boys, frightening them and causing Susie to become resentful. After a few weeks, though, they became less an oddity, and life settled into routine.

In February, Jim began to be troubled with bronchitis. Susie took him to a neighborhood doctor, who suggested that the problem lay in allowing Jim cold drinks with his meals. Susie dismissed this as absurd. The antibiotics that the doctor gave him didn't help, and Jim's condition was worsened, Susie felt, by her landlady, who believed that "fresh" air was necessary to good health and left doors and windows open even on the coldest days.

By the end of February, Jim had pneumonia. And Susie and John were sick as well. She took Jim to Taiwan Adventist Hospital—the best in Taipei, she'd been told—where the doctor insisted that he be admitted. She and John stayed with him, sleeping in the same bed. By the next day, disenchantment had set in.

"The toilet overflowed and I received a lecture, in Chinese, on why it was my fault," Susie later wrote. "Since I did not understand much of what was said, a nurse who knew a bit more English than the others came in to explain. It seemed that I had committed the unpardonable sin: putting toilet paper in the toilet. Where, I asked, was one to put it? 'In the trash can, of course, where everyone else puts it.' Their disgust at my ignorance was obvious and no one bothered to hide their feelings. That night the last straw arrived in the form of tribes of roaches which came out of the dresser drawers to feed off the sticky floors. I could not take any more and left the next morning."

The hospital stay cost $125, wiping out Susie's emergency reserve. And all of them were still sick. A friend at the Mandarin Center whose sister was a nurse came to Susie's aid. The nurse recommended antibiotics and the proper amounts to take. Susie bought them and she and the boys went to bed and stayed there for a week.

Their illnesses cost Susie ten days of classes, and she was hopelessly behind when she returned. She struggled to keep up but couldn't, and she decided she'd have to switch to a slower class. She was incredulous when, in applying for the transfer, an administrator ruled her absence unexcused. "You know the rules," she remembered him telling her. "You must notify us in advance if you are going to be ill."

She received the transfer anyway, and soon afterward a new opportunity opened for her. An English teacher at the Language Training and Testing Center lost his job because of political statements, and Susie was asked to fill in. She accepted to replenish her emergency fund.

Her life became even more hectic. She was up before 6 A.M. every day, getting the boys ready for day care. Once she got them off, she rushed to the bus stop for the long trip to the Language Center on the packed buses she so hated. She taught from 9 to 11, and barely had time to catch a snack on her way to her studies at the Mandarin Center. "I always wondered what it would be like to come to class prepared, but I never found out," she later wrote. After class, she had to run to make the bus home so that she would be there when the boys arrived. The bus stop was five blocks from her apartment, and she stopped to pick up groceries and other necessities as she made her way home. "As I shopped my way up the street, it was not always easy to keep smiling. I was really beginning to hate being 'the American.' "

With luck, she arrived home in time to change clothes and prepare snacks for the boys before they got there. "On the *good* days, there were letters from the States to read while I waited," she wrote. "I loved to see the little school bus arrive with the boys. It came to signal the victory over one more day."

Yet the day was far from done. She still had to cook dinner, bathe the boys, and put them to bed with a story, before she cleaned up the day's mess, got her own bath, and tried to find a little quiet time for study. The schedule had one advantage: it left little time for thinking about Tom.

Near the end of March, five days before Jim's fourth birthday, a call from home brought news of Paw-Paw's death, sending Susie into depression. By the next month, she was even more distressed. Even in the slower class, she was not able to keep up her studies. And Jim developed pneumonia again.

She later wrote about her thoughts at the time. "I had to make a major decision: how long should we stay? How dangerous was his condition? What was causing it? I was told that he suffered from a pollution allergy, but that was a vague diagnosis. The only thing I was sure of was that Jim was either on antibiotics or he was sick. He had always been cooperative and uncomplaining, but I was shredding emotionally. At this point, our landlady came to announce that she was allowing a Chinese couple to move into her room for the next three months. The thoughts of sharing our apartment and what little privacy we had were just too much. I knew that we had to move or leave. Our current situation had become intolerable."

Not only was the situation intolerable, she could see no hope of improvement. Completely frazzled, she decided she had but one recourse: to return home. That night, she put the boys to bed, read them a story, and lay down with them until they dropped off to sleep. She later remembered the night clearly.

"As we lay there, I looked at them closely, so beautiful and brave, learning a language, making new friends, succeeding in an alien environment with only one parent to provide all their security. I got up and made myself a cup of coffee and began to list all the things I *had* to do before we left. I decided to leave by the end of June and forget the language classes. I would concentrate all of my efforts on finishing my research. My second priority was to have enough time left to visit friends, take John and Jim to all of the major tourist sights."

Her visa was expiring, and she would have to get it extended to stay through June. When she ran into red tape, she called home in disgust. Her mother called Aunt Su-Su, who called her friend Jesse Helms, North Carolina's right-wing Republican senator, a strong supporter of the Taiwan government, and the problem soon was eradicated.

In May, Susie moved out of her apartment and in with Henry and Marie Ju. With the pressures of teaching and studying gone, she was able to relax some. She spent most of her time gathering information about Taiwan's history and economy for future graduate school papers, shopping for gifts to carry home, and taking the boys to museums and temples.

As the end of her stay neared, Susie began calling home with strange stories. She didn't think the government was going to allow her to leave, she said. She was being watched constantly. Two agents followed her wherever she went. The government even moved an agent into her apartment, prompting her move out.

"It was like an unfolding drama," recalled Annette Hunt, who was kept informed of daily developments by Susie's mother. "Susie said the government couldn't believe an American woman would come over there with two small children just to study. She said they thought she was a spy."

Frantic with worry, Florence called her sister Susie, who again called Jesse Helms and asked him to intercede.

"After that," Susie Sharp said later, "she came on home."

Later, Susie's friends in Taiwan were surprised to hear about this, for they knew of no such things happening, and Susie made no complaint about it while she was there. Neither did Susie mention it when she later wrote extensively about her stay in Taiwan for an advice book she wanted to publish for business women traveling in Third World countries. But the story seemed plausible to her family at the time, and only years later would anybody realize that this could have been the first clear indication that Susie was becoming emotionally unhinged.

Bie returned to Taiwan from Greensboro before Susie and the boys left, and they spent their last week with her, visiting friends and having a good time. On June 25, Susie and the boys got on a plane for home, with stops in Tokyo and Chicago. As the jetliner climbed into the sky, the pilot banked and Susie looked back on the place, with all its pollution, filth, and germs, she was so gladly leaving.

"A haze of reddish brown smog encircled the mountains and tarnished the clouds," Susie wrote. "As we flew higher the clear blue of the Pacific sky rose to meet us and I excitedly pushed the boys toward the window. 'Look! Blue sky!' 'Oh, yes,' said John, 'just like in America.' "

On the flight, Susie had time to contemplate the past six months. "We were not the same people who had left. We were a family unit; no longer three without a fourth. We had learned to rely on each other and on ourselves. But most important of all we had learned compassion for others and we had learned the most valuable lesson of all: that others do not think and believe as we do, that other people in other cultures do not have our goals, share our needs, or share our god. We met good people and bad. We found out what it means to be a minority, to be followed by the curious, to have little privacy, to live in a tiny apartment with little hope of a house with grass or trees. We had been lonely, tired and sick. We had been pushed to our limits emotionally but the three of us had held. The long road ahead to acquire those magic credentials so necessary for a job seemed shorter and conquerable."

When their plane arrived at O'Hare International in Chicago, where they were to make connections for Greensboro, Susie and the boys were met by her mother-in-law, who had driven from Louisville with Helen Stewart to see them during their brief layover. Susie, Helen later recalled, seemed almost happy to see Delores, and even

Delores said it was the only time she thought Susie was glad to see her. Delores bought lunch for Susie and the boys in an airport restaurant, then saw them off with hugs and waves on the last leg of their journey.

"We were exhausted on our arrival in North Carolina," Susie later wrote, "but this time—when it didn't matter—all of our luggage arrived."

The preceding year had been the most draining and unforgettable of Susie's life. Soon after her return, she wrote, "There is a wonderful Chinese proverb that applies to a woman on her own: 'Success is like a turtle climbing a mountain. Failure is water running downhill.' Someday, when I have time, I'm going to do it in needlepoint. For the past year, I have known what it's like to be a turtle clinging to the side of a mountain, and I'm too high up to let go."

When Susie Sharp came to see Susie and the boys, the first thing Jim said was, "Su-Su, I don't ever want to go to Taiwan again."

Su-Su was concerned about her niece, as were other members of the family. Susie looked haggard, wan, and frail. Su-Su thought she might have contracted some mysterious illness in Taiwan and urged her to get a checkup. Florence was worried, too. And she finally talked Susie into going to Reidsville for an examination by her uncle, Dr. Fred Klenner, who had delivered her and supposedly cured her of polio.

His diagnosis brought no relief. Susie, Dr. Klenner pronounced, had multiple sclerosis, a debilitating disease of the nervous system that in time can cripple and kill, a disease for which medical science claims no cure. But Dr. Klenner disagreed with conventional medical science. Susie should not worry, he said. He would take care of her.

22

The second floor above a drugstore in an old brick building in downtown Reidsville seemed an unlikely spot in which to find a doctor of such renown as Frederick R. Klenner, and some of his first-time patients who came great distances seeking his miraculous cures were dumbfounded upon encountering it.

An inconspicuous glass-top door bearing a hand-painted sign that said FRED R. KLENNER, DISEASES OF THE CHEST, LIMITED GENERAL PRACTICE led patients up a steep, dimly lighted, creaking wooden staircase to a hallway with rain-stained ceilings and plaster crumbling from dull green walls, dominated by an ancient, dusty refrigerator, its white finish yellowed by age. Doorways led to separate waiting rooms for blacks and whites—which Dr. Klenner maintained even into the eighties, defying anybody to do anything about it—to dingy, cluttered treatment rooms with antiquated furnishings, and to Dr. Klenner's homey office.

It often was said that walking into Dr. Klenner's office was like stepping back half a century in time. "If there ever was a prototype of the old-time family doctor, he was it," a friend said.

Two walls of his office were covered with more than four dozen official-looking certificates and diplomas, certifying his credentials. The furnishings were stout, antique, and masculine, and included a huge grandfather clock Dr. Klenner had bought at an auction; old medical instruments; a vintage, leather-bound Bible, always open; and two hornets' nests, which he had fetched from the woods and dangled from an overhead pipe.

An unbelievable clutter overwhelmed the shabby, rambling suite of rooms that made up the clinic. Medical supplies and medicines were scattered in disarray, some of the vials looking as ancient as the doctor himself. Bric-a-brac and crude handcrafts, gifts from worshipful patients, were everywhere. Few open spots were to be found on any wall, and those that appeared were quickly covered by notes, signs, schedules, notices, political posters, needlepoint homilies, and children's drawings.

Dr. Klenner's clinic told much about his political and philosophical beliefs. A huge red, white, and blue GEORGE WALLACE FOR PRESIDENT poster dominated one wall more than a decade after Wallace's failed campaign. A quote attributed to Thomas Jefferson proclaimed GOVERNMENT BIG ENOUGH TO SUPPLY EVERYTHING YOU NEED IS BIG ENOUGH TO TAKE EVERYTHING YOU HAVE. A sign that said THERE ARE NO GUNS IN THIS HOUSE had been altered so that the word NO was blacked out. Gun magazines were scattered through the waiting areas along with tracts from the John Birch Society, White Citizens Councils, and Billy James Hargis's Christian Crusade. Books and pamphlets decried public education as a forum for Communists, integration as a Communist plot, trade with Communist nations as treason, women's rights as sacrilegious, Franklin D. Roosevelt as a traitor, and Martin Luther King as a spokesman for the enemy.

"Very conservative," "ultra-conservative," "very much Old South, more Old South than anybody from the South" were phrases that close associates used to describe Dr. Klenner. A Civil War buff, he had been known to proclaim that the wrong side had won that war, and to speak favorably of the Ku Klux Klan. Some thought that strange, for nearly everybody in Reidsville knew that not only was Dr. Klenner devoutly Catholic, a religion targeted by some Klan groups and anathema to fundamentalist southerners, he also was a Yankee.

Fred Klenner was born in Johnstown, Pennsylvania, on October 22, 1907, the last of Frank and Mary Klenner's eight children. His parents had come to this country from Austria as youngsters, brought by their families in the great migrations from Europe late in the last century.

Drawn to Johnstown by the promise of jobs, both of their fathers found work in steel mills.

Johnstown sits at the confluence of Stony Creek and the Conemaugh River in Cambria County in the Allegheny Mountains of western Pennsylvania. The town was laid out in 1800, four years before the county was formed. In 1840 iron was discovered nearby, and a new industry sprang up to exploit the area's vast reserves of iron and coal. The town had one major problem: it was regularly flooded.

When he was eleven, Frank Klenner got a job making cigars. In his teens he went to work at Cambria Iron Works, later to become Bethlehem Steel Corp. On a rainy May 31, 1889, when Frank was eighteen, he was at work when a man on a white horse rode up at a gallop yelling for everybody to flee to the hills. A dam in the mountains northeast of the town had burst and a wall of water was racing with a fury through the long, narrow Conemaugh Gap toward Johnstown. Frank was one of the lucky ones who made it up the side of Prospect Hill, where he watched the water sweep much of Johnstown away. Mary, then a domestic for a wealthy family whose home was on high ground, later claimed that she had seen the whole thing in a dream three days before it happened. Their children grew up hearing many tales of the Great Johnstown Flood, which killed more than 2,300 people, 300 of them suffering the horrible irony of dying in fires started by the water.

When Fred was born, Frank and Mary were living on a farm near Johnstown, although Frank continued to go to work in the mill every day. One of their daughters, Gertrude, had breathing problems, and the doctor suggested that she might fare better in the country, away from the grime and smoky gray skies produced by Johnstown's blast furnaces. Gertrude died on the farm of pneumonia at sixteen.

Mary was devoutly religious, and she brought her children to mass every week at St. Joseph's Catholic Church, a grimy, fudge-brown cathedral with a slate roof, on Railroad Street close by the steel mill where her husband labored. Next door, in a squat, three-story yellow brick building, was the parochial school where Fred began his education. He was a smart child, some said the smartest of all the Klenner children, sensitive and earnest.

When Fred was eight, his family moved back into town, and he was able to spend more time at church, where he found much attention and great joy. He was an altar boy, and after school, eager to please, he stayed to wash windows and do other chores for the nuns at the adjoining convent.

In 1918, when Fred was eleven, a flu epidemic swept the country, felling hundreds in Johnstown. The hospitals were filled, and new patients were turned away. Whole families died. Fred and his sister Agnes, two years older, fell ill with high temperatures. The family feared that both would be lost, but Mary, a believer in herbal remedies, treated her children with large amounts of tea made from the leaves of the boneset plant, and both recovered. Years later, when he had become one of the early proponents of the healing qualities of vitamin C, Fred told his family that he'd had boneset tea analyzed to find out what was in it. He was not surprised, he said, to learn that it contained great quantities of vitamin C. Boneset tea was not the only herbal remedy that Mary used. She also made an all-purpose salve from a variety of plants and sent her children into the fields and woods to gather them.

Frank Klenner worked long hours, came home bone tired, and collapsed snoring on the sofa after supper. When he managed free time, one of his favorite activities and greatest joys was playing in an Austrian band. He had mastered several instruments, including the cornet, violin, harpsichord, and zither, and he urged music on all of his children. Fred learned the piano and played duets with his sister Agnes at school and family gatherings.

A proud man, Frank was a strict disciplinarian. "Typical German," his daughter Marie recalled. Yet it was Mary who really ruled the house with her gentleness and mystical religious fervor, and Fred became far closer to his mother. He was her favorite child, always singled out for special attention, her hope for the future.

When the Klenners first moved back into town after Gertrude's death, they lived in a two-story, shingle-covered frame house on Boyd Avenue in the eighth ward on the bluffs overlooking the river. Later, Frank built a brick house on a hillside at the end of Confer Avenue, two blocks away. Fred got a paper route in the neighborhood, delivering the *Tribune* on foot every afternoon after school.

Johnstown was a lively town while Fred was growing up, a mélange of ethnic groups molded into a strict social order, with the descendants of English settlers at the top, followed by Germans, Welsh, and Irish, the first immigrants to arrive. Eastern and southern Europeans, who came later, fit in below. At the bottom were the few hundred blacks who had been brought in from the South to work in the mills in a time of labor strife. They lived in a shantytown in the flats near the river, isolated from the rest of Johnstown. Fred had no contact with them, and his strongly outspoken feelings about blacks didn't surface until he moved south. There was another thing with which he had no contact in his youth, but about which he also later came to have strong feelings: guns. His mother wouldn't allow them in her house.

Fred grew tall and slim. In high school, he played on a football team that never lost a game, but unlike his teammates, he showed no interest in the girls who showered the victorious athletes with flirtatious attentions. His main interests were his studies and the church. And when he became one of the first graduates of Catholic High School in 1924 and announced that he wanted to become a priest, his mother showered Heaven with praises of gratitude.

None of the other Klenner children had gone to college. All either married or went to work young. But with the older children gone from home and no young ones waiting to be fed, clothed, and educated, Frank knew that he could find the money to allow his youngest child to escape the hard labors of the steel mills and become a servant of the Church. To have a priest in the family would be high honor.

Fred enrolled at St. Vincent's, a Catholic college at Latrobe, and later he told of living in an attic cubbyhole with inadequate ventilation and rising at 4 every morning to work in the fields. He also came in contact with a tubercular priest, and by the end of his first school year, he, too, had the disease. He returned home, where he remained for more than a year, nursed by his mother with her prayers and home remedies. During that time, he determined that the priesthood was not for him. Instead, he told his mother, his bout with illness had caused him to realize that he wanted to become a doctor. Eventually, he returned to college, this time at St. Francis in Loretto, where he majored in chemistry, and went on to get a master's degree. Later, he taught chemistry at Catholic University in Washington while working on a Ph.D., and on a research trip through the South, he stopped at Duke University in Durham, North Carolina, an institution endowed with the tobacco money of James Buchanan Duke, and decided that Duke was where he wanted to go to medical school. "He said it was one of the best," his sister Marie recalled.

At Duke, Fred met Annie Hill Sharp, setting the course for the remainder of his life. During his final year of medical school, another big flood hit Johnstown, and his sister Agnes's husband, Daniel, was one of those who drowned in it. Fred came home to be with his family, and he was filled with talk of the long-haired, dark-eyed nurse he had met. His mother was concerned. This girl wasn't Catholic.

Mary Klenner's concern paled compared to that of Annie Hill's mother, especially after Annie Britt Sharp accidentally discovered that her daughter had converted to Catholicism. There could be only one reason for that: Annie Hill intended to marry this brooding young Catholic from the North. Annie Britt made her opposition known in her strongest terms, but no amount of argument could sway her headstrong daughter. The opposition led Fred and Annie Hill to deceit. They married in Greensboro on November 24, 1937, while Fred was working on his residency at the tuberculosis sanitarium in Winston-Salem, but they kept it from her family. Not until the following fall did they tell their secret, and then they said that they had been married just three days before, prompting the Sharps to hold a wedding dinner and to unknowingly put a false notice of their marriage in the Greensboro newspaper.

Fred Klenner was the complete outsider when, in 1939,

he finally settled in Reidsville to begin his practice: a Catholic in a town which did not yet have a Catholic church, a northerner in the South, an unwanted son-in-law of one of the town's most prominent families. Perhaps that was the seed that caused a bunker mentality to begin to grow in him, family members later speculated.

But in the beginning, few signs of what were later considered bizarre thoughts and deeds were publicly evident, and the medical practice of Dr. Klenner, the husband of a Sharp, grew more quickly than expected. He encouraged this growth by giving free care to policemen, firemen, ministers, and pharmacists, who helped spread the word that he was a decent fellow.

"Fred was a darn good person," his sister Marie said. "Nice, sociable. He was too easygoing. He'd give too much all the time. He never was greedy. If people needed something, he'd give."

He proved her right by never sending bills to his patients, a practice he continued throughout his career. If a patient couldn't pay when treated, then he could pay when he could. And even if he couldn't pay and still needed a doctor, Dr. Klenner would be there, making house calls no matter the hour.

More and more people who went to him began to think of him as a trusted friend, not as a strange outsider. The only things that blemished Dr. Klenner's early years in Reidsville were his occasional outspoken support for the views of the Nazis of his family's homeland and his contention that Adolf Hitler was misunderstood, which continued even after the United States went to war with Germany. This brought great embarrassment to the patriotic Sharps when they heard gossip about it. James Sharp, after all, had been a champion war bond salesman in World War I, honored by the secretary of the treasury, and he would again do his part raising money for the war effort during World War II. After several people who heard Dr. Klenner's pro-Nazi statements challenged him, questioning his loyalty, the doctor became more circumspect.

During the war, Fred and Annie Hill began a family. Four days after the first anniversary of the attack on Pearl Harbor, their first child, Mary Ann, was born at

Duke University Hospital, where Annie Hill had gone so that one of her respected former professors could deliver her baby. Soon after Mary Ann was born, the Klenners moved into a two-story brick house on Huntsdale Drive on the southern side of Reidsville about a mile from the big Sharp home on Lindsey Street. In September 1944, a second daughter was born at Duke. She was named Gertrude for Fred's sister who had died a teenager.

Near the end of the war, Annie Hill went to her dentist with bleeding gums. He recommended pulling all of her teeth. When she told her husband about it, he thought the solution too drastic. He remembered reading about research using ascorbic acid—vitamin C—to cure chimpanzees with a similar problem. Why not try it? Annie Hill agreed, and after several shots, her gums stopped bleeding.

A short time later, Dr. Klenner tried vitamin C again, this time on an obstinate man who was "near death," as Dr. Klenner later described it, from viral pneumonia.

"I went to his house and gave him one big shot with five grams or five thousand milligrams of vitamin C," he told Greensboro reporter Flontina Miller years later. "When I went back later in the day, his temperature was down three degrees and he was sitting on the edge of the bed eating. I gave him another shot of C, five thousand milligrams, and kept up that dosage for three days, four times a day. And he was well. I said, 'Well, my gosh! This is doing something.' "

Soon afterward, when Mary Ann and Gertrude came down with measles at the same time, their father tried an experiment, first giving the girls large amounts of vitamin C, then withholding it. When he gave it to them, he later reported, the symptoms disappeared. When he withheld it, they returned. After he'd satisfied himself that the vitamin really was affecting the disease, he went ahead and gave them large dosages for five straight days and the measles went away to stay.

In May of 1946, Dr. Klenner delivered quadruplets to the thirty-six-year-old deaf-mute wife of a fifty-nine-year-old black sharecropper. The babies were tiny, three of them weighing only about two pounds each, the fourth a little more than three pounds, and in the beginning they had to be fed with medicine droppers. Dr. Klenner began giving them vitamin C immediately.

"A premature baby specialist from Duke said they had a fifty-fifty chance to survive," he later recalled. "I kept the humidity normal and kept giving them a lot of vitamin C, starting with five hundred milligrams a day and as they got older gradually increasing the amount."

The babies, all with the same first name, Mary, the only known identical quadruplets in the world, not only survived but thrived and proved a boon to their parents, Annie Mae and James Fultz. In exchange for using the girls' pictures in ads, the Pet Milk Company bought the family a 150-acre farm from Dr. Klenner's father-in-law, James Sharp, and built on it a modest house and a barn, complete with a mule. The quadruplets also brought Dr. Klenner his first national attention when, a year after their birth, his picture appeared in, of all places, *Ebony* magazine. Decades later, pictures of the quadruplets still hung in Dr. Klenner's office and home.

These cases led Dr. Klenner to other experiments with vitamin C, and in 1948 he published his first article in a medical journal about his success in treating pneumonia with it. Dozens more such articles would appear in coming years.

In 1949, a polio epidemic hit North Carolina, and Dr. Klenner soon was diagnosing the disease in dozens of young patients, all of whom he began treating with massive amounts of vitamin C. Among them were his young niece Susie Newsom and her cousin Nancy Miller. All of his patients, he claimed, recovered completely, and later he told of pleading with doctors at the polio hospital in Greensboro to give vitamin C to all of the patients there. He even offered to pay for it. But the doctors wouldn't listen to him, he said, and many lives were lost and many children were left crippled as a consequence.

In her best-selling book, *Let's Eat Right to Keep Fit*, published in 1954, nutritionist Adelle Davis wrote about one of Dr. Klenner's polio patients, an unidentified eighteen-month-old girl. As Davis described the child, she was paralyzed and unconscious, her body stiff, cold, and blue. The frantic mother thought her daughter dead. But a single, massive shot of vitamin C brought the child back to life. After a second shot four hours later, Davis wrote, the child was laughing and taking a bottle, and her paralysis had disappeared.

That wasn't the only miracle that Davis attributed to Dr. Klenner. She told of burns he'd healed quickly with vitamin C, without pain or skin grafts, leaving no scars. She allowed him to boast of putting arthritic cripples back to work, curing even the most hopeless cases within six months.

Not surprisingly, Adelle Davis's book had a big effect on Dr. Klenner's practice. Desperate people from all over the country, given little hope by their own doctors, began making their way to his clinic. His waiting room was filled every day, some of the patients carried up the steep steps in wheelchairs or on stretchers. Patients often waited hours to see the doctor. While they waited, veteran patients often entertained new ones with tales of wonder about the miraculous results Dr. Klenner had wrought with his vitamins.

"It was not with out justification that the new patient found the very air of the doctor's waiting room permeated with hope," one longtime patient, Bill Davis, wrote in tribute. "A very young Fred Klenner must have missed the day in school when the word 'hopeless' came before the class. It was not in his vocabulary."

"He got all the chronics," recalled Phil Link, a Reidsville pharmacist who admired Dr. Klenner. "He got all the ones the others had given up on."

And to each, regardless of condition, he offered hope.

"He really believed he could help anybody," said another pharmacist, also a friend of Dr. Klenner.

Dr. Klenner's very presence seemed to inspire hope and confidence. "He had an aura about him," a close family friend recalled.

Everything about him spoke authority, from his firm handshake to his commanding voice and powerful blue eyes that were at once calming and reassuring.

"You felt better when Dr. Klenner walked into the room," one longtime patient observed. "And when he touched you, you knew everything was going to be all right."

"When he told you something, you believed him, and

when he told you he could help you, you knew that he would," said another patient.

"He was the kindest, most caring and most giving man I've ever known," said yet another.

Many patients observed that once they were in the presence of Dr. Klenner he had a way of making them feel as if they were his only concern. His wife, too, shared some of these qualities. In the years when their children were growing up, she worked with her husband only occasionally, but in later years, she became his full-time nurse.

"When you were around them, you became very, very secure about whatever illness you had," a patient and family friend said. "You also became dependent on them. It became almost like a love affair."

Dr. Klenner's patients became dependent for one simple reason: they were convinced that he was making them well. "He helped just about everybody he treated," said his friend Phil Link. "If he hadn't helped them, they wouldn't've come back."

Most of them came back. And kept coming. They not only trusted Dr. Klenner, they adored him with utter devotion.

"To belittle Dr. Klenner to his patients is like slandering motherhood or the American flag to the Daughters of the American Revolution," Bill Davis wrote in his tribute. "His patients vie avidly to outdo each other in praising him."

"Dr. Klenner didn't have patients," observed a family acquaintance. "He had acolytes."

"His patients thought he was right next to Christ," said Phil Link. "They worshiped him. They thought there was nobody like Dr. Klenner."

If, to some, Dr. Klenner's patients seemed almost religiously dedicated, and if his shabby clinic seemed to become almost a shrine where the faithful brought their pain-racked bodies for the miracle of the master's healing touch, it was not surprising, for a religious fervor indeed existed between Dr. Klenner and his patients.

He quoted the Bible to them. He prayed for them and assured them that he would continue to do so. He gave them prayer cards that promised protection from evil forces. He even anointed some with what he said were sacred waters from Our Lady of Lourdes, the Catholic shrine in France where millions of the lame and desperately ill seek miraculous cures. In a way, his clinic was a miniature American version of Lourdes, with vitamins replacing the sacred waters.

As Dr. Klenner's experiments expanded, his fame grew. He was frequently written about in magazines and books, hailed by some as a genius, a medical pioneer. Irving Stone wrote about Dr. Klenner's work in his book *The Healing Factor: Vitamin C Against Disease*, as did the Nobel Prize–winning chemist Linus Pauling in his 1970 best-seller, *Vitamin C and the Common Cold*. Dr. Klenner told family members that Linus Pauling had used his work extensively but only mentioned him briefly. He didn't seem upset about it, though. "If he wants the big name for it, let him have it," Dr. Klenner's sister Agnes remembered him saying. "He doesn't know much about it anyway."

Dr. Klenner still depended on conventional treatments, but his practice grew more unconventional with the years. Some patients left with nothing more than a prayer and an old-time home remedy, something for which his mother's faith had instilled lasting belief in Dr. Klenner. But more and more, he came to depend on vitamin C as a cure-all.

"Ascorbic acid is the safest and most valuable substance available to the physician," he wrote in one of his medical journal articles. "Many headaches and many heartaches will be avoided with its proper use."

He used it against all the viral and bacterial diseases, for bursitis, arthritis, poisoning, spider bites, and a host of other ailments. He began touting its use in treating cancer, saying that fifty grams a day administered intravenously would control the disease. "Who can say what one hundred grams or three hundred grams given intravenously daily for several months might accomplish in cancer!" he told a magazine interviewer. "The potential is so great and the employment so elementary that only the illiterate will continue to deny its use."

"If you went to Dr. Klenner with an ingrown toenail,

he'd give you a shot of vitamin C," the local sheriff, Bobby Vernon, later noted.

In 1978, Dr. Klenner was rewarded for his work and long-held faith in vitamin C. On March 18, on the fiftieth anniversary of the discovery of vitamin C by Hungarian researcher Albert Szent-Györgyi, who received the Nobel prize for physiology, Dr. Klenner was presented a gold plaque at a special symposium of the World Congress of Health. The plaque bore the likenesses of four men: Albert Szent-Györgyi, Linus Pauling, Irving Stone, and Fred Klenner. Dr. Klenner considered it his proudest honor. "On a gold medal with two Nobel Prize winners! And Irving Stone!" he told Bill Davis with glee. "You can't get much higher than that."

That wasn't enough to satisfy some of his patients, though. "In my estimation, his work—works, I should say—were worthy of the Nobel Prize in several fields," said Virginia Wiley, a patient for more than thirty years.

But to his colleagues in Reidsville, the recognition and awards meant little. Just as Dr. Klenner had been an outsider in Reidsville and his wife's family, he also had become an outsider in his profession. Other doctors distanced themselves from him and his unorthodox treatments, especially after he began using large dosages of other vitamins to treat other ailments. They were skeptical of his claims, noting that they were based on clinical observations, not controlled experiments, that Dr. Klenner kept no records of his treatments and results. They thought that he held out false hope to those who had none and that his treatments were not only largely ineffectual but perhaps dangerous. They noted that few studies had been done to show the effects of massive amounts of vitamins on the body, particularly over long periods. They pointed out that some vitamins, such as A and D, which Dr. Klenner was using, were known to accumulate in the body in toxic quantities.

"Ridiculous," Dr. Klenner responded to charges that vitamin treatment could be dangerous. "Vitamins are innocuous substances. After it all breaks down, what you don't need, the body kicks out."

"He knew other doctors laughed at him," said a family

friend, "but he also knew what he was doing would save lives."

"Let's face it," said his friend Phil Link, "people called Dr. Klenner a quack. Used to make me damned mad. He was as dedicated and sincere as he could be. All he gave a damn about was his patients and his family."

What some doctors suspected was that Dr. Klenner frequently diagnosed diseases that people didn't have. That made curing them with vitamins easy. It became more evident that this was indeed the case after Dr. Klenner became a firm believer that massive amounts of B vitamins would cure multiple sclerosis, something that other doctors and the National Multiple Sclerosis Society denied. But as word spread about his treatment, more and more multiple sclerosis patients, many of them already crippled and given no hope anywhere else, began coming to Dr. Klenner, some of them moving temporarily to Reidsville from other states so that they could undergo long-term treatment. Dr. Klenner also began diagnosing more cases of multiple sclerosis. Many of these never had the disease, other doctors later discovered.

"I don't think he deliberately misdiagnosed," said one such patient, who held no bitterness about the fear Dr. Klenner's diagnosis had stirred in him or the unnecessary treatments he had undergone. "He just believed so much that this worked that he wanted it to happen. I'm very aware his ego was part of it. He wanted to be Louis Pasteur or something."

By the summer of 1980, when Dr. Klenner diagnosed his niece, Susie Newsom Lynch, as having multiple sclerosis, he no longer was a healthy man himself. The sixty-five vitamin tablets that he took every day—and had been taking for thirty-five years to stave off ill health—had not kept his blood pressure from rising or his heart from betraying him. A pacemaker stimulated his heart to action, and no longer could he climb the steep, creaking steps to his office without stopping to catch his breath. But he still did it every day, at seventy-three, a tall, shambling, stoop-shouldered man with solid white hair and a kindly face. And his waiting room remained filled with desperate and devoted patients seeking the hope that only he could give.

23

Soon after Susie's return from Taiwan, she began making weekly trips to Dr. Klenner's clinic in Reidsville. For an hour she lay on an ancient treatment table while massive doses of B complex vitamins dripped into her veins, her uncle's surefire cure for the multiple sclerosis he had diagnosed.

First came nicotinic acid, B_3, which dilated her blood vessels and caused her to flush crimson. This, her uncle explained, would allow her body to absorb more B_1, thiamin, which followed. Not only would the B_1 rebuild her diseased nerves, he said, it also would provide her with a natural source of energy.

Energy was one thing for which Susie had little need that summer of 1980. To family and friends she seemed almost frenetic, her usual hyperactivity running at more than full speed. She was worried about building a future for herself and her boys, and she set about laying the foundation for it. She enrolled once again in graduate school at Wake Forest University, this time to study anthropology, a subject in which she and her brother had shared an avid interest since childhood. Despite her bad experience in Taiwan, she still had not given up the dream of somehow working in China, perhaps as a liaison for some big corporation, maybe even for the State Department. She had become interested in customs and protocol, and she was convinced that anthropology would lead her where she wanted to go. Her mother thought that frivolous. She should study something more practical, Florence said, something that would hold out better hope for a decent job. She was, after all, a mother of two children with no husband. Susie scoffed at her mother's suggestions, reminding Florence that she was an adult fully capable of making her own decisions.

"Susie didn't tend to set limits on herself," said her friend Annette Hunt, who had been the only person to support Susie in her earlier decision to go to Taiwan. "Aim for the stars and see what happens, that was Susie. What seems ridiculous to most of us did not seem ridiculous to Susie. She did not put a lid on her jar."

Bob judiciously avoided involving himself in the differences between his wife and daughter.

"Bob just absolutely thought Susie could do no wrong," explained Annette.

"Bob just doted on her," said a neighbor. "He just thought the sun rose and set in Susie."

He was glad to have Susie home again, but Susie was not so pleased. She'd rather have a place of her own, she told friends, but that was simply financially impossible until she got her settlement from Tom.

Tom was in no condition to make a settlement at that time. His financial situation, if anything, had grown worse since he had been sending $500 monthly to Susie. He was relieved when he heard that she was returning early from Taiwan. In her first months there, she had written him a couple of times with news of the boys, and once she even arranged for him to telephone them. But it had been months since he'd talked with them and nearly a year since he'd seen them, and as soon as she returned to Greensboro he called and said he wanted the boys to come for a visit.

"There was a tremendous blowup," he recalled. "She said, 'Oh, no! There's no way. You can come and see them anytime you want, but they're not going to come out to New Mexico.' I got all upset. I didn't know what I could do. I mean, these were my kids. I ought to be able to see them. I thought I'd just call her up and we could arrange a visit and they could spend a month or so out here and we'd have a good time. There was never a question in my mind that there would be a problem."

In late August, Tom received a letter from Susie's lawyer, Sandy Sands, saying that Tom was not living up to the separation agreement. Sands noted that Tom had not sent Susie the title to her Audi Fox, that he hadn't paid the $1,500 for furniture she left behind, and that she needed an additional $300 a month for school and child-care expenses.

"Another problem, which will have to be determined shortly, is the disposition of the house," Sands wrote.

By then, Tom had consulted a lawyer, Mike Rueckhaus. A native of Albuquerque, Rueckhaus was thirty-eight, the father of three sons. Other local lawyers called him the Barracuda. "I don't know if it's deserved or not," he said with a grin, "but I sure want 'em to think I'm going to cut 'em up and spit 'em out."

His legal aggressiveness eventually led him to grow impatient with Tom.

"He's a rough son-of-a-gun to represent because he's too nice," he complained. "He's the kind of guy who's going to be able to get up and look himself in the eye in the mirror every morning. Mr. Nice Guy. Mr. Passive. He kept believing what she was telling him. He always wanted to give her the benefit of the doubt, and he was too willing to give in. When you've got somebody like Susie on the other side, that's just like throwing gasoline on a fire. Every time he gives in, it just gets worse."

Rueckhaus thought the best course was to get the jump on Susie by filing for divorce before she did, and on September 25, 1980, he filed in Bernalillo County. But he chose not to have notice served on Susie for two reasons: Tom didn't have the money to make a settlement and still hoped that Susie would let the boys come visit him at Christmas and didn't want to alienate her.

John and Jim had settled happily with their grandparents, John particularly so. He craved male attention and became close to his grandfather. Florence didn't like being called Grandma, so she told the boys to call her GG, for gorgeous grandmother. That went back to her high school days in Reidsville when she was in a play called *The Flapper Grandmother*, in which the main character insisted on being called GG.

Although Florence was glad to have Susie and the boys living in her house, the old, familiar clash of wills between mother and daughter soon surfaced. Florence was distressed about her daughter's slovenly housekeeping habits. Susie wouldn't pick up after herself, Florence complained. Susie allowed the boys to leave messes. And she seemed to expect meals to be cooked and laundry done with no contribution of her own. Things had to change, Florence said. There could be no misunderstanding about whose house this was and who was in charge. Susie's resentment about living with her parents grew deeper with her mother's ultimatums.

John started school late that summer, and Susie found a child-care center at a nearby church for Jim. Susie had some night classes, including one so late that she spent one night a week at Nanna's to keep from driving the twenty-five miles back to Greensboro. It had been only six months since Paw-Paw died, and Susie worried about Nanna being alone. On the night she stayed at Nanna's, Bob and Florence looked after the boys. They also were happy to keep them when Susie went out with Guy Martin.

Guy had been a friend of Susie and Tom in college and became close with Susie's family. After Susie's marriage, he maintained his friendship with Bob and Florence, Nanna and Paw-Paw, frequently stopping by to say hello. The previous Christmas, he had dropped in to wish the Newsoms happy holidays and been surprised to find Susie there, separated from Tom. They renewed acquaintance, and while Susie was in Taiwan, they corresponded. When Paw-Paw died that spring, Guy spent a lot of time with the family, running errands, doing whatever he could. To the family, it was almost as if he were filling in for Susie in her absence. As soon as Susie returned, Guy came calling, and they had been seeing each other since.

By that fall, Susie was aglow with romance. She gushed about Guy in letters to friends in Taiwan and Washington. Annette thought this was all sort of soon for Susie, especially when she began talking about marriage after a few months. What about her career? What about China? Could she be happy in the small country town where Guy was safely ensconced in business?

Apparently so, for Susie forged ahead. Her parents had his parents to dinner. Susie began talking about a garden wedding, perhaps at Nanna's. She sought Annette's advice on what to wear.

"All of a sudden," Annette recalled later, "bam! It was off."

Susie wrote to friends that the romance had fizzled, but she didn't offer reasons. Neither did she tell Annette why.

Later, Guy was reluctant to talk about it as well, saying only that Susie had become more and more absorbed in graduate school and her growing difficulties with Tom.

"She was pretty fiercely determined not to let Tom have time with those kids," he recalled. "And she had this almost unconscionable hatred for her mother-in-law. She just hated her and would express it frequently. She seemed to be getting wound tighter and tighter and tighter."

Susie sought relief for her tension at the Psychological Services Center at Wake Forest, where she began seeing Dr. Ron Davis, a tall, bearded, soft-spoken, contemplative staff counselor, a former Baptist minister, four years older than she.

"She was very alive, very energetic, bubbling over," Davis recalled. "Appeared to be very happy. Everybody in the office looked forward to Susie coming in because she was just a ray of sunshine when she came through the door. She could make a stone talk to her."

After a few sessions, Davis realized that Susie was "a little too light, a little too cheerful, a little too talkative, a little too animated," that it all was a cover for a great deal of distress and anxiety.

At first, Susie talked about the problems of being a single parent, going to school, and dealing with her children. She worried about how the boys were adjusting without a father. She was concerned that John was hitting kids at school.

Dr. Davis got her to bring the boys in and found them to be "very normal, delightful, bright, well-adjusted, just charming boys."

"They were different," he recalled later. "John was very aggressive. He was very articulate, bright. Jim was a lover. He was a people person, soft and warm and gentle. Climb up in your lap, liked to be held. John preferred distance from people."

Susie was overly invested in the boys, too protective of them, Davis thought, and he tried to get her to loosen her hold a little.

As their talks continued, he realized that Susie held a lot of bitterness for her estranged husband and mother-in-law. Tom, she told him, was a neglectful father who didn't want to see his children, but his manipulative mother was pressing him to get visitation rights. She didn't want the boys spending time with their father, not in New Mexico anyway, where, she said, "the environment" wasn't good for them.

"She certainly wanted to limit the amount of time he saw the boys," Davis recalled. "She wanted to place restrictions on his seeing the boys. She wasn't willing to bend. Well, she just wasn't tolerant of Tom's rights."

Later, Davis would be drawn into Tom and Susie's court fight over visitation, but in the beginning he was worried about Susie's condition.

"Susie was under a lot of stress. My concern was trying to get control of that so that it didn't spill over in ways that were damaging to her. She just wouldn't deal with it. She just refused to acknowledge the level of stress at which she operated. My concern was that she would just collapse with that stress level."

He wasn't the only one worried about Susie. Her cousin Nancy and Nancy's husband, Steve, came to visit in the spring of 1981 and noticed how distraught she appeared to be. They thought she needed a break and suggested that she come to Raleigh and do the town with them. Bob and Florence thought that a good idea and agreed to keep the kids. Susie went one weekend soon afterward.

Nancy and Steve took Susie to three different nightspots. At the first two, Susie ordered a glass of white wine but finished neither. At the third, she passed when drinks were ordered, and it was so evident to Nancy and Steve that she was having a miserable time that they suggested going home. On the way, Susie threw up on the backseat of Nancy's new station wagon. The rest of the night she lay on the bathroom floor, hugging the commode, refusing all offers of help.

Dead drunk on less than two glasses of white wine? Nancy and Steve found that dubious.

Susie spent the next day on the sofa in a snuggle sack, drinking hot tea, nibbling toast, and popping pills. From her pocketbook she fetched a freezer bag bulging with pills and capsules of many hues and sizes, a wad as big as a baseball. Vitamins, she said. She took them by the handful.

"I'm talking hourly, she'd pop those things," said Nancy, who was flabbergasted by it.

Nancy knew that Florence believed in Dr. Klenner's theories about vitamins as preventive medicine, that she always kept big jars of vitamins on the dining room table so family members could take them freely, but had had no idea that Susie was taking vitamins in such quantities. Considering Susie's condition, Nancy wondered if she might have something other than vitamins in the bag.

"She was an absolute wreck," Nancy said. "I can hardly describe her."

That Sunday, Susie talked for hours about two subjects: her parents, and Tom and his mother.

She hated living with her parents, she said, but she had no choice.

"She said her mother and daddy were crazy and they were warping her children's minds," Nancy recalled. "I kept trying to get her to tell me what they were doing. She said it was psychological the way they were doing it. She didn't like what Bob and Florence were teaching her children, but she'd never be specific. She said the boys were scared of Florence."

She also went on about how Tom had no interest in his children but was being pushed to see them by his mother, "the witch."

"All weekend she talked about what an SOB Tom was," Nancy said, "how he wouldn't settle up and give her the money he owed her."

Nancy was glad to see her cousin leave that weekend, but she felt sorry for Bob and Florence, whom she knew to have big hearts and gentle souls. Later, when the situation between Susie and her mother grew worse, Nancy sent Florence a bouquet in sympathy for what she was going through.

Despite what Susie said, Tom was indeed ready to settle up, but the lines of communication between him and Susie had grown brittle, their conversations, when they had them, were terse, tense, and crackling with hostility. Tom had asked Susie to let the boys come and see him at Christmas, and she again refused.

"I thought I had been cooperative monetarily as well as every other way, and I couldn't understand why I couldn't see these kids," he said. "It didn't seem to matter whether I was nice or not. She didn't want me to see the kids or have anything to do with them."

He turned the negotiations over to Rueckhaus. Tom's desires were simple: he wanted to be able to see his sons, and he wanted out of his marriage.

By the end of April, Rueckhaus thought that he had worked out an agreement with Sands. His understanding was that Susie would accept $15,500 in total settlement, with the support payments to continue as earlier agreed. The sum would include $14,000 for Susie's equity in the house, and $1,500 for the furniture she left behind. Tom said he would borrow the money from his mother. The money came in May, and Tom drew a cashier's check and gave it to Rueckhaus. He was confident that his troubles soon would be behind him, and he was looking forward to spending time with John and Jim that summer.

On June 1, four days after he got the check, Rueckhaus told Sands that he was ready to send Susie's money, and he requested that Sands confirm in writing that this would be full settlement. When he received no confirmation after three weeks, Rueckhaus called Sands again. Sands brought up a $2,400 student loan Susie had got, and said Tom was supposed to pay for it. Rueckhaus said that was not part of the agreement, and he brought up the question of visitation. Sands said he would talk with Susie and call back shortly.

Three days later, on June 26, Rueckhaus returned the check to Tom with a note telling him of developments and advising him to put the money into an interest-bearing account. A copy of the note also went to Sands.

"I made a deal with Sands, and he just denied it and reneged," Rueckhaus said. "I got really pissed off. The way I play the game, if you cut a deal, you cut a deal. You take notes and you try to make sure you understand what it is."

It began to become clear to Tom that his chances of seeing the boys that summer were growing slim.

"She had the kids basically as ransom," he said. "That was always the deal."

Rueckhaus agreed. "They were just intractable," he said of Susie and Sands. "You settle the financial stuff, then we will start talking about the kids. That was their position. They were using the kids as a wedge."

On July 8, Susie wrote to Sands: "Feel free to play hardball wherever you think it appropriate."

Two days later, Sands responded to Rueckhaus by letter, including a copy of the separation agreement, pointing out that it required Tom to pay Susie's expenses for graduate school. Clearly, Tom was obligated to repay the student loan, he wrote, as well as unpaid medical and dental bills for the children.

As for visitation, Sands went on, Susie would accept whatever Tom could work out with Dr. Davis at Wake Forest. She would not let the children travel alone. She would be willing to fly with them for a visit in Kentucky or New Mexico if all expenses were paid. Of course, Tom always could visit them in North Carolina with proper notice.

"I am concerned that the children are not seeing enough of their father," Sands wrote, "and I hope that this problem can be worked out."

Tom didn't want to pay to fly Susie to Kentucky or New Mexico or anywhere else. He simply couldn't afford it, he said. Neither could he afford to take off time from work and pay motel and food bills to visit at length with the boys in North Carolina. He wanted them to visit in a family setting at home.

"Just at the point where I'd think we'd worked out an agreement, there was always some little thing thrown in, some roadblock that would cost another thousand dollars that I couldn't afford," he said.

One such roadblock, Tom felt, was Susie's insistence

that the boys were too young to fly alone. In this stand she had found an ally in Dr. Davis. Davis thought one parent should put the boys on the plane, another be waiting for them at their destination. If the boys had to change planes—and there were no direct flights from Greensboro to Albuquerque—that meant either that Susie accompany them to Atlanta, where she could put them on a direct flight to Albuquerque, or that she put them on a flight to Dallas and Tom fly there to meet them and take them on to Albuquerque. Either case required considerable extra expense.

As Tom began to realize that another summer was likely to pass without seeing his sons, his determination not to give in to Susie's demands hardened.

The continuing conflict was showing on Susie, too, that summer. At one point, she took the boys to Raleigh to a family outing at the home of her cousin David Miller. John and Jim were playing kickball with the other children, and John, who didn't like to lose, began scrapping with his playmates. Other family members thought the children were just being kids, that John had committed no great offense, that the spat would pass quickly without adult interference. But Susie screamed at John and chased him around, hitting him in the head.

Her cousins were shocked. They had noticed that Susie treated John differently, and they thought it was because Jim was sweet and looked like Susie, while John was aggressive and looked like Tom. But they hadn't realized that the difference in treatment extended to abuse.

"He's just got to learn," Susie kept saying after the incident.

David was so upset that he told other family members he was going to call Tom.

"You can't just go call the ex-husband," his sister Nancy told him.

"Somebody's got to do something," he replied.

They came to regret not doing anything. "At that time," Nancy later explained, "we're thinking Tom's an SOB. But we realize there's two sides to every story and we're asking ourselves, 'Could you live with Susie?'"

* * *

Living with Susie was not easy in September, when she finally was served notice of Tom's petition for divorce. Tom had instructed his lawyer to take whatever action was necessary for him to see his sons. Susie was livid that the action had been filed nearly a year earlier and that she hadn't been told about it. She was frightened of the consequences that the petition might hold.

The action requested that all matters, including property and child custody, be settled in New Mexico. It further asked that the separation agreement, the terms of which both had agreed would be part of any divorce settlement, not be included.

The separation agreement granted custody of the boys to Susie, and later Tom said that he really didn't want custody at that time but agreed to let Rueckhaus include it in the suit as a bargaining tool.

Regardless of its purpose, it struck fear in Susie. She became convinced that Tom wanted to take the boys from her.

Sands immediately filed in Rockingham County to have custody and visitation settled in North Carolina, but Susie would still have to fight the New Mexico action, and he suggested that she hire a lawyer there. He recommended Barbara Shapiro, who worked in one of Albuquerque's largest law firms.

Shapiro, a native of New York City, had a Ph.D. in English from Harvard. She went to law school after moving to Albuquerque for her husband's allergies. She specialized in domestic relations, an area shunned by most lawyers. "I like it," she explained. "I like the counseling side of it. I like people and I'm a problem solver."

After studying the case, she told Susie that the law was on her side and she needn't worry about losing custody.

Two weeks after Susie got notice of the divorce action, she was served with more papers asking that she be held in contempt for refusing to allow John and Jim to visit their father. In an affidavit, Tom said that he couldn't afford to visit in North Carolina. "My children have expressed to me and to my mother their dismay in being unable to see me," he said.

On September 22, Tom called Ron Davis, the psychologist in Winston-Salem. Davis later remembered the call as "tense." An argument ensued about the children being too young to travel alone if they had to change planes.

"Dr. Lynch refused to listen to me and stated that my attitude was unreasonable," he stated in an affidavit.

Later, Davis remembered Tom saying, "They're children and children do what they're told to do."

"Children are people, too," Davis responded, "and you work with children instead of just telling them what to do."

Tom, in another affidavit, claimed that "Dr. Davis first insisted that visitation only be in North Carolina." He said Davis told him that children shouldn't "fly anywhere unless accompanied by an adult throughout." He said Davis also told him that Susie claimed he was a neglectful father who had no desire to see his children.

"I explained to him my financial circumstance and advised him that I was simply being hassled," Tom said.

The Uniform Child Custody Jurisdiction Act sets out rules by which courts decide custody issues when parents live in different states. North Carolina was a partner to the act, and in July of 1981, New Mexico accepted it, too. The act stated a preference for custody to be decided in the home state of the children, that being where they had resided for the previous six months.

In October, Barbara Shapiro filed a motion asking that matters of custody and visitation be dismissed from the divorce petition because the children lived in North Carolina and had done so for two years; therefore, the New Mexico court lacked jurisdiction.

In an accompanying affidavit, Susie reiterated her concerns about travel arrangements for the children. "I have always encouraged visitation," she said. "I am willing to have the children go to Albuquerque provided some arrangement is made to protect their safety if they have to change planes." She went on to say she couldn't afford to litigate the issue in New Mexico and thought the case belonged in North Carolina.

"Apparently neither of the parties can afford to litigate anywhere," Tom responded. "If I could just get reasonable visitation with my children and make some financial settlement, the case would be over."

The case was far from over. On November 17, it came before District Judge Gene Franchini in Albuquerque. Rueckhaus argued that the Uniform Child Custody Act did not apply because Tom had filed for divorce before it was enacted in New Mexico. Shapiro maintained that it did apply because notice was not served until after the act was in force.

Judge Franchini ruled that custody, visitation, and property settlement would be decided in New Mexico.

Susie was distraught, but a few days after the decision Judge Franchini left the bench, and Shapiro quickly filed for a rehearing. The motion came back to court in December before Judge Joseph Alarid, who turned the tables on Tom.

He agreed that the New Mexico court had jurisdiction, but deferred "to the Courts of North Carolina as a more convenient forum."

After months of litigation, incurring big legal fees that neither Tom nor Susie could afford (Tom's parents were helping with his; Nanna was helping with Susie's), the only thing that had been accomplished was a hardening of position and a deepening bitterness on both sides. Visitation and property settlement seemed as far from being resolved as ever.

Convinced that Tom's true intent was to take the boys, Susie was certain that if they ever went to New Mexico she never would get them back.

"Susie, if she had a fault," Sandy Sands said later, "it was her overprotectiveness toward those children. That seemed to be her sole purpose in life, protecting her children."

Tom, however, was not about to let another Christmas pass without seeing his sons. He demanded that they be allowed to come to New Mexico over the holidays, and once again the lawyers set to dickering.

The arrangement they finally worked out offended and angered Tom, yet he had no choice but to accept it if he wanted to see the boys. He would have seven days with them, but he would have to sign a $10,000 bond that would be forfeited if he took the boys out of New Mexico, did not return them on time, or if there arose "any dispute about the visitation that results in having to take court action or other action that incurs attorneys' fees or other expenses." Such a bond was allowed under the child custody act.

Tom would have to fly to Greensboro to get the boys and spend two days getting reacquainted with them at the Newsom house before taking them to Albuquerque. On the return trip, the children would be put on the plane in Albuquerque and go to Atlanta, where their mother would meet them. Tom would pay Susie's expenses back and forth to Atlanta.

Tom put up the deed to his house as security for the bond, and while Christmas drew closer and legal documents shuffled back and forth, he remained uncertain whether the process would be completed in time for the visit.

Only hours before he was scheduled to leave, approval finally came, and he flew to Greensboro to see his children for the first time in more than two years.

24

Susie's stress continued its effect on her stability.

In January of 1982, she dropped her anthropology studies at Wake Forest, calling her professors "idiots."

She then enrolled at the University of North Carolina at Greensboro, once Woman's College, where her mother and her aunts Susie, Louise, and Frances all had gone. This time she chose business—in effect, starting over. Her mother, who was trying not to interfere in Susie's life, shook her head and told a neighbor, "I think we've got a professional student on our hands."

The problems between Susie and Tom once again fell into stalemate. Tom still called regularly to talk to John and Jim, but he no longer made any attempts to reason with Susie. As another summer loomed with no visitation scheduled and no progress being made with Susie's lawyer in Reidsville, Tom knew that he would have to deal with the problem in North Carolina. He hired a lawyer in Reidsville, Bill Horsley, who was thirty-four. An Alabama native, Horsley had been an aspiring writer until rejection slips drove him to law school at Wake Forest in the fall of 1969, while Tom was beginning his senior year. He didn't know Tom at college but after talking with him, he got down a college yearbook and remembered that he had been on the basketball team. Drawn to Reidsville because he wanted to rear his children in a small town, Horsley was an accomplished trial lawyer well on his way to building a reputation for winning big claims in personal injury cases. He didn't mind domestic cases, had a record of success with them. That this case involved a member of the locally prominent Sharp family bothered him not at all.

On July 6, Horsley filed a motion in the General Court of Justice of Rockingham County asking that a schedule of visitation be decreed. A hearing was set for July 23. Susie sought to postpone it, knowing that a delay would leave little time for a visit that summer. Her motion was denied.

Several weeks prior to the hearing, Susie again took the boys to see Dr. Ron Davis, who had just left Wake Forest to enter private practice. Susie planned to have Dr. Davis testify at the hearing, and he wanted to know how the boys felt about visiting their father. He taped the session.

Both boys said that they liked their father, but both liked Kathy, their father's former dental assistant, who now lived with him, even more.

"I like Kathy more because we're not very used to Dad yet," Jim said.

"John, you like your daddy?" Dr. Davis asked.

"Yeah," he said.

"You like Kathy better," Jim put in.

"But I like Daddy, too."

Both agreed that they liked to visit their father and wanted to go back.

"Well, see, we want to go to Daddy's," John said at one point, "but we just don't want to get in trouble or anything."

"If you had your choice of going to see your daddy or going to a birthday party, which would you choose?" Dr. Davis asked.

"The birthday party," said Jim.

"Daddy," said John.

Jim again put in for the birthday party. "That's an easy choice," he said.

"Well, it's not for me," said John.

When Dr. Davis asked whether they'd rather visit their daddy's mother and father or stay in Greensboro, the answer was quick and unanimous: "Stay in Greensboro." Given the choice between visiting their daddy's mother and father and their daddy, they chose their daddy.

"If I ever went to Albuquerque if Kathy wasn't there, I'd be happy with Daddy there," Jim said.

"If Kathy wasn't there and Daddy was the only one, we'd have to stay by ourselves when he went to work," John said. "We could take care of ourselves. Yes, we sure could."

Asked what they liked best about visiting their father, both named playing his Atari game.

"What if he didn't have an Atari, would you still go visit him?" Dr. Davis asked.

"Yes," said John.

"I wouldn't," said Jim.

Jim was concerned about the dogs at his daddy's house. "See, there are two dogs who are bigger than Muffy, which is my dog friend. He's nice to me, isn't he, John?"

"It's a *she,* Jimbo," John said, laughing. "Only one is a he. That's Ashley. Two of 'em like us and one of 'em doesn't."

"Who doesn't like us?" Jim asked.

"Ashley."

John had the microphone and pretended to be a TV star.

"Is there anything else from the audience?" he asked as Jim giggled.

Dr. Davis had his answer. The boys liked visiting their father and wanted to go back—John more so than Jim, but both were essentially in agreement—and he could see no reason why they shouldn't.

Tom flew to Greensboro for the hearing and checked into a motel at the airport with his mother, who drove from Louisville.

The hearing was held at Wentworth, seven miles west of Reidsville, in the old red-brick Rockingham County courthouse, where a portrait of Susie's grandfather, James Sharp, hung in a spot of honor, and where, less than three years hence, Susie would bring the boys to unveil a portrait of her famous aunt, Susie Sharp.

The presiding judge was Peter McHugh, himself the father of three young sons. A native of Buffalo, New York, McHugh had married into a prominent Reidsville family. He had been in private law practice in Reidsville for three and a half years before being appointed a district court judge, a position he'd held for nearly five years. Judge McHugh had been introduced to Reidsville's most famous lawyer, Susie Sharp, at a bar meeting, but he'd never held a conversation with her and was unacquainted with any other members of the Sharp family. For a while he had worked in the same law firm as Tom's lawyer, Bill Horsley, and both lawyers in the case, as well as the judge, were friends. Horsley and McHugh were members of the same church, St. Thomas Episcopal.

The afternoon before, while Tom was on his way from Albuquerque, Horsley had been served with a last-minute motion requesting that the matter of child support also be considered at this hearing. The opening arguments were over that motion, which was rejected by the judge because it had been filed with insufficient notice.

The hearing got under way with Tom being questioned by his lawyer. Horsley established how little he'd seen the boys in the three years since his separation, then brought up a touchy subject he knew the opposition would pursue, asking if Tom lived alone in the house he and Susie once shared.

"No, I share the home with my girlfriend."

Horsley went on to show that Susie was aware of this situation before sending the boys for the Christmas visit and that the boys got along well with Kathy.

One other important question remained.

"Is it your intention to take the children back to New Mexico and there seek complete custody of them?"

"No."

Sands began his cross-examination with the implication that not seeing the boys was Tom's choice.

"Have you not been advised that you are welcome to see them any time that you want to in North Carolina?"

"Oh, yes."

As expected, Sands peppered Tom with questions about Kathy, trying to leave the impression that their relationship caused the failure of his marriage. He also tried to show that Tom had fallen behind in support and medical payments and hadn't lived up to the separation agreement. A testy exchange developed about the $1,500 Tom was supposed to pay for Susie's share of the household appliances she left behind. Sands also brought up another touchy subject—the bond Tom had been forced to post so he could see his children at Christmas.

"Are you resisting a bond on this particular occasion?"

"On the matter of principle, yes. If the judge so orders, I will sign the bond."

"Is that why you caused all the problems in New Mexico and cost her all that expense was because of principle?" Sands said to Horsley's objection.

"Mr. Lynch, you resisted completely the courts of North Carolina having jurisdiction over these children, didn't you?" Sands asked.

"I filed for divorce in New Mexico on the advice of my counselor because he wanted the courts in New Mexico to have jurisdiction over the divorce."

"Yes, sir, and y'all fought like the dickens to keep it out there, didn't you?"

"I don't know if you could say we fought like the dickens, but we had a couple of hearings with the judge. It was never my wish to have custody of the boys. . . . My own personal wishes are that the boys remain in the custody of their mother."

"You think she has been a good mother to the children, hasn't she?"

"I think so."

Sands brought up Dr. Ron Davis, the psychologist Susie had appointed to negotiate visitation.

"You have completely refused to cooperate with Dr. Davis in regard to visitation, haven't you?"

"Seems to me it is the other way around," Tom replied.

Horsley rose at the end of Sands's examination to ask Tom a question he considered crucial.

"Is it your intention to marry Kathy Anderson once you are divorced?"

"Yes, it is."

Susie wore a simple blouse with a Peter Pan collar as she took the stand. Her face was pale and powdered, her bearing demure and proper. She answered her attorney's questions in a soft voice, describing the boys' trip from Albuquerque the previous Christmas as "a rather unnerving flight."

"Do you feel the children will be able to fly on an airplane by themselves again?" Sands asked later.

"I would prefer that they did not."

Sands led her through questions about the boys' problems both before and after the breakup of her marriage. John had "severe emotional problems" prior to the breakup, she said, and she had sought help for him.

"The psychologist communicated to me that children usually show the first signs of trouble in a marriage," she said, before Horsley could object to the hearsay testimony. "He felt that John's emotional problem was due to our conflict."

She went on to say that after her return to North Carolina, she'd taken the boys to Dr. Davis because of "a great deal of conflict" between the two, but the conflict had since disappeared.

Susie recited a long list of plans she'd made for her sons in coming weeks before Sands asked, "Are you afraid of the children not returning if they leave again?"

"I would not have been except for the kind of conflicts we had over jurisdiction, and so currently I am, yes."

"Mrs. Lynch, your jurisdictional matter has been resolved, hasn't it?" Horsley asked on cross-examination.

"Yes, it has."

Dr. Ron Davis was a witness in Susie's behalf. He told of his telephone conversation with Tom the year before and of Tom's objections to his recommendation of a succession of short visits instead of a single, long summer visit, to keep the boys from becoming homesick and miserable. He described the children as apprehensive because of the uncertainty about their visits with their father.

Near the end of his questions to Davis, Sands brought up another call Dr. Davis had received, this one from Leonard Timpone, a Chicago lawyer who had been Janie's high school sweetheart and a chum of Tom. Davis had thought the call hostile and an attempt to intimidate him. Although he tried several times to get those impressions on the record, Sands was unsuccessful.

Delores had asked Leonard, the son of her old friends, Jackie and Mario Timpone, to make that call, although Tom and his father objected to it.

"She said, 'Look, Leonard's a big shot attorney. He'll do this and do that,' " Tom recalled later. "Not only was this way out of his jurisdiction, I got the feeling he wasn't really interested. Leonard's one of these blustery Italian guys, Mr. Personality, Wild Man. He would've been the perfect guy to alienate the entire state of North Carolina."

Horsley had one primary question of Davis, and it was about the boys.

"Do you think it would be helpful for them to see their father more frequently and have a relationship with him?"

"Sure."

Delores had sat through the hearing barely able to control herself, and as it was drawing to a close, without warning, Susie's lawyer called her to the stand.

"Mrs. Lynch, did you contact Mr. Leonard Timpone about representing you or your son on this particular matter?"

"Yes, I did."

"Was he retained to represent your son or represent you, or both?"

"I guess both."

Horsley had no questions, and Delores returned to her seat. Rarely had she said so little about something she felt so strongly about.

Thus the testimony came to its nondramatic conclusion. Only the judge's decision was left to be heard, and when it came, it was temporarily pleasing only to Tom. He could pick up the boys the following day, July 24, and after spending one day in Greensboro with them, take them to New Mexico. He would not have to sign a bond, and he must return the boys by August 12 so they could prepare for school. Final decision on a permanent schedule of visitation would be postponed to give Susie's lawyers time to take more depositions in New Mexico to be presented at a future hearing involving only the lawyers.

The only deposition Susie took that fall was from Tom. Her lawyer in Albuquerque, Barbara Shapiro, did that, asking mainly about property and financial matters. When her questions ventured into other areas, Tom's sullen answers were short and less than illuminating.

Shapiro wanted to know about the marriage breakup

and pressed Tom for his reasons for not talking to Susie about his divorce action.

"I didn't feel any need to discuss it with her," he replied. "You get divorced, you get divorced."

Shapiro also asked about Kathy, learning that she had quit work in 1981, was now studying at the University of New Mexico, and that she and Tom shared a joint checking account to which only Tom contributed.

When Tom responded that he hadn't declared Kathy as a dependent on his tax returns, Shapiro asked why.

"You mean I can?" Tom asked.

"Sure," said Shapiro.

Judge McHugh had set October 1 as the deadline for additional depositions from Susie. When none was received, he summoned the lawyers for final arguments. On November 22, he issued his order. In the summer of 1983, Tom would have the boys for the month of July. Each summer after that, he would get them for thirty-five days beginning on July 1. He would get a week at Christmas every other year, beginning in 1983, and a week at spring break in even-numbered years. He also would have the boys for spring break in 1983. He could visit them in North Carolina at any time with two weeks' written notice. Transportation arrangements would be Tom's responsibility, as would all costs. Until the summer of 1986, one parent would have to accompany the boys on one leg of the flight to assure that they changed planes safely. If that was Susie, Tom had to pay her expenses. After 1986, if Susie wanted to accompany the boys, it would be at her expense.

Tom's lawyer, Bill Horsley, had mixed emotions about the judgment. He thought the judge had compromised, trying to satisfy everybody. It wasn't bad as a beginning, he told Tom.

Tom had other ideas. He thought thirty-five days in the summer "ridiculous." The travel stipulation, he felt, had been put in to penalize him. Susie had won. Her name, he was convinced, had prevailed.

"I got hometowned bad," he said bitterly.

Delores was furious. She told friends that Tom never had a chance. The courts of North Carolina, she said, were under the thumb of "that old battle-ax," Susie's aunt, the retired chief justice.

Horsley knew that wasn't the case, but he never would be able to convince Tom and his mother of it.

"Peter McHugh is one of the best district court judges in the state," Horsley said later. "If anything he would have leaned over backwards to prevent that impression. I wasn't real happy with the decision, but I didn't feel like we got hometowned. I could see how they might feel that way."

The enmity between Delores and Susie had grown even stronger in recent months. No longer was Delores allowed to talk to the boys by telephone. She had the evidence on tape.

"Hello, Susie?"

"Yes," Susie said before the voice had fully registered. When the identification hit her, she sprang forth in a fury, "Delores, now listen! I can't allow you to upset the children anymore! These boys are settled and you're not playing games with them anymore! Now good-bye!"

"Now what in the world is the matter with her?" Delores later recalled thinking. "I didn't say anything wrong."

She called back immediately. "Susie," she said, her voice dripping artificial sweetness, "what are you talking about?"

"You know exactly what I'm talking about! And don't call back anymore!" Click.

Despite the judge's ruling, Susie was more unhappy than ever, more watchful and protective of her children. Neighbors noticed that she was the only mother in the neighborhood who went to the curb with her children to await the school bus every morning, who stayed with them until they were safely aboard, who hovered over them even at play. She bickered more frequently with her mother, who worried that Susie was too preoccupied with her children, too absorbed in her bitterness for Tom, about whom she had begun to speak in sinister tones. Florence worried, too, that Susie was pushing herself too hard to keep top grades, sitting up until early morning hours studying. And, frankly, Florence was irritated that Susie had a regular late-night caller, a visitor of whom she disapproved.

That visitor was Fritz Klenner, Susie's first cousin. Florence and other family members had always thought him odd. He seemed to prowl mostly at night, and he had a fascination for guns and intrigue. The family thought him a medical student at Duke University, soon to be graduated with honors, certain to step into his aging and ailing father's unusual practice in Reidsville. For years, he had assisted his father in his clinic on weekends, and Susie had renewed acquaintance with him when she began going to the clinic for her regular injections of vitamins. Susie was nearly six years older than Fritz, barely knew him as he was growing up, and rarely saw him for years, but now a close relationship had developed between them, rousing whispers of concern in the propriety-conscious Sharp and Newsom families. Most family members chose to believe that the cousins were simply consoling and supporting one another because both were going through divorces. Fritz's marriage had come apart in 1981, and he'd seemed to be having a hard time because of it.

Susie told friends that the boys liked Fritz and she felt safe when he was around. But her mother had begun to suspect that Fritz was more than a friend and protector, and she was mortified by the prospect. Fritz was coming around entirely too much, Florence thought, often far after midnight, when he would roust Susie from her late-night studies by pecking on the dining room window, sometimes disturbing the sleep of other family members. Occasionally Florence got up in the morning to find Fritz sleeping on her couch. She feared that Susie was becoming too dependent on her strange cousin, who had a disturbing way of looking at people. Fritz, she knew, was quick to see conspiracies, and she wondered what fears and exotic theories he might be pumping into her daughter's head. Was he encouraging the wild and scathing new tales that Susie had been concocting about Tom?

Susie even had brought up some of these tales to her lawyer. Tom was involved with drugs, gambling, and underworld characters, she told Sandy Sands just before the hearing that summer, and she was frightened by it.

"What in the world gives you that idea?" Sands asked.

She said that a friend of the family who was an FBI agent had told her. The FBI was getting ready to go after international smugglers, she said, and Tom was just "a small fish in a big pond," but he was apt to get caught up in it. Pressed for her source, she wouldn't reveal it, and Sands discounted the tale and quickly put it out of mind.

Later, Sands noticed Fritz at the July hearing, slinking around conspiratorially. He wondered what Susie's cousin was doing there, but it would be years before he realized that Fritz had to have been the source of Susie's strange tale about Tom and the underworld.

Fritz needed little evidence to persuade himself that Tom was involved with the Mafia. That Tom's dental partners and accountant all had Italian names was plenty. Add the judge with an Italian name who had ruled in Tom's favor and the intimidating call to Dr. Davis from an Italian lawyer in Chicago and that was evidence enough.

That Susie, too, came to believe such a farfetched notion, many who knew her would not doubt. They could conceive only one reason she had turned to Fritz: just as his father was saving her from deadly illness with his vitamins, Fritz would save her and the boys from deadly mobsters with his guns.

PART FOUR

SPIRALING MADNESS

25

From the time Fritz Klenner was old enough to sit unassisted, weapons were put into his hands. Rare is the childhood photo that shows him without a gun. At less than a year of age, he sits in a red barrel chair, a tiny toy pistol gripped tightly to his chest. At five, he poses defiantly in a fringed black cowboy suit, his hands on his six-shooters.

"I had to run around with one of those play guns hanging on me all the time," recalled his aunt Marie Jennings, his father's eldest sister, who came from Pennsylvania to tend Fritz each summer while his mother, a nurse, worked in his father's clinic. "He was Roy Rogers and I was Dale Evans."

Marie, who became Fritz's favorite aunt, remembered one time visitors came to the house when Fritz was about three.

"Don't let 'em in until I get my guns," he cried as he dashed to his room to fetch what had become even then the instruments of his security.

During his childhood, Fritz would possess hundreds of toy guns of every description—pistols, rifles, shotguns, machine guns, and other military armaments—all bought for him by his father. By the time he was eleven, he had his first real gun, a German Luger, a birthday gift from Dad. By then, too, he had acquired all of his father's fears, insecurities, prejudices, and eccentricities, as well as his hopes and dreams, becoming his father's worshipful clone.

Family, friends, and patients could not recall a happier time in Dr. Frederick R. Klenner's life than the day on which his son was born at Duke University Hospital—July 31, 1952, less than three months shy of the doctor's forty-fifth birthday. Dr. Klenner long had dreamed of having a son who would bear his name and eventually take over his important work, and now, nearly eight years after the birth of his youngest daughter, Gertrude, that dream had come true. He beamed to those who congratulated him, and passed out, not cigars, but a local product, packages of Lucky Strike cigarettes wrapped in blue ribbons. His friend Felix Fournier, manager of the American Tobacco Company plant that made Lucky Strikes, would become his son's godfather.

From infancy, the baby was called Fritz, and he was nourished not only with large quantities of vitamins but with his father's visions of miracles he eventually would perform with these wondrous natural chemicals. Fritz's Aunt Marie recalled that the child hated to take the vitamins and that she had to play story games to get him to down them, spreading the pills and capsules over a tabletop as if they were steps in an exciting journey, each step rewarded with chocolate milk.

That the boy would be molded in the image of his father was unquestioned, for Dr. Klenner brooked no challenge. "He had a Prussian attitude," recalled a family acquaintance who thought Dr. Klenner "an oddball, a kook." "His word was law and that was it. He never let the children live a normal life. His wife, Annie Hill, was a prisoner in that house. She was his slave. She didn't have a husband; she had a warden, and so did those children."

"He was dictatorial," said a family friend, "but he had a loving relationship with his wife and family. I'd say they were a very close couple. Her personality flourished under that rock he kept her under. She was a very sparkling personality."

"He was a very kind and caring man, but he was Prussian to the core," agreed another family friend who thought highly of Dr. Klenner. "An old German papa. He wanted to rule the family. He didn't try to completely isolate his children, but he didn't encourage his daughters' having any friends. He didn't like for them to go out to parties or do things that other girls did. And he kept Fritz close to himself."

The relationship between father and son was a picture of closeness, jealously guarded by the doctor. "Fred idolized Fritz," the doctor's sister Marie recalled. "He just idolized him."

"They were best friends," said Fritz's aunt Susie.

Fritz often didn't attend Sharp family gatherings. His mother and sisters went, but Fritz frequently stayed behind with his father, who never felt fully accepted by the Sharps and still nursed the scars of rejection they had inflicted, scars whose memory he transferred to his son. Fritz always looked forward, though, to visits with his father's family from Pennsylvania. The doctor had little time for trips back home, but now and then he drove his wife and children to Natural Bridge, Virginia, a halfway point, where he met family members from Pennsylvania. The reunions took place in the cavernous brick visitor center, with Dr. Klenner administering blood pressure checks to family members and Fritz romping around, sometimes firing his toy guns at passersby. Years later, Fritz would talk frequently of the good times he had at Natural Bridge.

Fritz had no childhood friends, even after he started going to school. Dr. Klenner discouraged his son from developing friends by forbidding playmates from the house, a forbidding place anyway, even to adults. Dr. Klenner considered the house his refuge, his sanctuary, and few outsiders were allowed to invade it. Those who were invited inside found dark rooms and unbelievable clutter. Books and papers and boxes and bric-a-brac were everywhere. In some rooms, little floor space was left for walking. Visitors sometimes had trouble finding a place to sit.

Dr. Klenner was an inveterate collector of stamps, coins, toys, electric trains, miniature wagons, clocks, German beer steins, miniature cannons, cut glass, and antique furniture, but his specialty was guns, particularly German army weapons. He bought and traded so many guns that he acquired a federal firearms license issued to dealers. He filled his house not only with his collections but also with cases of canned and preserved foods that he hoarded against coming calamities, with box upon box of vitamins and medicines, and with thousands of books and periodicals. His library was vast, and mixed with somber law and medical books were mystical religious tomes as well as the published near-hysterical rantings of conspiracy-minded right-wing doomsayers. Comforted by his magnificent clutter, Dr. Klenner sat late into the night listening to classical music, reading his medical journals, and writing papers extolling the wonders of vitamins.

Neighbors thought the Klenners secretive, reclusive, eccentric, "a little strange." They came to regard the Klenner house as an eyesore in the otherwise immaculate upper-middle-class neighborhood. The white paint peeled from the bricks. The shrubbery grew wild, the grass high. Stacks of decaying building materials, rusting vehicles, and unusual machinery parts filled the yard. Service people were reluctant to approach the house, fearing the big, ferocious-sounding German shepherd inside, a dog named Dorner that Dr. Klenner claimed to be gifted with extrasensory perception.

Years later, Fritz recalled a lonely childhood spent in this dark and cluttered house. He talked of filling his time practicing his cornet (an instrument his grandfather had played in an Austrian band), reading his father's books, and studying with growing fascination his father's weapons.

Over and over, he told one particular story that seemed to have great significance to him.

In the late forties, Dr. Klenner bought 256 acres of land at an estate sale handled by his father-in-law, James Sharp. The land was on the Dan River, fifteen miles west of Reidsville, near Leaksville, Spray, and Draper, three towns that later merged as Eden. It was rugged land, steep and wooded and rocky, and Dr. Klenner came to call it "the Mountain." He went there almost every Wednesday, the one afternoon a week he took off from the office, and often after mass on Sunday. He fancied himself an arborist, and there he planted trees and grafted limbs.

Almost always, Dr. Klenner took his son when he went to the Mountain. They tramped the steep hills, hiked along the river, fired Dr. Klenner's many weapons, set off dynamite charges. Dr. Klenner was convinced that caves lay under his land, and he frequently blasted holes searching for their entrances. He also believed that a legendary Bigfoot creature, locally called the Wampus Cat, lived along the river and prowled his land, and he and Fritz spent many hours searching vainly for the creature's lair. Later, Dr. Klenner made plaster impressions of unusual footprints he found and sent off samples of droppings to the Smithsonian Institution in attempts to confirm the creature's existence and identify it.

One day, when he was about ten, Fritz was supposed to go to the Mountain with his father. He was in his room playing with a radio when his father got ready to leave. His father called impatiently to him, but Fritz dawdled. By the time Fritz got downstairs, his father had gone without him. Fritz never got over it. He had failed his father, and his father had rejected him for it. He couldn't bear that.

Pleasing his father was Fritz's foremost goal in life. Everybody who saw the two together knew instantly that the son worshiped the father, but Dr. Klenner's expectations were high, and pleasing him was not easy.

Dr. Klenner demanded academic excellence of his children and sometimes dispatched his wife to their schools to argue with teachers over fractions in grade points. Town gossips whispered that Dr. Klenner gave his children amphetamines so that they could stay up late studying and be more alert for tests.

A classmate of Fritz, Charles Kimbro, recalled a time when their teacher was returning test papers and Fritz's came back with only a B-plus scrawled across the top.

"He just put his head down on the desk and started crying, because he was scared his daddy was going to find out about it," Kimbro said.

"He feared his father," said Randy Clark, who became Fritz's closest friend after moving to Reidsville when he and Fritz were in seventh grade. "There was no question of the authority his father had over him. It was almost militaristic, a timid submission. Yes, sir! No, sir! Acting on command. His father was god of the house."

Fritz attempted to please his father by becoming as much like him as possible. He became enamored of German history and Adolf Hitler, and drew swastikas on his school notebooks. "He was very prone to give a Sieg Heil! and a Remember the Third Reich!" Randy Clark remembered.

Fritz displayed his father's love for military paraphernalia by wearing an army fatigue jacket and other military attire to school years before that became fashionable among other youngsters. "He liked to be militaristic," Clark recalled. "He liked having an air of authority about him. He liked having a sense of superiority."

Neighbors sometimes saw Fritz marching in the yard, counting cadence, a rifle on his shoulder—but never in the front yard. He wasn't allowed to play there because his father feared kidnappers.

Of weaponry, military and otherwise, Fritz spoke with confident knowledge, being able to spew out the muzzle velocities and other vital statistics of a wide variety of guns before he was twelve. While other kids sneaked free reads of comic books at downtown drugstores, Fritz engrossed himself in gun magazines.

As he cloaked himself with his father's obsessions, he also parroted his father's religious and political beliefs.

He believed with his father in a superstitious and mystical Catholicism, rife with signs and omens, that harked back to the Middle Ages. He believed in demons and spooks and the power of holy water in confronting them, for he had seen his father expel such evil spirits with only a few drops of the magical liquid. He spoke often of Armageddon, the ultimate battle between good and evil predicted in the Book of Revelation, and he believed, as did his father, that that awesome moment of decision was imminent (his father on occasion claimed to know the actual date on which the great battle would begin).

Like his father, Fritz railed against blacks, liberals, and Communists. "Be A MAN, join the KLAN," he wrote in Randy Clark's yearbook in the ninth grade. "George Wallace for President in '68."

"He was increasingly paranoid in high school about blacks, the civil rights movement, Communists," Clark recalled. "He thought blacks were low-class, no-class, and all the civil rights movement was just a Communist plot to overthrow the government. He had such a hatred built up in him. It was almost as if he were waiting for Armageddon any minute."

More than in any other way, however, Fritz pleased his father by constantly expressing his wish to be a doctor. That was given, and he accepted it as if it had been preordained by his genes. After school and on Saturdays, he spent time at his father's clinic observing him carefully, getting to know patients, assuring all that one day he would be assuming his father's work. On his belt, he regularly carried a pouch filled with vitamins and medical supplies. In tenth grade, when a girl fainted in class, he was quick to revive her with an ammonia ampule.

Fritz was so intent on pleasing his father that he had little time for play or other activities. Randy Clark would remember playing only one game with him: spy. They carried attaché cases with toy pistols inside and fantasized exotic James Bond intrigues. Only later did Clark realize why the game so appealed to his friend. "He liked being secretive. For Fritz, secretiveness was very important. If a person knew a lot about you, you couldn't maintain your secrecy. You don't want anybody to know about you."

At school, Fritz had no trouble maintaining secrecy. Most students steered clear of him, considering him weird, a nerd. He was shy and quiet, almost withdrawn, and except for Clark and Kimbro, he had no friends. If he had an interest in girls, he never displayed it. He shunned most school activities. He was too uncoordinated and inept for sports and never developed an interest in them. He joined Demolay, a secretive, teenage version of the Masons, was a member of the French, Latin, and Library Clubs, and became an audio-visual assistant in the library. He played cornet in the concert band, and other band members would remember him as being nervous and sweating before every performance.

Fritz took fast-track classes, and, at his father's insistence, concentrated in science. Although he made good grades, he never quite achieved the high level of academic excellence for which he strived so diligently.

Spring of 1969 not only marked the end of Fritz's junior year in high school, it also brought the end of his studies at Reidsville High. Plans were announced to fully integrate Reidsville's schools that fall, and Dr. Klenner would not allow his son to attend. Fritz was in full agreement. He had vowed never to sit in class with "niggers."

Instead, Dr. Klenner chose for Fritz what he considered to be a more suitable, and more white, environment at Woodward Academy, an expensive boarding school on thirty-six acres near College Park in Atlanta. Three years earlier, Woodward had been a military school. But it had become coeducational and was known for its strong discipline and heavy Christian emphasis. At Woodward, Fritz belonged to the rifle team, rifle club, pep club, and band. He took first place in the science fair. To patients and friends who inquired of Fritz's well-being, his father replied that he was doing fine and boasted that his son was the roommate of the son of Jimmy Carter, the Georgia governor (who, six years hence, would become president). In the spring of 1970, Fritz graduated ninth in his class of 138. His father could barely contain his pride.

Fritz's choice of college had long been decided. Like his sisters before him, he would attend the University of Mississippi. His father had chosen Ole Miss because he thought it would be the last academic bastion of white supremacy, and although James Meredith had integrated the university with the help of federal troops in 1962, Dr. Klenner had been impressed by the institution's defiance and he continued his support of it. He had made donations to the school library and even had given $2,500 to have planted on the campus magnolias and dogwoods, both of which, symbolically, flowered white.

When Fritz moved onto the campus in the fall of 1970, his life was right on the track laid for him by his father, but all of that was soon to change.

26

In the summer of 1972, after his second year in college, Randy Clark was visiting in Reidsville when he happened by the Klenner house on Huntsdale Road. He spotted Fritz in the yard and stopped to chat. Fritz had finished his second year at Ole Miss, and the old friends caught up on what had happened since their days at Reidsville High.

Randy was surprised to learn that Fritz, whom he'd never known to have a date, was planning to marry. He'd met his fiancée at college, Fritz said. Her name was Mary Carolyn, and she was from a wealthy family, he noted, a debutante.

"He was very serious about her," Randy recalled, "but I got the feeling that the marriage was more like an arrangement between prominent families than a real love affair. He seemed very stern about it. Very resolute."

As they talked, Randy, who was studying religion and thinking of the ministry, realized that the hatred he long had seen in Fritz, especially for blacks, had grown even stronger. Fritz told of using karate to single-handedly fend off a group of blacks who jumped him in an elevator on campus. The story sounded dubious to Randy, but Fritz seemed to need for him to believe it, so he displayed polite awe; but later, as he was leaving, he wondered how long it would be before the hatred in Fritz built to an explosive level.

In coming years, Fritz not only repeated to others the story of being jumped by blacks in an elevator at Ole Miss, he also told of working as an undercover narcotics agent on campus, wearing a concealed pistol to classes, belonging to a campus vigilante group that "kept the niggers in their place," and undergoing secret military training in Georgia. But one thing he did not talk about was what happened to his marriage plans.

Those plans went so far that at one point his fiancée's name was painted on a wall plaque of the Klenner family tree, but before Fritz's college days were through, the wedding was abruptly canceled, and friends and relatives beyond immediate family never learned what happened.

Whatever interests and outside activities Fritz had at Ole Miss, they served as distraction from study, and after four years, he still hadn't accumulated enough credit hours for his degree in biology. His grades were only slightly above average and included some Ds, hardly the kind of record apt to win him quick entrance to the Duke University Medical School, the next step in the life course his father had so carefully charted. With that weighing on his mind, he entered summer school in 1974 and finished all of his requirements except for a three-hour language credit. He had successfully completed nine hours of German, a language in which he and his father sometimes bantered, and that fall he signed up for a correspondence course for the three hours he still needed. He never finished it, but he dared not tell his father. Instead, he went home at Christmas with the news that he had graduated. His diploma, he said, would be coming in the mail.

When the diploma hadn't arrived by May, Dr. Klenner called the university to find out why. A dean wrote to tell him that his son could not have graduated in December, for the university had no commencement then. Records showed that Fritz still needed a three-hour foreign language requirement to win his degree. Confronted by his father, other family members later learned, Fritz claimed that enemies in the language department who had opposed his extracurricular campus activities had intercepted his work and kept him from getting a final grade on his correspondence course. He would straighten it out, he promised.

As he waited for the problem to be corrected, Fritz worked as an unlicensed assistant in his father's clinic. He and his father agreed that this practical, on-the-job training would benefit him greatly after he started medical school. Patients liked Fritz. He had the bearing of a doctor, they thought, and he was as concerned and caring as his father. Beyond that, many exclaimed, he had the softest touch with a needle they'd ever felt.

His father's side of the family thought Fritz the very image of Fred as a young man: tall, lean, and handsome, with a shock of dark hair across his forehead. His nose was not quite so prominent, and his eyes, true, were not the gentle grayish blue of his father but the soft brown of his mother—Blackwell eyes, they were called by the Sharp brothers and sisters, for they had come from their mother's family.

Family members weren't the only ones to notice the resemblances, however. On the street one day, a longtime acquaintance encountered Dr. Klenner and his son.

"Fred," the man said, "as long as Fritz is alive, you're going to be on this earth. He looks like you. He walks like you. He talks like you. He even puts his hat on like you."

Dr. Klenner smiled broadly. Few compliments could have pleased him more.

If the day of Fritz's birth was the proudest day in Dr. Klenner's life, surely the second proudest was the day late in 1976 when Fritz announced his acceptance at the Duke University Medical School, which his father had attended. In January of 1977, Fritz drove off to Durham in the new BMW 320 his father had bought for him. For $240 a month he had rented a one-bedroom apartment, 5-G, in Holly Hill Apartments on LaSalle Street, just a couple of blocks from the Duke campus. Each Saturday, he returned to Reidsville to work in his father's clinic and talk about his studies. His father soon was boasting to patients about how well his son was doing at Duke.

By that spring, Fritz was spending a lot of time in a gun shop in Hillsborough, a small colonial town west of Durham, where he came to know the owner, John Forrest. The two shared a love for guns and BMWs. At first, Forrest thought of Fritz as just another gun nut with money enough to indulge his hobby. Fritz bought many guns— shotguns, sporting rifles, handguns, and military weapons, particularly Belgian and German army rifles—

but he also brought many back to trade for others. "He never could make up his mind what he wanted," Forrest said.

Fritz had a fetish for knives, too, Forrest discovered, always wearing one supersharp knife sheathed on his lower leg, another under his clothing on his back. Forrest had had some training in explosives in the navy, although he was by no means an expert, as well as some experience with fireworks, and when Fritz learned that he peppered Forrest with questions about how to make and use different charges.

"What he thought I knew and what I knew were two different things," Forrest later recalled. "I'd say, 'What you want that crap for anyway, Fritz?' He had a real fixation on that kind of stuff."

As Forrest got to know him better, Fritz began to confide in him. "He said he had a real unhappy childhood," Forrest remembered. "Kids treated him as if he were different. People made fun of his dad, and other doctors ostracized his father. He went on and on about his dad. He had his dad up on a pedestal, no doubt about that."

Forrest had a garage behind his house where several nights a week he and two fellow gun and car fanciers, Bruce Robinson and Sam Phillips, both mechanics, worked on BMWs, and soon Fritz began hanging out at the garage with them. Often he wore a white doctor's coat with a Duke emblem on it and a stethoscope in his pocket. If anybody knicked a finger or had a cold, headache, or any other ailment, Fritz would fetch a doctor's satchel from his car and offer treatment. He passed out vitamins freely and touted them as the preventive for all ills.

Fritz first told John Forrest that he was a medical student at Duke, but later led the group to believe that he had received his M.D. and now was engaged in research. All three wondered how a doctor involved in such important work could afford to spend so much time hanging around a garage, but they realized that he had a deep need of companionship and they accepted his company, even though they sometimes wondered if he'd ever leave. If they stayed until one or two o'clock in the morning, so, usually, would he, and only when they began making motions to leave would he say, "Well, I'd better go make the rounds at the hospital" or "I need to go check on the dogs at the lab."

"He had no friends," Sam Phillips said, although he didn't realize that until later. "We were his sole support group."

When Fritz was not talking about guns, explosives, the benefits of vitamins, or his work at the hospital, his conversation centered on only two other subjects: his father and the coming holocaust. He talked about both incessantly, and with both, his three new friends realized, he was obsessed.

"He believed something catastrophic would happen in the not-too-distant future," said Sam Phillips, who, with the others, agreed it was possible and enjoyed talking about it.

Nearly every fluctuation in the news brought new certainty to Fritz's fears that the end of civilization was at hand. A Mideast war would shut off oil supplies. A truckers' strike would initiate a run on supermarkets. Communist-fomented internal strife would bring down the government. A financial crisis would destroy the world economy. Starving hordes would pour across the Mexican border. The Russians would launch a surprise attack. Everybody would have to fend for himself and fight for his existence, Fritz said, and he intended to be ready. He and his father stockpiled food, medical supplies, survival gear, and plenty of guns and ammunition at his Reidsville home, he said—and he had gold hidden away, too. When the big fall came, he would retreat to his daddy's farm and take his friends with him, and anybody would pay hell getting them out of there.

"He was always in this fantasy world about how when the shit hit the fan, we'd all hole up," John Forrest recalled. "He was really into that crap. He really believed it."

While Fritz was working with his father in 1976, he met and began dating a young woman who came to the clinic with her mother, a regular patient. Her name was Ruth Dupree, and she was a student at Meredith College in Raleigh, just twenty miles from Durham. They dated regularly after Fritz moved to Durham, and in 1977 they became engaged. A Christmas wedding was announced. Invitations already had been sent when Fritz told Ruth that he wouldn't be able to go through with the marriage; his father had diagnosed him as having cancer. The wedding was canceled.

Within a year, Fritz revealed that his cancer had been cured by his father's vitamin treatments, and the wedding was rescheduled for Christmas of 1978. It took place on December 23, at Our Lady of Grace Catholic Church, an imposing granite structure in Greensboro. Ruth later confided to friends that, on their wedding night, Fritz left her alone for several hours, saying that he had to make hospital checks.

The newlyweds moved into a two-bedroom apartment on Maiden Lane in Reidsville, only a short distance from the Klenner home. Ruth became a teacher in the Reidsville city schools. Fritz continued his routine of working in his father's clinic on weekends—patients sometimes were still there at midnight on Friday—leaving every Monday morning for Durham, where he remained until Friday.

His father had begun boasting more and more of Fritz's accomplishments at Duke. Fritz was in his third year now, an honor student, his father told patients. Eminent doctors thought highly of him. He was involved in important blood research, as well as other projects. Dr. Klenner even took blood samples from patients for Fritz to analyze.

At one point in 1979, Fritz became ill and told of a hush-hush research accident that had infected him and several doctors with a rare form of hepatitis. The doctors died, Fritz later told acquaintances, but his father saved him with vitamins.

Fritz told several stories of this type. One involved radioactive materials that killed two researchers, while Fritz was shielded from harm by vitamins. Another was about the first known incident of airborne viruses infecting researchers with a rare cancer. Fritz was the only member of the team who didn't contract the disease, and vitamins got the credit.

In the fall of 1979, Cynthia Phillips came home from a PTA meeting to find a stranger in the wingback chair in her living room. He rose when she came in, and her husband, Sam, introduced his friend Dr. Fritz Klenner. Cynthia had heard her husband speak of this friend he'd met at John Forrest's house, but she'd never met him. She was slightly embarrassed that her husband would bring a doctor to their modest house, but she was immediately impressed with Fritz's friendliness and sincerity.

He seemed almost too young to be a doctor, clearly younger by several years than she, a little reserved, almost shy. She thought him cute, though, with a certain rakish air about him, accentuated by his Australian bush hat on a nearby chair. He intrigued her. She was flattered that he immediately included her in the conversation. When she spoke, he paid rapt attention, his dark eyes transfixed on hers.

Soon Fritz was coming to the Phillips house at least one night a week, sometimes more frequently. Cynthia looked forward to his visits. She found him an entertaining conversationalist with a wide range of interests. His friendship was an exciting interlude in an otherwise ordinary life. The Phillips' two young sons also liked Fritz and enjoyed his visits. He talked with them about guns, camping, Indians, and karate.

Fritz sometimes stayed so late that Sam, who had to be at work early, often excused himself and went to bed, leaving Cynthia to talk with him. She discovered that Fritz would stay as long as she allowed, and frequently it was one or two o'clock in the morning before she'd tell him that she'd better be getting to bed.

Fritz talked about postgraduate studies at Duke and research projects, but he talked much more about his father and his father's work. He loved to talk about the Mountain, the farm where he and his father went to shoot, blast for caves, and hunt monsters. He was fascinated by religion and would talk about it for hours. After he and Cynthia became closer, he talked at length about his childhood and his loneliness.

"I never had any really good friends until Sam and you," he confided one night.

Gradually, Cynthia learned some of Fritz's eccentricities. Although he seemed to be in marvelous shape, he was terribly insecure about his lean, muscled body and was always buying and using gimmicky exercise equipment. A childhood disease, he said, had left him with atrophied muscles in his side and back. At times, he wore ankle weights. He frequently carried squeeze devices to build the muscles in his hands and arms. He was addicted to Tab, a diet soft drink, yet he constantly gobbled high-calorie packaged pastries—pecan twirls, fudge brownies, and Little Debbie delights. He was fanatic about germs and was quick to combat them with spray cans of disinfectants and bottles of antiseptics. And although he loved dogs and talked regularly about his big German shepherd, Dorner, who was, he said, wildly protective of him and his father, he was afraid of cats. One night, when the Phillips' cat jumped onto the back of the couch behind him, Fritz yelped and leaped up into a karate stance.

He had a fetish about jewelry. He loved to fondle it and see it glitter, and he was constantly buying and trading it. If the $8,000 gold presidential Rolex on his wrist went unnoticed, he somehow managed to draw attention to it. Once he showed Cynthia a heavy gold necklace, thick with diamonds, that was so beautiful it nearly took her breath away. He said it was his mother's, but it was the kind of thing, Cynthia thought, that only a queen or a movie star might wear. She couldn't imagine how much it cost.

To Cynthia, these were but mild eccentricities, and she found herself utterly charmed by Fritz. In June of 1980, after she had finished her school year, he came by one day while Sam was at work and invited her to a nearby park. He stopped in an out-of-the-way spot to talk. Soon, he drew her to him and kissed her. "I love you," he said, and she found herself yielding to his embrace and his affection.

"He just got you so wrapped up," she recalled years later, trying to explain her actions. "He was your protector, your confidant, your best friend. He just consumed you. He was really sweet and always so delighted to see you. He made you feel that everything you said was interesting and you were the most important person in the world."

Soon after his profession of love, Fritz and his wife left on a long-planned trip to the West that was to take several weeks. For the trip, Fritz had bought a new Chevrolet Blazer, a bulky, four-wheel-drive vehicle designed for rugged terrain. While he was gone, Cynthia found herself thinking about him almost constantly.

Several times during the trip, Fritz called to say that he was thinking of her, too, his love unchanged. Then he called from Utah to let her know that the trip was being cut short. Fritz had stopped on a roadside to take in a vista, leaving Ruth in the Blazer. While he was across the road, a car careened into the Blazer, demolishing it and injuring Ruth. Others were also hurt, including one man who died, despite Fritz's self-described heroic efforts to save him. Ruth was not seriously injured, and as soon as she was released from the hospital, she and Fritz returned home. Fritz hurried to Cynthia to tell her how much he had missed her and how the trip had made him realize the depth of his feeling for her. More than ever he knew that he belonged with her and not with Ruth. His wife didn't care for him, he said, and he told sordid tales about her that only later Cynthia learned to be lies. He was trying to get his marriage annulled, he said, and he was so sincere that Cynthia believed him.

Cynthia began stopping by to see Fritz at his apartment. At first, she couldn't believe the place. It was almost cavelike, dark and cluttered. Quilts and blankets hung over the draped windows, preventing light from entering or escaping. Votive candles were everywhere, and Fritz burned them whenever he was home. An old enamel table in the dining room was covered with vitamins, medicine bottles, and vials of blood. An antique desk was buried under stacks of medical books and papers. Military gear and camping equipment occupied the sofa, leaving no place to sit. The footstool, made from a camel saddle, another oddity his father had picked up, offered no room for feet. The bedroom, at the end of a short hall, didn't escape the clutter either. An old chest, a lamp table, an ancient pedal sewing machine, all suffered equal burdens. Under the bulky, four-poster, antique mahogany bed were stacks of mercenary magazines filled with pictures of grotesque dead bodies and articles about exotic weapons and killing techniques.

Cynthia had known for some time that her marriage

was in the doldrums, but now, with Fritz in her life, she began to question whether it was worth saving. By the end of October, she wanted to get away alone and think. A girl friend invited her to visit in the mountains, and when her husband told her that she couldn't go, she considered that the final blow to their relationship and told him that she wanted out. He packed his clothes and left home, renting an apartment in a complex on the same street as Fritz's apartment and not far away.

Fritz was supportive. "Everything's going to work out," he assured her. "This is the way it's meant to be."

It was just a matter of time now, he told her, until they could be together permanently, man and wife.

"I can't wait for Daddy to meet you," Fritz said. "He's going to love you. We're going to have so much fun as a family."

Sam Phillips knew nothing of his wife's affair with his friend, and he and Fritz continued seeing one another regularly at John Forrest's garage. Fritz pretended concern to Sam about the breakup, and offered to help work out the problems. For several months, he told Sam of his attempts to get Cynthia to reconcile their differences.

Cynthia, meanwhile, was completely happy with Fritz's love and attention. "I guess I was mesmerized," she observed later. Friends told her that she'd never looked better or seemed happier. One day Fritz took her to see the Mountain, the rugged farm about which he had talked so much. He pointed out the hillside spot where someday they would build their love nest, a stone house, their own fortress against the world. His daddy would come to see them regularly, he said, and they would plant trees together.

"The next time you come up here," he told her with a broad smile as they were leaving, "you're going to be pregnant with my baby."

On another occasion, Fritz took Cynthia and her sons on an outing to Raven Rock State Park on the Cape Fear River near Lillington. Cynthia was especially pleased at how Fritz lavished attention on her sons. He always made time for them and talked with them about their interests. He brought them presents and took them places. "They were crazy about him," she said. At Raven Rock

Park, he guided them on the hiking trails, pointing out different plants and wildflowers, talking about all the flora his father could identify on sight. He clambered alone onto the huge rocks overlooking the river, and when he reached the peak of the highest one, he stood looking down at the water and let out a bloodcurdling Indian yell that startled Cynthia and her sons. It was so intense and primitive, Cynthia knew, that for a moment Fritz had become an Indian of yore, master of the wilderness. It was almost comical, and she wanted to laugh, but she checked herself.

"You didn't laugh at Fritz," she explained later. "I don't think you would ever be safe laughing at Fritz."

The seriousness of Fritz's demeanor was prominently manifested in his religious beliefs, and his Catholicism, Cynthia realized, was deeply entwined with mysticism. He carried protective prayers that he had gotten from his father. He believed them to be so powerful that by praying them he could have whatever he wanted.

When Cynthia expressed guilt about her relationship with him, he invited her into the dark cave of his apartment, and with votive candles flickering, he told her to kneel before him and began a ceremony of affirmation. He held her hands, looked deeply into her eyes, recited prayers, and asked her to repeat vows of love and dedication. She was embarrassed, but she went through the ritual to please him and made no mention that she thought it weird. When it was over, Fritz told her that now they were married in the eyes of God and that was all that mattered.

"It was as if he thought, 'I've got this special relationship with God and I don't have to follow the rules everybody else does,' " she recalled later.

Despite his vows of love, his talk of marriage and of having a son of his own, as the spring of 1981 approached, Cynthia not only sensed that Fritz was drawing away from her, she realized that he had a wall around him that she had never been able to penetrate. What she did not know was that he was involving himself in the lives of other women.

*   *   *

One was Betty James, a victim of multiple sclerosis. Her doctor had told her that little could be done for her condition, but then she heard about Dr. Klenner and his miracle vitamins. She lived out of state, and in the beginning she was making as many as three twelve-hour round-trips a week to Reidsville to get injections. She met Fritz soon after she began coming to the clinic, and she could tell immediately that he was interested in her. He seemed to single her out for special attention, and she considered him to be nearly as wonderful as his father, whom she thought to be the kindest and greatest man she'd ever encountered.

"He was extremely gentle," she later said of Fritz, "and his hands were so soft they were like a baby's hands."

Like all of Dr. Klenner's patients, she knew that Fritz was completing his medical training at Duke and soon would be joining his father in practice. He told her he had been a Green Beret in Vietnam, and he liked to tell gory details of accident victims on whom he'd worked in the emergency room at Duke Hospital. She knew, too, as all the patients knew, that Fritz was married, but when he asked her out, she said yes. He began calling her regularly, and she went out with him as often as possible when she came for treatment. He made her feel important and desirable, and his marriage, he told her, was fast coming to an end. Ruth was too resentful about his many hours at the hospital, he said. And she was jealous of the time he spent with his father.

"I just can't handle a woman being jealous of my father," he told her.

At about the time Fritz began entertaining Betty James, his friend Ned White began wondering about Fritz's relationship with his wife. Ned and Wanda White were the parents of a small child who had been stricken with a rare disease that had caused doctors at major hospitals to give up hope. The Whites read of the miracles Dr. Klenner was claiming with vitamins and turned to him in desperation. Dr. Klenner began massive doses of vitamin C, which the Whites were certain had saved their child's life. But despite all of Dr. Klenner's reassurances that he would make the disabled child whole again, there had been but slight improvement. For years, one or the other of the Whites had brought the child to the clinic every day for injections of various vitamins. They spent thousands of hours with the Klenners and became not only intimately close with them but emotionally dependent as well. Dr. Klenner, who never charged them, had become almost obsessed with the case and had made the child's restoration a personal crusade.

Gradually, Ned White realized that his child's situation was hopeless. He began to think that his family's dependence on the Klenners was insane, that it was depriving them of a normal family life. He wanted to wean his family from false hope. But his wife refused to give up, refused to break from the Klenners, and as they argued about it, an already strained marriage began to disintegrate. As their situation worsened, Ned noticed that Fritz seemed to be getting closer and closer to Wanda, who was several years older than Fritz.

At one point, Ned had thought himself Fritz's only real friend. They had spent hours talking about everything from Armageddon to medicine, had even discussed becoming business partners. Fritz had proposed that Ned build a new clinic to lease to him and his father after he got his medical license and joined the practice.

Ned, an intelligent and well-educated man, enjoyed listening to Fritz's stories about his studies and work at medical school. "He told me some of the damnedest things that happened at Duke," Ned recalled. "He would create these incredibly detailed scenarios about things that happened in the emergency room or the lab. The stories were very, very medical, so complex, and he was so thorough in the way he would tell them."

The stories usually were filled with intrigue or disaster, and Fritz inevitably came through with narrow escapes or emerged the hero, but they were always convincing.

In the spring of 1981, Ned and Wanda White separated, and within days Ned started seeing Fritz's Blazer at his house on a regular basis.

People who knew Fritz thought that his behavior was becoming stranger and stranger that spring, the spring that should have seen him graduating from medical school. One day he came into John Forrest's gun shop in Hillsborough and displayed scratches on his arms and ribs. People were out to get his daddy, Fritz said. Somebody had taken a shot at his daddy in the night, and he had shoved him out of harm's way, getting himself creased by the bullet in the process.

"He was extremely paranoid always, but he was even more paranoid than ever," Forrest recalled.

Soon afterward, Fritz hinted to Forrest that he had killed a man. He was secretive about it and offered no motive. From what Fritz said, though, Forrest got the feeling that if somebody went digging on his daddy's farm, they might find a body.

Sam Phillips thought Fritz was beginning to fall apart emotionally. He talked more and more of the coming holocaust, and Sam realized it wasn't something that Fritz merely feared and wanted to be prepared for, it was something he wanted to happen. "He was really looking forward to and hoping for a collapse," he said. "He dreamed of setting up some sort of feudal society and he would be the kingpin."

Fritz was wearing his hatreds more and more on the surface, not only the ones for blacks and Communists, but also the ones for his mother's family, the Sharps, who, he said, had denigrated his father and never accepted him.

Sam discovered something else about Fritz. He was acquiring cyanide, making cyanide capsules and cyanide-tipped bullets, an unseemly activity, Sam thought, for a man who was a healer.

"He didn't have any value for life," Sam later recalled. "One day he told me, 'If things really get bad, you can always take something as worthless as human beings and make something valuable out of them—like fertilizer.'"

To Sam, that kind of thinking simply didn't jibe with being a doctor.

Earlier, Sam and his friends John Forrest and Bruce Robinson jokingly had come up with a nickname for Fritz. Behind his back, they called him Dr. Crazy. Now they were more convinced than ever that they had been right in dubbing him that.

ABOVE LEFT: Delores Lynch. At sixty-eight she remained a hovering presence in her children's lives. (Courtesy of *Greensboro News & Record*.) ABOVE RIGHT: Janie Lynch. At thirty-nine, she looked far younger. She was sweet and without her mother's guile. (Courtesy of *Greensboro News & Record*.) BELOW LEFT: Janie with her last boyfriend, Phil Pandolfi, fourteen years her junior, at the University of Louisville's dental school. BELOW RIGHT: Phil took Janie to the senior prom shortly before her graduation from dental school, only weeks before her death.

ABOVE: The house on Covered Bridge Road. Delores isolated her paranoia in fourteen rooms protected by iron bars and alarms. BELOW: The parking area beside the Lynch house has been marked for evidence by police. Delores's body lies by the garage door. The killer probably lurked behind the car nearest the house as Delores arrived home from church.

Lieutenant Dan Davidson of the Kentucky State Police. He had investigated so many grisly homicides that he couldn't remember them all, but the Lynch case became the biggest of his long career.

Detective Sherman Childers of the Kentucky State Police took one look at Delores's and Janie's bodies and said, "This was a hit. A pro took these people out."

Lennie Nobles of the Oldham County Police had been a detective for only five weeks when he was assigned to the Lynch murders, his first homicide.

ABOVE: Paw-Paw and Nanna's house in Winston-Salem, where the lesson of love was always present until brutal murder intervened. (Photo by Gerry Broome, courtesy of *Greensboro News & Record*.) BELOW: An ambulance bears Nanna's body away from her house. (Photo by Gerry Broome, courtesy of *Greensboro News & Record*.) OPPOSITE TOP LEFT: Rob Newsom knew something was wrong when his parents didn't return home as scheduled. OPPOSITE TOP RIGHT: Hattie Newsom. At eighty-four, Nanna still gardened, cooked chicken pie suppers for her church, and tended her big house. People who knew her could not imagine a more unlikely murder victim. (Courtesy of *Greensboro News & Record*.)

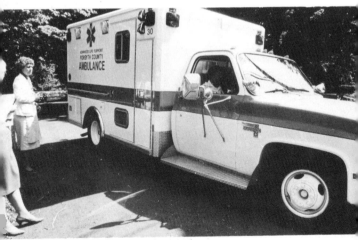

BELOW LEFT: Florence Newsom had retired from family teaching shortly before her death. Strain from family problems depressed her and seemed to turn her hair white overnight, but she was a woman of great will. Police thought she had struggled with her killer, who savaged her body. BELOW RIGHT: Robert Newsom, former tobacco company executive, civic leader, devoted son, was preparing to move into his mother's house to look after her. Friends were shocked that a man so gentle should die so violently. (Photo by Lorillard Co., courtesy of *Greensboro News & Record*.) RIGHT: Detective Sergeant Allen Gentry of the Forsyth County Sheriff's Department was drawn between two loves, fast cars and police work. He thought the Newsom murders were executions.

ABOVE: Annie Britt Sharp, standing behind sofa, with four of her children and three grandchildren. Standing with his mother is James Sharp, her youngest son. Seated, left to right, are Annie Hill Klenner, with her daughters, Mary Ann, on end of couch, and Gertrude, Judge Susie Sharp, and Florence Sharp Newsom at right. Susie Newsom, called Susie Q, sits between her mother and Judge Sharp. (Photo by Mrs. Bernadette W. Hoyle.) BELOW: At five, Susie Newsom reigned as Queen of the May, but her temper tantrums were so bad that her mother tried to deal with them by putting her under cold showers. (Photo by Coppedge.)

LEFT: Judge Susie Sharp, Su-Su, Susie Newsom's favorite aunt, for whom she was named, became the first woman elected chief justice of a state supreme court in America. *Time* magazine named her one of America's twelve most important women. (Photo by Dave Nicholson, courtesy of *Greensboro News & Record*.) BELOW: Susie posed for a photo layout of fraternity sweethearts at Wake Forest University, where she met Tom Lynch. INSERT: Yearbook photo of Susie as a graduate student at Wake Forest, while she waited for Tom to receive his degree.

ABOVE: Tom Lynch, number 21, on the Wake Forest basketball team. His best friend, Jerry Montgomery, number 11, was team captain. LEFT: Tom's yearbook photo at Wake Forest in 1969, when he was a junior.

ABOVE: Tom and Susie's wedding proceeded with great tension because of bickering between Susie and Delores. But both families posed amicably afterward. Left to right: Florence Newsom, Bob Newsom, Delores Lynch, Chuck Lynch, Susie, Tom, Susie's cousins, Nancy Dunn and Mary Ann Klenner Palmer, and Janie Lynch. BELOW LEFT: Susie with her Aunt Su-Su at her wedding. BELOW RIGHT: Susie poses with Tom's parents, Delores and Chuck. Later she would refuse to visit them.

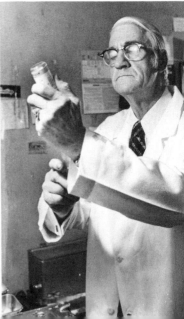

OPPOSITE TOP: Dr. Frederick R. Klenner and his wife, Annie Hill Sharp Klenner. Their marriage greatly disturbed the Sharp family. (Photo by Richard T. Davis, courtesy of *Greensboro News & Record*.) OPPOSITE BOTTOM RIGHT: Dr. Klenner was a pioneer of vitamin treatments, particularly vitamin C, his cure-all. He was internationally recognized for his work and considered a genius by some. Patients flocked to his run-down clinic in Reidsville, North Carolina, in hope of miraculous cures. (Photo by Dave Nicholson, courtesy of *Greensboro News & Record*.) OPPOSITE BOTTOM LEFT: Entrance to Dr. Klenner's clinic. (Photo by Dave Nicholson, courtesy of *Greensboro News & Record*.) RIGHT: Frederick R. Klenner, Jr., was called Fritz from childhood. His father sent him to a private academy in Atlanta to escape racial integration in his senior year of high school. (Courtesy of *Greensboro News & Record*.) BELOW: At Reidsville High School, where he was in the Library Club, Fritz, second from right in back row, was thought to be a nerd. He wore military attire to school, worshipped guns, and spoke favorably of the Ku Klux Klan and Adolf Hitler. His best friend, Randy Clark, peers over his shoulder.

Fritz's life was mapped out for him by his father, who dreamed that his son would take over his important work. Father and son worked together at the clinic while family members and patients were led to believe Fritz was a medical student at Duke University. (Courtesy of *Greensboro News & Record.*)

Fritz's worship for his father and his deep need to please him led to a secret life that grew more and more bizarre. (Photo by Richard T Davis, courtesy of *Greensboro News & Record.*)

ABOVE LEFT: Tom Lynch had to go to court to see his sons. At Christmas 1983, he and his new wife, Kathy, had a happy reunion with Jim, front, and John. ABOVE RIGHT: Delores rarely got to see her only grandchildren. She wasn't a typical grandmother. She was happy to see John and Jim, but she was happy when they left, too. They had visited her and her dogs in the big house on Covered Bridge Road in the summer of 1983. BELOW: On their summer visit in 1984, Tom took John and Jim to a ranch in Wagon Mound, New Mexico, where they rode horses and heard ghost tales around a campfire. BOTTOM: John, Jim, and Kathy on a visit to Delores in 1984.

ABOVE LEFT. In November 1984, Tom visited the boys in North Carolina, but the main purpose of his visit was to court Susie's family in the hope of winning support for more visitation. ABOVE RIGHT: Tom and Kathy took John and Jim to Disneyland in the spring of 1985. John cried and pleaded not to have to go back home to his mother. BELOW: The O. Henry shopping center in Greensboro, where Ian Perkins twice secretly taped conversations with Fritz, trying to trap him into an admission of murder. (Photo by John Page, courtesy of *Greensboro News & Record*.) BOTTOM: Rear view of Susie's apartment, second from right, top floor, being roped off by police after shoot-out with Fritz. (Photo by Joseph Rodriguez, courtesy of *Grensboro News & Record*.)

RIGHT: SBI agent Ed Hunt commanded the operation to trap and arrest Fritz. (Courtesy of *Greensboro News & Record*.) BELOW: Fritz's Blazer after the explosion. Lieutenant Dan Davidson took one look inside, saw what he feared he would see, and turned away. (Photo by Duane Hall, courtesy of *Greensboro News & Record*.) BOTTOM: Bomb-disposal truck pulling up to Susie's apartment after explosion. (Photo by Joseph Rodriguez, courtesy of *Greensboro News & Record*.)

BELOW: Ian Perkins, left, surrendering to authorities with his lawyer, Jim Medford. (Photo by Joseph Rodriguez, courtesy of *Greensboro News & Record*.) RIGHT: Site of final pursuit and explosion.

"We all realized how sick he was," Sam recalled.

Forrest began to get suspicious of Fritz's abilities as a doctor. Once Fritz had talked of a new cure for heartworms in dogs, and Forrest had allowed him to treat his dog, but the dog died. Later, Fritz offered to cut a wart off Forrest, and Forrest noticed that he was extremely nervous as he did it. Afterward, to ensure quick healing, Fritz gave Forrest a shot of vitamin C that almost sent him into shock. Forrest had hired a manager for his gun shop and later sold him the business. One day the man suffered a fatal heart attack while Fritz was alone in the store with him. Instead of trying to save the man's life, Fritz ran up the street to a dentist's office for help, and the dentist administered CPR.

"I decided this SOB ain't no doctor," Forrest recalled.

Cynthia Phillips was wondering what was happening to Fritz. He didn't call much anymore, and although he assured her that he loved her and wanted to see her, he said it without enthusiasm. He kept making excuses. He had to go to Reidsville. He had lab work to get done. He was sick. When she did see him, they never had fun anymore. He was not his usual self. He was clearly depressed, at times scared.

One time Cynthia went to see him when he was trying to come up with a disguise. He had connections in the FBI, he said, and he'd been warned that his life was in danger. (This was not the first time he'd spoken about his FBI connections. Once, early in their relationship, Cynthia mentioned that she had been to a couple of meetings of Students for a Democratic Society in college, and she wondered if the police had a record of it. Later, Fritz said that he had brought this up to a friend in the FBI, and his friend had checked and discovered that there was indeed a file on Cynthia's attendance at the radical meetings, but his friend had seen to it that the file was destroyed.) Fritz was secretive about these threats on his life, but at one point he showed Cynthia parts of an intimidating letter he said he'd received. She noticed that all of the words he commonly misspelled also were misspelled in the letter. She thought that he was beginning to come apart emotionally.

He couldn't make up his mind what he wanted from life, she knew, and he obviously was tormented about it. What he seemed to most want and need was to hide from the world with a little circle of dependent people around him that he could care for and defend. But she didn't want to hide from life, nor did she want that for her sons. Too often her times alone with Fritz became psychological torture tests, with Fritz talking for hours about his unhappiness, his doubts and insecurities, his illnesses, his fears, always seeking reassurances.

"I would come out of there so drained," Cynthia later recalled. "He would drain everything out of you. He relied on that kind of strength."

Fritz needed help, she realized, and she wanted to help him. The root of his problems, she thought, was his father. At one of those draining sessions, when Fritz complained that he was not what his father wanted him to be and couldn't be what his father expected, that he never could be the brilliant and gifted man his father was, Cynthia encouraged him to have a confrontation, tell his father that he had to be his own man, live his own life.

"What's he going to do, disown you?" she asked.

But even as she said it, she knew that finding the courage to stand up to his father was impossible for Fritz.

"I knew that was probably what he needed to save himself," she said later, "but he couldn't do it."

Late in that spring of crisis, in another of their draining sessions, Fritz presented an alternative to Cynthia. He asked her to join him in suicide.

"It can be easy," he said. "It can be painless. We can be together in Heaven."

She was stunned to disbelief.

"There's no way," she said coldly, and walked out.

"I'm certain that if I'd said, 'Yes, let's do it,' he'd have done it right then," she said later. "He would have taken that way. I think he was scared to do it by himself. He didn't want to be alone. He wanted somebody to be with him."

From that point, Cynthia knew that she couldn't help Fritz alone and that she had made a big mistake and would have to find some way out of the relationship.

One day not long afterward, her telephone rang. "This is Ruth Klenner," said the voice on the other end. "I think we need to talk."

A long pause followed as Cynthia tried to gain her composure.

"Yes," she replied. "I guess we do."

"Fritz had a gift," Sam Phillips said years later. "He could sit down and talk to you and in an hour's time he could feel you out and understand what your needs were, and he would come right at you from that angle."

"He had a very acute instinct for sensing a weakness and exploiting it," John Forrest said.

"Fritz would always have the appropriate emotions," Sam said. "His emotions would be perfect for what he would be telling you. I always had the gut feeling that he hated women, but to women he had some of the charismatic appeal that somebody like a Manson had. He was a chameleon. Whatever you wanted or needed, he could provide. He was the knight on the white horse who'd come charging up and save you."

All of that was in retrospect. That spring of 1981, when Sam discovered that his wife was in love with Fritz and that Fritz had been having an affair with her while pretending to help him resolve their problems, Fritz's psychological makeup was of little concern to him. At first, he intended to kill Fritz. "And I would have if he'd kept seeing my boys," he said later.

After Cynthia became almost deathly sick from a series of vitamin treatments that Fritz gave her, Sam became concerned that Fritz might bring harm to his sons with some of his treatments. Like his friend John Forrest, he, too, began to wonder about Fritz's credentials as a physician. John Forrest's wife worked at Duke, and he had her ask around the hospital what was known about Fritz.

Four years earlier, Sam Phillips had been treated at Duke Hospital for lymphatic cancer, which now was in remission. He'd heard Fritz mention his doctor's name on a few occasions. So he called his doctor and asked what he knew about Fritz. The doctor had never heard of him.

John Forrest's wife hadn't been able to find anybody who knew Fritz, either. Their suspicions now even more aroused, John and Sam checked the admissions office at Duke. Only one Frederick R. Klenner had ever been enrolled there, they discovered, and he had been graduated in 1936.

Fritz was a fraud. He'd been pulling a scam not only on them, they realized, but probably on his family, and perhaps even on himself.

"He lived in such a fantasy world that I'm convinced you could've put him on a lie detector machine and asked him if he was a doctor and he would have passed," Sam said. "He knew what was right and wrong and he knew what was moral, but I truly believe he did not know what was real and what wasn't."

Sam went to his house and seized several bottles of prescription medicines, syringes, and other medical paraphernalia Fritz had given his wife. His intention was to take it to the police and have Fritz arrested for practicing medicine without a license and illegally dispensing drugs. In turmoil, his wife did not want to believe what he was telling her about Fritz, and she would not until later. She pleaded with him not to go to the police and press charges, and out of concern that she might not let him see his sons if he did, Sam agreed that he wouldn't.

Sam still thought that something should be done to stop Fritz, and on May 1, he talked to to Mike Kelly, an agent for the State Bureau of Investigation who regularly brought his car for service to the garage where Sam worked. He told Kelly that Fritz was posing as a doctor and treating people, although he had never been to medical school; that Fritz was dispensing prescription drugs that he got from his father; that he was paranoid and carried lots of weapons. He didn't want to press charges, he said, but he hoped that the SBI would start its own investigation, and he offered to turn over the bagful of medicines he'd taken from his house.

Intent on ending Fritz's masquerade, Sam also called Reidsville and told Annie Hill Klenner that not only was Fritz involved with his wife but he had never been enrolled at Duke.

"I got nowhere with his mother," Sam said later. "She was noncommittal. She told me I'd better be aware of what I was saying, that they would put an attorney on me. Later, I found out from Ruth that he had told his mother I might be calling, that I was a patient of his and had a brain tumor and was psychotic. 'If he calls, don't pay any attention to him,' he told her."

Mindful of all the weapons Fritz carried in his Blazer, and of the bumper sticker on the back that said DON'T GET MAD, GET EVEN, Sam took precautions. He started wearing a bullet-proof vest wherever he went, and every time he returned to his car, he checked it for explosives.

Cynthia Phillips met Ruth Klenner at a Pizza Hut near Fritz's apartment. Despite initial tension, their meeting was amiable. Each felt empathy for the other as they discovered how much they had in common. As they talked over a long lunch, comparing stories, learning the truth behind Fritz's many lies, they were dumbfounded by the extent of his elaborate deceptions. His whole life, they realized, was a sham. He was cunningly sick, and they were his victims. They parted with new perspectives and the knowledge that they would have to free themselves.

Soon after that painful meeting, Cynthia went to see an elderly priest in Durham. She carried with her the folded pages of exotic prayers to archangels she had taken from Fritz's pocket.

"A person I know seems really obsessed with these," she said, "and I'd like to know what they are."

After glancing over them, the priest seemed reluctant to talk.

"Do you know what magic is?" he finally asked.

"Yes."

"Then you know there's good magic and black magic, right?"

He went on to explain that these were ancient religious writings that had been spurned because of their magical thrust, black magic cloaked as white.

"Whoever is dealing with this, you don't want to know," he said, "because they are dealing with evil. This is the work of the devil."

Ruth left Fritz at the end of May, taking the BMW with her. She moved into the same apartment complex in Durham in which Sam Phillips lived, and she became friends with Sam and Cynthia, all bound by their bizarre experiences with Fritz. All were angry at Fritz, but they agreed that he was sick and needed help. Ruth and Sam talked of trying to have him committed to a mental institution, and later discussed it with a lawyer, only to learn that it was virtually impossible.

Cynthia and Ruth decided that the only way to end Fritz's subterfuges and get him to seek help was to go to the source of the problem—his father. They called the Klenner home several times, only to have Fritz answer and thwart them. When Dr. Klenner finally answered one of their attempts, they poured out their story: Fritz never had been to medical school; he had affairs, lived a life of dangerous fantasy and lies; he was sick; he might hurt himself or somebody else; he desperately needed help.

The response wasn't what they expected. "It isn't your problem," Dr. Klenner told them coldly. "You shouldn't concern yourselves with it."

As both women sought to persuade him to do something, they heard Fritz burst into the room shouting. They listened in disbelief while Fritz wrested the phone from his father, screaming at him, "I'll blow your god-damned head off!"

Suddenly, Fritz came on the line, cursing, crying, threatening. He had a .45 in his hand, he said, and he was going to kill himself.

"Go ahead, Fritz," Ruth taunted. "You don't have the courage."

From an extension phone, Cynthia pleaded for him to see a psychiatrist. He stopped her with one command, the last words he would ever speak to her.

"Get . . . the . . . fuck . . . out . . . of . . . my . . . life."

But the voice wasn't Fritz's. It was guttural, cold and alien, a voice unlike any Cynthia had ever heard, and minutes after she'd hung up the phone she still shivered from its effect, convinced that she had heard the very voice of evil.

27

Only bits of information about the troubling incident at the Klenner house filtered down to the Sharp family that summer. Fritz had blown a fuse, word had it, suffered some kind of temporary breakdown. He had pushed his mother down the stairs, and, most unbelievable of all, threatened to kill his father. But as usual, the Klenner secretiveness prevailed, and few details were ever forthcoming. Sharp family members thought that stress brought on by the breakup of Fritz's marriage, about which they also knew little, probably provoked the trouble.

Soon after the incident, Fritz stopped to see John Forrest in Hillsborough, and Forrest quickly made it clear that he did not condone deception and wife stealing. Fritz was apologetic, sorry, he said, that it all had happened.

Forrest asked what Fritz planned to do now that his parents knew that he was a fraud and had wasted more than four years of his life, not to mention vast amounts of money his father had supplied for tuition and expenses. Fritz said that he wasn't sure.

"Our relationship is ended," Forrest told him, "but I won't ever do anything to hurt you."

"Well, John," Fritz replied, "you meant a lot to me and you never have to fear anything from me either."

Forrest couldn't help but notice that Fritz was wearing a Second Chance bullet-proof vest, and he passed the information on to Sam Phillips, who still was wearing his vest, too, in case Fritz was not quite so humbled as he appeared.

Ruth talked to Fritz several times that summer of 1981, and she later told friends that he sounded contrite. He said he was glad that everything was finally out in the open, happy that he no longer had to pretend. He still talked of medical school, but Duke's wasn't the only one in the world, he said. He might just go to one overseas.

Instead, he enrolled that fall at Durham Technical Institute in a two-year dental laboratory course, keeping it secret from everybody but immediate family. It was a demeaning step down for someone who had so long thought of himself as a doctor, and his heart wasn't in it. Although he would attend the full two years, his presence would hardly be remembered by teachers and classmates, and he would complete only 60 percent of the required work and never receive a degree.

The front of contrition that Fritz presented to his wife and John Forrest turned out to be merely another pose. The elaborate structure of pretense that he had built to prop up his life proved formidable and enduring. Neither he nor his parents could face the humiliation of disassembling it, and with his parents' knowledge and complicity, Fritz continued his masquerade. He still worked at his father's clinic; still led patients, friends, and family—including his cousin Susie Lynch, who came regularly for treatment—to believe that he was continuing at Duke Medical School, now involved in postgraduate studies and research, and that he eventually would take over his father's clinic. To strangers and casual acquaintances he presented himself as Dr. Klenner, still tramped about publicly in a physician's coat with a stethoscope in the pocket, still carried a medical satchel loaded with vitamins and prescription drugs, which he dispensed as freely as ever. So long had he lived in fantasy that fantasy now seemed his only reality, and, feeding on itself, it grew.

Fritz continued seeing Betty James sporadically, but he spent more and more time with Wanda White and her sons, and all the time he was getting closer to his cousin Susie and her two sons, John and Jim. By the fall of 1982, however, just as Susie's mother, Florence, began to

Jerry Bledsoe

grow concerned about her daughter's relationship with
her cousin, Fritz was about to enter another love affair.

Amanda Jones met Fritz soon after moving to Durham in
1979, and friendship soon developed. They became much
closer after Fritz confided that he had incurable cancer,
and her maternal sympathies reached out to him. He
presented himself as a Duke medical student, but led her
to believe that he was involved in clandestine work for
the army's antiterrorist Delta Force, work he'd been
drawn into while serving as an intelligence officer for
Special Forces in Vietnam. Although secretive about his
work, he frequently spoke of political and military stirrings in exotic parts of the world, about which Amanda
had little concern. She thought of Fritz as an "inside-
track man."

"He always knew people who knew the real situation,
no matter what it was," she recalled.

In the summer of 1980, when she gave birth to a
daughter, Ann, her only child, Fritz quit seeing her without explanation, and she feared for what might have
happened to him. Not until the spring of 1981 did he
suddenly reappear, relieving her anxieties but offering
only vague excuses for his absence. Their friendship grew
closer early in 1982, when Amanda's marriage began to
fall apart. By then Fritz had grown a full beard, giving
him a dark, brooding, and more mature appearance, and
he seemed always to be there to comfort and reassure
her. After she separated from her husband, she began to
feel other stirrings for Fritz, whose cancer, he now assured her, had been cured by his father. By 1983, she was
in love with him. That summer, her parents, who dis-
trusted Fritz and wanted to protect their daughter from
another disastrous relationship, checked at Duke and
discovered that Fritz had never been enrolled there. Presented with the evidence, Amanda chose not to accept it
and not to confront Fritz about it, reasoning that even if
he hadn't been to Duke he needed the medical identity
as cover for his clandestine work.

"It didn't make any difference to me," she later recalled. "I needed to have a relationship with somebody."

Amanda kept a diary, and in it she recorded her love affair with Fritz.

November 10, 1982: I am constantly emotionally anticipating that perhaps Fritz and I will develop an affair. We've been thru so much together in these years—his divorce as well as mine, Ann's birth and his cancer and at one time seeming sure death. I long for a deeper relationship, but I am not sure of its consequences. We may not have as much in common as we think.

February 2, 1983: And my relationship with Fritz continues to grow. I always look forward to touching but we're both slow.

February 16: I had a chat with Fritz today and my head still reels. I know now that he is seven years younger than I am, a Catholic of some breeding and I am twice divorced. It seems a ridiculous match. I do seem to attract curious people. He is a survivalist, which I can understand and certainly have leanings toward, but where I'm for retreat he is for action. Too much Vietnam. And religion. He's ready to defend his fellow man and has reason to believe that necessity will come about in the imminent future. If you believe that, then it's hard to see any reason to work for today. I mean if all life is to be dismantled, does it really matter if I get a shelf put up in my closet?

February 23: I had a long visit with Fritz last night. Whether he's clairvoyant or a crazy remains to be seen. But he definitely foresees nuclear war and he plans to be a survivor. Romance of romance, he has invited Ann and I to go along and despite all I agreed. So there is his cousin Susie and her two boys, his sister Mary Ann and her daughter Lynn, and Ann and I so far that I know of in the party. The tea leaves or whatever he reads say between now and the spring thaws in Europe are the times to worry the most. And naturally it is with great reasonableness and justification that he reads these messages. And I try to roll along in my normal pattern wondering once again if there will be a tomorrow. But, too, there still is romance, and I must admit Fritz has charmed me.

April 6: Last night I actually went out for supper with Fritz. Not very prepossessing but I did enjoy it. Fritz has bought property in Idaho and wanted to know if Ann and I would move out there. "In theory" anyway. At least he's beginning to dream of something other than disaster.

May 25: I had a funny dream about Fritz. I went to visit him at his place and he fell asleep—probably not too unrealistic. That's what worries me about Fritz. He doesn't see much joy in life.

June 28: Fritz came in last night. It's been a month since I'd seen him. He brought me another towering pile of flowers with a lily kind of thing on top. It's charming to have a fellow bring you flowers. He also brought me a pair of jade earrings. He says he's going to remount the jade into gold pierced earrings, that these aren't gold but had better jade. Anyway, it's nice to have him back in the country.

July 8: He brought me more flowers and has some pearls for Ann and I that he'll bring later. I've never encountered such a gift giver and am somewhat per- plexed how to handle it. He seems to have a very thick shell that I find hard to pierce. His defense is innate. I almost look forward to making love to him just to remove the physical layer of clothes. There are so many more layers remaining. I can't imagine really seeing in. Meanwhile, he is gentle, kind and thoughtful.

July 18: So I did see Fritz again and then he's off for a couple of days. But I did tell him I loved him. It was smooth and easy for us both. Not a shocking revelation, but perhaps a letting down of barriers.

August 5: I haven't heard from Fritz in over a week. That situation always chafes me. I'm so much a waiter.

It's just like all my affairs with married men—I'll hear from him. Except he's not married. I keep hoping our communications will improve. Right now I don't know if he's in Chad or Reidsville. He's got so many roles I wonder if he keeps them straight.

August 10: I'm sure Fritz is off in North Africa. I think there is a lot going on in Chad and Libya that we are concerned about. I'm pretty sure I would have heard from Fritz if he'd been in the U.S. I do miss having him to talk to tho he's never really been that available.

August 19: Fritz came by last night. Again momentarily and back off to Chad and the unknowns. But I am cheered.

September 17: And always I am waiting for Fritz. He called me Friday before I left work. His "I miss you and I love you" were enough to keep me warm again.

September 20: I haven't often been as depressed, mad and disappointed. It's Fritz. He called Fri. night that it would be the first of the week that he'd see me. It's Tuesday night and no word. He could be in N. Africa or Reidsville for all I know. He has promised time and time again to do things for me, yet he's never come thru. He never has time for me or him. I feel like I've reached the end.

October 25: Fritz has still not appeared. The world is currently rocking and close to war on all fronts. 200 or so Americans were killed in Lebanon on Sunday. Few of the relatives have been notified and so few names released. The only thing that gives me cheer is that Fritz said someone would come to Ann and I and give us some money were anything to happen to him. So no news is good news. I just pray he returns before the world explodes. It really seems imminent.

The image that dances into my head is what a complex, intelligent and sensitive soul the Lord has created in Fritz, and the reduction of that to a mass of blood and tissue would not be sensible. The Lord must have more in mind for him than that and I need to keep that faith.

December 18: Speaking of Fritz, still no word. Either he's lost in the jungles of S.E. Asia looking for POWs, or he's in a loony bin. I really can't decide what's up. The strange thing is not feeling at liberty to call his dad.

December 20: I called Fritz's mom today. I broke all the barriers. What the hell. Is he alive, dead or in a loony bin? The former or the latter I guess. I still can't be sure. She said they saw him last Sunday, that he is working hard but ok. Did he owe me any money?

January 1, 1984: I didn't mention that Fritz called. Sometime maybe Christmas Eve, or the Monday after. Wished us all a merry Christmas and said he'd see us in the first of the year. I was not overly friendly and tried to express some of my indignation. Oh well. I have that relationship still on Freez-dry. We'll see what comes.

Amanda never heard from Fritz again. Not until more than a year and a half later would she discover that all the time she had spent longing and waiting for Fritz, while she thought him off surreptitiously fighting for his country in North Africa and Southeast Asia, he was right in North Carolina, much of the time in Durham, plodding through mundane dental lab classes while living a fantasy life that was growing ever richer and more adventurous. Nor would she know until then that all that time she had been but one of several women in Fritz's crowded life, and that by the time she last heard from him, he had focused his attentions on only one, his cousin Susie—the cousin he had planned to include in his little survival brood with her and his sister and their children.

28

January of 1983 brought the long-brewing final confrontation between Susie and her mother. It came after a neighbor told Florence that Fritz had been spending weekend nights at the Newsom house while Bob and Florence were in Winston-Salem at Nanna's. Florence could not tolerate that. No matter what was happening in the house when she and Bob were not there, the appearance was scandalous and it had to cease.

"Propriety was so important to them," Bob's sister Frances later explained. "How one appears to other people is as important as what one really does."

For several months, the spats between Susie and Florence had been growing in frequency and intensity. Florence confided to her sister Louise that she feared Susie was becoming mentally ill. It worried her that Susie was so consumed by her bitterness toward Tom and her protectiveness of her children, that she was becoming so dependent on Fritz and wouldn't talk about her problems.

"Susie Q didn't confide in Florence," Louise said. "She was very difficult and she got more difficult as time went on. Florence was so good to Susie. She never deserved the treatment she got from her."

The family whispered that Susie had undergone a personality change and that its roots lay in Albuquerque.

"Nobody knows what went on in Albuquerque," Florence said.

Annette Hunt, whose corner house on Fairgreen Drive was separated from the Newsom house by an intersecting street, Redwine Drive, saw the confrontation building and tried to keep clear of it. She was Susie's best friend, but she also loved Bob and Florence and didn't want to take sides. Other neighbors found themselves in the same situation. The Newsoms were gracious hosts, and their big house was a neighborhood gathering spot. In warm weather, neighbors gravitated to their spacious back porch to chat, sip cool drinks, and admire the roses Bob tended so lovingly. All of them were aware of the tension between Susie and her mother, and none wanted to get involved.

Annette had watched the relationship build between Susie and Fritz. At first, it seemed centered on Susie's boys. Annette felt sorry for John and Jim. She knew that they needed male attention, John particularly. Fritz doted on the boys, played with them, took them places, did things a father would do, and Susie was plainly grateful.

Susie told Annette that Fritz longed to have sons of his own but couldn't. He'd had leukemia while she and Tom were living in Kentucky, she said, and although his father cured him, the treatments left him sterile. "I guess that's why I care so much for John and Jim," she said Fritz told her.

Annette knew the power Fritz held over children, because he had become close to her own sons, talking to them about camping, hunting, guns, and the arts of the Ninja, the secret hooded assassins of ancient Japan. She knew how much John and Jim looked forward to his visits.

"They adored Fritz," she said. "The children really looked up to him."

Although Susie didn't talk much about Fritz, as time passed Annette realized that not only had Susie, too, come to have deep feelings for him, she seemed dependent on him.

"He wanted her to need him," Annette said. "He wanted her to feel dependent on him."

He wanted her to believe his fantasies, too, Annette later was certain, and he went to extraordinary measures to convince her they were true. Once, Susie had become excited when Fritz invited her to attend a medical school dinner at Duke, at which, he told her, he was to be honored for his scholarship and research. She bought a new dress, and for weeks she talked to Annette about the upcoming event. Famous doctors were to attend, and Susie, who always had been impressed by doctors, was to sit beside a noted medical school professor. She even read about him so she could converse knowledgeably. On the day of the dinner, she left her sons with her parents and drove off to meet Fritz at his apartment in Durham.

"Well, how did it go?" Annette asked when she saw Susie the next day.

"We didn't get to go," Susie said, crestfallen. "I got down there and Fritz was sick and throwing up. All I did was sit and hold his head while he threw up all night."

Although Annette could see Fritz's Blazer across the street when Bob and Florence went out of town, she didn't want to believe that Susie was having a physical relationship with her cousin. But she realized that Florence, who long had thought the growing closeness between Fritz and Susie improper, might now be facing that possibility and that she could not abide it.

Florence had even expressed concern about the relationship to her sister Annie Hill, Fritz's mother. But Annie Hill saw no harm in it. Fritz and Susie were just close friends, she said. Fritz was good with the boys, and Susie just felt better when he was around. They were comfort to one another in their troubles.

Florence was certain that the relationship was not so innocent. She suspected that Susie and Fritz were sleeping together and adding insult to injury by doing it in her house, and she knew she would have to confront Susie about it. She knew, too, that nobody said no to Susie without paying a price, and she was proceeding cautiously in bringing up the matter. But before she could do it, a minor incident provoked a blowup.

Florence fixed elaborate breakfasts on Saturday mornings. One Saturday at the end of January, Fritz showed up at breakfast and was invited to eat. During the meal, Susie mentioned that her cousin in Washington, Jim Taylor, had bought a chow.

"I think somebody would have to be stupid to get a chow," Bob observed.

It was an offhand remark, but it threw Susie into a rage.

"I don't have to take this kind of shit!" she said, slamming down her fork.

Susie stormed from the table and left the house, taking Fritz and the boys with her. She didn't return until Sunday night, when Florence confronted her, not only about her behavior but also about Fritz. A loud and bitter argument developed, and rumors later circulated through the family that Susie struck her mother, claiming that Florence's body language had been threatening. The conflict ended with Susie gathering up her children and her belongings and leaving her parents' home permanently.

The boys later mentioned little to their father about what happened that night, John saying only that they'd had to leave "because GG swore at Uncle Fritz."

Florence confided the events of that night to only one person, her sister Susie, who, at Florence's request, kept them secret even from other family members. "It was so terrible, and Florence was so humiliated and embarrassed by it, that she didn't want anybody ever to know," Judge Sharp explained.

After Susie left that night, Florence, distraught, called her son Rob and his wife, Alice, who were living in Illinois. Susie had gone, she said, but she didn't say why. She was worried that Susie didn't have enough money to take care of herself and the boys. If Susie called, Florence wanted to know about it.

Susie did call Rob and Alice a few days later. She said she'd moved out but wouldn't say where she was living. She left a phone number where she could be reached, however.

"She just said she had this big fight and she would never tell anybody what had been said, never," Alice recalled. "She said that her mother was just shrieking. I said, 'That doesn't sound like your mother.' "

Weeks passed before Bob and Florence even learned Susie's whereabouts. Florence was especially worried about the boys, whom she and Bob loved dearly. She told her sister Louise that John cried at leaving and she had taken him into the bathroom to console him.

"You know Grandpop and I don't want you to go," she told him. "This is your mother's idea."

A few weeks after the confrontation, Florence spotted

the boys outside an ice-cream parlor in Friendly Shopping Center and hurried to chat with them. Susie emerged from the store to snatch up the boys, screaming at her mother to keep away. Publicly humiliated, Florence fled home in tears.

Susie had long wanted to be out of her parents' house and on her own but simply couldn't afford it. Now she could. At least for a while. Shortly before Christmas, her divorce had become final.

In the settlement, Susie received $23,500—$14,000 for her equity in the house, $1,500 for the furniture she left behind, $5,300 for her share of Tom's dental practice, $2,000 in attorney fees, $500 for medical bills, and $200 for unpaid alimony. The $100 monthly alimony was dropped in the settlement, but the $400 support that Tom was paying for the boys was raised by $100 each month. Susie was to receive $8,000 in cash, which was provided by Tom's father, who would be dead in less than a year. Tom was to pay the remaining $15,500 at $200 a month, with 10 percent interest annually. He left in a bank account the $15,500 his mother had sent earlier and used the interest to help pay the additional $200 he sent Susie each month.

With the $8,000 as a cushion for survival, and $700 in monthly income, Susie rented for $475 a month, utilities included, a two-bedroom upstairs apartment at 28-L Hunt Club Road in Friendly Hills Apartments, a huge complex on Greensboro's western edge near Guilford College, less than two miles from her parents' house. Without telling family members about it, she had put a deposit on the apartment four days before the confrontation with her mother.

The family knew that a blowup had occurred and Susie had moved out, but they didn't know why.

"Bob and Florence just didn't talk about it," said Susie's cousin Nancy Dunn.

"They didn't tell us a whole lot about the trouble that was brewing," said Nancy's mother, Frances Miller, Bob's sister. "It was something they could not share. They did not discuss it with us. They were very moral and circumspect people. It was hurtful to them for people to know those things. Over and over I would be surprised at things I learned. All I knew, I got from Mother."

Bob and Florence even kept the details of the incident from Rob. "They were very mum about it," he said. "All I know is it must've been pretty bad, but they never discussed it with us."

At that time, Rob was creating his own worries for his parents. On the day after Florence called to tell Rob and Alice that Susie had left, Rob was fired from his oil company job.

Bookish, brilliant, and devout as a young man, Rob had won a William Neal Reynolds scholarship to Duke University, but he declined it to accept a National Merit Scholarship at the University of the South, an Episcopal college in the green hills of southeastern Tennessee near a small town called Sewanee. Sedate and proper, the University of the South was where aristocratic southerners sent their sons and daughters to ensure that their Republican and Episcopalian foundations remained firm. Professors wore academic gowns to class, and male students were expected to wear coats and ties and be gentlemen at all times.

"I was sort of impressed with its claim of being the Oxford of America," Rob said later in explaining why he chose Sewanee, as the university usually is called. "I was an arrogant little jerk at the time. I liked that elitist nonsense that went with it."

Rob went to Sewanee with the idea of becoming an Episcopal priest, but later decided against the ministry and turned his studies to philosophy. After his graduation, he enrolled in law school at the University of North Carolina in Chapel Hill. He was the only member of his class to be sworn to the bar before the North Carolina Supreme Court, a privilege arranged by his aunt Su-Su. It was a proud family moment, the tradition of law passing to a third generation of the Sharp family.

Rob became an assistant state attorney general in 1977, and two years later, he accepted a job with an oil company, Conoco, in Houston and moved to Texas with his young family, which by then included three children. By 1981, Rob had realized something that his parents didn't want to accept: he was an alcoholic. He had started drinking to win acceptance of his peers when he was fourteen—his "redneck training program," he called it. He picked up the pace when he got to Sewanee and entered the "southern gentleman training program." The combined programs had simply produced at age thirty-two a southern drunk who was having more and more difficulty dealing with life. He gave up alcohol and took a new job with Marathon Oil Company in Robinson, Illinois. But the after-effects of his drinking caused him to become, in his own description, "a basket case." The result was his dismissal. His parents encouraged him to come home, and only three weeks after Susie and her boys moved out of Bob and Florence's big house, Rob and his family arrived, soon to move in.

At a time when they should have been thinking of retiring and enjoying life in peace, Bob and Florence had only turmoil and tribulation. Those close to them knew that they were grieved and hurt, but they chose not to talk about it and tried not to show it. Although he was drinking more, Bob was more successful at keeping his disappointment hidden than was Florence. Family members worried that she might have a nervous breakdown. Her lifelong sense of humor departed. She grew depressed, lost weight. Her hair seemed to turn white overnight. She looked strained.

"She was brokenhearted, just completely brokenhearted," said a close friend.

"She felt defeated," said her sister Louise. "She felt like she was a failure as a parent."

In an attempt to escape her problems, Florence threw herself into work, taking on extra duties at the business college where she taught.

"She wrapped herself up in the job," said her sister-in-law Frances. "She stayed busy. She was a good teacher and she didn't do a sloppy job of it."

Nanna did not have to be told when somebody in her family was suffering. She knew it instinctively, and she reached out to comfort. She reached out to Bob and Florence, and, when she learned Susie's whereabouts, she reached out to her, too. Susie didn't want her comfort. When Nanna called and asked to come and see her, Susie made excuses. Nanna was deeply hurt.

Susie not only turned her back on her parents, she spurned her entire family except for the Klenners, whom she visited often. Defying family, she turned to Annie Hill, the only Sharp who had defied family. On one of Susie's trips to Reidsville to see the Klenners, Louise invited her to bring the boys to the big Sharp house for lunch. She wanted to try to get to the base of Susie's split with her family in the hope of bringing about a reconciliation.

"I tried to find out why," she said. "I couldn't get any satisfactory answers."

After he moved in with his parents, Rob went several times to call on his sister, occasionally taking his children to play with her boys, and although she was cordial, she made it clear that she didn't want to talk about Fritz or her parents and had no intention of making amends. After several months, Rob quit going to the apartment. Soon after moving there, as if in deliberate defiance of her parents, Susie bought a black chow puppy that she named Shiao Shiong, Chinese for "little bear." The boys called him Chowy. The dog grew huge and ferocious, and Rob didn't like being around him. "Chows give me the willies," he said.

Friends, too, felt Susie's withdrawal. Annette went to her apartment several times to visit. "I felt like she was ill at ease with my being there," she said later. "I think she didn't want me to realize how much she was seeing Fritz."

Susie even shut out her namesake, Su-Su, the aunt she loved and admired above all others, the one about whom she so frequently had boasted. Susie Sharp used the occasion of John's ninth birthday at the end of August to reestablish contact.

"I wondered what I'd done to be excommunicated," she said when she called her niece.

"I just thought you'd never want to see me again," Susie responded.

Su-Su invited her to come to Raleigh and bring the boys for a birthday celebration. She took them to a department store restaurant for cake and ice cream, then to Pullen Park for the afternoon.

"I couldn't get Susie to talk about anything I wanted to

talk about," she later recalled. "If anybody mentioned Fritz to her, she just immediately bristled and shut up."

What Susie wanted to talk about was Tom, how awful he was and how he was involved with the Mafia. The judge thought that her niece was sorely in need of help, but she didn't push her for fear of breaking the new contact. Still, at departure, she could not resist a stern admonition.

"Susie," she said, giving her a hard look that many a defendant had known to fear, "make peace with your mother."

"A lot of things will have to change before that happens," Susie said.

29

Spring of 1983 found Delores Lynch still stewing about the decision in Tom's hearing the summer before, and a few days before John and Jim were to fly to Albuquerque for their first spring visit, she called Tom's lawyer in Reidsville, Bill Horsley, to vent her unhappiness.

She was particularly upset about Tom's having to pay to fly Susie to Atlanta with the boys so that they wouldn't have to change planes alone.

"This is costing fifteen hundred dollars," she complained, "five hundred of which is to fly her back and forth from Greensboro to Atlanta to meet their plane twice. Now, she has a perfectly good broomstick she could use, as you and I well know.

"Really, Bill, there's something wrong with that girl. She's a strident, loud, abusive female. I don't know how Tom did it for ten years. I just really don't. My first remark was, 'Well, I'm surprised it lasted this long.'

"I don't think she gives a damn for those kids. All she wants to do is break Tom.

"It's harassment. It's a flagrant violation of our decency, and I think we're a lot better people than those funny people down there. I'll send you a picture of our house. We have a fourteen-and-a-half-room house with four bedrooms on four acres and its a showplace. But they treat us like we're from the wrong side of the tracks.

"That judge didn't give visitation rights. He sentenced those children. They love Tom. They want to be with him. But they aren't allowed to mention his name.

"That's why she won't let me talk to them on the

phone. I never mentioned his name but this one time when little Jimbo got on the phone.

"He said, 'My school's going along just fine and I don't want to talk about my daddy.' I said, 'Well, honey, what's the matter? Didn't you have a good time in Albuquerque?' 'Well, yeah.' I said, 'Why don't you want to talk about your daddy?' Well, there was a set speech. Now what kind of a mother sets her children up with set speeches like this? He was five years old then.

"Tom wouldn't even call her up because she'd scream at him. I said, 'Why don't you call her up and reason with her, honey, there's no sense to all of this.' This was before. He said, 'Mom, you can't talk to anybody who gets hysterical and screams.'

"I wake up at night and I think, My God, what has happened to my nice son? He never knew people like this existed. Neither did I.

"So, I don't know, Bill, I'm just real unhappy for Tom. You might tell Sands Tom is a gentleman, as you can tell, but I'm no lady. I'm a she wolf and I'll defend my cub if I have to."

Horsley listened with great patience, as he always did. Delores called him far more frequently about the case than Tom did, and she continued to seethe about the injustice she thought had been inflicted upon her son— especially the financial injustice. She railed against the judge and complained that the entire North Carolina judicial system was "under the thumb of that old bat," the former chief justice, Susie's aunt. Nothing Horsley said could dissuade or appease her. His feeling was that while Tom hadn't been particularly happy with the judge's order, he had accepted it and wanted to get on with his life with as little contact with Susie as possible. But Delores, he thought, would not be happy until she had pushed Tom to try to change the situation and confront Susie once again.

Delores's friends knew that she was nearly obsessed with Tom's problems with Susie. "Delores lived and breathed that thing with Tom," Susan Reid said. But her friends also knew that wasn't the only reason for her growing unhappiness that spring. She seemed equally upset about

Tom's pending marriage to his former dental assistant, Kathy Anderson, who had been living with him for more than three years.

She'd done everything she could to stop it, she told Susan Reid and Joyce Rose. She couldn't understand why Tom wouldn't listen. After all, hadn't she been right about Susie? Wouldn't he have saved himself a lot of pain and trouble if he'd listened to her then?

"She said this girl's family was far below her son," Joyce later recalled.

"Delores was a woman, it didn't make any difference who it was, they weren't good enough," said Susan.

Kathy never knew that Delores had such feelings about her. She had a genuine fondness for Delores and made every effort to show it. She thought that Delores felt the same way about her.

Despite her misgivings, Delores went to Albuquerque for the wedding, taking Janie and leaving behind her hospitalized husband. The wedding took place June 11 in the chapel at the University of New Mexico with nearly two hundred family and friends present. Kathy's family stayed at Tom's house, and Delores got a room at the Sheraton. With the boys soon to arrive for their first full summer visit and both of their families visiting, Tom and Kathy decided against a honeymoon. But before Delores left, they promised to come to Kentucky later in the summer and bring the boys.

Less than three weeks after the wedding, John and Jim arrived in Albuquerque. They looked sickly, and Tom was not only distressed with their appearance, he was disgusted with their plaque-encrusted teeth. The boys came with a load of vitamins and medicines. The huge doses of vitamins sometimes made them nauseated, but they insisted they had to take them or their mother would be angry. Tom threw away most of the pills and assured them that their mother would never know.

The boys were reticent at first, seemingly fearful of saying the wrong things. John sometimes elbowed Jim when he began to say something, and Jim would check himself. When Tom went to work, leaving the boys alone with Kathy, they said disturbing things about their father and grandparents.

"Daddy was a jerk. Daddy was dumb. Daddy was stupid. Stupid and dumb. Stupid and dumb. Delores and Janie and Chuck were mean. They were stupid and dumb. GG and Granddaddy were mean to us. They kicked us out of the house. Daddy used to be mean to us."

"I'd say, 'Where did you get that idea?' " Kathy recalled. "Everything was 'Mother said.' "

Tom tried to spend as much time as possible with the boys. He took them to Wagon Mound, New Mexico, to a ranch owned by friends who also had a young son. The boys rode horses, jumped on a trampoline, and searched a canyon cliff for arrowheads. At night the had cookouts and sat around the fire with the ranch hands telling ghost stories. One night during the story telling, a cowboy galloped in on his horse and jumped the campfire, a cape flying from his neck, his six-shooters belching smoke.

Back in Albuquerque, Tom and Kathy took the boys on the world's longest train ride up Sandia Mountain, 10,600 feet high. They went with them on the Wild Water Slide and took them to Uncle Cliff's Amusement Park, where Jim stepped into the cage to face a baseball-pitching machine and knocked the first pitch out of the park, creating a memory his father would always carry.

"He's going to be the next Joe DiMaggio," Tom predicted.

Jim was not nearly so athletic as John, who clearly was his father's son. Not only did John look like Tom, he was a natural athlete. He loved sports. He could do anything with a ball and was the fastest kid in his class. But he never got to play sports, except during school recess, he told his father, because his mother wouldn't allow it. She rarely let him and Jim play outside, he said, and discouraged them from making friends.

John, sensitive and highly competitive, was obviously frustrated and on edge much of the time. Tom also knew that he craved affection. John's second-grade teacher, Shirley Thorne, had written to tell him that John was the only student who gave her a big hug on leaving each day.

Both John and Jim were bright and studious. Tom knew that they did well in school because of his correspondence with their teachers.

Jim was much different from his brother. Tom could

see that he had the soul of a poet, an artist, a philosopher. Jim saw images in the clouds and pointed them out. He had the heart of a peacemaker, and was always trying to quell the acrimony between his parents. Less aggressive than John, he rarely stood up for himself, and seemed more fearful.

Jim was a ladies' man, too, his father could tell, a charmer. Girls gravitated to him. He quickly made friends with several in the neighborhood.

Jim's first-grade teacher, Julia Cooper, had written to Tom that Jim was the "most caring child" she'd ever taught. "No one could help but love Jim," she said.

Near the end of the summer visit, Tom borrowed a motor home from his neighbors, Hank and Irene, and drove to Kentucky with Kathy and the boys. Delores had complained because she never got to see the boys and couldn't even talk to them by telephone anymore. She sometimes made fudge and cookies and mailed them to her grandsons, but the boys told Tom that their mother threw the packages out because the food in them might be poisoned. That infuriated Delores.

The boys seemed to enjoy their visit with their grandparents. They played with Delores's dogs, banged on her piano, got running starts and slid in their socks on her highly polished floors. Delores piled into the motor home with them to see Mammoth Cave and to visit a friend of hers who raised miniature donkeys. She rented a room at the Melrose Inn, only a few miles from her house, so the boys would have a swimming pool to play in, and she splashed in the water with them.

To Tom and Kathy, Delores seemed to have a good time and enjoyed the boys immensely, but after they were gone, Delores told her friends that she was relieved. She complained that the boys messed up her house. She called them "brats."

"She wasn't a typical grandmother," said Joyce Rose. "She was anxious to see the boys, but she was anxious to see them leave, too."

That summer, John and Jim began to tell their daddy about "Uncle Fritz." They had mentioned Fritz a few times on earlier visits, but Tom hadn't paid much attention. He knew that Fritz was Susie's cousin, but he'd seen him only a couple of times. He'd noticed Fritz at the custody hearing the summer before. That had struck him as odd, but other things were on his mind and he didn't think about it.

Now the boys told him that Uncle Fritz sometimes stayed with them, that he took them camping and to gun shows. They seemed to like him.

Tom couldn't understand why Susie would be spending so much time with her cousin. She'd never been close to him before, had hardly ever mentioned him. Indeed, Tom had the impression she'd thought her cousin peculiar, as he did. "A nerd for life" was how he'd always pictured Fritz.

"I thought he was a little strange, but I thought he was basically harmless," Tom said.

He had troubles enough with Susie, though, without questioning why she was spending time with her peculiar cousin.

While the boys were with their father that summer, Fritz was telling Amanda Jones about Susie and her boys. Amanda, who was in love with Fritz, knew that he spent a lot of time with his cousin, and asked about her. Susie and her boys were, after all, among the select few who would be joining them in Fritz's little survival group when worldwide calamity struck, and Amanda was curious about her. Fritz said that he had to look after Susie and her boys because her parents had thrown them out of their house and wouldn't do anything for them. He didn't like it that the boys were in New Mexico with their father. Tom used the boys as a front to haul drugs into the country from Mexico, he said.

"He knew a border guard who'd told him all about it," Amanda remembered.

30

As spring of 1984 approached, Susie called Tom to tell him that snow days had cut short the boys' spring break, so they couldn't come for their scheduled visit. Instead, she was taking them on a brief trip to Washington to visit Senator Jesse Helms, whom she greatly admired.

Delores was so angry when she heard about this that she wrote a letter to Judge McHugh in Reidsville telling him that this was an unfair violation of his order. She asked him to intervene and proposed an alternative: a weekend trip to Louisville for the boys at the end of March, when Tom would be there for an American Dental Association convention.

"It could be a nice visit even tho short," she wrote. "It would be the third time I have seen them in their lives. . . . My husband will not be here to enjoy them. He died of a heart attack on Nov. 5th."

Delores enclosed some snapshots of the boys with Tom, along with a couple of her house, but she showed the letter to her friend Susan Reid before she mailed it.

"Okay, Delores, you've written it," said Susan, who thought Delores had no business meddling in her children's lives and had told her so. "Now tear it up."

Delores mailed it anyway, enclosing a stamped, self-addressed envelope with a request that the pictures be returned.

The letter was not enough to win Tom a visit with his sons in Louisville. Nor were any pleas to Susie. Tom's lawyer had to file a motion before the judge allowed the visit. That Tom had to go to court and spend more money just for a weekend visit only added to the growing tension.

That spring, Dr. Klenner found himself unable to go to his clinic to treat the hundreds of desperate patients who were dependent on him and his vitamins. The heart problems that had plagued him for several years made him too weak to climb the steep stairs. His wife, Annie Hill, who referred to him as Doctor, was nursing him at home. On a Saturday in late May, she went upstairs to check on him.

"Doctor was sitting up there in our bedroom on the side of the bed talking," she later recalled. "He just dived on back and just plain went out. Fritz resuscitated him, gave him oxygen, got him stabilized, got an ambulance, and got him to a hospital. So Fritz knew what to do, and he knew how to do it, and he did it in quick order."

Although Annie Penn Hospital was less than a mile from the Klenner house, Dr. Klenner was taken to Morehead Hospital in Eden, fourteen miles away. Several years earlier, he'd given up his privileges at Annie Penn in a dispute over his controversial methods, and after the dispute he would have nothing else to do with that hospital.

Dr. Klenner died the following day, Sunday, May 20, with his son at his side. He was seventy-six. The family received visitors at the big Sharp house on Lindsey Street because the clutter at the Klenner house allowed no room for callers. Hundreds of patients came to see Dr. Klenner lying in state at Citty Funeral Home, and Fritz moved among them, calm and reassured, comforting one and all.

"That was a very interesting phenomenon," observed Dr. Klenner's friend Phil Link. "It was as if Dr. Klenner had gotten inside Fritz's body. He had all of his mannerisms and expressions. 'Well, we have to forge ahead,' he'd say, just as if Dr. Klenner was saying, 'Don't worry about me.' That was the strangest thing I've ever seen, him just assuming Dr. Klenner's identity."

The funeral was May 22 at St. Joseph of the Hills Catholic Church in Eden. Years earlier, Dr. Klenner had left Holy Infant Church in Reidsville in a huff after a dispute with the priest, and had refused to go back, even after the priest had long been gone. Normally, Reidsville doctors sit in a group at the funerals of other local physicians. Only one attended Dr. Klenner's funeral—ironically, a black woman.

After the service, Fritz again went through the large crowd, consoling patients. He was so much like his daddy, many said. They asked when he would be reopening the clinic. He was supposed to take his "national boards" that very week, Fritz told them, but the tests had been postponed because of his father's death. Soon, he promised.

Dr. Klenner was buried at Greenview Cemetery in Reidsville, next to a big magnolia, one of his favorite trees. No graveside service was held. Fritz allowed no one but himself at the gravesite for his father's burial.

"Fritz has been very emotional over his father's death," his mother observed later.

About a week after the funeral, Fritz appeared at Park Chevrolet in Kernersville, halfway between Greensboro and Winston-Salem, where he regularly had his Blazer serviced. He'd come to know several of the mechanics there. They thought of him as a tough guy. He'd told them stories of fighting with the Green Berets in Vietnam, of being trapped behind enemy lines, of saving his buddies and barely escaping with his life. His Vietnam stories were so detailed and convincing that even Vietnam veterans to whom he told them believed him.

When the mechanics offered condolences about his father's death, Fritz began telling how he'd tried to revive his father at the hospital. In the past, he'd told many stories about saving his father from death in many circumstances, but this had been reality, not fantasy, and neither Fritz nor vitamins could pull him back. Once again, his father had gone to the Mountain without him. Fritz had failed him ultimately.

He burst into tears trying to tell the story and began sobbing uncontrollably in the crowded waiting room.

Fritz's onetime friends Sam Phillips and John Forrest heard about Dr. Klenner's death and wondered how it would affect Fritz.

"I knew in the back of my head that something was

going to happen one day after his father died," Sam Phillips said, "because his daddy was the only thing really keeping him in this world."

"I always said if old man Klenner ever dies, look out world," said John Forrest, "because that son of a bitch Fritz, won't anybody have any control over him anymore."

Not long after Dr. Klenner's death, Fritz began seeing selected patients at his father's clinic. He had his name included on a soon-to-be-printed 1985 calender listing area doctors and their telephone numbers. He wrote prescriptions that were filled by local pharmacists, who assumed he was a physician. But his aunt Susie Sharp had become suspicious, and she asked her friend Terry Sanford, the president of Duke University, to check on her nephew. When Sanford reported back that Fritz never had been at Duke, the retired chief justice had a talk about the law with her sister Annie Hill, and to make sure that it was understood, she had a chat with the Klenner family lawyer, Allen Gwyn, son of the judge who had claimed the judgeship her father had coveted and become her high school debating coach. Soon afterward, Dr. Klenner's clinic quietly closed for good. Many patients, offered no explanation, were left desperate for their regular vitamin treatments and wondering what had happened to "young Dr. Klenner."

Susie Sharp also called her sister Florence to tell her about her discovery. Should they inform Susie Q?

"I don't know," Florence said. "Let me talk with Bob."

Florence called back, saying, "Bob said don't say anything to Susie about this."

"Why? Are you afraid something might happen?"

No, Florence replied, she and Bob thought that if they told Susie, Susie would think it was just another trick to try to separate her from Fritz, and that it would drive her further from family and deeper into isolation.

"She wanted to keep somebody in the family to whom Susie would talk," Judge Sharp recalled later.

Several weeks after Dr. Klenner's death, Nancy Dunn got a call in Raleigh from Susie. Nancy hadn't seen her cousin since Susie moved out of her parents' house a year and a half earlier. She'd talked to her only a few times by phone, and those times Susie had seemed distant, not like herself. Nancy still didn't know the reason Susie had left. She had no idea that Fritz was living with Susie much of the time. She didn't even know that Dr. Klenner had died until Susie called.

"Where are you?" Nancy asked, happy to hear from her cousin.

"I'm in Durham," Susie said. "I took the boys camping and I had to stop over at Fritz's apartment."

"Well, look, if you're going to be there, I want to come and see you," Nancy said.

But Susie made excuses. "I'm so busy," she said. "You know Fred died and left the biggest mess you've ever seen. He had absolutely no money. He left that poor woman destitute. I'm helping Fritz get his old coins appraised."

After that conversation, Nancy wondered about several things. The way in which Susie talked about Dr. Klenner's death and all she had to do because of it made her sound almost as if she were a Klenner, not a Newsom, as if her own father had died. Just what was her relationship with Fritz anyway? And what was this business about camping? Susie camping?

"The Queen of England does not camp," Nancy said.

While Susie was helping Fritz straighten out his father's affairs, the boys were in Albuquerque for their summer visit. They arrived, as usual, looking pale and sunken-eyed, and this time they had fresh scars on their faces. Uncle Fritz had cut off moles, the boys said. That concerned Tom. From the little medicine he had studied, he knew that moles generally weren't removed until after puberty.

"Don't worry, Dad," Jim said. "Uncle Fritz is a doctor."

Tom had never heard that Fritz was a doctor. He thought he was just a physician's assistant who worked with his father.

"No, he's just a doctor's helper," Tom said.

But the boys insisted that Uncle Fritz was a doctor and said he also gave them shots.

That wasn't the only thing that Tom heard about Uncle Fritz that disturbed him that summer. The boys told of spending the previous Thanksgiving camping in the mountains with Uncle Fritz and their mother, eating cold turkey sandwiches for Thanksgiving dinner and getting so cold that night that they thought they would freeze.

Tom could never have imagined Susie camping. When he had suggested they go camping after moving to Albuquerque, her response had been "Only if there's a Holiday Inn."

Fritz kept coming up in the boys' conversations that summer. At one point they mentioned that he had an Uzi.

Tom enjoyed guns himself, and he had a cabinetful at home. When the boys had come on their first visit, he'd showed them the guns, all hunting rifles, told them they were not toys, and instructed them to keep away. He couldn't imagine why somebody would have an Uzi.

"I was beginning to get a little concerned," he said later.

But that was something to worry about in the future. Now he had a full schedule planned for the boys. He taught them to ride the used bikes he had bought and fixed up for them. He and Kathy took them back to the ranch at Wagon Mound, where they rode horses, and to the Grand Canyon, where they rode donkeys down the precarious trails cut into the cliffs to the murky Colorado River. They returned to Albuquerque to find a gift mailed to the boys by their mother—T-shirts picturing Clint Eastwood peering over the barrel of a .44 magnum, saying, GO AHEAD, MAKE MY DAY. Tom was disgusted that Susie would send such shirts and threw them away.

In mid-July, Tom and Kathy rented a cabin at Lake Vallecito in the mountains of southern Colorado and took the boys there for a weekend with their friends Duke and Betty Halle and their two children, Kelly and Kyle. Jim had a crush on Kelly.

The weekend seemed almost jinxed. Things went wrong from the beginning. Duke's car broke down in a small town in northern New Mexico, and they had to leave it and take a rental. On Saturday they rented a houseboat and had a nice outing with a cookout that evening. But that night, two water-skiers collided on the lake, leaving one young man drowned and missing, and the next day the water was covered with rescue workers dragging for his body, making further pleasure outings too gloomy to contemplate. Instead, they went to a ski resort named Purgatory, rode the chair lift, and whooshed down the Alpine Slide. On the way home that night, heavy rains engulfed them, and in the town of Bloomfield, a child on a bicycle darted out of the darkness into the path of Duke's car. Everybody ended up waiting at the hospital while the child, who wasn't seriously injured, was patched up.

It was after midnight when Tom and Kathy and the boys finally got back home, and they expected the phone to ring at any minute. Delores usually called two or three times a week and always when she knew they were due back from a trip, even if it meant that she had to sit up half the night because of the two-hour time difference.

But this night Delores didn't call, and Tom and Kathy figured that she must have fallen asleep waiting for them to get back home. When she failed to call Monday, both Tom and Kathy thought it unusual. Maybe she was wrapped up in something with her theater group. If she didn't call Tuesday night, Tom said, they'd call her.

But Tuesday afternoon, as Tom was hurrying to leave his office to meet Kathy and the boys at the Hiland Theater, the police department chaplain showed up, and the summer turned to sorrow.

That night, Susie was one of many people Tom called to tell about the murders of his mother and sister. He was going back to Louisville, he told her, but the boys would stay in Albuquerque with Kathy. They'd be fine, he assured her. So stunned was he by events, that later he wouldn't recall her response.

Another person Tom called that night was his lawyer, Mike Rueckhaus. Tom knew that he was going to be heir to a lot of money, but if his plane crashed on the way to Kentucky, he wanted to make sure that none of it went to Susie through the boys. Rueckhaus worked all night drawing up a will that created trusts the boys would not receive until adulthood.

* * *

Only hours after Delores's and Janie's bodies were discovered, Susie's lawyer, Sandy Sands, arrived at his Reidsville home from a beach trip to find his telephone ringing. Susie was calling. It was the first of three calls she made to him that night, and she was nearly hysterical.

"She just went bananas," he said.

Susie told him that Tom's mother and sister had been found dead in a "gangland-style killing," and she was scared because the boys were with Tom. Mobsters had killed Janie and Delores, she said, because Tom owed them money and needed his family inheritance to pay it. She was afraid that something else was going to happen, that the boys might be killed or kidnapped, and she wanted Sands to help get the boys home immediately. Sands managed to calm her and convince her that Tom no doubt needed the boys at a time like this. They should let John and Jim stay for the few remaining days of their visit, he said. He did not ask how she knew that the mob had killed Delores and Janie and that the murders had been "gangland" style. At that time, Kentucky police had said only that the murders appeared to be related to a robbery, and no details had been released.

When Tom returned to Albuquerque five days later, after burying his mother and sister and undergoing the suspicious questioning by the police, he again called Susie, this time with a nearly tearful request. Could the boys stay a little longer, maybe through his birthday? He really needed to be with them now, he said.

Susie's answer was quick and curt. No. Impossible. She had plans for them. They were going camping. Tom couldn't believe that she could be so cold and insensitive. Later he would remember that she didn't even say she was sorry.

"That's when I resolved to use all the money to get the boys back," Tom said, referring to his inheritance.

On August 5, on schedule, Tom flew to Dallas with his sons so they could catch a direct flight to Greensboro. In the airport during their wait, he got a pocketful of quarters and played video games with them. John not only beat him, he scored so high on one machine that he got to add his initials to the list of top scorers. He strutted around proudly, like a football player who'd just raced ninety yards for a touchdown, but he cried when his father put him on the plane. He always cried on leaving.

31

Bob and Florence sent flowers to Delores and Janie's funeral, and Tom used that as an opportunity to reestablish contact with his former in-laws.

On August 27, 1984, just before leaving Albuquerque to return to Louisville to deal with estate matters and face his third lie detector test for Detective Dan Davidson, Tom mailed them a five-page, handwritten letter.

Kathy and I want to thank you for the lovely floral arrangement. During a time like this, it's knowing people care that is helping us deal with this terrible tragedy and senseless loss.

I've wanted to correspond with you before this but I felt awkward. Since the divorce, I wasn't sure how you felt about communicating with me. There really shouldn't be any reason for us not to correspond. You are the only grandparents John and Jim have. Since this tragedy and having lost my father in November, I am much more aware of how precious life is and the importance of having a close relationship with the boys.

Tom went on to recite a litany of concerns and complaints. He was worried that the boys took too many vitamins and medicines, concerned that they had no beds, slept on the floor, never got to play outside or participate in sports. He didn't like it that they weren't allowed to see Bob and Florence.

The thing that worries me most is the boys' mental state. I am told by the boys that they are not allowed to call us collect, say prayers about me, send school pictures, cards or letters, or even talk about us. I see absolutely no reason for this and it could cause problems for the boys as they seem to feel guilty about it.

It bothers me, too, that the boys are so secretive about their lives. They seem to have certain subjects they aren't allowed to talk about. I can't understand the need for such secrets.

One of my biggest regrets is that the boys were never allowed to have a close relationship with my family and didn't get to spend more time with them.

I don't want to put you in an awkward position, but I love the boys and I'm concerned about them. I know you are concerned for their welfare, too.

Two weeks after receiving Tom's letter, Florence mailed a reply.

"Yes," she wrote, "we agree it is very important that the boys have a strong and good relationship with their father."

She said she had little knowledge of the boys' day-to-day activities and that she had offered beds for them but Susie had refused.

It would be nice if you could come and spend a few days and go through their daily routine with them. Also, I'm sure the boys would like for their teachers and friends to meet their father.

Bob and I feel that you should maintain as much contact as you can with the boys, and as they get older they will make more decisions for themselves.

We do what we can to maintain contact and have told Susie and the boys to call us at anytime they need us. We are here to help when our help is wanted or needed.

Tom made a copy of the letter he sent to Bob and Florence and enclosed it with a thank-you note for her sympathy card to Florence's sister Louise, who lived in

the big Sharp house in Reidsville. She responded immediately, telling Tom that John and Jim were sweet children but she and other family members saw them
infrequently.

> Susie brought them to see me when she came to
> Reidsville to Dr. Klenner's office, but she has not
> been here since his death. Florence rarely sees her,
> so she can give me little news. One-sided communica-
> tions are hard to pursue.
> I don't know why Susie is being so difficult. Flor-
> ence feels that she is making her a scapegoat for her
> unhappiness. Of course, we don't know what hap-
> pened in Albuquerque to break up your home. Susie
> can be awfully bossy and stubborn.

She closed by saying that she hoped Tom and Kathy
would come for a visit.

There was purpose in Tom's courting of Susie's family.
He and Kathy had been collecting information about
children of divorce and how to develop cooperative plans
to care for them, giving more balanced roles to the parents. They had consulted family counselors and a psychologist, who told them that the time Tom was allowed
with his children was well below the norm. Tom wanted
that time extended, wanted more influence in his sons'
lives. Down the road, he hoped the boys might choose to
come and live with him. First, he wanted to know how
Susie's family felt.

"I wanted to see who I was fighting against," he recalled, "whether I was having to deal with the whole
family or just her."

He decided to involve Louise, the guardian of Sharp
family heritage, for two reasons: "Number one, to get as
much information as we could. Number two, to find out
how things looked from Reidsville.

"We wanted everybody to know how the boys were
being treated out here and to ask them how the boys
were being treated back there. We were relying on Louise to feed us information we didn't even ask for, the
more information the better."

Uncertain how to proceed, Tom decided to take Florence's suggestion and come to North Carolina to see the boys and meet their friends and teachers. The trip had other purposes as well.

"We wanted everybody to see me and make sure I wasn't some kind of ogre from out west and also to meet Kathy and let them see how she got along with the boys," Tom recalled.

In October, Tom gave Susie the two weeks' notice required by the court. He and Kathy flew to Greensboro the first week in November for a five-day visit. Wanting to have plenty of space for the boys, Tom rented an apartment at Guest Quarters. Not until he arrived did he realize the apartment was in the same complex as Susie's, only a short distance away.

Susie was hostile when Tom picked up John and Jim. "She looked like a harpy," he recalled. "Her hair was all disheveled and she had a weird look in her eyes. She looked like she was coming unraveled. She just threw their luggage at us."

That morning, Susie had called her brother Rob, and with great urgency in her voice asked if she could come and talk with him. After moving in with his parents in March of 1983, Rob had gone to his uncle, Fred Klenner, for a couple of B vitamin treatments for his alcoholism. But the effects of the heavy drinking he'd given up two years earlier still lingered. He suffered from short-term memory loss that had caused great problems when he tried practicing law for several months, problems that attracted the attention of the state bar. He stopped practicing in September of 1983 and gave up his license in July 1984. Meanwhile, he had begun treatment at an alcoholism clinic in Southern Pines that was having good results, and he had taken a job as an alcoholism counselor with Guilford County. He agreed to meet Susie at his office on North Eugene Street.

Their conversation lasted nearly two hours and caused Rob concern and distress. Susie was filled with fears, frightened of Tom's purpose in his trip, frightened of Tom himself, convinced still that he wanted to snatch the children. Earlier, she had said things that indicated that she thought Tom had criminal associations and was abusing prescription drugs. Now she said that she knew for certain that Tom was involved with the Mafia, that his underworld enemies had murdered his mother and sister, and that she feared that she might be murdered, too. She never went anywhere without her pistol or her dogs, she said. Since Rob last visited her apartment nearly a year earlier, Susie had bought another black chow, this one a female named Mai Ling, called Maizie by the boys. Susie took a .25-caliber Browning semiautomatic pistol from her purse and showed it to Rob, making him uncomfortable.

"Have you got a permit for that?" he asked. She said that she did and returned the weapon to her purse.

Rob reminded her that carrying a concealed weapon could get her arrested.

"That's a heck of a lot better than being dead," she said.

Rob, ever the lawyer, sought proof of her allegations against Tom. "I talked to her and tried to determine on what basis she believed these things," he recalled later, "and never got any answer that was satisfying to me. Whenever I would ask her why she believed it, she said she and Fritz had friends in the federal government, that Fritz was an employee of the Central Intelligence Agency and had access to all of this information."

When Rob quizzed his sister about her relationship with Fritz, she said that he visited often to make certain that she and the boys were safe and sometimes took them camping. "She said she felt safer with him around and checking on them frequently," he said later.

Rob didn't believe any of the things Susie was saying about Tom, nor did he believe that Fritz was connected with the CIA.

"My initial thought was, Why don't I call mental health and have her committed?" he said. He remembered his mother's cousin who'd gone off the deep end and killed her estranged husband and herself, and wondered if nuttiness might be in the blood. When he suggested that Susie ought to seek counseling, she responded that she and the boys were already seeing a psychiatrist, Dr. Andrew Courts, whom Rob had also seen briefly.

After Susie left, Rob was so disturbed that he called his parents, who were at Nanna's that day. He told his father about the conversation and said he thought that

Susie was acting irrationally and seemed deluded. He warned that they should be circumspect and cautious over the weekend, because Susie had seemed very excitable.

"I wasn't worried about Susie so much as I was about Fritz," he said later. "I suspected all along that this was bull that Fritz was feeding her."

He wasn't certain how his father received his call. "I had the distinct impression that Dad only half believed me," he said. "I wasn't sure my testimony was given great weight, that maybe they weren't sure how far along the road to recovery I was."

Although Rob didn't know it, his parents were scheduled to meet Tom and Kathy for lunch on Friday, and his testimony was given more weight than he realized, for, after his call, Florence called Tom and canceled their appointment, suggesting that they meet at Bob's office that afternoon instead.

Tom and Kathy were unaware of the reason that made the Newsoms change the time and place for their meeting, but they realized that something wasn't right.

"They were nervous," Kathy recalled. "Mrs. Newsom acted very strange. She sat not facing us. She wasn't talking. She didn't say much."

Tom thought this was because of the awkwardness of the situation and meeting Kathy for the first time. Kathy, too, was nervous, wanting to make a good impression. "I was scared to death," she said.

Tom and Bob did most of the talking. Tom began by essentially repeating what he'd said in his letter.

"I said I didn't think the boys were being handled properly and there had to be some solution to this so I could see them more and they could be exposed to a more normal life-style. Mr. Newsom agreed. He basically said that we had seen the boys more than they had in the last couple of years. He said they wanted to keep the windows open for the boys so they could always have opportunities. He felt the same way I felt. There wasn't any difference of opinion. He said that when the boys reached the age they could talk to the judge, 'I'm one hundred percent sure the boys will come to live with you, Tom.' He said that was fine."

Tom said if that should happen, he would be glad to pay for the boys to come back regularly for visits.

"He asked me if I would pay for college," Tom remembered. "I said there would be no doubt they would go to college and I would handle whatever it cost."

Tom was surprised at some of the things Bob said about Susie that day, all of which Tom had already observed. She had to have her way, Bob said, had to be in control. She was spoiled, stubborn, bossy, and "pathological in her possessiveness of the children." At one point, he called her a "smartass" and said he didn't know what to do about her.

Before he and Kathy left, Tom had a question.

"What is the relationship between Susie and Fritz?"

Bob remained silent.

"We really don't know," Florence finally said.

Not until this trip did Tom realize that Fritz was actually living with Susie. He saw Fritz walking the two chows at 8 A.M., an unusual time for somebody just to come calling. The boys said that Fritz stayed there most of the time now, and Tom didn't like it. Neither did he like the boys' appearances. Their shoes were too small, their toenails long and curling, their hair dirty. They wore crosses and St. Christopher medals on chains around their necks.

Tom and Kathy went shopping for new shoes and clothes for the boys. They took them to see the movie *Gremlins*. They went to their school and met their teachers. On Saturday, Tom and his friend Bob Brenner of High Point, a former Wake Forest football player who had been an usher at Tom's wedding to Susie, took the boys to Raleigh to see their first live college football game between North Carolina State and South Carolina. Later, Tom bought a kickball for the boys and went out to play with them, but the boys were too concerned about soiling their clothes to have a good time.

"Mother will kill us," they said.

On Sunday, Tom and Kathy took the boys to Reidsville to have the lunch buffet at the country club with Louise Sharp. Bob and Florence came, and so did Annie Hill

Klenner. Bob and Florence had a good time with the boys, whom they hadn't seen for several months. Later, Louise took Tom and Kathy on a tour of the big Sharp home. She showed the boys photos of the tragic, long-dead twins, their great uncles whose names they bore.

On Monday, Tom and Kathy had lunch with the boys at school, and John's teacher told them that John had been crying all morning because his father would be leaving the next day. She told him to keep John for the afternoon.

"I won't tell his mother," she promised.

Taking the boys back to Susie was difficult.

"John was crying," Kathy remembered. "He kept looking at me and looking at her."

Tom and Kathy wanted to see the apartment, see the boys' room, but Susie made it plain that they weren't welcome. She swept the boys up before they had a chance to give good-bye hugs and took them inside.

Tom and Kathy flew home the next day, election day, feeling sad about leaving the boys but good about the effect of their trip. They felt they had made a good impression with Susie's family and possibly had won support for the future.

Judge Sharp missed little that went on in the family. Having been informed of Tom's earlier letter to Louise, she knew his purpose, and after hearing about the Sunday meeting in Reidsville, she called her niece at Florence's suggestion and asked her to lunch at the K&W Cafeteria in Greensboro. Actually, it was Rob who had suggested to his mother that his aunt Su-Su meet with Susie to see if she could get a reading on his sister's mental condition and the situation with Fritz, although his aunt was unaware of that.

As Tom and Kathy were flying westward, Susie Sharp was waiting at the cafeteria for her niece to arrive. "I thought maybe I could get her to talk," she said later, "but she showed up with Rob. I was thoroughly thwarted."

After lunch, Su-Su stopped at Bob's office to report her conversation to Bob and Florence. She found them in a low mood. Although they had evaded mentioning it to

Tom and Kathy, they remained deeply distressed about Susie's relationship with Fritz and greatly worried about its effect upon the boys.

"Florence and Bob were at their wits' end," Judge Sharp recalled later. "They just didn't know what to do. They were very apprehensive that something terrible was going to happen. They were afraid Fritz was going to kill the children with his doctoring."

On November 10, Louise wrote to Tom: "It was good to see you, Kathy, John and Jim last Sunday. Your concern for your boys is commendable and heart-warming."

She went on to write about the election, family visits, and other affairs, before reporting the cafeteria meeting arranged by her sister Susie.

"After lunch she met Bob and Florence at Bob's office for a talk before returning to Raleigh. I believe she has Susie Q ready to find bunk beds for the boys and to go to Bowman Gray for a medical check-up. She looks pretty but is too thin."

Susie did pick out bunk beds for the boys, and Su-Su sent a check to pay for them. John and Jim argued the first night about who would sleep on top. Later they sent thank-you notes to Su-Su. John called the new beds "neat." Susie also took the boys to her parents' house for Thanksgiving dinner. Susie had been made aware that if Tom went to court again, it would be in her best interest for the boys to have a closer relationship with their grandparents. Susie stayed only long enough to eat, but despite the strain, everything went well.

On December 13, Kathy wrote long, almost identical letters to Bob and Florence and Louise:

It is hard to believe that Christmas is just around the corner. Usually, this is my favorite holiday, but this year with all that has happened, it is hard to get into the spirit. Tom and I are going through the motions. We were supposed to be in Kentucky this Christmas, and we were hoping John and Jim would have been able to join us for a couple of days.

Both of us are trying to keep busy so we won't be reminded of how empty this Christmas will be. Tom needs me now more than ever. I feel so frustrated at times because sometimes no matter what I say or do makes Tom feel better.

We have gotten our shopping for John and Jim finished. We just have to get their gifts in the mail. Tom says he hopes the boys will be allowed to play with their presents from us because in the past the items were given away or put up. The same was true when Delores sent their gifts, so she used to send everything here for the kids to enjoy.

Tom says he will be surprised if he gets a Christmas card, phone call or thank-you note from the boys.

I am still concerned about Tom. He has been through so much this year with the loss of his mother and sister. It doesn't help that he is always worrying about John and Jim and that he misses them a great deal.

I know the Lynches loved John and Jim very much and they were upset that they weren't allowed to see them. Tom says he knows Susie has painted a distorted picture of his family because she never wanted anything to do with any of his relatives while they were married. The boys have told us the awful things their mother has said about Chuck, Delores and Janie. All this has hurt Tom terribly. Tom says Susie tried to dominate him and alienate him from his family just like she is trying to keep John and Jim away from him, you and the rest of her family.

We understand that Susie Marshall bought bunk beds for the children. That was a thoughtful and generous thing for her to do. The boys are pleased that they finally have beds. Tom is happy the boys came for Thanksgiving dinner and he feels it was our trip to North Carolina that prompted them to go. The boys are still very secretive and we get all kinds of conflicting stories from them. Tom says the boys are still being told what to say and what not to say. When talking to the boys on the phone we can always tell when their mother is there by the way the boys act. Jim and John say they want to spend more time with us but are afraid to tell anyone. We would also like to see more of them. Thirty-five days in the summer (when they get ninety days off from school), every other Christmas and every other spring break is not enough time to form the kind of close relationship the kids need.

Florence answered Kathy's letter five days before Christmas.

We are looking forward to our Christmas Eve dinner here. It will be our last Christmas dinner in this house. Susie and the boys are coming and we will be delighted.

I had a nice surprise last week. Bob asked me to go to lunch with him, and he took me to the Hilton—it turned out to be a surprise retirement luncheon for me by the staff and faculty of Rutledge College.

Tom and Kathy learned about Christmas at the Newsoms when they returned from a holiday trip to her parents' home in Nebraska and found a letter from Louise.

Susie and the boys had come to the big Christmas Eve dinner, and Susie had seemed her old self. The boys looked well. They got jogging suits from Bob and Florence, pajamas from Nanna, and games from Louise.

Florence served a big, traditional meal: ham, turkey, dressing, gravy, cranberries, yams, green bean casserole, squash casserole, wild rice, biscuits, coffee, egg nog, mincemeat and pumpkin pies, fruitcake, and cookies.

"Poor Florence worked like a Turk," Louise wrote. "She did not eat until we all left. Bob carved the meat and Nanna helped cook. Nanna spent the night. On Christmas Day the Newsoms went to Raleigh to be with the Millers.

"I feel sure that your fall visit to Greensboro did a lot of good."

Thus the worst year of Tom's life came to an end. The new year, he thought, would have to be better. Surely it would bring him more time with his sons.

32

Neither Tom nor anybody in Susie's family realized that Susie and Fritz had become so close that they were now calling themselves husband and wife. Neighbors at Susie's apartment complex assumed them to be married, and although Fritz and Susie seemed somewhat secretive and kept largely to themselves, when they did have contact with neighbors they did nothing to dispel that impression. At nearby businesses they frequented together, Fritz referred to Susie as his wife in her presence and to John and Jim as his sons. He wanted the boys to call him Papa instead of Uncle Fritz, and they usually did.

In February of 1985, Fritz presented Susie with an elaborate valentine "to my loving wife," and she tucked it away for sentimental keeping.

Early in March, Fritz moved out of his apartment in Durham, which had stood largely unused in the previous year. He left behind a telephone, smoke-permeated walls, and a big, perfectly round hole burned in the center of the living room carpet, causing the property manager to wonder what strange activities this young doctor had been up to. No request was made for the return of the security deposit.

Fritz moved many of his things into Susie's second-floor apartment, which became as cluttered as the Klenner house always had been. He hung blankets and camouflage sheets over the closed window blinds in the bedrooms, shutting out all light, and while Susie went about her routine of getting the boys off to school and diligently attending her classes at the University of North Carolina at Greensboro, where she was nearing completion of her work for a master's degree in business administration, Fritz continued his habit of sleeping through most of the day and prowling late into the night. He still presented himself as a doctor, and even some family members still thought he was one. The previous fall, when his cousin Vera Luteri, the only child of Fritz's favorite aunt, Marie, was dying of leukemia, Fritz drove to Pennsylvania with his mother, arriving late on a Thursday. Marie wanted him to hurry to the hospital because Vera was near death. "He said, 'Aunt Marie, I've got to get cleaned up. I'm a doctor. I've got to get cleaned up and look like one,' " Marie later recalled. "We just assumed that he had got his papers." Fritz continued to freely offer medical advice to casual acquaintances and strangers. Neighbors and others who encountered him on a regular basis assumed that he worked a late hospital shift.

One neighbor, Larry Robinson, a Vietnam War veteran who lived in the adjoining apartment, overcame his curiosity by asking Fritz where he practiced. Fritz told him that he'd taken over his father's clinic in Reidsville. Robinson wondered how he could keep a clinic going by working such odd hours.

Robinson had come to know Susie in the spring of 1984, and frequently chatted with her when he encountered her outside, often talking about Oriental cooking, an interest they had in common. But getting to know Fritz had taken longer. Fritz was quiet and seemed mysterious. Sometimes days would pass and he wouldn't appear at the apartment, then he'd be around for a week without leaving. And he was always shuttling military gear and weapons back and forth between the apartment and his ominous-looking black Chevrolet Blazer. Several times Robinson had seen Fritz loading weapons and field gear into the vehicle at 2 or 3 A.M., causing him to suspect that Fritz was involved in something other than medicine.

By Christmas of 1984, Robinson had noticed that Fritz was now at the apartment almost all the time. One day he struck up a conversation with him and asked about all the guns. Fritz explained that his dad had left him a large gun collection and that he did a lot of buying, selling, and trading. Later, after thieves broke into several cars in the parking lot, including Susie's new S-10 Blazer, from which a radar detector was stolen, Fritz and Robinson spent a night together in a patch of trees, drinking coffee from a Thermos and watching the parking lot in the hope that the thieves might return. Robinson could tell that Fritz had more than normal caution about intruders. Fritz talked of wiring his apartment with burglar alarms and of putting extra dead bolts on the doors, and as they kept watch through the night, he suggested with no hint of facetiousness that they should rig a car with a trip wire and a claymore mine for the thieves' return.

"When he started talking about explosives, the man was very, very knowledgeable," Robinson said.

Mostly that night, though, Fritz talked about his experiences in Vietnam, telling gory details about ambushes, two-week patrols, and the fall of Saigon. He'd been there for the collapse, he said, and described it at great length.

"He talked a damn good game," Robinson recalled months later. "You just don't tell somebody who was in Vietnam that you've been there unless you were. He was very convincing. He knew the names of all the places. He knew what it was like. He was so damn convincing, it's kind of scary now. I would've bet my life that he was a combat soldier."

Fritz was equally convincing to others he encountered in this period. He spent a lot of time at News 'n' Novels, a bookstore in the Kroger Shopping Center on West Market Street, only a couple of miles from Susie's apartment. There he bought large numbers of mercenary, survivalist, and gun magazines, as well as poetry by Rudyard Kipling. He became friendly with Lynne McNeil, a clerk, and talked with her about medicine and poetry. The *Rubaiyat,* by Omar Khayyam, she later remembered, was one of his favorite works. (In the past he had given copies of the book to women he liked.)

Fritz had brought Susie and the boys to the store and introduced them to Lynne as his wife and sons. He also offered her medical advice on occasion, and she had no reason to suspect that he was not a doctor. Later, remembering Fritz, a single poignant incident stood out most in her mind.

One day she was wearing a brooch she had made from an odd little hand-painted trinket she'd found in her grandmother's jewelry box. Fritz noticed it and told her it was a decoration from horse-and-buggy days that had been used to festoon harnesses on special occasions. His dad knew all about them, he said, and when he saw him, he'd find out more for her. He never brought it up again, and later she was surprised to learn that Fritz's father had been dead for many months when he told her that.

Fritz was a regular customer at the Kroger store, a twenty-four-hour supermarket, in the shopping center. He usually came in after midnight, wearing either camouflage fatigues or a white doctor's smock with a stethoscope in the pocket. One night he arrived in a green surgical suit that appeared smeared with dried blood. Several employees got to know him and regularly sought medical advice from him. They thought him nice but a bit peculiar. He frequently spent fifteen or twenty minutes talking on the pay phone at the front of the store, causing the employees to wonder why a doctor would come to Kroger to use the telephone. That wasn't all they wondered about. His purchases intrigued them most.

He bought vitamins in vast amounts. He filled a shopping cart one night with bottles of rubbing alcohol, rolls of adhesive tape, and boxes of gauze, more than $300 worth. Why would a doctor buy medical supplies at Kroger? One night, he bought every box of Hershey's cocoa on the shelves, and the checkout clerk could not contain her curiosity.

"Somebody must be about to have a chocolate fit," she quipped.

Fritz smiled and said that cocoa was an appetite suppressant. In desperate situations, he explained, a person with cocoa could get along without food.

Another night, Fritz became agitated when the bill for the customer ahead of him in line came to $6.66. Those numbers represented the mark of the beast in Revelation, Fritz pointed out, and he began to talk about the Battle of Armageddon and the end of time.

"Before I'll take the mark of the beast," he said, "I'll take my wife and my two boys and we'll go so far back into the mountains that not even the devil can find us."

Phil Farlow knew that Fritz was preparing for some kind of battle, but he was unaware that it was for one so drastic as Armageddon. Farlow operated the Army-Navy Surplus Store on Lee Street in Greensboro where Fritz had been an occasional customer for several years. But late in the fall of 1984, Fritz started coming to the store on almost a weekly basis, sometimes more often, and he continued on through the winter. He usually arrived late in the afternoon, often just before the 6 P.M. closing time, but Farlow kept the store open as long as Fritz wanted to shop, sometimes for three or four hours.

Fritz told Farlow that he was a doctor and had taken over his father's practice in Reidsville. He occasionally offered medical advice to other customers, and once left some medicine for a customer whose dog was having a difficult time recovering from an encounter with a car. But Fritz never said why he was buying so much military gear, and Farlow never questioned. He assumed that Fritz must operate a commando or survival school, because he usually bought several of the same item.

Over a period of about six months, Fritz became the store's biggest customer. He bought knives, bayonets, canteens, field rations, sleeping bags, compasses, packs, field jackets, uniforms, camouflage materials. And he never looked at prices. He spent hours in the store's book section, and carried books to the checkout counter by the stack—military manuals on arms (including heavy armaments, explosives, and combat skills), plus books on mercenary tactics, guerrilla warfare, survivalism, and killing techniques. Fritz rarely left without buying several hundred dollars worth of books and gear, and he usually peeled off hundred-dollar bills in payment. He always paid in cash, just as his father had done.

Throughout his life, Fritz's father had been Fritz's only source of income, and he continued to be so. Dr. Klenner had made Fritz the beneficiary of a $25,000 life insurance policy, and although Fritz distrusted banks, as his father had, he had put the money in a Reidsville bank the summer before. By the spring of 1985 only a little more than $1,000 was left.

Fritz had used some of the money to help Susie buy her new Blazer, but the bulk of it had gone for military equipment and weapons. He never missed an area gun show, and he usually took Susie and the boys with him. Gun dealers later remembered Fritz and the two boys, because they all came dressed in jungle fatigues, and the boys seemed so worshipful and obedient to him.

Fritz regularly ordered weapons and parts by telephone from faraway mail-order houses, using Susie's Visa card to pay. He usually bought only the best, and at one point he had three of the expensive M-10 MAC automatic pistols so popular with drug dealers. He traveled regularly to a big gun store in Tucker, Georgia, where he bought several thousand dollars worth of military weapons. On the black market, he was buying stolen military grenades, mines, and other explosives, and was storing them at his mother's house in Reidsville without her knowledge.

But most of his weapons dealing was done at a small, heavily barred, two-story brick building next to an overpass in a seedy section of Winston-Salem. McHargue Guns and Coins was owned by Curtis McHargue, an employee of R. J. Reynolds Tobacco Company, and operated by his wife, Dot, and sons, Mike and Steve. They had known Fritz, whom they called Fred, for about six years, since he had first come in with his father. In the past year, they also had come to know Susie and the boys well. At Christmas, Susie brought them homemade fudge. She told Dot that she was thinking of making fudge for businessmen to buy as gifts in airports and she was eager to know how they liked it. When Susie and the boys came with Fritz, the boys usually read gun magazines or books while Fritz talked with Steve and Mike and Susie chatted with Dot. Usually, Susie talked about the boys or her classes, but she also liked to talk about guns.

"She loved to shoot," Dot later said.

So, Dot said, did the boys. From the McHargues, Fritz bought them .22-caliber versions of the AR15 assault rifle and was teaching them to shoot. They were doing well, too, he boasted, filling their paper targets with holes near the bull's-eye.

The McHargues believed that Fritz and Susie were married because Fritz told them so, and Susie later confided to Dot that they'd had to go out of state for the

ceremony because first cousins couldn't wed in North
Carolina.

Fritz, too, confided in the McHargues, who loved intrigue as much as he did. He told them things that he told
few others. These things were top secret, he said, but he
could tell them, because he knew that he could trust
them. He told that he was a contract operative for the
CIA, that he was a special member of the Delta Team,
the quick-response commando group stationed at Fort
Bragg. He gave vivid descriptions of several operations
on which he'd been involved for both groups, descriptions that the McHargues later would not reveal because
Fritz had told them they had to be kept secret at all costs.

The McHargues believed him, just as they always had
believed him to be a doctor and a Special Forces veteran
of Vietnam, because Fritz clearly was a man in the know.
Four hours before news broke about the Russian downing of a Korean airliner in September 1983, Fritz told
them about it, Dot McHargue said. A month later, and a
full day in advance, Fritz told them about the U.S. invasion of Grenada. He also told them stories that didn't
make the news. One was that four Russian submarines
had been sunk off Cape Hatteras, but nobody would ever
know about it, Fritz said, because both sides chose to
keep it secret.

Susie, too, joined in the story telling, confiding to Dot
that she also had worked as an agent, assisting Fritz on
"courier runs" by dropping off satchels full of money, the
purpose of which she was not llowed to know.

If anything ever happened to him, Fritz said, the government would deny any knowledge of him, perhaps
even surreptitiously spread lies about him, but the
McHargues would know that he had died in the service
of his country.

Death clearly was on Fritz's mind in the spring of 1985.
He told the McHargues that two recent attempts had
been made on his life, as well as Susie's.

"He didn't give a lot of details," Dot McHargue remembered. "He was just worried."

As usual, Fritz also had bigger things on his mind. He
was convinced that Armageddon would be set off by a
nuclear explosion in the United States that would result

345

in panic, civil disorder, and invasion from all sides, he told the McHargues. He pictured it vividly and warned that they should be ready.

"He never told me he knew when it was going to be exactly," Dot McHargue said, "but he knew everything was near the end of time."

33

In March of 1985, Judge Susie Sharp was honored with a portrait hanging at the Rockingham County Courthouse in Wentworth, her portrait joining that of her father. She invited Susie, who kept the boys out of school for the ceremony. Su-Su insisted on having the boys pose with her for photographers, and the pictures appeared in area newspapers. The boys looked stiff and ill at ease, especially John. His clothes were rumpled and ill-fitting, his eyes dark circles in his sad face.

Louise snipped the pictures from newspapers and mailed them in a letter to Tom and Kathy on March 22.

> You may like to see how John and Jim made the news here. They did well and we were proud of them. The portrait hanging was sponsored by the Rockingham County Bar Association, and Sandy Sands is the president.
>
> John and Jim looked fine. They are growing fast. Jim is almost as tall as John. Susie is too thin but seems full of vitality.

She went on to talk of other family members and to mention Fritz before closing.

> Annie Hill frequently has supper with me. When she comes we watch "Wheel of Fortune" after supper before she goes home. She backs out at the last minute when Fritz shows up at home for supper

unannounced. I have no idea how or where he spends his time, but he seems to have little consideration for his mother.

On the day Louise wrote that letter, Tom wrote to his lawyer in Reidsville, Bill Horsley.

Enclosed are most of the correspondence between Susie's family, Kathy and me. The relevant parts have been highlighted and we've made comments in the margins that should be of interest to you. Notice especially that our visit to North Carolina last November prompted Susie to at least put on a cosmetic display of family unity over the holidays and permitted the boys a little more freedom. However, the situation seems to have returned to the pre-Christmas position, i.e., Susie and the boys are not spending much time with the family except Annie Hill.

As for the visitation, I would like about 70 days starting this year on June 14 through August 19. This is from a Friday to a Monday, which should be the rule summer after summer. This will maximize the number of weekends Kathy and I can spend with the boys. I also want to ask for every spring break, thus preventing the long periods of time in between visits and this would make for a more consistant visitation schedule. The length of time in the summer will enable us to get in a routine as a family rather than just spending a few weekends with a goodtime father.

I would like to get that part of the visitation changed that requires one of the parents to accompany the boys on their plane trips out here. This provision is a real financial and logistical problem. It usually takes a travel agent two days to coordinate the schedules and naturally doubles the cost of the visitation. On a couple of occasions, Susie has driven the boys to Atlanta and cashed in the tickets. I firmly believe this obstacle was put in as a purely punitive measure to make it more difficult and expensive to see the kids. I don't think that my desires in this matter should be negotiable. You'll need to notify Susie of my desires while I have the boys in Disneyland (April 3–9). I do not expect her to cooperate.

Bill, I can not express to you in any stronger manner how committed I am in this. The information you glean from these letters is not half of the story, but I won't put down on paper my feelings about how Susie is raising the boys. I do think that at this time even her family questions her methods.

The plan to take the boys to Disneyland had originated a year earlier, when Tom discovered that his regular spring visit had been cut short by snow days. He made it known then that he wanted a full visit the next year, and he had taken up the plan of the Disneyland trip with his and Susie's lawyers well in advance. The boys had been enthusiastic about the idea, but Susie was not, and arranging it, as usual, had been a problem. Bob and Florence thought the trip a grand idea, and on the day the boys were to leave on a direct flight to Los Angeles, where Tom and Kathy had flown to meet them, Florence wrote to Tom and Kathy, sending along some snapshots made at Christmas.

John and Jim and Susie came over for a belated birthday dinner for Jim. He and John were quite excited about leaving this a.m. to meet you in Ca. I know you all will have a good time and I think it is great you are giving the boys such a wonderful vacation.

Well, I have finally finished teaching. I am now officially retired from Rutledge and am full-time secretary for Bob. He is keeping me busy.

The renovation in Winston is very slow and still not finished. I imagine it will be June before it is completed.

Bob and I will go to Reidsville to church with Louise, Susie and Judge Bobbitt Sunday. We always go to Mother's church on Easter and place flowers in her memory since she died on Good Friday and was buried on Easter. Easter is a very sad time, but also a glorious time. The trees and flowers here are beautiful.

Tom, Kathy, and the boys had a wonderful trip. The boys were a little wild on arrival—"like barbarians," Tom later described them—but he soon got them settled. They checked into a fancy hotel, where the boys bounced on the beds and tried escargot. They frazzled themselves taking in so many rides and shows at Disneyland. When the boys begged to try the shooting gallery, Tom, an avid hunter, agreed. The boys missed most of the targets.

The boys got to visit Granny Goose and Opa, their former Albuquerque neighbors, who now lived in Anaheim, and Jim went to sleep in his favorite Granny Goose chair. For three days, Tom, Kathy, and the boys visited friends in San Diego. They went to Sea World and roasted hot dogs and marshmallows on the beach.

On this trip, Tom talked to the boys about spending more time with him. John was happy with the prospect, but Jim was reluctant.

"Just tell your mother you want to stay longer," Tom told Jim.

"We can't say that to Mother," Jim said.

"Yes, you can. You're going to have to stand up to her and just tell her."

"You want us to come back with a broken arm?" Jim asked.

Both Tom and Kathy noticed a funny thing on this trip. Three or four times, the boys called Tom Papa, something they'd never done before. After saying it, they acted almost as if they'd slipped and said something wrong.

"Where'd you get that?" Kathy asked once, but neither answered.

John acted different on this trip, as if he wanted to talk about something but couldn't bring himself to do it. When Tom or Kathy asked if something was bothering him, he denied it.

Yet, on the drive back to Los Angeles to put the boys on the plane for home, John cried most of the way.

"Daddy, don't drive so fast. We don't want to have to go back any sooner than we have to."

At the airport, John cried worse than he'd ever cried before on leaving. "Don't send us home," he pleaded.

"I tried to explain to him, 'You have school to finish, and if we don't send you back, your mom's going to have the law after your daddy,' " Kathy remembered.

Tom told him that it would be only a matter of weeks before he and Jim would be coming back to Albuquerque, and he promised that he would see to it that they got to stay longer this time.

"It's going to work out," he said. "Don't worry."

But nothing placated John, and even as Tom and Kathy strapped the boys into their seats on the plane, John clung to them, crying and begging not to go home.

"Do you know what it's like when you're hugging them good-bye and kissing them and telling them we're going to work it out and not to worry . . ." Kathy later said tearfully. "But our hands were tied. What could we do?"

As soon as Tom got home from Los Angeles, he called Bob Newsom. He really needed to spend more time with the boys, he said. If he went back to court to seek longer visitation would Bob be willing to testify that he thought it beneficial for the boys?

"I won't have any trouble at all with that," Bob said.

Tom wasted no time in calling Bill Horsley to tell him that the Newsoms were now willing to help.

On May 2, Horsley filed a motion for extended visitation, and a hearing was set for May 23. Tom again called Bob to fill him in and tell him that he should expect a supoena.

Nine days later, on the Saturday before Mother's Day, Bob and Florence left for Silver Spring, Maryland. The primary purpose of the trip was for Bob to attend hearings in Washington the following week for one of his clients. But Bob also wanted to take Florence out of town on Mother's Day to lessen the pain of having Susie ignore her. As usual, Bob and Florence were planning to stay with Marvin and Taki Mundel, close friends of long standing that Bob had made through his work with the national society of industrial engineers.

The following Wednesday, a sheriff's deputy appeared at the Newsom house with a subpoena for Bob. The subpoena caught Rob by surprise because his father had not told him about the upcoming hearing or his plan to testify. When Bob and Florence arrived home the following afternoon, Rob told his father about the subpoena.

"I knew it was coming," Bob said, and went on to tell his son why he intended to testify on Tom's behalf.

"Have you told Susie about it?" Rob asked.

"Not yet."

Thursday night, Tom called Susie's apartment to talk to the boys.

"John," he said, "we're going to have a hearing next week to see if you and Jimbo can't spend some more time out here with us this summer."

John said little, and Tom was certain that it was because Susie was listening and he didn't want to upset his mother.

Jim objected. "I thought I told you we don't want to stay any longer," he said.

"We'll just let the judge decide," Tom told him.

"Jim always wanted to keep peace," Tom later said of Jim's reaction. "He knew a big stink was coming."

On Friday morning, Bob steeled himself to tell his daughter of his intentions.

"That Friday when I left for work, he told me he was going to call her," Rob said later, but he would never know the contents of that conversation.

At 3:30 that afternoon, Susie and the boys arrived in Reidsville at the office of her lawyer, Sandy Sands, for a scheduled appointment to talk about the hearing, which was set for the following Thursday. Susie was carrying a plastic bag containing two small stuffed toy animals, a green dragon and an orange-and-black tiger. The throats of each had been slit.

When Susie was ushered alone into Sands's office she was trembling, crying, her voice quivering.

"Susie was as scared as any human being I've ever seen in my life," Sands said. "She was terrified."

She showed him the toy animals and told him that sometime in March Tom had called and asked for a longer visit in April. She'd said no. They'd argued. She'd hung up on him. Shortly afterward, she came home from class to find the two animals, toys the boys usually took when they went to Albuquerque, with their throats slit.

"Did you call the police?" Sands asked.

No, she said. Nothing else was disturbed, and there was no sign of forced entry. She went to the complex office, where passkeys to all of the apartments were kept on a panel on the wall, but the one for her apartment wouldn't open the door, she said. She figured that somebody had taken the right key and replaced it with another.

Soon after finding the animals, Susie went on, she got an anonymous call.

"Two down and two to go," the caller said, and hung up.

Susie said she took it to mean that the Lynch murders were the two down. The two to go, she feared, were her children.

After the anonymous call, she said, Tom called again, renewing his request, and she was afraid not to grant it.

After Sands calmed Susie, they talked about the upcoming hearing. Sands told her that her father would be testifying for Tom, but he realized from her reaction that she already knew about it. They talked about what evidence might be presented and what they should present.

Sands wanted to put the boys on the stand to say that they didn't want to spend more time with their father, and he called them in for a thirty-minute session without their mother. Among the things Sands asked them were what activities they were looking forward to with their mother this summer. Hiking and camping, they both agreed.

Sands liked the boys. He found them quiet but polite, erudite, well read for their ages.

"They were the kind of kids who could've impressed a judge," he said later, "the kind that judges would listen to."

After talking with the boys, Sands told Susie that he might also want to call the psychiatrist she and the boys had been seeing, Andrew Courts, to testify that they were handling their situation together well. Susie said that she and the boys had an appointment with Dr. Courts on Monday and that she would mention it to him.

The meeting lasted two hours, and as Susie was leaving, Sands assured her that it was not unusual that her father would testify for the other side. Grandparents often thought that the other parent should have more time with the children, he said. He thought she was satisfied about that.

"When she left here," he said, "there was no reason for her to worry about her parents' testifying."

After leaving Sands's office, Susie drove the short distance to the Klenner house, where she and the boys joined Annie Hill and Fritz for supper. Hearing from Susie that her father was planning to testify in Tom's behalf, family members later learned, Fritz responded gravely, "I never dreamed Bob Newsom would turn traitor."

During the meal, Annie Hill later reported, she suggested that if Susie were having to go back to court, she should try to get more money from Tom for the boys. After all, wasn't he a millionaire now that he had inherited his family's fortune? Susie said that she intended to do just that.

After the meal, she and the boys returned to Greensboro. Fritz left for Virginia, telling his mother that he was going camping in the mountains with Ian Perkins, a neighbor from down the street, the son of longtime Klenner family friends, a student at Washington and Lee University.

As Fritz was leaving, Ian was already waiting for him on Roanoke Mountain, thinking that he would be joining Fritz on a CIA mission to Texas. Not until several hours later, after Fritz finally showed up at his room in Lexington, did Ian learn that there had been a change in plans. Their mission would take them instead to North Carolina. First stop: Winston-Salem.

On Saturday morning, May 18, a day that would end in murder for the Newsom family, Annette Hunt, who lived next door to the Newsoms in Greensboro, got a surprise call from Susie.

Annette once had been Susie's closest friend, but she'd rarely heard from her in the past year and a half. Annette thought it was because Susie didn't want her to know how close she'd gotten with Fritz.

"What are you doing?" Susie asked.

"Nothing much."

"Can I come over?"

"Sure."

Susie stayed several hours. She and Annette spent some time catching up, but mostly Susie wanted to talk about the upcoming hearing. She was convinced that Tom wanted to take the boys away from her and she couldn't understand how her father could testify against her. She was clearly upset.

"She just went on and on about it," Annette remembered later. "She said she just couldn't believe he was going to do that. I said, 'Susie, please go talk to Bob. Go talk to him.' I wanted to see them work things out."

Before Susie left, Annette told her that if she had to go back to court, she should try to get Tom to pay to send the boys to camp each summer. It would be good for all of them, she said. She gave Susie some material about a camp her boys had gone to, and Susie saw that it had a rifle program.

"The boys," she said, "would like that."

Charlie and Juanita Clarke were on their way home from a country barbecue that Saturday evening when they passed a road that triggered something in Charlie's mind. Yadkinville Road led past Green Meadows, the small development where Bob and Florence Newsom once lived. The Clarkes had spent many pleasant evenings visiting there with the Newsoms.

"Know what I'd like to do?" Charlie said. "Let's go see Bob and Florence."

"Not unless we call," Juania admonished.

Charlie and Bob had grown up together. Charlie's father was the pastor of the church Bob and his sister attended with their father. Charlie and Bob were close friends in high school and roommates at North Carolina State after Charlie convinced Bob that he should give up his dreams of a music career to pursue industrial engineering.

Charlie dropped out of college and went into defense work, but he later returned, got a degree in civil engineering, and moved to West Virginia to work on government hydraulic projects. For years he didn't see his old friend at all, but in 1960 he returned to Winston-Salem to work for a construction company, and he and Bob picked up their friendship again.

He knew that Bob and Florence were spending weekends at Nanna's now and soon planned to move there. The Clarkes drove to their home in Lewisville, just west of Winston-Salem, and Charlie called Nanna's house. Bob answered and sounded delighted to hear from him.

It was about 8 P.M. when Charlie and Juanita arrived at the big house on Valley Road. Bob and Florence met them at the back door with smiles, handshakes, and hugs. Bob took Charlie on a tour of the house, showing the renovations. Florence and Juanita went off in a different direction. Nanna wasn't feeling well, Bob said, and was resting in her bedroom.

While Charlie and Bob were taking in the new downstairs rooms, Charlie asked about the children.

"Rob is getting along just fine," Bob said. "He's with the county now, doing just great. They're living with us, you know."

"Oh," Charlie said; he didn't know.

"Susie's living in an apartment and going to school at UNC-G getting a master's degree in business," Bob went on. "Just getting along great."

"He wasn't the type to tell you his family problems," Charlie observed later.

Upstairs, where Florence was showing her the new guest room, Juanita was hearing a different story.

Florence asked about the Clarkes' daughter, Marsha, whose wedding she'd attended four years earlier.

"She's just fine," Juanita said.

"That was the nicest wedding," Florence said. "Is she happy?"

"She just seems to be happy beyond words."

"I certainly hope that lasts," Florence said. "I tell you, we're having a problem with Susie. She's having a hard time, and I don't know how that's going to end."

Florence shook her head, then laughed and changed the subject.

Later, the four gathered to chat in the living room, and Nanna came out in her nightclothes to join them. Bob and Juanita sat on the sofa with an ashtray between them. Juanita was smoking cigarettes, Bob puffing his pipe.

"We don't need the TV," Florence said, flicking it off. She removed her shoes and settled comfortably in the recliner.

Charlie told a story over which they'd laughed dozens of times in the past, about the time Bob borrowed his transit to survey a property line and thought he'd lost the crosshairs from it. Then Bob and Charlie started reminiscing about their childhood neighborhood. Nanna joined in the story telling, and the Clarkes marveled at her memory for names and incidents.

About 9:15, Charlie noticed Bob stifle a yawn and figured he was tired.

"Well, we've got to be going," Charlie said.

The leave-taking took several minutes. Outside, Bob mentioned a problem with water running off the back of the house, and Charlie stepped over to examine it, leaving a footprint in the sand next to one of the broad new windows.

"What you need here is a drain," Charlie said.

A new round of good-byes followed before the Clarkes walked out to their car under the big oaks. It was a dark night, turning cool, but the thing Charlie later remembered most about it was the eerie quiet that enveloped them. As they got into their car and pulled away at about 9:30, the Clarkes looked back and saw Bob and Florence still standing in the big windows, smiling and waving to them.

PART FIVE

THE UNRAVELING

"O haggard queen! to Athens dost thou guide
Thy glowing chariot, steeped in kindred gore;
Or seek to hide thy damned parricide
Where peace and justice dwell forevermore?"
—EURIPIDES

34

Nancy and Steve Dunn were already in bed at their home on Raleigh's western edge when the phone rang shortly before midnight on Sunday, May 19, 1985. Nancy was surprised to find her father, Bing Miller, on the line.

"Nancy," he said with no preliminaries, "I've got some bad news. Nanna and Bob and Florence have been murdered."

Nancy started screaming uncontrollably, and Steve took the phone to find out what had happened. They would be right there, he said.

They dressed quickly and rushed to their car, Nancy trembling so that she hardly could open the door. As Steve drove across town, Nancy began screaming again.

"Susie did this!" she cried. "I know she did!"

"It was the first thing that came to my mind," she recalled later. "I just knew how weird she had been acting. I don't know why, but I just started screaming that. I couldn't say it enough."

Nancy arrived to find her mother packing. She was startled by her mother's calmness until she realized that she must be in shock. "She was calm," Nancy said, "and not there."

Nancy's brother, David, arrived shortly, and Nancy went out to greet him.

"Susie has done this," were the first words he spoke.

Inside, Nancy and David continued to insist that Susie had to be involved, bringing their mother from her stunned refuge.

"Don't say that," Frances said. "You don't know that. She's family."

Nancy¹ decided to go with her parents and brother to Winston-Salem while Steve returned home to stay with their two sons. Nancy drove her parents' car, and she drove fast. For the first seventy-five miles, nobody even spoke, each in a cocoon of personal thought and pain.

"It was like we were going to get there and find out it wasn't true," Nancy later recalled. "The faster we got there, the faster we'd find out it wasn't true."

Susie was much on the minds of others that night. Rob had tried several times to call her after he became concerned about his parents and grandmother, but he never got an answer. He tried again after the call came from Winston-Salem that something was terribly wrong. Friends and neighbors who gathered at the Newsom house that night kept calling without success after Rob left for Winston-Salem.

A little after midnight, Dr. John Chandler, a dentist, a neighbor, and a close family friend of the Newsoms, called again. This time Susie answered. She'd just gotten home from a trip, she said.

Dr. Chandler told her that an accident apparently had happened at Nanna's. He had no details yet. Rob had gone over.

Susie seemed little concerned. She asked no questions, and when Dr. Chandler inquired if she needed somebody with her, she said no; she'd be fine.

Later, when a call came to the Newsom house confirming that Bob and Florence and Nanna were dead, all murdered, Rob's wife, Alice, called Susie again.

"I'd rather your brother be here to tell you this," Alice said, fighting back tears as she went on to tell what had happened.

Later, Alice remembered that Susie showed no shock. She didn't cry. For a long moment, she offered only silence.

"Well, there's nothing left, is there?" she finally said.

Again, Susie declined when Alice offered to have somebody come to get her or stay with her, and Susie broke off the conversation by saying, "Well, my dog has run off. I've got to go find him. I'll talk to you later."

A strange reaction, Alice thought, to the revelation that her parents and beloved grandmother had been murdered.

Rob was then at the home of Fam Brownlee. His friend, Tom Maher, was with him, and so was his father-in-law, Fred Hill, as well as the Newsom family's minister from St. Paul's Episcopal Church, Dudley Colhoun. Detective Allen Gentry, who'd quietly assumed charge of the case, had come to the house to interview Rob, and Rob had told him of the murders of his sister's former in-laws in Kentucky. Gentry took down Susie's address and telephone number, as well as Rob's, and suggested that Rob go home, take care of his family, and try to rest. Somebody, he said, would come to talk to him later.

As Rob was getting ready to leave, Dudley Colhoun called Fam Brownlee aside.

"Do you know Susie?" Colhoun asked.

"I do not. I've heard her name."

"If she should come by here or call, would you please have her get in touch with me or the police or with Rob, because they can't find her."

"Yeah, she's probably involved in this," Fred Hill added.

Brownlee was taken aback by this statement. "I find that very difficult to believe," he said.

"Oh, he's probably right," said the minister.

These comments, coming from people so close to the family, flabbergasted Brownlee, and while Colhoun was talking with Rob, Brownlee pulled aside Rob's friend.

"I don't want to be stirring up anything," he said, going on to tell what he'd just heard about the possibility of involvement by Susie.

"I wouldn't be the least bit surprised," Tom Maher said. "Her or her boyfriend."

As soon as the group left his home, Brownlee sought out a detective and told him what he'd just heard, but that information never got to Allen Gentry.

* * *

Rob had been gone for nearly an hour when Nancy pulled her parents' car up to the gate of her grandmother's home.

"We are the family," Nancy said to the officers stationed there. The officers directed her to the Brownlee house and said that somebody would talk to them shortly. While Nancy and her family waited in the car, they saw the SBI's big mobile crime lab pull up to the house. This lab had come from Raleigh. A regional lab was stationed in an adjoining county, but its operator was sick that night and another one had to be sent.

Shortly, a detective came to the Millers' car.

"It's my mother," Frances said. "Tell me what has happened."

The detective began, but had to stop when tears began coursing down his cheeks.

Frances said that she wanted to go into the house and see for herself.

"You can't go in" he told her. "You just can't do that."

Nanna's minister, John Giesler, was still at the Brownlee house, and when he and Brownlee learned that the Millers were outside, they went out to offer comfort and invite them in. Giesler called a Holiday Inn not far away and got a room for them. The Millers told the detectives where they would be and went to the motel, where a night clerk, upon learning of their tragedy, opened the closed restaurant and made coffee for them.

Near dawn, Detective F. G. Crater came to the motel and gave the Millers a sketchy rundown of the facts. The Millers peppered him with questions, most of which he said he couldn't answer.

Crater had some questions of his own.

"Do you know anybody who would do this?"

Frances said no, and despite their earlier convictions that Susie had to be involved, Nancy and David kept silent.

"We thought we were the terrible ones to be thinking that," Nancy later explained.

"Do you know where Susie Lynch is?" Crater asked.

They all said no.

"Do you know anything about the divorce in Albuquerque?"

"I just know that it was bitter," Frances said, then went on to tell about the murder of Susie's in-laws the summer before.

After the detective left, the Reverend Giesler came to the motel and told the Millers all that he had seen at the house.

Frances sat with her head in her hands. "This can't be true," she said.

At the Newsom house, while the crime lab crew went about its work, officers drank coffee fetched from a nearby fast-food place and theorized about the murders.

Despite the evidence to the contrary, some still thought robbery the motive. Others thought somebody high on drugs might have done it. Ron Barker, the commander of the criminal investigation division, was certain that the murders had been executions. When he heard that Bob Newsom sometimes dealt with labor problems, his first thought was that this might have been a mob crime. "I thought, 'My God, if it's organized crime, it's going to be a long case.'"

Allen Gentry wasn't joining in the theorizing, although he, too, thought that the murders looked like executions. "For what we're used to, it looked incredibly professional," he said. He'd told this to his friend Tom Sturgill, when Sturgill arrived at 2 A.M.

Tall, gaunt, and bald, Sturgill was the SBI's lead agent in Winston-Salem. He was quiet and soft-spoken, never acted impulsively, and had a reputation for building solid cases. Gentry, himself meticulously thorough, liked Sturgill, had worked with him on several cases, and thought they made a good team. Sturgill had but one comment after going through the house: "This is going to be a tough one."

It was going to be made even tougher, Gentry knew, by the prominence of the victims. Not until a couple of hours after he arrived did he learn that Florence Newsom was the sister of Susie Sharp, the former chief justice of the state supreme court. "A little additional pressure," he later called this news, but it didn't bother him.

"I don't get nervous," he explained. "You get down and do everything as best you can. You go at it in a deliberate and methodical way and try not to worry. You just take the steps you can, and if you run out of things to do, then you worry."

On this case, he knew, he was not apt to run out of things to do anytime soon.

By 7 A.M., Gentry had accompanied Dr. Lew Stringer, the Forsyth County Medical Examiner, through his on-scene examination of the bodies, had completed a thorough search for clues, and had assigned officers to canvass the neighborhood and talk with construction workers who had been at the house. He hurried home to get a quick shower and shave, and abandon his informal attire for a coat and tie, his usual dress. He stayed barely long enough to tell his wife, Lu Ann, that this was indeed a big case, three prominent people murdered and few clues in sight. Then he rushed off without breakfast to rejoin the investigation at the house.

While Gentry was gone, District Attorney Donald Tisdale arrived. At forty-two, Tisdale, a Wake Forest graduate, had been DA for ten years, and he had not been fainthearted in his work. "Far from shying away from controversy," the *Winston-Salem Journal* once noted about him, "he seems to relish it." Tisdale liked cops and sometimes rode with them on drug busts and undercover activities. They returned his respect. Rarely did an officer make a big move without first consulting him.

Lieutenant E. B. Hiatt called Tisdale that morning, and Tisdale, who lived only a mile from the Newsom house, dressed and drove there before heading to his office, where he was preparing for a big and controversial trial. Tom Sturgill and Captain C. C. McGee of the Forsyth Sheriff's Department showed him through the house and filled him in on what was known. Tisdale thought it significant that the death blows were all wounds to the head. This had to be a drug-related killing or an execution, he said, and these were hardly the type of people to be involved with drugs. But why would anybody want to execute them?

Near Nanna's telephone, the detectives had found a calendar on which she jotted comments about her life and daily activities. Tisdale picked it up and thumbed through it. Some of the entries were touching. On February 4, Nanna wrote: "Bob's birthday. 65 years ago was raining and cold. Dr. stayed all night."

On March 18, Tisdale noted, she'd planted lettuce and onions. On the twenty-seventh, she'd worked in the garden and mailed Jim's birthday card. On the following day, the first asparagus appeared in her garden.

Tisdale flipped over and read all of May's entries:

5. Went to church.

6. Worked in garden, planted squash, painters still here.

7. Circle meeting, chicken pie bake, septic drain fixed, painters still here.

8. Painters finished.

9. Beauty parlor. Dr. Sutton. Went to Bob's for supper.

10. Friday. Charlie and Bolly worked all day.

11. Bobby worked till lunch, left 2:07, went to Washington.

12. Frances came, took me out to dinner. Had a nice day.

13. Floor finishers here. Get wedding gift. Cloudy.

14. Went to get monitor fitted. Floor finishers done. I can't do much. Dust everywhere.

15. Got monitor off. Floors beautiful.

16. Finish men working. Washed. Cut broccoli.

There were no further entries.

But on the opposite page was a quote from Emily Dickinson: "A little madness in the spring is wholesome even for the king."

Tisdale was also a gardener—"a two-bit farmer," he liked to call himself—and after he put down Nanna's calendar, he went outside and walked alone in her garden, trying to cleanse from his mind the images of agonized death he'd seen inside. The garden was coming alive with morning, the mist rising, the squash Nanna had planted just days earlier already peeking from the damp and fertile soil. The broccoli was beginning to produce, the broad, blue-green heads glistening with dew. Such a fruitful and peaceful place, Tisdale thought. How could somebody who nurtured something so beautiful and lifegiving be cut down so cruelly?

"That affected me," he said later.

Not far away, at the Holiday Inn on Cherry Street, Nancy Dunn called her cousin Rob in Greensboro. She wanted to know how he was doing and whether the police had told him anything more than she and her family knew. She also wanted to know what he'd told the police, or might be going to tell them about his sister's behavior.

"He was scared," she recalled later. "I said, 'Rob, I'm going to tell them everything I know.' He said, 'I guess I will, too.' "

35

Susie's friend Annette Hunt, Bob and Florence's neighbor, was unaware of the turmoil that was going on next door until another neighbor called to tell her about the murders on Monday morning.

"I was just reeling," she recalled later. "I could not believe it. I wanted to get to Susie. I kept thinking, 'I've got to get to Susie, I've got to get to Susie.' "

She ran across the street to the Newsom house, only to find that Susie wasn't there. Rob was expecting her, he said. He'd called and asked her to come over. Annette said that she'd drive to Susie's apartment and get her. A friend, Shirley Darden, went with her.

They found Susie sitting alone at the kitchen table, dressed and ready to go. Annette hugged her.

"I just can't believe it, you know?" Susie said.

Susie fixed tea. Fritz was asleep, she said, and she didn't want to awaken him. She'd sent the boys to school without telling them what had happened.

"I think you've done the best thing," Annette said.

But Susie was worried about the boys, concerned that somebody might try to snatch them or harm them, and Annette made her call the school and leave word that nobody was to pick them up but herself.

Afterward, Annette drove Susie to her house. Susie immediately got on the phone, calling people. She called the university to report that she would not be at class and to reschedule a test. She called Dr. Courts, her psychiatrist, to cancel an appointment that day. At one point she broke into tears on the phone.

Annette made iced tea, and Susie took three huge orange pills from her purse and began to swallow them.

"What on earth are those?" Annette asked.

"B vitamins," Susie said. "They're stress tablets."

Later, she took more pills. "She was just chugging handsful of things," Annette recalled.

Annette accompanied Susie to her parents' house across the street, where family and friends were coming and going and the phone was constantly busy.

"Doesn't somebody need to call Tom?" somebody asked at one point.

"The son of a bitch can learn it from his lawyers," Susie said.

That was precisely how Tom was learning it. He called Bill Horsley's office in Reidsville that morning to make sure that the hearing was still scheduled for Thursday. He had to get airline tickets and he'd waited until the last minute in case the hearing was canceled. He expected some such trick by Susie's lawyer.

The first news reports of the murders in Winston-Salem had been on radio by then, but they were only sketchy, and word had begun to circulate by phone. It had reached Horsley's office only a short time before Tom's call. Horsley's secretary told Tom that there had been some trouble at the Newsom house in Winston-Salem. Somebody had been killed. She didn't know details.

Tom hung up and called Rob.

"It's Tom Lynch," Rob was told when he was summoned to the phone at his tense and crowded house.

"Rob, don't talk to him," Susie said, but he ignored her.

"Susie and Fritz have done this," Tom told himself after talking to Rob. "This is too big a coincidence."

He picked up the phone again and dialed the number of Kentucky State Police Post Five in La Grange.

Detective Sherman Childers, who long had been frustrated about the murders of Delores and Janie Lynch, took the call from Tom and listened with building excitement. He'd see what he could find out from North Carolina, he told Tom, and call him back.

Just a couple of weeks before, Childers's friend and partner, Lieutenant Dan Davidson, who was in charge of the Lynch case, had taken all the records home to pore over them at night. Davidson was almost obsessed with his inability to solve the Lynch murders, and he and Childers talked about it constantly. Davidson was away at an FBI Academy retraining conference, and Childers couldn't wait to tell him about the call from Tom.

"It sounds odd," Childers said when he finally got through to Davidson.

"Yeah, it damn sure does," Davidson said. "If it's a coincidence, it's a funny one. Well, let's just see what it is. I don't want to get my hopes up again and get shot down."

"We were optimistic," he explained later, "but we'd been hurt bad. We were not going to let ourselves get in that predicament again."

Childers called the Forsyth County Sheriff's Department to say that he had a case that might tie into the Newsom murders and to find out who was in charge of the Newsom case. He called Tom back with the name and number of Allen Gentry. Tom called, but Gentry was unavailable, and he left his number.

"We'll give them a few days to get their case together," Davidson told Childers, "and then you and Lennie can go down there and see what you can find out."

After visiting with the Newsoms on Saturday night, Charlie and Juanita Clarke drove to Raleigh on Sunday morning to see their daughter Marsha. They left for home after breakfast on Monday, and after stopping several times along the way for shopping, arrived at about 3 P.M. The afternoon was warm and pleasant, and Charlie took his small boat onto the lake behind his house for some fishing.

A little after 5 P.M., the phone rang at the Clarke house. Juanita answered, and her daughter Marsha asked, "Are you standing?"

"Yes, why?"

"Sit down."

"Okay, I'm sitting. What's wrong?"

"The Newsoms have been murdered."

"Marsha, you have to be kidding. I don't believe it."

Juanita went onto the high deck at the back of her house where she kept a cowbell for summoning her husband to supper. She rang it frantically.

Charlie muttered, reeled in his line, and paddled to shore to see what was wrong. The fish had just begun to bite.

After telling her husband about the murders, Juanita called Katy Sutton, the wife of Nanna's doctor and an old Newsom family friend.

"I've just heard what happened," Juanita said.

Katy told her that she and Homer had discovered the bodies.

"Oh, dear me, Katy," Juanita said. "We were just over there Saturday night."

"You were? What time?"

"We were home by quarter to ten."

"I'm sure the sheriff's department would want to know this," Katy said, "because they aren't sure when they were killed."

Charlie called the sheriff's department to report that he might have some useful information about the Newsoms.

Allen Gentry spent Monday morning at the Newsom house, going through Nanna's belongings, coordinating the investigation, and assessing the information that had begun to pour in. Reporters arrived at the foot of the driveway early and remained, clamoring for information, but all the officers avoided them.

A little before noon, the bodies were removed, each departing in an ambulance filmed by TV crews. Shortly afterward, Gentry and several other officers went to a nearby restaurant for lunch. When he returned to the house, Gentry got a call from Sheriff Preston Oldham, who had received a call from Rockingham County Sheriff Bobby Vernon saying that he had some information that might be pertinent to the murders. Oldham thought Gentry should go to Rockingham County.

Early that morning, Susie's lawyer, Sandy Sands, had received a call from Annie Hill Klenner, who wanted to know if it was true that Florence, Bob, and Nanna had been murdered. Sands called Vernon, who confirmed the murders. Sands then went to Annie Hill's house to tell her. Afterward, Sands called Vernon to say he had information, and Vernon called Oldham.

Gentry got Walt House, a young SBI agent, to go with him. House, a close friend, had been a Forsyth County sheriff's deputy before joining the SBI. After talking with Vernon, they went to Sands's office near downtown Reidsville.

Sands not only filled in the officers about Susie's divorce and the bitter battles over visitation, he went on to tell about Susie's fears, her belief that Tom's underworld connections had killed his parents, and her visit to his office just three days earlier.

"The trip was not all we were hoping for," Gentry recalled later. "Sands was trying to lay it all at Tom's doorstep, but I couldn't figure out how Tom could benefit from the death of Susie's family."

Gentry left Sands's office confused and tired—very tired; he'd been going for nearly thirty-six hours on less than two hours sleep. He and Walt House dropped by the Rockingham County courthouse in Wentworth to pick up copies of the documents in Tom and Susie's court struggles, then headed for Winston-Salem.

On the way, Gentry stopped by Susie's apartment to meet her and arrange a later interview. His knock was answered only by a ferociously barking dog that kept slamming into the door from the inside. He left his card in the door and drove on to Winston-Salem.

The lab team had quit for the day by the time Gentry and House returned to the Newsom home at 7:30 P.M. Gentry went home, had a cheese sandwich, fell into bed and immediately went to sleep.

Susie was at Annette Hunt's house that evening, having dinner with Fritz, Annie Hill, and the boys.

The talk in the beginning was of the events of the day. Susie didn't mention her parents, but she did talk about her grandmother. Nanna was a great student of the Bible, she said.

"Greed," said Susie. "Nanna always said that was the ultimate sin. You could boil it all down to one word: *greed*."

She went on to talk about what a wonderful woman Nanna was. It was hard to think of her gone, she said.

"She was such a sweet person," Fritz added.

"Fritz never did have a tremendous amount to say," Annette said later. "He never made any comment at all about Bob and Florence."

But Fritz's chair at the dinner table had a view of the Newsom house. "It's hard to have to look over there," he observed at one point.

After dinner, Fritz went outside to talk with Annette's son, Joey, who was seventeen and had long looked up to Fritz, sharing his interests in weaponry and martial arts. While they talked, Fritz noticed Rob come out of his house across the street, and he walked over and offered condolences.

"He just said, 'I'm sorry,' and I said, 'Thank you,' " Rob said later.

Fritz had to drive his mother to Reidsville, and Annette said that Joey could take Susie and the boys home. Before Joey left, Fritz slipped him a loaded pistol and told him to be very watchful. Joey's mother was upset later when she found out about that.

When Joey didn't return promptly, Annette called Susie's apartment to make sure everything was okay. All was fine, Susie said. Joey was walking the dogs for her.

"The sheriff came by," Susie said. "He left his card in the door."

36

The Newsom murders were the top story on area TV newscasts Monday night, but the reports were sketchy, and newspapers in Greensboro and Winston-Salem could offer few more details in their Tuesday morning editions.

Most of what reporters had learned came from Homer Sutton, who had found the bodies, and John Giesler, Nanna's minister, who also had gone to the house before police arrived, but even they hadn't said much. One story noted that Dr. Sutton declined to answer many questions because Sheriff Preston Oldham asked him not to talk.

Oldham had little regard for the press, and on Monday he had circulated a memo through his department warning that information about the murders was to be released only through him, and he was inclined to release little.

Oldham's reputation as a tough cop was hard-earned. He'd wanted to be a policeman since his childhood in a local orphanage, and he went at his work with uncommon zeal. His undercover narcotics work, during which he rode for two years with a motorcycle gang, was legendary, his adventures the stuff of movies. Once called Mule because of his stubbornness, he remained dedicated, driven, and distrustful of nearly everybody after twenty-two years in law enforcement. Humorless and blunt, he was short not only with the press. "I don't have time to be a social worker," the *Winston-Salem Journal* once quoted him as telling a local group. "I just kick ass and take names."

Early Tuesday morning, the detectives involved in the case gathered at the sheriff's department in the basement of the modern, seven-story justice building in downtown Winston-Salem to go over what they'd learned and decide assignments.

Afterward, Gentry called Rob to set up an interview. An appointment was made for 3 P.M. Gentry also called Susie about an interview. Sorry, not today, she told him, sounding, as he later described it, "perfectly chipper and happy." She had other appointments.

"I thought that was a little odd," he said. "If my parents and grandmother got murdered, I'd think talking to the police about it would be high on my priority list. It obviously was not on hers."

Whenever something bothered Gentry, he ran it by somebody before forming an opinion. "Does this sound right to you, or is it me?" he said to SBI agent Tom Sturgill, telling him about Susie's reaction.

"We both felt things weren't quite kosher," he said, "but at that point it was just a feeling."

At 10:43, Gentry called Tom in Albuquerque. Tom told him about the murders of his mother and sister, and Gentry would not forget the date, July 22; that was his birthday. Tom told of Susie's dislike for his mother and of Bob's plan to testify in the upcoming hearing. Susie had been acting strangely, he said, and he wasn't sure what was going on. She also had an unusual relationship with her first cousin, Fritz Klenner.

This was the first mention of Fritz's name that Gentry had heard, and he misunderstood it, writing it on his notepad as "Clennerd."

Fritz was a weird guy, Tom went on, a gun lover, some sort of survivalist. Tom thought he should be checked out. He would be, Gentry assured him.

Frances Miller and her family had returned to Raleigh Monday after stopping in Greensboro to see Rob and Susie. They picked up clothing and other necessities and drove back to the Holiday Inn on Cherry Street in Winston-Salem, where they were joined by the fifth member of the family, the youngest child, Debbie Parham, who had come from her home in Atlanta.

Although they had not slept Sunday night, sleep had not come Monday either.

"We stayed up all night and started playing detective," Nancy remembered. "We were obsessed with it."

They drew maps, charts, and diagrams, and they were frustrated with their lack of information. They wanted answers from the police, and they thought they might get them Tuesday morning. Officers had invited Frances to come to her mother's house. They wanted her to tell them if she saw anything missing or out of the ordinary.

Frances was met at the house by SBI agents J. W. Bryant and Walt House, who explained what they wanted. "You talk," Bryant said, "we'll listen." Frances entered through the broken storm door with Nancy on her arm. The officers guided her away from the foyer where Bob's body had been lying less than twenty-four hours earlier and straight ahead to Nanna's bedroom, where the drawers from the chest were still stacked on the floor. The experience seemed somehow unreal to Frances. Entering the bedroom where just nine days earlier, on Mother's Day, she and Nanna had sat giggling over all the things Nanna couldn't bring herself to throw away, Frances was flooded with memory: *"I sure hope, honey, that you don't have to come in here and take care of all of this stuff if something happens to me."*

As soon as she stepped into the room, Frances saw her mother's expensive gold-and-pearl bracelet on the floor. That answered one of her questions. Surely, this had been no robbery.

The officers guided her upstairs, where Bob's briefcase lay open on the floor of his bedroom.

"It's empty," she said. "He would never have carried an empty briefcase. What was in here?"

"We don't know," one of the officers said.

While her mother looked around the room, Nancy spotted some letters in Florence's knitting basket next to the bed. She picked them up and glanced through them. They were copies of the letters exchanged between Tom and Kathy and Florence and Louise. Frances and her family had not known about the upcoming hearing, nor had they known of Bob's plan to testify on Tom's behalf. Nancy grew excited as she read the letters.

"Here it is!" she said. "This is it! Take these. This is the motive right here. Have you read these?"

The officers said little about the letters, but later Nancy learned that they had read them and made copies before returning them to the basket to see if Frances would notice them.

The letters convinced Nancy that Susie and her problems were behind the murders.

Rob and Susie drove to Winston-Salem in separate cars Tuesday morning to make arrangements for their parents' funeral. Susie went first to St. Paul's Episcopal Church, which she had attended until her marriage. She hadn't been to the church in years, and the Reverend Dudley Colhoun invited her into his office in the church annex. He knew of Susie's troubles with her family. He'd been briefed by Rob's in-laws, who were members of the church and suspicious of Susie's involvement in the murders, and he was curious to see how Susie was acting.

"I'm certainly sorry about what's happened," he said.

"It could've been anybody in Forsyth County who did it," Susie responded. "There have been all kinds of workmen in that house, you know."

The way Susie talked about the murders was almost as if she were talking about somebody else's family, perhaps something she'd read in the newspaper, Colhoun thought. He realized that in cases of sudden death, family members sometimes have trouble letting out their emotions, and he thought this might be the case with Susie.

He asked what she'd been doing. She told about going to Taiwan. She was at UNC-G now, she said, about to get her master's degree in business, and she was thinking about returning to China.

She asked about his son, Chuck, whom she'd taught in Sunday school.

"Know where Chuck is?" Colhoun said smiling. He pointed out the window behind him to the apartment building next door. "He lives right there, he and his wife."

He tried to stir her emotions by recalling happy family

moments from the past, but he realized that he wasn't getting through. Susie turned conversation to the service, and after they'd gone through the order of it, she made ready to leave.

"How can I help you?" Colhoun asked, but she offered no suggestions. The meeting lasted only twenty minutes.

"It was a weird thing," Colhoun said later. "There was no feeling whatsoever, no sense of remorse or loss."

After Susie left, Colhoun made an observation to the church's director of education, Wilma Smiley, who had been a friend of Florence. "Something's not right," he said.

Rob and Susie met at Vogler's Funeral Home, only a short distance from Nanna's house, where they were joined by their aunt Frances. Susie seemed hyperactive and very talkative to Frances, who found her behavior unusual. "It would not have been normal to anybody who loved their parents," she said later. "I was looking for some signs of sorrow. I could find none."

While Frances planned her mother's funeral, Rob and Susie picked out a casket for their father, an urn for their mother's ashes, and saw to other arrangements. At her request, Florence was being cremated. Bob would need a suit in which to be buried, the funeral director noted, and Rob said there was a new one at Nanna's house. He'd pick it up if the police would let him and drop it off. Susie went to the house with him to look for some of her mother's belongings. Officers accompanied them as they went through the house. Later, they stood on the patio at the back of the house, chatting with Captain Ron Barker.

"We talked about their childhood days and how much fun they'd had there as kids," Barker recalled later. He also remembered Susie making some mention of Nanna's will, an inappropriate time for that, he thought.

He thought a couple of other things were odd about Susie's behavior that day.

"I've investigated a lot of murders," he said. "Usually, the family asks you all kinds of questions. They stay on you constantly. Not one question did she ask."

The other thing he noticed was this: "She was cheerful. She didn't seem remorseful at all."

Rob was late getting home for his appointment with Gentry, and Gentry and SBI agent Walt House were waiting for him. They talked for several hours, going over family background, the events of the past week. They talked about wills. Rob estimated his grandmother's estate at nearly $1 million, his parents' at about $750,000. He mentioned that his grandfather once kept large sums of money at the house, causing concern in the family that somebody might find out about it and rob him. After Paw-Paw's death, $15,000 had been found hidden away. Perhaps somebody thought money was still stashed there. He told about the upcoming hearing and his father's plan to testify in behalf of longer visitation. He said that his sister suspected Tom of criminal activity, but he would be surprised if it were true.

What Rob did not mention was his own suspicions. On the way home from Nanna's house Sunday night, he and Tom Maher had talked about who might have committed the murders. They had agreed that Fritz was the most likely suspect. But Rob said nothing of this, nor did he tell about how his family was troubled about Susie's relationship with Fritz. Only when Gentry asked, "Does anybody in the family have an unusual interest in weapons?" did Rob speak his cousin's name. Later, Gentry would have trouble understanding that. But Rob had reasons for failing to mention his suspicions about Fritz, he said later. First, Fritz was still coming to his house, still a potential danger to him and his family; second, he had given Gentry all of the information on which he had based his suspicions and thought he could figure it out for himself; but the third and major reason was something that was forming in the back of his mind, something that he would keep to himself for a long time.

At 4:30 Tuesday afternoon, Nancy Dunn called the Forsyth County Sheriff's Department and said that she wanted to talk to a detective. John Boner, a tall, heavyset veteran detective who wore glasses, sported a mustache, and smoked cigars, took the call and said that he would come right out. He first went by the home of Stephen Carden, a young, boyish-looking detective, to pick him up, then drove to the Holiday Inn. Nancy, her brother David and sister Debbie went with the detectives to a private room so they could be away from their mother, who still didn't want to believe that Susie might somehow have had a part in the murders. The letters Nancy had read that morning at Nanna's house had convinced her that the time had come to do what she'd earlier told Rob she was going to do: tell everything she knew.

First she had questions. Earlier that day, she'd "given the third degree," as she put it, to the SBI agents at the house, but she got few answers. "We don't know," they'd answer. Or "We can't say anything about that now." She got much the same responses from Boner and Carden.

Giving up her questioning, Nancy spilled out her suspicions. When she and her brother and sister had tried to figure out who might have wanted these murders done, Nancy said, they came up with only one name: Susie.

"Boner nearly swallowed his cigar," she recalled later.

Why did they think that? Boner asked, and Nancy reeled off the reasons. Later, Boner listed them in his report.

Susie had a bad divorce, which was traumatic, and she had a change of attitude and short temper.

When Susie returned from New Mexico, she and her two boys moved in with her parents.

Susie moved out when she, Robert Jr. and Florence had a big fight.

The fight occurred when Robert Jr. and Florence confronted her about her relationship with her first cousin, Fritz Klenner.

It was thought in the family that Susie and Fritz Klenner were too close and probably slept together.

Also Fritz was giving Susie and the two boys injections of what they thought was probably vitamin C.

When Susie left she did not return, even sent someone to get her clothes and other belongings.

Susie cut off her ties with the family, even Big Susie, Susie Sharp, whom she idolized and Big Susie idolized her.

Susie carried with her a plastic bag of medicine that Fritz prescribed for her and the boys.

Fritz was supposed to have gone to medical school, Chapel Hill or Duke, and flunked or dropped out.

Robert Jr. and Florence tried to keep the fight low-keyed and not let the family know too much.

Susie is too cool and calm and shows no emotion about the murder of her parents and grandmother.

Robert Jr. and Florence, or Robert Jr. alone, was to testify on behalf of Dr. Tom Lynch four days after the murders for Dr. Tom Lynch to have more visitation of the children.

Nancy also mentioned the possibility of Susie's involvement in the Lynch murders in Kentucky.

"We thought at the time that somebody should question her," she said, "but nobody ever asked us, so we thought we were crazy."

While Rob talked with Gentry and House on Tuesday afternoon, Susie was shopping with Nancy Holder. Nancy, who had been Bob's secretary at R. J. Reynolds for seventeen years, was now herself a Reynolds executive. She had remained close to the Newsoms. Rob and Susie had grown up calling her Aunt Nancy. Susie had called and asked Nancy to help her shop for clothes for the boys to wear to the funerals.

Nancy tried to present a cheerful front. "I tried to keep off sadness as much as I could," she remembered later.

Susie talked at length about John and Jim and how proud she was of them. She spoke bitterly of Tom and said she didn't want the boys spending time with him.

"Susie, he's their daddy and he's bound to want them," Nancy said.

But Susie would hear nothing of that. Tom, she said, was up to bad things. She had a friend high in the CIA who'd told her about them.

Susie told about going to Nanna's house earlier that day and how upset it had made her.

"It was just devastating to walk in there," she said.

"Everything's sprayed black and they've cut holes in the carpet. It was awful."

Susie said she dreaded the funeral. She had no intention of riding in the family car.

"I just can't," she said. "I just don't like hearses and limousines."

"Would you like for us to drive you?" Nancy asked.

"No, Fritz said he'd drive us."

That was the only mention she made of Fritz all afternoon.

Nancy bought suits for the boys, and afterward, she and Susie drove to the K&W Cafeteria for supper. On the way, Nancy talked about Bob and Florence.

"You know how fine they were and how much I loved them," she said.

"I know."

Nancy went on to say that she'd always felt more like family than friend with Bob and Florence and that she was glad that Rob and Susie had included her at such a time. "Thank you," she said. "I do love you both."

Susie burst into tears and reached to hug her.

"Hey," Nancy said, "Cut that out. I don't drive too well as it is. I can't drive at all if you get me crying. I've already cried so many tears over this that I don't think I have any more left."

Fritz had taken John and Jim to Annette Hunt's house on Tuesday morning and left them for the day. Nancy brought Susie back to the Newsom house across the street at about 8 P.M., and when Susie went to Annette's to get the boys, she said, "Ride with me to the apartment."

Annette thought that she needed company, so she went with her. At the apartment, they bathed the boys, took the dogs for a walk, and returned to put the boys to bed and talk.

Soon afterward, Fritz arrived, angry and shouting.

"He was really upset with her," Annette recalled later. "He was fussing at her for not having contacted him that afternoon. He was beside himself. 'Why didn't you call?' he kept asking. He didn't want her out on the highway that late. She wasn't too concerned that he was upset. She tried to calm him down, but he was just beside himself. I just kind of sat there and tried to fade into the wall."

37

On Wednesday morning, the Newsom murders were relegated to an inside page of the *Winston-Salem Journal.* An anonymous source was quoted as saying that a fire had been set near the bodies, that the Newsoms appeared to have been shot, and that the house "had been ransacked from top to bottom." Nanna's next-door neighbor, Jerrel Bell, said deputies told her "that there was no sign of a struggle and that investigators thought it was possible the Newsoms knew their attacker or attackers."

Bob and Florence had two children, the report said. Rob had declined comment. Susie couldn't be reached. Then, almost as if it were unrelated, came the revelation that Susie's former husband had talked with a detective the day before.

"He asked me if I knew anything that might help them there, but I didn't," Tom had said. "I just thought it was strange, having been through something similar myself."

Only then did the story mention that Tom's mother and sister had been shot to death the previous July in Kentucky.

Preston Oldham was a man who wore a uniform well and proudly, and always for press conferences. At 10 A.M. on Wednesday, when he walked into a sheriff's department briefing room filled with TV cameras, reporters, and newspaper photographers, his uniform was form-fitting and freshly starched. TV lights reflected off the gold eagles on his collar as Oldham revealed that the murders had taken place some time after 9:30 P.M. Saturday, that all three victims had been shot and each suffered at least two fatal wounds. One victim, he said, was also stabbed, but he would not say which.

"The apparent motive appears to be robbery," he said.

He confirmed the details revealed by the *Journal's* anonymous source.

"I don't know if the fire was set to destroy evidence or what," he said.

Oldham said that fourteen officers were working on the case, and described the investigation as "multiple focus."

"There has been no central focus made on a particular individual or suspect," he said, "but I think that will come in time."

Had family members been ruled out as suspects?

"It wouldn't be fair to make any comment on that," he said, going on to say that nobody had been ruled out.

The reporters wanted to know about links between the Newsom and Lynch murders.

"We have not established a connection," he said, but that was "high on the priority list."

The atmosphere between Oldham and the frustrated reporters was not one of amiability, and at one point the exchanges grew sharp. Asked when the autopsy reports would be released, Oldham said that they wouldn't be if he could get a court order to stop it.

What difference could it make to the case if the nature of the wounds was made public? a reporter asked.

"I've spent twenty-two years on the street," Oldham said. "You haven't. You'll just have to trust my judgment on this one."

Contrary to what Oldham said at the press conference, the investigation had found a focus, and at the very moment the sheriff was denying it, Allen Gentry and Tom Sturgill were talking to her in Greensboro. After hearing what Nancy had told Boner and Carden the day before, Gentry and Sturgill were eager to know what Susie would say. But they had no intention of pressing her or letting her know that she was suspected in any way. "We were kind of on a friendly interview," Gentry explained. "We wanted her to talk."

Chowy answered their knock, hitting the door from

inside like a fullback crashing the line. Susie put the dogs up before opening the door.

"She was just charming," Gentry said later, "almost bubbly, bouncy."

The detectives were taken aback by the incredible clutter in the apartment. Susie invited them into the living room, where she introduced Fritz.

"This is my cousin," she said. "He helps us out."

Both detectives noticed that Fritz was wearing a folded knife in a leather case on his belt.

Susie cleared books and papers from two wicker chairs so the detectives could sit. She sat on an ottoman. Fritz perched close behind her on a short stool.

Trying to appear friendly, the detectives made small talk, but Fritz didn't join in.

"He didn't have much to say at all," Gentry remembered later. "He just kind of sat there and judged us."

Susie was different. "She was all sweetness," Gentry said. "It was like she was interviewing for a job instead of talking to officers about the murder of her parents and grandmother."

Gentry led into the questioning by asking when she'd last talked with her parents. She said her father had called Friday morning before leaving for Winston-Salem, but she didn't mention that the purpose of his call was to tell her that he planned to testify for Tom, as the detectives already knew.

She was close to her grandmother, she said. Nanna had helped her with legal expenses in her divorce. Nanna often gave money to her grandchildren, she said, including sizable checks every Christmas. She believed that Nanna might have kept large sums of money stashed at her house, and offered this as a motive.

She was upset about the condition of the house after going by the day before, she said, and was especially concerned about all the fingerprint dust. Would it come off? The detectives assured her that it would. The dusting was necessary to help solve the crime, they explained. She was also worried about the whereabouts of her grandmother's silver flatware, mink, and jewelry.

Gentry asked if she'd mind going over her activities for the previous weekend, and she graciously complied.

She'd had dinner at Annie Hill's in Reidsville Friday night. Fritz had gone camping in the mountains. She spent much of Saturday at Annette Hunt's house. She seemed vague about the rest of Saturday but remembered taking the boys to McDonald's that night, then returning to the apartment. On Sunday afternoon, Fritz called from Lexington, Virginia, and asked her to meet him at Natural Bridge for dinner. She drove there with the boys, nearly a four-hour trip. They ate in the cafeteria in the big entrance building, took a short hike, and drove back to Greensboro, arriving about 11:30. As soon as they opened the apartment door, Chowy ran off, chasing a cat, and Fritz spent four hours looking for him.

"Isn't that right?" she said, turning to Fritz and touching his knee.

Fritz nodded agreement.

About midnight, Susie went on, John Chandler, a neighbor of her parents, called and said there'd been an accident at Nanna's. She thought it was a minor auto accident and wasn't concerned. Later, Alice called and said that her parents and Nanna were dead. She didn't believe it and called Annie Hill, who told her that it probably wasn't true, not to worry, that she would try to find out something about it in the morning. Fritz went to sleep on the floor, but she stayed up all night working on a school paper. Rob called about 3:30 A.M. to tell her of the deaths, but not until Annie Hill called to confirm the news the next morning did she really accept that it was true.

When Gentry asked if she knew anything about the Lynch murders, she became very vocal.

"It was professional," she said. "Nothing was taken."

Gentry chose not to press by asking how she knew that.

Her former husband was involved in "shady dealings," Susie said. He'd tried to get her to sell stolen trucks for him, and he was involved in drug trafficking. She didn't think that Tom would have killed his mother and sister, she said, but he owed money to underworld characters, and they'd had them killed so that he would inherit money and be able to pay them. She said that Delores had a big estate and that she'd been trying to get her lawyer to get part of it for her sons.

She went on to tell about finding the boys' toy animals with their throats slit and the mysterious "two down and two to go" call.

She was scared for herself and her boys, she said, but Fritz was protecting them.

While the detectives were talking, they had been glancing around at the clutter of the apartment, taking note of what they saw. Behind a screen that separated the living room from the dining room, they noticed what appeared to be big piles of military field gear, but no weapons were visible. As they made ready to leave, they saw that the front door was rigged with a motion detector. A huge floodlight and a strobe light were aimed at the door to blind intruders. What appeared to be a gas grenade was fastened above the door. They thanked Susie for her time and help, and as they started to leave, Gentry asked Fritz for his address and telephone number. Fritz gave him his mother's address and number in Reidsville.

"What kind of work do you do?" Gentry asked, as if he were just curious.

"I'm a physician," Fritz said, "but I'm not licensed in this state right now."

"Is it just me, or did that seem strange?" Gentry asked after they got into Sturgill's cruiser and jotted down the license numbers of the two Chevy Blazers parked in front of the apartment.

Sturgill agreed that all did not seem right.

"It didn't make sense," Gentry explained later. "Rob was upset about his parents and grandmother. He was really torn up. But as far as Susie was concerned, it was like there was no problem, that nothing had happened to her."

Susie had an appointment for a haircut and permanent on Wednesday afternoon. Annette went to her apartment to look after the boys. Fritz was there, fooling with camping gear. John and Jim were supposed to be cleaning their room. They squabbled, and Fritz broke it up. Annette had a headache and asked Fritz if he had anything for it.

Fritz opened a kitchen cabinet, and Annette had never seen so many bottles of pills outside a drugstore—mostly vitamins, she noticed. He gave her two Tylenol tablets. She took them and went into the boys' room to lie down. Maizie jumped onto the bed with her.

"She just wants to cuddle," Jim explained, but Annette shooed the dog back to the floor.

The boys and dogs played while Annette rested. Fritz loaded the camping gear into his Blazer and left without explanation.

Shortly, Annette got up to finish Susie's ironing. She gathered some clothes, put them on hangers, and took them into Susie's bedroom, where the door had remained closed. The room was a mess, the closet packed so tight that she couldn't even squeeze in a T-shirt.

"All I could see was Fritz's stuff," she recalled later. "There was no place to put anything. I said, 'I shouldn't be in here.'"

She retreated, closing the door behind her, certain that Susie's relationship with Fritz was more than Susie had acknowledged to her.

Wednesday evening turned stormy. Tornadoes and severe thunderstorms ripped through Winston-Salem and Greensboro and continued on to the east, uprooting trees, damaging buildings, downing power lines, flooding streets, and pounding the crops of area farmers with hail. Frances Miller and her family received friends at Vogler's Funeral Home, not far from Nanna's house, shortly after the storms passed. Detective Steve Carden posed as Debbie's escort at the funeral home to see if any suspicious characters showed up. Neither Susie nor Rob came, choosing instead to receive visitors in Greensboro. Nancy Holder represented them at the funeral home.

Among the visitors who arrived early at the Newsom house in Greensboro that evening was Chris Severn, Susie's close friend from college, now Chris Waters, a teacher who drove from Greenville, two hundred miles to the east. She arrived to find that Susie had gone to Reidsville to pick up Annie Hill, and she waited for her return.

Like Susie's other friends, Chris had great affection for

Bob and Florence, and she had continued to keep up with them even when she no longer heard from Susie, always calling them or stopping to see them when she happened to be in Greensboro, and she was greatly distressed by their deaths. Only occasionally had she seen Susie since their years in college, usually by accident when she stopped to see Bob and Florence. Susie had been in Chris's wedding, and she had attended Susie's. Chris had seen Susie briefly after Tom finished dental school, then largely lost touch after Susie's move to Albuquerque. She encountered her again soon after Susie left Tom, and visited after Susie dropped her anthropology studies at Wake Forest. Susie had told her a convoluted tale about strange requirements Wake Forest had tried to put on her and that had kept her from her degree. "It was the most cockamamy story I ever heard," she recalled later, and it caused her to wonder what was happening to her friend.

Susie seemed astonished to see Chris. They hugged, and Susie introduced her to John.

"Oh, you look so much like your father," Chris said, realizing instantly from Susie's change of expression that she'd said the wrong thing.

"I knew him at Wake Forest," Chris felt obliged to explain.

"Well, you don't know him now," Susie said.

Because most of the people at the house were Rob's friends, Susie took Chris next door to Annette's house, where they sat at the kitchen table and talked with Annette and Annie Hill. The conversation centered on that night's TV news, which had quoted Tom asking for an investigation to determine if the murders of his mother and sister were connected to those of the Newsoms. Only a short time earlier, while waiting at Rob's, Chris had learned from a neighbor about the murders of Delores and Janie, and it had immediately caused her to remember how much Susie disliked her mother-in-law. Now Annie Hill remarked that this was probably Tom's way of getting his foot in the door to obtain custody.

"They were talking about things I didn't know about," Chris later recalled, and she was too polite to pry.

Finally, Susie changed the subject and began talking

about Chris's family and remembering old times, particularly their weddings. She recalled that Chris had given her a sterling nail file as a bridesmaid's gift. "I still have it," she said.

They laughed when Susie recalled how much she hated the dress that Chris wore to her rehearsal dinner.

Soon, Chris left. She drove back to Greenville with the feeling that something about Susie had changed, that a terrible void lurked within her.

As Chris was leaving, Linda Crutchfield, Susie's best friend from high school, now Linda Chris, was arriving from her home in Chapel Hill. She hadn't seen Susie in years, and Susie broke into tears at the sight of her, then took her around, introducing her to the people at the Newsom house. Linda was a little taken aback that Susie was so calm, but she thought that perhaps the shock had not had time to seep in yet and that Susie was maintaining the façade that her family background demanded for such occasions.

Soon Susie took her to Annette's, where they sat and talked about what had happened.

"The police seem to think that we all are in some sort of danger," Susie said.

She told about being questioned earlier that day. "It's almost as if they're treating us as if we're the criminals. Can you believe it?"

She went on to talk about the holes the police had cut in the carpet at Nanna's house and other things they had done there.

"She seemed to be upset that they had not had a respect of property," Linda recalled later. "I thought that was sort of strange, that concern."

While they talked, Annie Hill came in carrying a suit in a dry cleaning bag for Susie to wear to the funerals next day.

"Oh, thank you," Susie exclaimed. "I don't know what I would do without you."

Susie introduced Annie Hill, and shortly afterward, Linda began making ready to go.

"Please don't leave," Susie pleaded. "I want you to meet my sons."

She took Linda upstairs, where the boys were engrossed in a TV show.

"I'd like you to meet Mrs. Chris, whose husband has the restaurant in Chapel Hill I've told you about on our trips to Raleigh," Susie said to them.

The boys seemed more interested in the TV than in Linda, and Linda turned to Susie and said, "If you've been to Raleigh, why didn't you ever stop and see us?"

"I was afraid if I came through and found you weren't still there I would break the illusion," Susie said.

Linda had no idea what she meant. Did Susie prefer the illusion of a friend to a real one? She thought the remark strange indeed.

Back downstairs, Susie and Linda joined in conversation with Annette and Annie Hill. Susie got Linda to talk about her family, and Linda began telling about her daughter's learning problems and how diligently they had worked to overcome them.

"I wish I had done that with Fritz," Annie Hill said, causing Susie to turn and pat her shoulder.

"You need not trouble yourself," Susie said. "You've done the best you could."

Later, as Susie was walking Linda to her car, she started talking about Tom.

"I have made some decisions that are unpopular with the family," Susie confided, without amplification. "Tom wants extended visitation rights in the summer. The boys do not want to be with him."

"But he *is* their father," Linda put in.

"I've been real active with the boys," Susie said. "We go hiking and camping. You'd be proud of me. While I can I'm going to keep up with them."

As Linda started to leave, Susie smiled and said, "You know, Linda, I had the greatest time at your wedding. I still have the dress I wore. I cut it off to tea length, and I've worn it many times."

When Linda arrived at her father's house in Winston-Salem that night, her stepmother mentioned that they'd heard on the TV news that the police were looking into the possibility that a family member could have been involved in the Newsom murders.

"Who could that be?" she asked.

"I don't know," Linda said, "but something is wrong."

38

Thursday morning's newspapers headlined robbery as the motive for the Newsom murders. Both the *Winston-Salem Journal* and the *Greensboro News & Record* made extensive mention of the Lynch murders, saying that Sheriff Oldham intended to give high priority to determining if the cases were connected.

The *Journal* quoted Lieutenaut Dan Davidson of the Kentucky State Police as saying he planned to send two investigators to Winston-Salem the following week.

"The reason we are looking at it is because Dr. Lynch's ex-wife is the daughter of the victims," Davidson said. "That is quite a coincidence. We just want to make sure there is no connection. There is a lot of similarity there."

The story pointed out the similarities: "In both murder cases, the victims' homes were ransacked, pointing to robbery as a motive. Both victims in the Lynch murders were shot twice, and both sets of murder victims were members of prominent families who lived in large, secluded homes."

The *Journal*'s lead editorial that day also concerned the case.

"Popular as the news media are these days, Sheriff E. Preston Oldham may well be considered something of a folk hero for the way he handles public information these days, which is, essentially, by keeping it under wraps," the editorial began.

It recited several recent cases in which the sheriff had withheld information and tried to keep reporters from doing their jobs.

"How do you allow the police to operate in privacy

and still remain comfortable that they are operating in a responsible, effective manner?" the editorial asked.

It concluded: "Arrogance is not an appropriate pose for a sheriff or any other public official, especially one who serves in elective office. But after arrogance comes suspicion: What's this person got to hide, anyway, that he won't release any information? Or the standard media suspicion surfaces: If this person won't reveal any information, is there any information to reveal or is the object simply to hide the fact that the police don't know anything? After suspicion comes fear: If you don't know what's going on in a police department, chances are you become afraid of policemen."

Some who saw him that day said the sheriff was not in a good mood.

At 10 A.M. on Thursday, family and friends filled the granite cathedral of St. Paul's Episcopal Church in downtown Winston-Salem for the funeral of Bob and Florence. Susie and the boys arrived separately, driven by Fritz in Susie's Blazer. Susie wore a black dress with a white jacket and black earrings. Her hair was tied into a bun. The boys were dressed in the new suits Nancy Holder had bought for them. Susie and the boys joined the rest of the family in a small anteroom from which they were to enter the sanctuary as a group. As they started in, Fritz appeared in a stairwell, wearing a three-piece blue suit, a light blue shirt, and a burgundy tie.

"Here, Fritz, you get in here," Susie said, pushing him ahead of other family members.

The Millers were startled by Fritz. "It made your flesh sort of creep the way he just appeared out of nowhere," Frances later recalled.

Frances and members of her family were disturbed at having to sit behind Fritz, thinking all the time that he probably was the reason for these funerals.

In her daily diary, Louise Sharp later wrote this about the first funeral:

> *Fritz, John, Susie Q and Jim sat on bench in front of me at St. Paul's. Fritz pawed John the entire time and held onto him as though John were his ticket. Fritz*

walked out of church first behind Bob's casket—let Su-
sie Q and Jim follow him and John. Fritz's beard had
been shaved.

The service was formal and conventional, as Bob and
Florence would have wanted it. The choir in which Bob
had once sung so lovingly performed his favorite hymns,
"A Mighty Fortress Is Our God" and "Lead On, O King
Eternal."

After the service, Fritz and Susie hurried from the
church with the boys.

"They came out of the church, down the sidewalk,
didn't speak, cut through the Sunday school building,
dodging everybody," Nancy Dunn remembered. "A lady
stopped Susie and asked if there was anything she could
do for her. 'Could we keep your children?' But Susie
said, 'Oh, I'm taking the children back to school.' I
thought, 'She's lying about what she's doing with those
kids for no reason.' She was keeping those children away
from everybody." Did the children know something that
Fritz and Susie were afraid they might innocently reveal?
Nancy came to wonder.

Most who attended the service for Bob and Florence
rode in a procession the five miles to the modern Bethabara
Moravian Church for Nanna's funeral at 11. Fritz parked
behind the church, and when Susie spotted her parents'
neighbors, John and Martha Chandler, getting out of a
car nearby, she hurried over and asked Martha if she
could leave her purse in their car. Martha thought it a
strange request but agreed. The purse was so heavy that
Martha almost dropped it when Susie handed it to her.

"What have you got in here, textbooks?" Martha asked,
but Susie offered no explanation. Only later would Martha wonder if the purse had held weapons.

Nanna's service was simple and appropriate. The Reverend John Giesler read from Paul and Philippians. He
spoke of Nanna's "sweet reasonableness," of her devotion to church and family. She always reached out to
those who were troubled, he said, and so many had been
touched by her life. Several people later said that they
saw tears coursing down Fritz's face during the eulogy.

After the service, Linda Chris saw Susie and the boys

getting into her Blazer behind the church and hurried to speak to her. She arrived to find Fritz hovering over Susie's door, as if shielding her. It was the first time she had seen him, and she found him disturbing. Susie rolled down her window when she saw Linda, and Fritz stepped aside so they could speak.

"He sort of glared at me," Linda recalled later. "I said, 'I just wanted to tell you good-bye.' She started crying. I said, 'Don't forget you're coming to Chapel Hill.' "

At noon, a graveside service was held at Forsyth Memorial Gardens on Old Yadkinville Road, less than two miles from Nanna's house and just a short distance from Green Meadows, where Bob and Florence had once lived. The procession wound up the hillside along a drive lined with hemlocks to the family plot where Paw-Paw already lay.

Family members kept looking for Susie during the service but couldn't spot her. They thought she hadn't come. But she, Fritz, and the boys were standing away from the crowd at the back of the funeral canopy. When a TV cameraman approached, Fritz and Susie herded the boys between them, and Fritz turned his back to the camera. Detectives Boner and Carden, who'd been assigned to the funerals, made note of this in their reports.

Dudley Colhoun, the minister from St. Paul's Church, also missed Susie when he made his rounds after the service to console family members, but he spotted her preparing to leave and went to her. While he spoke to her, John and Jim grabbed him around the legs and hugged him with tight desperation.

Family members and close friends had been invited to Nanna's church for lunch after the services, and Susie was first to arrive. She came alone. Fritz had taken the boys and his mother for fried chicken, she told John Giesler when he greeted her, and they would not be attending.

Giesler was struck by something he thought odd as he chatted with Susie: "She didn't seem to be upset at all. She showed no sign of grief."

Only one thing seemed to be on her mind—that morning's news stories linking the two sets of murders. She was outraged at Sheriff Oldham.

"The gall of him," she said.

"She was seething with anger at him," Giesler later recalled. "She was just burning up with this thing."

Soon, other family members arrived, and Giesler turned his attention to them, but some of them, too, were wondering about the way Susie was acting.

"Susie's behavior baffled everybody," Frances said later. "It was as if it were a wedding reception or something. She just bubbled around."

Shortly, Susie went off into a corner with Jim Taylor, her cousin from Washington whom she hadn't seen in a long time. She spent the remainder of the lunch with him, talking about chows.

As Susie talked with her cousin, her namesake aunt, Judge Sharp, approached Frances and quietly asked, "Frances, do you think there could be any connection between this and that Kentucky killing?"

"I don't know," Frances said.

Judge Sharp had begun to wonder if Fritz could be involved.

Earlier, she had been in her room at the family home in Reidsville when the telephone rang. She picked up the extension only to find that Louise had already answered. Her sister Annie Hill was on the line, and Judge Sharp could hear that Fritz was trying to tell his mother what to say.

"Tell Fritz to shut up," Louise said. "I can't hear you."

Fritz took the receiver from his mother. "I'll leave," he said, "but you tell Judge Susie that it has just occurred to me that the murderer may have thought he was killing her instead of Florence. You know they often have been mistaken for each other."

Judge Sharp said nothing, and Fritz did not know she had heard him. She had never known Florence to be mistaken for herself and she couldn't imagine why Fritz would say such a thing. Could it be a threat?

Later that day, Allen Gentry asked Nancy Dunn, her brother Steve and sister, Debbie, if they would come to the sheriff's department. Each went with two detectives for separate interviews, Nancy remaining with Gentry and Sturgill. She again went over everything she knew about Susie's problems with Tom and her family and her relationship with Fritz. Even as a child, Susie had defied her mother, Nancy said, but in recent years her behavior had been in complete defiance, all of it seemingly designed as a slap in her mother's face. Murder and mutilation, she didn't have to point out, was defiance at its utmost.

"Nancy is somewhat direct," Gentry said later. "When she walked out of my office, there was no doubt in my mind about what she thought had happened, and I can't say the same for anybody else I talked to. She thought Susie and Fritz had done it."

39

On the morning after the Newsom funerals, Gentry and SBI agent J. W. Bryant drove to Reidsville to talk with Annie Hill.

"We were trying to get some more background on Fritz before we went back to see him," Gentry explained later, "to see if we were going to catch him in a lie."

As at Susie's apartment, the detectives were greeted by fierce barking, and heeding the BEWARE OF DOG sign, Bryant slid his foot against the door.

Annie Hill, alone in the house, invited the detectives in and directed them to a large formal dining room to the left of the foyer. She was a pleasant woman, short and plump and graying, with quick, dark eyes. The house had a shabby appearance, Gentry thought, and the clutter was even greater than at Susie's apartment. Seemingly unperturbed by the mess, Annie Hill cleared books and magazines from dining room chairs to make places to sit. Bottles of pharmaceuticals and cartons of books were everywhere.

Annie Hill talked first about Susie. She and her mother were much alike, she said, and Susie always had been defiant of Florence. She told how Florence had quelled Susie's childhood temper tantrums with cold showers. She was surprised by the breakup of Susie's marriage, she said, because she thought that Tom was devoted to her. But Tom had told her to take the boys and leave, and Jim had told Florence that his daddy threw things and yelled. Along with the rest of the family she worried about Susie when she was in Taiwan, especially when it looked as if she wouldn't get out of the country because the government thought she was a spy, but Jesse Helms had worked that out.

The problem that brought the break between Susie and her mother, Annie Hill said, was the boys. The boys worried Florence; she fussed at them, and they were afraid of her. Susie turned to her because she couldn't get along with her mother, she said, and now Susie visited her instead of her mother.

Doctor, as she called her husband, helped Susie and the boys financially when he was alive, she said, but he'd left very little after his death because he'd had no investments.

Now, she went on, Fritz was trying to help Susie and the boys.

"She said some people thought there was more to it than that," Gentry recalled later, "but her mind wasn't in the gutter and she didn't think there was anything to it."

"Fritz is very protective of the boys," she said.

She knew that Fritz lived at Susie's some of the time, but it was only to look after them. He'd trained Susie's dogs to protect them when he wasn't there, Annie Hill said. Once Susie had been attacked on her way to the trash dump at her apartment, but the dogs had driven off her assailants. Susie thought the attack might have had something to do with Tom's underworld involvement.

Fritz was a good boy, she said. He had been very close to his father and very upset at his death. He and his father loved to go out to the farm and shoot. His father collected guns and Fritz had liked guns since he was a little boy. His father wanted him to have the farm, and she was going to leave it to him, she said.

When asked about Fritz's medical training, Annie Hill said that he'd worked with his father but he'd never been in medical school. He'd pretended that he was at Duke and had fooled everybody, she said, even his wife, but he'd admitted the problem sometime around Easter of 1983.

"He was embarrassed," she said. "He wanted to be like his father so much."

Fritz had always been timid and humble, she said, but he'd really come out a lot lately since he'd been involved with this special unit that had given him extensive training in guns and explosives. Thinking that Fritz might belong to some private mercenary or commando group, the detectives questioned her about this.

"She said, 'No, it's government,' " Gentry said later. "This was something special, some hush-hush organization. She kept saying initials. She hit all around CIA, but she never could figure out just what letters he worked for."

She'd been afraid to ask questions about it, she said, out of fear that he or she might be killed.

One day during the previous fall, she'd come home and found a mysterious package at the front door, addressed to Fritz, delivered by UPS, she said. She'd called Susie's apartment to tell Fritz about it.

"Don't touch it," Susie told her. "We'll be right there."

When Fritz and Susie arrived, she said, he used an electronic device to check the package and announced that it was a bomb. He carried it carefully away and later said he'd disarmed it.

Up until she started talking about all of this, Annie Hill had seemed lucid and logical to the detectives. "It was just as if she'd wandered off into never-never land," Gentry recalled. "She was as serious as a heart attack."

The next thing she said had the detectives exchanging wondering glances. Recently, she told them, Fritz had been stopped by SBI agents who searched his Blazer. "She said they just tore it all to pieces and she had to give him three thousand dollars to have the car fixed," Gentry recalled. "I was having trouble keeping a straight face."

Had Fritz ever been hospitalized or had professional help?

No, she said, but he nearly died from Rocky Mountain spotted fever before his marriage. His fever had gone to 107, but Doctor had saved him with vitamin C.

Did Annie Hill remember if Fritz and Susie had made any out-of-state trips in July of 1984?

They'd gone to Atlanta one weekend, she said, but she couldn't remember the exact date. She thought it was the last weekend in the month, though. The boys were in Albuquerque with Tom then, she remembered, and Gentry put an asterisk by this in his notes to remind him that

Susie would have been free to go to Kentucky with Fritz at the time of the Lynch killings.

The officers asked if she knew about Susie and Fritz's activities over the previous weekend.

Susie and the boys had come for dinner Friday night, but she didn't hear from them again until Susie called late Sunday night to tell her something had happened. Annie Hill told her not to worry, that she'd try to find out something in the morning.

Fritz had come by Friday to let her know that he was going camping in Virginia with Ian Perkins, she said. Ian, she explained, was the son of family friends who lived down the street. He was a student at Washington and Lee University. Fritz was supposed to meet him at Roanoke Mountain on Friday night, but Ian called to say Fritz hadn't arrived and he had returned to Lexington. Not long afterward, Fritz called to say he was at the mountain and couldn't find Ian. She told him that Ian had returned to his room, and Fritz said he would go on there. Fritz had called Susie from Lexington on Sunday, she said, and Susie and the boys had driven to Natural Bridge to meet him for dinner. She was sure that all of this could be easily verified. Fritz, she said, no doubt used the telephone credit card from his father's office to make the calls, and she gave the officers the number.

So here was Fritz's alibi, and it all sounded very convenient. Too convenient, Gentry thought.

As the officers were making ready to leave, Annie Hill said something that both found interesting. Susie's children, she said, were the only common denominator in the two murder cases.

"She just threw that out," Gentry said. "Obviously, she'd been thinking about it. I thought she was dead on the money."

Gentry and Bryant drove to the Reidsville Police Department, and Gentry called Ian's house. Ian's mother, Camille O'Neal, answered and said that Ian wasn't there.

Could he be reached?

He was at school, she said, and she thought that he was attending a seminar all weekend, so it might be difficult.

"Who is this?" she asked, and Gentry identified himself.

"This doesn't have anything to do with the Newsom murders, does it?" she asked tentatively.

"Yes, ma'am, I'm afraid it does."

"Oh, my," she said.

"I just need to verify an alibi," Gentry told her. "Nothing more."

Susie came by her parents' house late that afternoon and went rummaging through it. Rob wasn't there, and Susie wouldn't tell Alice what she was looking for. Others had been there that day to take items that belonged to them but had been in the possession of Bob and Florence, or items that they cherished and wanted for keepsakes, but such things did not seem to be the object of Susie's search. Later, family members would speculate that Susie was looking for letters between her parents and Tom and Kathy, letters her parents had kept at Nanna's. When Alice offered Susie some of her mother's silver, Susie responded, "I don't want it."

"Well, I'll just put it away and keep it for the boys when they get married," Alice said.

"Frankly, Alice," Susie replied, "from what my children have seen of my marriage, they don't want any part of marriage."

Before leaving, Susie told Alice, "I'm going to be making four corporate moves in the next seven years," but she was not specific about what they might be.

As Susie was leaving the house that evening, she spotted Annette across the street. Annette was helping her son Joey get ready for his high school prom. He was thoroughly tuxedoed. His car gleamed with polish. His mother had even scrubbed the whitewalls. Annette called Susie over to show off Joey in all his splendor.

"You're overdoing this thing, you know," Susie said to her friend.

"Someday, you'll be doing the same thing for your sons," Annette said.

"No," Susie said, shaking her head gravely.

Later, Annette cried when retelling that incident. It seemed to her almost as if Susie had accepted that John and Jim never would live to see their prom nights, that nobody could have changed her gloomy outlook.

Captain Ron Barker was pleased when Gentry and Bryant returned from talking with Annie Hill Klenner on Friday and told him that they had an alibi for Fritz.

"That was what I was wanting," he recalled later. "I said, 'Okay, we have got him. You're going to break this guy.'"

Gentry was eager to talk with Ian Perkins, and wanted to go to Virginia on Saturday to find him. He was hoping that Tom Sturgill could go with him, but Tom had a conflict, so Gentry asked Walt House to go. On Saturday, though, Sturgill called and said he thought they should hold off.

"Let's let Fritz tell us his alibi rather than just taking his mother's word for it," he said.

Besides, he thought, it might be better to let Ian stew a few days, worrying about when the police might appear. Surely his mother would get word to him that they wanted to talk with him.

On Tuesday, May 28, a little before 11 A.M., Gentry and Sturgill appeared unannounced at Susie's apartment. She came to the door wearing slacks and blouse, drying her shoulder-length hair with a towel. The detectives asked to see Fritz, and she invited them in, apologizing for not being dressed for company, and went to fetch him. He emerged from the bedroom shortly, bleary-eyed, yawning, wearing a one-piece olive-colored flight suit, socks but no shoes.

The detectives were still being friendly. "Somebody with education and money, you don't just go in and ask for a confession," Gentry said later. "They're not going to roll over. They'll say, 'Talk to my lawyer.'" Gentry and Sturgill wanted to get everything they could out of Fritz before matters reached the lawyer stage. They asked if he'd mind coming with them to the SBI office for an interview, and displaying no alarm or concern, he agreed.

Fritz went back into the bedroom to dress, and returned wearing khaki pants and a sport shirt. He had a sheathed knife on his belt, and he stuck a small flashlight into his rear pocket, causing the detectives to wonder why he thought he might need a flashlight for a short trip in broad daylight.

The SBI office, a small, cinder-block building hidden behind an Interstate 40 motel near the airport, was only a couple of miles from the apartment, and the three rode there in near silence, arriving at 11:05. They went into the conference room, where a big table was surrounded by chairs. Gentry removed his jacket and hung it over the back of a chair. He wore an unusual pistol, an H&K 9-millimeter German squeeze cock, and he wanted Fritz to see it in the hope that he might mention it and start talking about weapons. If the weapon didn't catch Fritz's eye, surely he would notice the distinctive John Bianchi holster in which Gentry wore it, but Fritz said nothing about either.

The detectives knew that Fritz's mother would have informed him of all that she'd told them, and they wanted to know his reaction to it.

"I believe you said you were a physician but you weren't licensed in this state," Gentry began.

"Well, I've trained as a physician," Fritz said curtly. "I have no formal degree. I don't see that this is relevant to anything."

Gentry nodded and went on to what was relevant: Fritz's activities for the weekend of the Newsom murders.

He'd left his mother's shortly after Susie and the boys arrived for dinner on Friday, Fritz said. He was going camping and was supposed to meet Ian Perkins at Roanoke Mountain, but he was late getting away.

"I'm always late," he said with a faint smile.

He got to the mountain and couldn't find Ian, talked with a park ranger, then used the credit card from his father's office to call his mother. She told him that Ian had gone back to Lexington, so he went there, arriving about midnight, and he and Ian drove to the Blue Ridge Parkway. They went to Peaks of Otter Campground and set up camp near dawn.

In fact, he said, he still had the campground receipt, and he produced it from his wallet. Gentry wrote down the camp space number: B-3.

They slept until nearly 2 P.M., Fritz went on, then went

to the lodge for lunch. Afterward, they gathered firewood and made ready for a night hike they had planned to the peak of Flat Top Mountain. They left about 8, and as they neared the peak, they got rained on and stopped to build a fire to warm and dry themselves. They didn't get back to the campsite until well after midnight. They rested and later fixed breakfast before breaking camp about noon.

Back at Ian's room, Fritz said that he took a shower, then called his mother and Susie, again using the credit card. Susie had made all A's in her classes and wanted to celebrate, so he told her to bring the boys and meet him at Natural Bridge for dinner. He liked Natural Bridge. He'd had happy family times there as a child.

After they all ate in the cafeteria and took a short hike, he followed Susie and the boys back to Greensboro, arriving about midnight. Chowy bolted from the apartment and ran off, chasing a cat, as soon as they opened the door, and it took hours to find him. By the time he found the dog and returned it to the apartment, Rob had called to tell Susie about the murders.

"What was her reaction?" Gentry asked.

"She was stunned," Fritz replied.

Susie and her mother had problems, Fritz said, but he, Susie, and Rob always had been close, and he felt responsible for Susie and the boys.

Did he know Delores Lynch?

Yes, he'd met her at Susie's wedding and seen her again at the visitation hearing in 1982. He knew Tom, he said, and got along well with him. He'd been divorced himself, and knew what it was to go through such a trying experience.

He'd heard that Delores had wanted visitation with the children for herself before her death, he said, and he was aware that Tom now wanted to double his. He thought that Susie's troubles with Tom about extended visitation might have had something to do with the threatening calls she'd been receiving and other mysterious acts. He told about somebody tampering with Susie's car and slitting the throats of the boys' toy animals. He'd secured Susie's apartment, he said, but the apartment managers apparently let somebody make off with the key for the new dead bolt lock he'd put on her front door.

As he told about this, Fritz took out a key chain, and Gentry noticed something unusual on it: a handcuff key.

"I know that only two kinds of people carry handcuff keys," Gentry said later, "the police and the bad guys. Since he wasn't a cop, I thought this was very strange. I know that no decent, honest citizen carries handcuff keys."

Had Fritz had any military training?

No, he said, but he was a gun enthusiast. His father had been a gun collector and had loved handguns, but most were gone now. They once had had a third-class license to buy and sell guns, he said.

Did he and Ian often do things together?

They'd really only gotten close in the past year, Fritz said. They'd been camping together, and several times he'd taken Ian to his father's farm to teach him such things as compass and map reading, rappeling, and rock climbing.

Had he ever been to Hattie Newsom's house?

No, he said, and he was unaware of any problems she might have had with anybody. He couldn't imagine anybody wanting to kill her.

On the way back to Susie's apartment, the detectives attempted to feel out Fritz's reaction about the murders. He said he'd been shocked along with everybody else.

"It just must've been terrible what they went through," he said, hanging his head with a look of sadness.

Gentry and Sturgill thanked him when they let him out at the apartment.

"He was putting on a little show for us there," Sturgill said with a smile as Fritz made his way up the stairs. "A real acting job."

"He's a real cool customer," Gentry agreed.

Both detectives realized after this interview that they never would get much out of Fritz that would be helpful to them. But they had been given someplace to turn.

"The problem was going to be Ian," Gentry said later. "We didn't know what to expect."

But before they confronted Ian, the detectives had to take another step. That night, Lennie Nobles and Sherman Childers, the detectives who had been so long frustrated by the Lynch case, arrived in Winston-Salem and checked into a motel. Early Wednesday morning, they met at the sheriff's department with Gentry, Sturgill, Barker, and other detectives investigating the Newsom murders. The detectives spent a full day going over all the details of both cases.

After the session with the North Carolina officers, Nobles called Dan Davidson. Months earlier, in a moment of despair, Nobles had gone to talk to a veteran homicide detective in Louisville about the Lynch murders, hoping for some guidance that might lead him to a break in the case. "That family has a dark cloud in it somewhere," the detective told him. "Find that cloud and you've found your killer." Nobles had passed this on to Davidson.

When Davidson answered the phone that night, the first thing Nobles said was, "I think we've found our dark cloud."

40

The detectives knew little about Ian Perkins other than that he was a neighbor of the Klenners. But the relationship went much deeper than that. Ian was tied to the Klenners from birth. His grandfather, Felix Fournier, was Fritz's godfather. Like Dr. Klenner, Fournier came to Reidsville an outsider. Like Dr. Klenner, his family was European, his religion Catholicism, and these things drew the two men together. But Fournier's manner made him even more of an outsider than Dr. Klenner in the country town.

"He looked like a foreign diplomat," said his friend Phil Link. "He had this formal bearing about him. He was the most perfect gentleman that I ever knew in my life. He was an old-school gentleman. He didn't want to hear any gossip about anybody. He didn't want to hear a dirty joke. He wasn't a prude. He just didn't care for that sort of thing."

Fournier moved to Reidsville from Richmond in the forties to become a foreman of the American Tobacco Company plant. He brought with him his wife, Maria, and their only child, Camille, and they settled into a modest house near the country club. Later, when Fournier became manager of the tobacco plant, he built a larger, brick house on Huntsdale Road, a one-block street on which his friend Dr. Klenner lived.

A shy and gracious man, Fournier loved music, played the violin, and aspired to write fiction. He and his wife belonged to the Reidsville Studio Group, which delved into the arts. His wife painted with watercolors, and he wrote stiff and formal short stories in a nineteenth-century style. Once, after much persuasion, Fournier agreed to play his violin for the group, but he was so shy that he insisted on playing in a separate room, out of sight of his audience.

Fournier died of a heart attack after church one Sunday in 1960, five years before the birth of his only grandson.

Camille Fournier had been advised not to have children. As a child, she was diagnosed as having polio by Dr. Klenner, who treated her with vitamin C and won credit and undying gratitude from her family for saving her life. The childhood disease and her petite size would make childbearing difficult, Dr. Klenner told her, but after her marriage to Tom Perkins, an engineer with strongly conservative political leanings at American Tobacco Company, she wanted to try. Dr. Klenner cared for her during her difficult pregnancy with plenty of vitamins and later delivered Ian. If not for Dr. Klenner, Camille later told friends, Ian would not have been.

"Dr. Klenner was not an open subject with her," said a former co-worker. "She worshiped the ground he walked on."

Camille became managing editor of the *Reidsville Review*, and in February of 1971, she wrote a long and glowing article about Dr. Klenner and his work, tying it to the publication of Linus Pauling's book *Vitamin C and the Common Cold*, in which Dr. Klenner's vitamin experiments were noted. She later reprinted the article "at popular request."

When Ian was four, Tom and Camille Perkins adopted a second child, a daughter they named Lori, Camille telling friends that she didn't want Ian to grow up a lonely only child. Some wondered later if she'd been successful in that goal.

"Ian always just struck me as a very lonely little boy," said a family friend. "I always felt sorry for him as a little boy. He was an idolized son in a strange sort of way. He was idolized and dismissed at the same time. But he was always idolized as a symbol instead of a person. They just had so many hopes pinned on Ian. He blinked a lot. He held his body in a way that always looked as if he felt he was in the way."

When Ian was thirteen, his parents divorced, and he, his mother, and his sister moved first into an apartment, then into a house on Ann Ruston Street in a middle-income neighborhood not far from downtown. In July of 1972, Camille left the newspaper to take a job producing a company newsletter for Fieldcrest Mills, a textile plant in nearby Eden. There she met Jim O'Neal, an executive who worked in government relations. They married a year after her divorce, and later they moved into her family home, just down the street from the Klenners, to help care for her aging mother.

In high school, Ian was quiet and studious, a good student who favored science and won an award for a chemistry project. He was president of an amateur radio group and belonged to the Bible Club. After his graduation in 1982, he was accepted at Washington and Lee University in Lexington, Virginia. A family friend recommended Washington and Lee to him, and he was drawn to its proud traditions. He began as a chemical engineering major but was less than an outstanding student and later switched to philosophy.

As highly patriotic as he was devoutly religious, Ian joined the National Guard during his freshman year and spent his first summer break in basic training. After his sophomore year, he had to choose a military job specialty, and he picked field medic. Dropping out of school for a quarter, he went off to training at Fort Sam Houston, Texas, on August 15, 1984. He completed the training on November 2 and returned to Reidsville. Soon afterward, he ran into Fritz, and they began talking about his training. Fritz spent hours instructing Ian on what he should have learned but wasn't taught.

And Ian was grateful. He felt special being offered help by Fritz. Like all of the other Klenner family friends and acquaintances, he thought Fritz a doctor, a graduate of Duke Medical School. He knew there had been some problem, because Fritz had kept the clinic operating only a short time after his father's death, but he thought Fritz was finishing his residency, had a provisional license, and would eventually reopen the clinic.

Ian had known Fritz all of his life, but they had never been close. Fritz occasionally came to Ian's house with his mother for dinner, but there was an eleven-year difference in Fritz's and Ian's ages.

"Ian looked up to Fritz like an uncle," a neighbor said later.

As they got together to talk about medical and military matters, their friendship grew closer, and Fritz told Ian that when he came home from school one weekend they would go shooting at his father's farm.

"We'll have to get out some rifles and see how good you are," Fritz said.

Fritz and Ian also shared another interest, one that they hadn't discussed yet. Ian was thinking about going into intelligence work after he finished college, perhaps becoming a covert agent. He had a great-uncle, Gerald Fournier, who was a secret agent in Europe, and after Ian returned to college in January, where his friends took to calling him "Doc," because of his new training, he wrote to his uncle, asking advice. His uncle sent the following reply.

> *I appreciate you requesting my advice about your career plans. It is not difficult to get accepted for the line of work which I have devoted my life to because it's an occupation that grows on you. It gives you job satisfaction, but it is frustrating at times. Your mother asked me in the early sixties during her visit with your grandmother to Europe the nature of my job. Although I could not answer her because of classification, I did however ask her to read the book War of Wits by Ladislas Farago. But I do not know if you will be able to retain that book now.*
>
> *Ian, what you want to get into will have to be your choice. However, if you choose to be employed by the CIA, I can put you in contact with a friend of mine who works out of Roslyn, Va. He can evaluate your educational background and assess your capabilities. He can then take you to the CIA screening officer for formal application.*

During his midterm break in late February, Ian returned home and dropped by the Klenner house to see Fritz. Fritz had a bandage on the middle finger of his left hand and a splint on his ring finger. He'd found a small homemade bomb taped to the gas tank of Susie's car, he said, and it had gone off after he removed it. He claimed that he had suffered nerve damage to the middle finger and sprained his ring finger.

He knew who'd put the bomb there, he said. He was certain that Susie's former husband, Tom Lynch, had contracted with the mob to have her killed. This hadn't been the only attempt on her, he said, going on to talk at length about Tom's involvement with the mob. Tom had his own mother and sister killed, he said, so that he could inherit the family fortune and pay off mob debts. And Tom still owed Susie for paying his way through dental school, Fritz said.

They went to the farm, where Fritz got out an AR15 assault rifle, an Uzi submachine gun, and a .45 pistol, and they fired hundreds of rounds of ammunition.

Between rounds, they talked of Ian's dream of becoming a secret agent, and Fritz hinted that he might be able to help. Later that weekend, Ian showed him the letter he had received from his great-uncle.

On another weekend trip home a couple of weeks later, Ian again went to the farm with Fritz. This time Susie and the boys also came along. Ian rode in Fritz's Blazer with Chowy, Susie's protective big male chow. Susie and the boys rode in her Blazer with Maizie, their female chow. Maizie was in heat, and after they got to the farm, Fritz tried to keep Chowy in his vehicle, away from Maizie, but Chowy, protesting, bit him.

That day, Fritz made "shape charges" by softening dynamite with water and pressing it into wine bottles he'd cut in half. He used them to blow holes in the ground, looking for "lava tubes" that he said lay under the surface. He wanted to get into one of the tubes and look around, he said, but he hadn't been able to find one.

They all fired weapons that day, the boys shooting their .22 assault rifle replicas. Susie wore a .45 pistol in a cross-draw holster, but she chose to fire her .25-caliber Browning.

"Imagine a big, ugly black mugger is about to do something to your children," Fritz told her as she took aim at the target, and she began firing with such a fierce intensity that she didn't stop pulling the trigger even after the pistol had run out of ammunition, and Fritz practically had to pry the weapon from her hands.

That day Fritz told Ian that he'd like to come see the campus at Washington and Lee, and Ian said he'd be glad to show him around anytime.

In late March, Fritz came. He brought with him what appeared to be a camera, but later he disclosed it to be a weapon capable of firing a shell at an unsuspecting subject. Ian took him on a tour of the historic town, with its brick streets and restored buildings, as well as the hilltop campus of Washington and Lee, with its Victorian buildings, and the adjoining campus of the Virginia Military Institute, with its Gothic barracks, its military museum, and its ramrod-straight cadets.

Afterward, they sat and talked in the darkness by Lee Chapel, and Fritz disclosed that he was a contract agent for the CIA, that he'd been recruited years earlier when he was at Woodward Academy in Atlanta. He also spent a lot of time at the John F. Kennedy Special Warfare Center at Fort Bragg, he said, and mentioned the Delta Team, but quickly added that these were things Ian didn't need to know about. He did talk of missions that on occasion had nearly cost him his life. They had brought him much closer to God, he said with a great show of emotion. One of those missions had been to search for POWs in Vietnam, he said.

Ian was flattered that Fritz chose to tell him these things. At last he understood all of Fritz's mysterious comings and goings, all the exotic weaponry and military gear. He was amazed that he hadn't realized it sooner.

But he could tell no one about it, for Fritz swore him to secrecy. Fritz knew that he could trust Ian, he said, because Ian, too, wanted to be a "Company man," and Fritz was going to give him the opportunity to prove himself worthy. He had been authorized to take Ian on a mission to see how he functioned under pressure. Even Ian's great-uncle Gerald had given his approval. The mission would be to Texas. It would take only four days, and it would involve a "touch," a necessary killing, but

Ian would not have to be part of that. His role would be support only. Would he be interested?

Ian couldn't say yes quickly enough.

As they rode toward Lexington, Virginia, to find Ian on Thursday morning, May 30, Allen Gentry and Tom Sturgill felt good about the way their case was developing.

"Let's say we were cautiously optimistic," Gentry said later. "In this business you don't want to get too excited, because we've all had cases where we felt like we knew who was responsible but couldn't get all the pieces together to prove it."

The detectives arrived in Lexington a few minutes after noon and went straight to the neat, story-and-a-half, shuttered home of Violet Firebaugh, a widow who rented spare rooms to college students. Mrs. Firebaugh had company and said that Ian was not there. He likely would be in a little later. The detectives went to lunch and returned to find Ian nervously awaiting them, clearly frightened.

"We need to talk to you," Gentry said. "Would you mind coming out to the car?"

Ian accompanied them to the four-door Ford Crown Victoria and got into the backseat. The detectives got into the front. Ian lit a cigarette, and both detectives noticed that he trembled as he smoked it.

Gentry asked first for biographical information, then went straight to the camping trip with Fritz less than two weeks earlier. Would he mind telling them about that?

Fritz had called about 3 that Friday afternoon and asked him to meet him at Roanoke Mountain at 6, Ian said. He'd gone there and waited until the overlook closed, but Fritz didn't arrive. He drove back to his room in Lexington and called Fritz's mother, who told him that Fritz had left several hours earlier. A little later Fritz called from Roanoke Mountain and said that he'd come on to Lexington. He arrived before midnight and they struck out for the Blue Ridge Parkway. They went to Peaks of Otter, set up a camp and got to sleep about 6 or 7. They slept until about 1, had brunch at the coffee shop, and returned to prepare for a night hike. They left about 5 and got caught in a rainstorm near the top of the mountain, where they stopped and started a fire to dry themselves. They got back to the campsite well after midnight, went to sleep, got up late, made breakfast, broke camp. Fritz brought him back to his room, took a shower, called Susie and told her to meet him for dinner at Natural Bridge, then called his mother. After Fritz left, Ian said, he just stayed in his room the rest of the evening.

Ian lit another cigarette as he talked. His mouth was obviously dry, his tongue sticking. Now and then his voice cracked. The fine bead of sweat that broke out on his forehead and upper lip didn't go unnoticed.

Had Ian seen Fritz since then? Gentry asked.

Yes, he'd talked to him just the night before. Fritz had called to find out how he was doing. And Fritz had come back to Lexington on the Wednesday night following the camping trip to help him study for his final exam in his medical ethics class. Ian went on to explain that Fritz was a doctor—of course, he realized, the detectives probably knew that—although he wasn't practicing right now.

"He's not a doctor," Gentry said. "He was never even in medical school. He just pretended that he was. His own mother told us that."

Ian looked startled, and Gentry pushed on with his questions. Was Ian aware of any weapons Fritz might own?

Yes, Ian said, they'd gone shooting together several times. They'd fired a .223 assault rifle, a .45 and a .22 pistol, he said, failing to mention the Uzi submachine gun. The last time they'd gone shooting was on Mother's Day, just a few weeks before.

Gentry paused in his questioning and consulted his notes, leaving Ian, who still puffed nervously on his cigarette, to ponder what they'd just been over.

"You know," Gentry finally said, "this just isn't going to fly. Something's wrong here. Fritz claimed that y'all left out on your hike about eight, but you said five. Fritz said that y'all didn't go to bed when you got back, that you just laid around and talked, but you said you went to sleep. Which way is it?"

Ian gulped noticeably and took another quick puff on

his cigarette. The detectives could see panic welling in his eyes.

"You know," Gentry pushed on, "in the time you say it took for this hike, ya'll could've driven to Winston-Salem, murdered three people, and returned to Virginia."

He didn't have to say any more. Ian broke into tears and began sobbing loudly, his head in his hands.

The detectives were surprised by his sudden outburst and looked wonderingly at one another, saying nothing.

"I'm thinking, 'This is too easy,'" Gentry said later. "Usually, you wind up having to get a little ugly and go back and forth with 'em before something like this happens."

Gentry and Sturgill sat quietly as Ian struggled to control himself. After a couple of minutes, Gentry broke the silence.

"You want to tell us what really happened?" he said softly.

It was true, Ian said, that he and Fritz had been to Winston-Salem that night but he had not known of any plan to murder the Newsoms. Fritz had recruited him for a CIA mission to go after arms thieves, drug dealers, traitors. He went on to tell the whole long story of how he'd dreamed of becoming a secret agent, how Fritz had finally told him that he was with the CIA and had invited him on a mission to Texas. The mission had been planned for a couple of months, he said, but after Fritz came to pick him up for the camping trip that was to provide their cover story, he had changed the plan. They were going instead to North Carolina, first to make a "touch" in Winston-Salem. There Fritz would steal a car, and then they would go on to Charlotte for a second operation.

Gentry and Sturgill had heard a lot of stories in their years in law enforcement, but never one like this.

"I'm writing," Gentry recalled later, "but we kept looking at each other like 'Is this guy for real?' It was almost too incredible to believe." But Ian was so rattled and so sincere that neither of them doubted that he now was telling the truth.

He and Fritz had gone to Peaks of Otter and camped just as he'd told them earlier, Ian said, but instead of going on a night hike, they had left at about 5 P.M. for

Winston-Salem. Questioning Ian carefully about times and locations, the detectives were able to put together the exact route Fritz had taken across Winston-Salem. And when Ian described the shopping center where he had turned to let Fritz out nearby in the darkness, the detectives knew its location precisely. It was just down the hill from Nanna's house. The time, Ian said, was about 11 P.M.

When Ian told of Fritz's reappearance in the gold car and of his fear when the police car stopped Fritz later, the detectives grew excited. Surely there would be at least a radio record of the stop. From that they would learn the officer's identity and perhaps he would remember Fritz. Regardless, it would still be corroborating evidence for Ian's story.

After Ian told them of Fritz's decision to cancel the Charlotte part of the operation and of Fritz's return to the scene to leave the car, the detectives questioned him closely about the trip back to the mountains and all the stops to dispose of evidence. Their hope was to recover some of the items.

When Ian had finished his story, Gentry asked if he hadn't been concerned after he heard about the Newsom murders. Ian said that he had been "stunned" at the news, but that he thought the murders had occurred on Sunday night, not Saturday, and that it was all just a big coincidence. Besides, he said, he trusted Fritz and couldn't believe he would do that. True, he knew that Fritz had killed three people, but he believed that was sanctioned by the CIA and thus all right.

Gentry thought that Ian's naïveté was a spectacle to behold, but even with such a handicap, Ian should have known that the CIA couldn't operate in such fashion without stirring official interest.

"It's not like James Bond where somebody goes through and kills people and nobody asks why," he said.

Perhaps fear was what had kept Ian from linking his and Fritz's activities to the Newsom murders and coming forth earlier, Gentry thought. Regardless, he was now clearly repentant, and seemed eager to do whatever he could to make amends.

Ian had mentioned in his story that Fritz had paid him

three one-hundred-dollar bills for his part in the mission, and he had deposited them in an automatic teller at Dominion Bank shortly after Fritz left on Sunday. He still had the deposit slip, and the detectives wanted that for corroborating evidence. He also had mentioned the Colt Gold Cup National Match .45-caliber pistol Fritz had given him, and they asked him for that as well.

Both detectives went with Ian to his room to fetch these, and they again grew excited when Ian mentioned something that had occurred on Fritz's return trip to Lexington the previous Wednesday. Not only had Fritz told Ian that his superiors at the CIA had been very impressed with how Ian handled himself, Fritz had changed the slide on the pistol he'd given Ian. Would he have put the slide from the murder weapon onto Ian's pistol? It would be easy enough to check. The two empty shell casings found at the Newsom house had ejection markings on them that could be matched with the slide.

Gentry and Sturgill asked Ian to go with them to the Lexington Police Department, where they again went over the details of his story and asked if he would accompany them the next day to retrace the stops he and Fritz had made on the way back from Winston-Salem and search for the abandoned evidence. Now angry about being duped by Fritz, Ian quickly agreed.

After warning Ian not to make any mention of their visit should Fritz call or come back, Gentry and Sturgill dropped him off at his room, then stopped at a nearby gas station telephone booth to report to their supervisors.

Gentry called Captain Ron Barker.

"He was elated," Barker recalled later. "I knew what he was going to say."

Sturgill called his commander, Ed Hunt, and also called the SBI ballistics lab in Raleigh to alert them to have somebody standing by, because he and Gentry were bringing in Ian's .45 to see if it could be matched to the shell casings.

Earlier that afternoon, not knowing how long it might take for the local officers to make a case against Fritz, the Kentucky detectives, Sherman Childers and Lennie Nobles, left Winston-Salem to return home with the information they had gathered so they could begin plotting strategy with Dan Davidson.

"I've got a good feeling about today," Ron Barker told them before they left. "Don't go more than two hours without calling me."

Nobles called when they stopped in Asheville for supper.

"If I were you, I'd turn that car around and drive back to Winston-Salem about as fast as you can drive," Barker told them.

"We're on our way," said Nobles.

Less than two hours later, the detectives hurried into Barker's office and asked, "What's up?"

Barker grinned and reached for two bags beside his desk. Earlier, local officers had promised Childers and Nobles visitors' gift packages of sample local products, but the officer who was to pick them up let it slip his mind until Childers and Nobles already had gone.

"We finally got these gifts for you," Barker said, "and I didn't want y'all to go home without 'em."

Then, without allowing time for Childers's and Nobles's colorful mutterings to abate, Barker said, "We got him! We got him!"

At 2:30 P.M. on Thursday, as Ian was telling his strange tale to detectives in Virginia, Susie called her lawyer, Sandy Sands. First, she thanked him for being supportive, but that wasn't the purpose of her call.

"She was even more terrified than when I saw her that Friday before the murders," Sands recalled later. "I could tell by the breaks in her voice, just the way she talked, that she was petrified."

Her fear was that she was going to be murdered and that the boys would be kidnapped or murdered.

"She felt she and the boys were next," Sands said.

She told of slipping the boys into the back of the church at the funerals and of shielding John and Jim from photographers at the cemetery to make it less easy for kidnappers or killers to spot them. She was certain that the mob was after them. Fritz had gone to pick up the boys now at school, she said, to protect them.

"What happens to my inheritance if I die?" she asked.

Sands explained that it would go to the boys, and if anything happened to them, it would go to their father.

"That can't happen!" she cried. "They'll kill me and the kids just to get it. What can we do?"

Sands said that he could draw a will for Susie that would leave everything to her children in a trust to age thirty. If anything happened to them before they reached thirty, she could have the inheritance go to her brother's children.

Susie told him to draw up the will. She said that she wanted to take it to the newspapers and make it public so that anybody planning to kill her and the children for the inheritance would know that it wouldn't do them any good.

Sands said he'd work on it and have it to her to sign by the coming week.

After getting Gentry's call, Ron Barker and Detective John Boner went to the Winston-Salem Police Department and listened to the radio transmission tapes from the night of the murders.

They heard an officer stopping Nanna's car. "What we were sitting there just praying for was for him to come back and say, 'I want a license check on a Fred Klenner.' " Barker recalled. But the officer merely came back to clear himself from the stop.

Still, Barker was hopeful when he learned that the officer was Jim Hull. He'd known Hull for years. "He's a sharp, fine officer," Barker said later. "I knew if anybody would remember a routine stop, it would be Jim."

At the SBI lab in Raleigh, Tom Sturgill and Allen Gentry learned that the shell casings found at the murder scene had not passed through the slide Fritz put on Ian's .45. But this was only a minor disappointment to cap off an otherwise productive day, and they arrived back in Winston-Salem after midnight, tired but ecstatic, confident that they soon would be closing in on Fritz.

Fritz was not at Susie's apartment earlier that night when Annette Hunt stopped by to see how Susie was doing. Susie fixed tea and began to talk about the murders.

"The police seem to think the motive was robbery," she said. "It's not robbery. That's obvious. Sixty percent of murders are covered up by making it look like robbery."

"She had a theory that Bob was working on a case in Washington, some kind of secret work he'd been up there to testify about, and maybe somebody had followed him back to kill him," Annette recalled later.

Susie went on to talk about her fears that she and the boys might also be murdered because of Tom's mob connections. Annette urged her to tell the police about all of this, but Susie said they already knew. The hopelessness that Annette had sensed in Susie the week before now seemed overwhelming.

"It was like there was nothing they could do and they were all doomed," she said later.

Early Friday morning, the detectives assigned to the Newsom case gathered at the sheriff's department in a jovial mood. Flush with success, they were eager to hear in detail what Gentry and Sturgill had learned from Ian and to plan their next moves.

They had two main hopes for this day: that in their search with Ian they might find physical evidence to tie Fritz to the murders; and that James F. Hull, the Winston-Salem police officer who had stopped Fritz shortly after the murders, would remember it and be able to identify him.

After the briefing, SBI agent J. W. Bryant decided to go to Virginia with Sturgill and Gentry. Boner, Carden, and Barker would question Hull, who was as yet unaware of how close he came to death that night.

A few hours later, Hull was summoned before the Forsyth County officers. He looked apprehensive.

"He didn't know whether he'd done something wrong or what," Barker later remembered. "I felt sorry for him. We had to prolong his apprehension. We couldn't tell him anything. He had to be treated like a witness."

The officers asked if he remembered stopping a car shortly before midnight on May 18.

He didn't, and the officers provided hints: a slow-moving vehicle; a drunk-driving check perhaps?

Still nothing.

Not until they mentioned the trailing Blazer was Hull's memory jogged. He had stopped a car going especially slow, but the driver showed no sign of drinking and said he was having engine problems and was trying to nurse the car home. Hull remembered the motor knocking. He couldn't run a check on the driver's license or car tag because the computer was down that night. He had a vague memory of the driver, who, he thought, had a couple of days' growth of beard and was wearing olive-colored pants. He couldn't recall the shirt.

"We knew then that he wouldn't be able to pick out Fritz in a lineup," Barker said.

Barker got Boner to write several names on a sheet of paper, one of them Klenner, others similar. Shown the list, Hull couldn't pick out one with certainty.

"There went all hope," Barker recalled. Hull would be a poor witness.

"I know you're in suspense," Barker told Hull. "The man you stopped that night had just murdered three people."

The detectives left disappointed.

Later, Hull claimed to a reporter that he had picked out Fritz's name but told Barker he couldn't be 100 percent certain. He also said he was sure he could have identified Fritz. He again described Fritz as having a couple of days' growth of beard and this time recalled him as wearing camouflage fatigues. The detectives knew from Ian, however, that Fritz had had a full beard, and that he was not wearing fatigues but dress slacks and a windbreaker under which he was holding a .45 that he planned to use to shoot Hull in the head if the officer had asked him to step out of the car.

Gentry, Sturgill, and Bryant arrived in Lexington in late morning to find Ian looking haggard. He was still upset and had slept little, but he was ready to help. The detectives had little hope of recovering any items Fritz had tossed into dumpsters and trash cans on the way back to Virginia, but they'd brought metal detectors to search for those he buried, particularly the knife he'd used to stab Florence and slit her throat.

Guided by Ian, they went to Peaks of Otter to begin

their search. Luck was not with them. They dug up barbed wire, soft drink caps, beer can tabs, pork and bean cans, but no knife. Ian showed them where Fritz went down to the lake to dispose of the gun barrel, and if necessary, the detectives decided, they could later have divers search the bottom.

They did pick up the registration envelope Fritz had filled out at the campground, and they couldn't help but smile over it. "Dr. Fred R. Klenner, Jr.," he had written on it.

At Roanoke Mountain, the detectives found a park ranger who remembered talking to Fritz, but this would be of little use to their case. After fruitlessly retracing all Fritz's stops, the tired and dejected detectives returned to Lexington in early evening.

Other SBI agents also were busy in the case Friday. The SBI discovered that it had a file on Fritz, the memorandum sent to headquarters by agent Mike Kelly in 1981 when Fritz's friend Sam Phillips tried to get the SBI to investigate Fritz for practicing medicine without a license. The memorandum noted that Fritz was "a very paranoid person, and usually carried several weapons with him along with his black medical bag."

That day both Sam Phillips and John Forrest, the former gun shop owner who had been Fritz's friend, received calls from the SBI.

Phillips said he told the agent who called that Fritz would be heavily armed, that he likely would have automatic weapons, possibly explosives, and that he was extremely dangerous—"kind of a dormant caged animal."

"I said, 'This guy is going to come out shooting,' " Phillips recalled later. "I knew he would go out and take as many people as he could with him if they tried to arrest him."

"I told him they'd better be damned careful," John Forrest recalled telling the agent who called him, "that he went around continuously with knives and guns and that the guy was a psychopath and if they tried to arrest him, he probably was going to kill somebody, that if he ever got to the farm in Reidsville, they'd have a hell of a time getting him out."

Frances Miller was at her mother's house that Friday with her friend Katy Sutton. They were going through Nanna's belongings and trying to put her affairs in order, when Susie appeared at the door. Frances was uneasy about her showing up unannounced, and the private guard she had hired to look after the house was apprehensive, too. Whenever anybody in the Miller family sought a solution to the murders, only two names ever came up—Susie and Fritz—yet nobody in the family had said anything to Susie about it.

"None of us wanted to confront her with that," Frances said.

Susie said that she had come to pick up her mother's and father's belongings, so Frances accompanied her through the house, pointing them out.

When they walked into the upstairs bathroom, Frances saw Bob's partial plates in a glass where he had left them the night he was killed. This was the first time she'd noticed them, and it nearly moved her to tears. Not Susie.

"She didn't respond at all," Frances recalled later. "She just gathered everything up as if they'd sent her over there to pick it up for them."

Susie was concerned about some formal dresses that had belonged to Aunt Su-Su, dresses that Judge Sharp no longer could wear and had sent to Florence to try on. Florence had told Frances that she could have some of the dresses, but Susie snatched all of them up. Several times Susie mentioned her mother's fur. It was in storage, she complained, and nobody knew where the receipt was.

"I thought, 'Who cares about fur coats?' " Frances remembered later.

While she and Susie were going through the house, the telephone rang and Frances answered it. Nancy was on the line, and she immediately detected strain in her mother's voice.

"Mother, you don't sound right," she said. "What's wrong?"

"Well, nothing."

"Something's wrong," Nancy said. "Who's there?"

"Oh, Susie's here. I'm helping her gather up her parents' things."

"Is anybody else there?"

"Yes, Katy's here, and the guard. Would you like to speak to Susie?"

"Yes," Nancy said.

Shortly, Susie came on the line.

"Hi, Nance, how you doing?"

"It was like nothing had happened," Nancy remembered later. "She just started bubbling on about something."

"Why haven't you talked to any of us?" Nancy finally asked.

"I'm trying to keep the boys away from the press and off TV," Susie said. "Can you imagine two better kidnap targets?"

Nancy wasn't sure what Susie meant, but before Nancy could say anything, Susie said, "My attorney told me not to move."

"What do you mean move?"

"You know, it would look awfully strange for a person who had inherited all that money to move quickly."

"All what money?" Nancy asked.

"You know, Delores left all the money to the boys in a trust. All of my daddy's money and Nanna's money was split up, and all that went to the boys in a trust."

Nancy knew no such thing had happened, but she also knew that something strange had happened to Susie during the course of this conversation. Her mother was noticing it, too. Susie's voice had changed, growing louder, the words slower and more deliberate.

Suddenly, she was talking about the murders.

"They say it was robbery, but I told the SBI it was professional killers. I've told them but they don't believe me."

She went on to say that professionals had killed Tom's mother and sister because of his mob connections, and now they had struck here.

"I've tried to tell everyone that this was a professional killing. We're all going to have to accept the fact that professional killers are never caught. That's why they are professionals."

As quickly as she'd changed before, Susie changed again, reverting to her previous bubbly self.

"We're going to have to keep in touch," she said. "Nobody knows your address."

"I'll mail it to you," Nancy said, thinking fast.

"That was the strangest telephone call I ever had with anybody," Nancy said later. "I was scared to death. All I could think was, How am I going to get Mother out of the house?"

She asked Susie to put her mother back on the line.

"I'm going to call the sheriff," Nancy told her mother. "I want you to go out back and stand near the guard until he gets there."

A sheriff's deputy arrived within minutes and pretended that he was just checking by while Susie cheerily loaded her parents' belongings into her Blazer and departed.

Gentry, Sturgill, and Bryant arrived back in Lexington that evening certain only about their next move: supper. Ian said he didn't feel like eating and went to his room to rest, so the detectives went across the street to the Country Cookin' Café, where a huge sign in the window proclaimed the house special: SIRLOIN STEAK, UNLIMITED SALAD, VEGETABLE, AND DESSERT, $2.99.

During the meal, they discussed what their next move should be. Ian's story was so fantastic that it might be hard for a jury to believe without stronger proof, they decided. Why not put a wire on Ian and let him try to trap Fritz into a confession? Would he do it? After supper, they took their idea back across the street to find out.

"We told him, 'You know this guy's dangerous,' " Gentry recalled. " 'He's killed three people and probably at least two more.' But there was never any doubt on Ian's part. He said, 'Yes, I'll do it.' Ian was feeling so bad about what had happened that I think he would have willfully done almost anything we'd asked him to. He was that upset."

41

After agreeing to help the detectives, Ian followed them to Winston-Salem in his bright orange Honda Civic and was put up at the Inn at Winston Square, a motel just two blocks from the Hall of Justice.

The officers were worried that he was too nervous to go through with their plan to entrap Fritz into a taped admission of guilt, but Don Tisdale, the district attorney, agreed that Ian's story was too incredible for a jury to believe otherwise and instructed them to go ahead. They decided to make the attempt the following day, Saturday, June 1.

The plan was simple. Ian would call Fritz and tell him that three detectives had come to question him on Friday and requested that he take a lie detector test. He would say that he was scared, needed to talk, and ask Fritz to meet him in the parking lot at Pennrose Mall, Reidsville's major shopping center.

To protect Ian, five unmarked police cars with at least two officers in each would be close at hand, and an SBI observation plane would be overhead. Ian would be accompanied by Steve Carden, a sheriff's department detective who looked young enough to pass as a college student. Carden would be posing as Chris, a friend from Washington and Lee, who'd come to spend the weekend with Ian. The officers gambled that Fritz would be reluctant to harm Ian knowing that somebody knew about the meeting.

The detectives gathered at the sheriff's department on Saturday morning with their jittery informer, who, though obviously scared, assured them that he wanted to go ahead. Several narcotics officers were assisting with the surveillance, and the police caravan drove to the SBI office near Greensboro. Ian called Susie's apartment only to learn that Fritz wasn't there, although Susie expected him soon.

The officers drove on to Reidsville and regrouped at the police department, where the chief, James Klenner Festerman—named for Fritz's father, who had delivered him—assigned a detective to assist them. When Ian called again, Fritz answered and agreed to meet him. Ian said he was with a college friend who needed to go to the mall and suggested that they meet there so they could talk while his friend shopped. The drive from Greensboro would take half an hour, giving the officers plenty of time to take positions.

Nervously smoking, Ian waited in his car with Steve Carden. A small, flat recorder was taped to his back, under his shirt, a tiny transmitter secreted on his belt. Ian and the officers were aware of the risk he was taking. They knew that if Fritz detected the devices, Ian could be killed before anybody could get to him.

Allen Gentry and SBI agent J. W. Bryant were parked at a nearby Hardee's with the receiving equipment. When they asked for a check of Ian's transmitter, Ian said, "Say a prayer for me."

The airplane followed Fritz from Greensboro, and the SBI agent on board kept the officers at the shopping center advised of his location. When Fritz pulled into the parking lot and stopped, Ian got out and walked to the Blazer. Carden went into the mall, where he kept watch out of sight.

Ian got in with Fritz and said he'd told his friend they were just going to sit and talk for a little while.

"Let's ride somewhere," Fritz said, immediately starting the engine and causing consternation among the officers.

Ian told Fritz about Gentry and two SBI men coming to talk to him the previous day as Fritz pulled away from the shopping center, police cars following at a discreet distance.

"What did the SBI people look like?"

"Oh, cop types."

Ian tried to describe them and recall what they'd asked. He said he'd told them about the camping trip just as Fritz had instructed.

"They told me the murders had taken place on Saturday night," Ian said. "I was sweating. I hope I didn't seem too nervous. I was scared to death."

They were in traffic, and the noises made it difficult for officers to understand all that was being said.

"Well, what do you think?" Ian asked.

"Well—first off, we had nothing to do with that."

"Right. I know that."

"We're just the fall guys."

Fritz asked the agents' names, and Ian said he wasn't sure about them.

"It's quite possible the third guy was a Company person who was there to judge your reactions." Fritz said, then remarked on some new construction they were passing.

"I told Chris I wasn't going to be too long," Ian said nervously. "We were thinking about going and seeing *Rambo* today. I've got to get my mind off this."

Fritz gave Ian a capsule that he identified as papaverine, a drug for calming muscle spasms. It would slow his heart and respiration, Fritz said, telling him to take it.

"No, Ian," Gentry said as he listened in his car, but it was obvious that Ian was swallowing it.

"Oh, Lord," Gentry said. For all the officers knew, the capsule could have contained cyanide.

Fritz asked Ian to repeat everything he'd told the officers, and Ian began reciting the litany of the camping trip. When he got to the part about calling Annie Hill, Fritz interrupted. "That'll be on the phone records."

Fritz was turning now into Greenview Cemetery, not far from the mall, the trailing police cars keeping well behind, advised of the Blazer's location by the agent in the airplane that was circling overhead. The police cars slowed and headed to different vantage points as the Blazer wound down the hill and through the tombstones. Ian was completing his version of the camping weekend as Fritz pulled up under the big magnolia tree next to his father's grave. After shutting off the engine, Fritz got out a map.

"Show me exactly what you showed them," he said. "Where did you show them that we started from?"

Ian pointed to a spot, and they began talking about the trail.

"Okay, about tomorrow morning," Fritz said. "There will be, back at the rock, off the trail, there will be remains of a—"

"A fire," said Ian quickly.

"—of a fire. You don't have anything to do tomorrow, do you?"

"Tell him yes," Gentry said to himself.

"I got this polygraph thing."

"Oh, it's tomorrow morning?"

"Oh, no, Monday. I was going to go back to Lexington tomorrow."

Fritz went back to the trail, tracing it on the map. "Now, I'll meet you somewhere tomorrow morning," he said.

"I'm going to be with Chris tonight. I could probably change that. I don't know. I'd have to talk to him."

"No, Ian, no," Gentry muttered, coaching helplessly. "Tell him you can't go."

"That's fine," Fritz said. "I was just thinking we could go up there tomorrow and hike a section of that trail." Suddenly he changed thoughts. "Okay, you do not have to take the polygraph."

"Be kind of suspicious if I backed out of it. I'm going through with it. I've just really got to get myself composed."

"That's a tactic people like that use. If they really were going to give you a hard time, they would want you to do the polygraph then, not give you three or four days to think about it. See, that's psychological. They want to get your head screwed out. You always have the option to tell them that—"

"You don't see any need for it?" Ian offered helpfully.

"All you have to say is that"—Fritz took a long pause—"you're privy to information that falls under the National Security Act."

"What if they ask me about that?"

"Say nothing."

"Name, rank, and serial number deal. I think I can

remember that. I'm sorry. This has been eating me up. I didn't sleep at all last night."

"Never say I'm associated with anybody," Fritz said, as a train screamed past on the nearby mainline Southern Railway tracks, again blotting out what officers could hear. "Just say . . . that you . . . you can always say that . . . like Gordon Liddy and the Watergate thing . . ."

"Uh-oh," Gentry said, when he heard that. A Liddy admirer. He wouldn't break easily.

". . . that you don't belong to any organization," Fritz was saying as the train receded. "Just say that you have been advised that taking a polygraph, that, just say flat that you are not to take one under any circumstances because of information that could be divulged indirectly in questioning. See, this is all mind games. They like to play with your head."

"Yeah."

Fritz reached into the back of the Blazer for his medical bag.

"I'll give you a phenobarb tablet to take so you can get a good night's sleep tonight. Take it about thirty minutes before bedtime."

He got out several capsules. "That's papaverine. Take one of these about every twelve hours."

"I feel better just talking to you," Ian said.

"Okay, now what you've got to do the next forty-eight hours, you have to develop a mindset. You have to tell yourself you were in Peaks of Otter."

"It has to be the truth," Ian said.

"That's right. You were not in Winston-Salem, so you can't say that you were in Winston-Salem. I'll lend you something that Dad gave me the first time I ever went on any type of covert operation."

He brought out a small cloth patch. On it was a figure of the Virgin Mary with a crown on her head. Flames leaped from a heart on a cross. He also took out a small card, encased in plastic, bearing another religious figure with a prayer to a saint.

"These are scapulars that come from, it would be in East Germany today. This one was his mother's sacred heart, and this one was his father's. They got those as children at the Shrine of Mary of the Hills on a pilgrimage the night before their family came to this country."

His voice became heavy with emotion, almost tearful. "I've always found great comfort in these," he said deliberately.

Ian accepted the objects and later gave them to the police.

Suddenly, Fritz changed the subject, talking again about prescription drugs and their effects. Ian said he'd heard of people taking downers before undergoing a polygraph test.

"I think Valium's probably a very good drug for that," Fritz said. "I've got some."

"I better be getting on back," Ian said.

Fritz cranked the engine and backed away from the gravesite. He drove slowly back toward the mall.

"I don't think I'll ever be as scared as I was yesterday," Ian said.

"Ian, if anybody ever asks you anything about being nervous, you know, just out of the blue, well just out of the blue people like this descend on you, anybody in their right mind's going to be nervous. Gracious."

Gentry couldn't help but smile over that. When he and Sturgill had descended out of the blue on Fritz, he hadn't been nervous at all.

"Did you ever think, Ian, you don't have to prove anything?" Fritz asked. "What they are doing—they have nothing. See, they are fishing."

"When they told me it was late Saturday night that this happened," Ian said, "I almost—it took sheer force of will to keep from falling apart right there."

"I still haven't heard any actual confirmation of when it occurred," Fritz said. "There's been nothing official, and the papers have had everything from Friday night to Sunday morning."

Fritz turned in at the parking lot and pulled into a space beside a car in which a small dog was barking squeakily and incessantly.

"Now, I do want to see you sometime tomorrow before you take off because I want to see how this medicine's working."

"What really scared me was when they said a forty-five

was used," Ian said, using some of the material he'd been coached to say. "That's probably the biggest coincidence I've heard about."

"They said, uh, they said . . ." Fritz paused, as if collecting his thoughts. "They haven't given a caliber that's been released in the paper that I'm aware of. There was an article yesterday in which they were saying it was not the same type gun as what was used out in Kentucky. What I suspect was that it probably was a fairly professional thing, that Tom had his sister and mother killed, and I would not be surprised if he were not behind this.

"Even if it was a forty-five, Ian, for a professional, that's not much of a coincidence at all. I mean forty-fives and twenty-twos are the most commonly used weapons because they are subsonic."

"I don't think they picked up on anything," Ian said.

"Don't worry about it. See, people read body language, but it means nothing."

"It's the first time I've ever been really confronted, you know, asked questions by a policeman."

"Like I said, that third person might very well have been a Company person judging the type of reaction you would have, how well you kept your cool."

"I'm going to go on and get Chris," Ian said.

"What do you want to do?" Fritz asked.

"I'll call you," Ian said, trying to open the door. His hands were so sweaty that he couldn't pull the lock up. Fritz reached behind him to get it, sending a rush of fear through Ian that he might detect the recorder on his back.

"If I don't get you at Susie's, I'll get you at the house," Ian said with relief as the door opened. "Well, I'll be talking to you."

After his meeting with Ian, Fritz drove to his mother's house. Later that afternoon, he walked across the street and chatted with Dr. David Henderson, a pediatrician, who was building a new house. Henderson, who had met Fritz a couple of months earlier, invited him in for a tour. They chatted about the construction, the neighborhood, medicine. Later, Henderson described Fritz as "nice, calm, peaceful, and pleasant."

"He was not nervous," Henderson told a reporter. "He seemed like a fairly normal person."

He was looking forward to getting to know Fritz better, Henderson said.

That evening, Fritz drove his mother to Susie's apartment for dinner. Susie had a guest, Taki Mundel, her mother's close friend from Maryland. Bob and Florence had spent most of the last week of their lives at the home of Taki and her husband, Marvin. The Mundels had been on a business trip when Bob and Florence were murdered and were not able to come for the funeral. When Taki called Susie to apologize and offer condolences, Susie asked her to come whenever she could. Taki had arrived the day before, and that night she took Susie and the boys out for a Chinese dinner.

Taki was staying with Rob's family, and early on Saturday Susie picked her up to go shopping. Susie said she wanted to buy a new blouse and shoes in anticipation of job interviews she was planning. After the summer school session she was now attending, Susie said she needed only one more course to complete her master's degree in business. She anticipated having it by December, and she was trying to decide what she wanted to do after that. She was thinking about moving to Atlanta, she said. Taki helped her pick out a silver-gray blouse and a pair of low, dressy black shoes. Susie seemed pleased with them.

To Taki, Susie was cheerful and didn't appear to be acting abnormally. "Same ol' Susie," she said.

The only thing out of the ordinary was Susie's strong fear that the boys might be kidnapped, but Taki didn't question her closely about it.

Taki was of Japanese origin, and Susie enjoyed talking with her about Japanese culture and Oriental cooking. Taki had promised to cook one of Susie's favorite meals for dinner, and that afternoon, after helping Susie straighten her apartment, Taki set about putting the kitchen in order for the meal.

Taki made an asparagus salad with sesame oil. She steamed broccoli and whipped up a spicy dish of ground beef, onions, tofu, and bean paste served over rice. For dessert, she had fresh strawberries.

As they ate, Taki began talking about Bob and Florence. She hadn't mentioned the murders earlier, and neither had Susie, but now Taki brought up the subject.

"Who in the world could kill such nice people?" she asked.

Nobody said anything, and the question was left hanging.

After dinner, John and Jim nestled under Taki's arms and hugged her.

"We're so glad you're here," Jim said.

"Yeah," said John. "Thank you for a yummy dinner."

Fritz and Annie Hill left soon afterward, and Susie and the boys drove Taki back to Susie's parents' house.

Taki planned to stay several more days. Susie said that she had to study all day Sunday for a test on Monday, but she wanted Taki's assistance in sorting some of her mother's things later. Taki said she would be glad to help.

"I'll see you Tuesday," Susie said cheerily as she left for home.

Ian took deep, nervous breaths, trying to calm himself. The recorder strapped to his back took note.

This was Sunday, June 2, a little after noon, and Ian was about to try once again to trap Fritz into admitting he'd murdered the Newsoms. His first attempt the day before had proved less than successful. It had confirmed his hard-to-believe story of the supposed CIA mission, but it had brought out no hard evidence about the Newsom deaths. The detectives were concerned that in court Fritz might be able to explain the whole thing away, and with their lack of physical evidence the case might be lost.

"We wanted to do everything possible to get a perfect case," Gentry recalled later. "We were being very, very careful trying to make all the right moves, to do everything we could to make a good, solid case."

After Saturday's tense meeting between Ian and Fritz, the detectives had taken Ian back to Winston-Salem, where they decided that a second attempt would be necessary. For this, they concocted a story. Ian was to tell Fritz that the detectives had returned to talk to him

Saturday night at his mother's house. They had asked him to accompany them to Winston-Salem, and they took him past the scene of the murders. Not only had he realized that it was just up the hill from where he had let Fritz out on the night of their mission, he had seen in the driveway at Nanna's house the car Fritz had been driving when he was stopped by the police.

This time the detectives planned to have the meeting take place at Carolina Circle Mall at Greensboro's northeastern edge on U.S. 29, the main highway between Greensboro and Reidsville. The surveillance cars were already spread out around the mall when the officers discovered that no outside telephone booth was handy from which to call Fritz. They had to drive a short distance up Cone Boulevard to the O. Henry Shopping Center before finding one. Ian reached Fritz at Susie's apartment. Something had come up, Ian told him. The cops had come for him again. They had taken him to Nanna's house. He needed to talk right away.

"Where are you?" Fritz asked.

"I'm at the Zayre's store on Cone Boulevard," Ian answered.

"Stay right there," Fritz said. "I'll be there in a few minutes."

Fritz's impulse caused the surveillance cars to be moved hurriedly into new positions, and this time the officers had no notice of Fritz's progress because the SBI airplane was grounded with a flat tire.

Now Ian, who seemed even more nervous than the day before, waited with Carden, who was again posing as his friend Chris. The day was hot, and Ian sweated as he waited, trying to remember all of the specific points the officers had instructed him to bring up. One of those points was Susie. Another was Fritz's medical credentials. A third was the mission to Texas. From the time Ian had told them that the original mission was to Texas, the detectives figured that it really was to New Mexico to kill Tom Lynch. They wanted to know if Fritz still had that in mind.

Fritz took nearly twenty minutes to arrive, and when he pulled into the parking lot, Ian got out of the Mustang, leaving Carden watching from behind the wheel.

Ian took several deep breaths to brace himself and quickly approached the Blazer.

"Really scared the shit out of me last night," he said after crawling inside. "Tell you what. Showed me the house. I saw the gold car and went in the house. It was a mess. It was right down the road from where I dropped you off.

"I believe we were on a government mission, but I think there's something that just ain't kosher here. I'd just like to know what's going on. I'm going to stick with the story."

"Gold car," Fritz said deliberately. "What gold car did they show you?"

"The one you had."

"The car I had was brown," he said with subtle sternness.

"They showed me a car. It was right down the road from where I let you off. That scared me. I didn't know what was going on then. I didn't know what to think. I don't think you're lying to me or withholding anything."

"How many cars did they show you?"

"Just the one."

Fritz reached behind the seat, brought out a file folder, and handed the folder to Ian.

"I want you to look at that. Names have been deleted from that that you didn't need to see."

Inside the file were official-looking documents marked secret. They purportedly pertained to the mission Fritz had completed that night two weeks earlier. Some parts were blacked out.

"There's some pictures in there," Fritz said.

"But what exactly happened?" Ian asked. "I don't understand. We were so close."

"Ian, I have never been to Nanna's house. I do not know where it is. It could have been in the same area. I couldn't take you there if my life depended on it."

"I'm not trying to doubt you or anything, but, you know, it was scary. I just didn't really know what to do. 'Course, I'll stick to the story. I won't tell them anything other than that we were camping."

Fritz wanted him to go over everything the officers had asked and what he'd told them. Ian did.

"They asked me if I wanted to change my story," Ian

said. "I said no. They seemed a little hesitant just to leave it at that, but they didn't ask me anything else."

"They're just fishing."

"I remember you telling me I better get a little better control of my nerves, but I was just—I'm not good at this. The only reason I got any sleep last night was because of that pill you gave me. I did sleep very well."

"How have those capsules been doing for you?" Fritz asked in his best bedside manner.

"They've been working pretty good. I'm not shaking."

"I've got some Valium tablets for you, too," Fritz said, taking the file Ian was holding. "I wish that had not had some stuff deleted, but you understand. At this point, you just do not need to know."

Fritz withdrew some photographs and gave the file back. "These are the people who were in the house. They're the ones who went down the other night. That's the one I had to hit five times."

"God," said Ian, his voice filled with awe.

"The one with the hat is one of the big—"

"One of the big guys," Ian put in.

"Yeah."

"I told Chris I just wanted to see you a minute before we go back to tell you how the medication was doing," Ian said.

Fritz was still showing pictures. "He was on the patio."

"Which one did you use the knife on?"

"I used the knife on this guy, and I used the knife on . . . on this one because he was still showing signs."

"I'm sorry to keep bothering you with all of this," Ian said. "I hate to seem like a big chicken, but I just didn't know how to deal with all of this."

"Where *was* the house?" Fritz asked.

Ian explained, and Fritz drew a diagram showing that he had gone off on another street near the house.

"How many cars were there?" Fritz asked.

"Just a couple."

"There should have been, unless Rob has picked the car up, there should have been three cars."

Ian said he was so nervous that he'd thrown up the night before, and Fritz gave him some Valium.

"Are you still going to see them tomorrow?" Fritz

asked, wanting to know about the polygraph test Ian had told him he was to take.

"I told them to delay it, postpone it indefinitely," Ian said. "They didn't seem too pleased, but they didn't push it."

"See, what they are figuring, that they can play mind games with you. They found very little physical evidence. In fact, nothing to connect anything to anything. See, they figured you're the youngest—actually, it should make you mad—they figured if I was a pro, if I'd done something they weren't going to get apeshit with me. They figured you're the youngest, that you were the weak link, you were the one if there was anything to pick."

"Well, I feel like I'm sort of letting Uncle Gerry down by getting so overworried about all this."

"Well, Ian, if I'd had any notion that anybody was going to, I mean, you talk about the luck of the draw. I almost shit in my pants about that."

"I want to do the right thing," Ian said. "I won't crack. I don't know if they'll leave me alone after this, but I don't think I'll have any problems. You know, they tried to tell me you weren't a doctor. 'Course, I didn't believe that . . ."

Gentry slapped the dashboard of the car in which he was sitting behind a nearby convenience store. "Let *him* talk, Ian."

"I know you've been in medical school," Ian was going on. "I know you were doing your residency when Doctor died. Tried to tell me Annie Hill told them that."

"Ian, the reason I have not started practice—I went to Duke—I told you, I've been doing stuff. I first got contacted when I was at Woodward and off and on over the years, when they check anything—when I went to Duke I was enrolled there, which is in the process of being straightened out now. When Dad died was an inopportune time."

"They gave you your provisional license?"

"Oh, yeah. When I was traveling, see, I went to several meetings and places you don't need to know about right now."

"I don't think I want to."

"But when I was in school, it was better for all concerned that I wasn't traceable back to Reidsville."

"Let me ask you about this thing in Texas. I'm not going to have to do anything with that in the near future, are we?"

"No."

"Good. Because I think it's going to take a while to steel myself down to even think about this again—I feel a lot better now. I tell you that."

"The car I had was a gold car," Fritz said. "What type of car?"

"It looked like a Granada or a Monarch to me. I didn't get that close to it."

"The car I had was gold, but it wasn't a Maverick. Something similar to a Maverick."

Gentry realized immediately that Fritz had just contradicted himself, having earlier said the car he had was brown, and he was hoping Ian would catch it and call him on it, but Ian didn't. Instead, Fritz gave Ian more papaverine. "Take one of these."

"I'll take 'em if I feel like I need to," Ian said, remembering the stern admonitions from the officers that he was to swallow nothing that Fritz gave him, "but I don't think I have anything to be nervous about."

"Anytime they want to talk to you or anything like that, you take one of these. Give an hour for it to work."

"How's Susie and everybody taking the whole mess?" Ian asked.

"They're numb. Susie's just really—numb. Ian, what they're trying to do is to get you to panic and say something. If I had been involved and they had something concrete to go on, they would already have done something about it."

"I'm trying to imagine what kind of state I'd be in if I'd been there actually with you," Ian said. "You know, had to help you. I'd probably be a pile of mush."

"See, what they're going on, supposedly a little while after dark, one of the neighbors at Nanna's house heard the dogs barking and looked out and said there were two men standing on the lawn. They thought with all the workmen that it was just two workmen, so they brought the dogs inside and that was it. There may have *been* two men on the lawn."

"Sergeant Gentry said that, uh—Florence, is it?"

"Florence."

"That they had company that night, but I don't remember what time he said they left."

"I think it was before dark."

Fritz mentioned that it wouldn't be hard to arrange to find somebody who saw them on the mountain trail if they needed a stronger alibi.

"That's cool," Ian said.

"I wanted you to see this," Fritz said, taking back the report, "so you'd have something to sink your teeth in. I know you trust me."

"I've got no reason not to. I've known you for years."

Fritz handed him a spray can. "Take that with you."

"Will that keep your odor down?" Ian asked.

"That has aluminum chlorohydrate in it, which is a prescription thing they use for people who have over-perspiration."

"You must've noticed that my T-shirt smells a little."

"Anytime you have to talk with anybody, spray the palms of your hands, your feet real good. Saturate a cotton ball, wipe your face. That'll keep you from perspiring."

"Yeah. That reminds me of a deodorant commercial I saw. It's like, it's okay to be nervous, it's just not okay to let 'em know."

If the police wanted particulars about what they had been doing on the hike, Fritz told Ian to say they were running checks with compasses and a barometer.

"Okay, thanks. 'Preciate it. Oh, I feel so much better."

"Here, take this regularly," Fritz said, offering more pills, vitamins this time. "That's B complex. That's nature's tranquilizer. You can take like three of those three times a day. That stuff's amazing."

Ian said he'd call if he had problems.

"I'll be at one house or the other," Fritz said. "Oh, another thing. I've checked the lines. I don't think any of the lines anywhere are tapped."

"If I get any nervous anxiety attacks or they come call me again, I'll call you for sure," Ian said.

His breathing came much easier as he walked back to his car.

The detectives were more pleased with the second tape, although they were upset with Ian for answering his own questions and blabbering on when he should have been listening. Fritz had at least admitted killing people on the night of the murders, though not the Newsoms, and he had acknowledged being in a car similar to the one stopped by Officer Hull. He even had tripped himself and said the car he had been driving was gold colored. But Fritz was still playing his fantasy games, and the detectives were uncertain whether this was the solid evidence they needed to take to court.

On Sunday night, five detectives involved in the case gathered at Ian's motel room in Winston-Salem to play the tapes for District Attorney Don Tisdale. All along, Tisdale had had trouble believing Ian's story, and because he had been so entangled in the big trial he was conducting, he had not yet met Ian.

"I was quite surprised," he recalled later. "We were dealing with a very intelligent, almost innocent person. If you'd told me his story apart from him, I couldn't have believed it. I don't think I could picture anybody being that gullible. But after I met him I believed it. There wasn't any doubt about it. Scared me to know there were people out here like that, but I believed it."

The detectives had been debating whether or not they had enough evidence to draw warrants for Fritz and arrest him. Gentry and Sturgill wanted to try one more time to entrap Fritz. They were afraid that Fritz might be able to wriggle out from the evidence they had.

"We might have had something if Ian hadn't talked so much or if he had pushed on the issue of the cars," Gentry said later, "but we really didn't have the response that we thought Ian could get."

Their suspicions about Susie were one reason they wanted to try again. "We had absolutely nothing to show Susie had done anything wrong," Gentry said. "It's safe to say I thought she had more than just a passing interest in what had happened. It's almost incredible to believe this series of events could take place and her not have the slightest idea what was going on."

After listening to the tapes, Tisdale agreed that another try might produce more incriminating results, and he gave the go-ahead for the following day.

The detectives needed another cover story for Ian, one that would cause Fritz to know that they were getting closer to him. To this point, Fritz was unaware that the detectives knew that a police officer had stopped him in Nanna's gold Voláre on the night of the murders. Maybe the time had come to let him know.

42

And there were voices, and thunders, and light-nings. And there fell upon men a great hail out of heaven.
—Revelation 16:18–21

Sherman Childers and Lennie Nobles, the Kentucky detectives, stayed after Ian's confession and went along as observers for his first meeting with Fritz. By then, they were not only out of clean clothes but money as well, and late Saturday afternoon they headed home to replenish their stocks and pick up their commander, Lieutenant Dan Davidson, who wanted to be present for Fritz's arrest.

Childers and Nobles got home early Sunday, and by that afternoon they were on their way back to Winston-Salem with Davidson. They arrived after midnight and checked into the Innkeeper, only a short distance from the motel where Ian was spending another restless night.

The long trip gave Childers and Nobles a chance to fill in Davidson on all the details of the relationship between Fritz and Susie, her troubles with her family, and the long struggle with Tom over the boys. Davidson, like all the detectives in the case, believed that Susie surely had to be involved in the murders. If she was completely innocent, wouldn't she have suspected something and acted upon it? Regardless of whether a case could be made against her, though, he felt certain that her mere association with Fritz was enough to prove her an unfit parent and allow Tom to take custody of John and Jim. In the ten months that he had been investigating the murders of Delores and Janie, Davidson had developed a fondness for Tom, whom he called Doc.

"The way things are working out," Davidson said on Monday morning as the three detectives were trying to jolt themselves awake with strong coffee, "looks like ol' Doc might be able to come and get his kids for good pretty soon."

At 9 that morning, Davidson, Childers, and Nobles joined Ian and a group of Forsyth County officers and SBI agents at the sheriff's department in the basement of the Hall of Justice.

The plan this time was to let Fritz know that the game playing was over. Ian was to call and tell him that he had been served a legal paper summoning him for a lineup. For this a bogus document was required, and Gentry typed up a "nontestimonial order," misspelling the Newsom name in the process.

> *Offense: Homicide.*
>
> *Facts which establish probable cause: On Sun. May 19, 1985, the bodies of Hattie Carter Newsome, w/f age 85, Robert Wesley Newsome Jr., w/m, age 65, and Florence Sharp Newsome, w/f, age 66, were discovered inside the residence of Hattie Newsome at 3239 Valley Rd., Winston-Salem, N.C. Autopsies and subsequent investigation have revealed that the 3 victims were murdered on Sat. night, May 18, 1985.*
>
> *Facts which establish reasonable grounds: A Winston-Salem officer stopped a gold 79 Plymouth, N.C. license #PSL-360 at 12:02 a.m., May 19, 1985, on University Parkway in Winston-Salem. Said vehicle is registered to victim Hattie Newsome of 3239 Valley Road. Said vehicle was driven by w/m with facial hair, and said vehicle was followed by a black Chevrolet Blazer. The Winston-Salem officer has identified the gold Plymouth belonging to victim, Hattie Newsome, as the vehicle he stopped on May 19, at 12:02 a.m.*

Gentry signed the order, then scribbled the name of an assistant DA into the space requiring a judge's signature. Ian was given the pink carbon, and he folded it and stuck it into his rear pocket.

This ploy put Ian in more danger than the previous two. It would reveal to Fritz that Ian now knew for certain that Fritz had been in Nanna's car and that his story of a CIA mission was a lie. It also would let Fritz know that the police were closing in on him. Ian was instructed to tell Fritz that when the officer who stopped Nanna's car failed to identify Ian as the driver, Fritz surely would be called next for a lineup. Ian was to directly confront Fritz about the murders.

From Winston-Salem, the task force of detectives went again to the SBI office near Greensboro, only two miles from Susie's apartment. After a briefing, more than half the officers prepared to set up surveillance of the apartment. Although the airplane was in service, the officers wanted to be sure that Fritz was kept in sight from the ground as well. By noon three cars were on station.

One of those was a tan Buick Riviera driven by A. G. Travis, a detective with the Greensboro Police Department. Travis was a liaison officer assigned to assist. He had no knowledge of the case before that morning. In Travis's car was Ed Hunt, a short, neatly groomed man, who was supervisor of the SBI's northern district and the commander of this operation. "He's a good cop," District Attorney Tisdale later said of him. "He's as smart as any police officer I've ever worked with." In the backseat of Travis's car were Ron Barker, the chief of detectives for the Forsyth County Sheriff's Department, and Dan Davidson, who was along only as an observer.

Soon after the officers arrived at Susie's apartment complex, they saw Fritz leaving alone in his Blazer.

When Ian called from the SBI office, Susie said that Fritz had gone out but that she expected him back shortly.

Fritz drove to the Kroger Shopping Center on West Market Street, which he often frequented, and went into the Radio Shack. He emerged a short time later, got into his Blazer, and took a roundabout way back to the apartment, causing the officers to worry that he might have spotted them tailing him. Several times he cut onto side streets and doubled back. Near Quaker Village Shopping Center, he pulled onto a side street and stopped under a tree. He sat for more than fifteen minutes, and because of the black-tinted windows in his Blazer, the officers,

observing from more than a block away, couldn't tell
what he was doing. Had he bought a police radio monitor? Was he now installing it?

While Fritz was out, Susie called Bob Connolly, her
professor of managerial economics at the University of
North Carolina at Greensboro. "The way things are going,
I don't think I'm going to get there for class tonight," he
later remembered her saying. She seemed calm and collected and told him she would come in Tuesday to take a
scheduled test and talk about her progress.

Soon after Fritz returned to the apartment, Ian called
again from the same spot he had used the day before.
The time was 1:07.

"We've got problems," he said. "We've got to talk
right away."

Fritz agreed to meet him and left the apartment eight
minutes later. Most of the police cars were already set up
at the Zayre's store. At 1:26, the airplane advised that
Fritz was five minutes away. Seven minutes later he
pulled into the parking lot.

"Hold onto your seats, gang," Ian said over his transmitter as he saw Fritz's Blazer. "This is going to be a
doozie."

Ian got into the Blazer and told Fritz about being
served the order for the lineup. Fritz asked to see it, and
Ian handed it to him.

The officers listening in their cars heard first the rus-
tling of paper, then only static, no voices. As the silence
stretched on, Gentry began to worry. "I thought something had gone wrong with the wire," he recalled later.

Ian's voice calmed his fears.

"The stuff on the back is what got me," Ian said.

"I didn't have a gold car that night," Fritz said. "I had
a brown car."

"Something's wrong here," Ian said. "Level with me,
Fritz."

Fritz paused as if in contemplation.

"I'm not playing games with you, Ian."

"Fritz, did you murder the Newsoms?"

"Ian, I never *murdered* anybody."

"Something's sure fishy here."

"Ian, I'm not going to let you be involved. Nobody saw you. Nobody can involve you."

Ian said he was sure the cop wouldn't be able to identify him because he hadn't been in the car. But the police weren't going to stop there, he said. After that, they'd call Fritz in for the officer to see.

"If they tie you in to this thing, that's going to take me down with you," Ian said. "I've got some grave doubts, Fritz."

"I'm being set up, for what reason I don't know," Fritz said. "I'm about to take a royal screwing. I'll pop a capsule. I will not—"

Fritz's voice had changed. His bedside manner was gone. He sounded preoccupied, impatient.

"I'll write a paper saying you were not knowingly involved, that you believed you were on a covert mission for the government," he said.

It was clear that he was ending the conversation and wanted to get going.

"I've got things to do," he said.

As Ian started to get out, Fritz said, "I won't see you again."

Ian trembled with relief as he got back into his car with Carden. The meeting had lasted fourteen minutes.

The officers were uncertain about their next move as Fritz headed back to Susie's apartment, a nine-mile drive by the shortest route. All were aware that this operation was being closely monitored by higher-ups in Winston-Salem and Raleigh, and they knew that whatever they did, it would make big news. Mistakes might not only endanger the case but careers as well, and they didn't want to make any.

They knew from what Fritz had said that they couldn't use Ian anymore and that they were not apt to get more evidence against Fritz. It seemed apparent that Fritz was about to make a run. They knew that they would have to move against him soon. But they knew, too, that he was well armed and arresting him might not be easy. Should they try to take him before he got back to the apartment? They had no warrants.

As Fritz drove slowly back, three of the trailing police cars stopped at a phone booth at a Sunoco station at the corner of Battleground Avenue and Cone Boulevard, and SBI agent Tom Sturgill called the district attorney's office in Winston-Salem.

Tisdale was at a crucial point in an emotional and controversial trial that was making big news. Amid charges of frame-up and racial discrimination, he was trying a young black man for his life for murdering and raping a beautiful young copy editor for the *The Sentinel* as she arrived for work early one morning the previous summer. Tisdale had to request a recess to take Sturgill's call, and more than fifteen minutes passed before he got to the phone.

Sturgill filled Tisdale in on what had happened.

"Have we got enough to make an arrest?" he asked.

"Yes, you have enough to charge him," Tisdale remembered telling him. "You can't go any further, and he is a potential danger."

"Do we need a warrant?"

"No, we can get a warrant later. Just go ahead and pick him up, but proceed with caution. You cannot let him hole up in that apartment."

By that time, Fritz was already back at the apartment, which was being watched by two surveillance cars.

The officers at the Sunoco station realized that they might have a problem with communications. All had hand radios with which they could communicate from car to car and with the SBI airplane. All but one of the cars, however, were Forsyth County cars, and their radios were out of range and ineffective if further help was needed. The command car, driven by Travis, could communicate only with the Greensboro police dispatcher. The officers decided that an SBI car would have to be used, despite its easy recognizability, so they would have a radio connection to the state highway patrol.

All three cars left the Sunoco station and drove to a small shopping center a few hundred yards from Susie's apartment. The command officers stopped at a Big Star supermarket from which they could see Fritz's Blazer. Bryant, Gentry, Sturgill, and Boner continued on to the SBI office to swap cars and pick up Carden, who'd returned there with Ian.

At the SBI office, Sturgill and Gentry came up with a

plan. Why not just call the apartment and ask Fritz to come in for another interview? As confident as he'd been earlier about matching wits with the officers, Fritz might be cocky enough to do it, they thought. Gentry was looking forward to telling Fritz that he was under arrest. Knowing Fritz's admiration for G. Gordon Liddy, Gentry had picked out a Liddy quote for the occasion: "In a battle of wits, you came unarmed."

Sturgill dialed, and Susie answered. He identified himself and asked to speak with Fritz.

"He's not here," Susie said.

"Do you know when he will be?" Sturgill asked.

"You can try about six-thirty or seven."

Neither Sturgill nor Gentry was surprised that Susie had lied.

Sturgill, Gentry, and Boner returned to the Big Star in a gray SBI Ford and joined the debate on how best to attempt the arrest. Carden rode with Bryant in a burgundy Chevrolet Impala and took up a position east of Susie's apartment.

The officers didn't want to risk a shootout in the crowded apartment complex, and they realized that they could not evacuate the apartments without attracting Fritz's notice. They considered sending two officers to the door but rejected that as too dangerous.

Because all of the officers involved were detectives in civilian clothes, all the cars unmarked, Ed Hunt finally decided that a uniformed officer in a marked car should be on hand before any attempt was made to move in on Fritz, and at 2:38 Travis radioed that he needed assistance from a uniformed officer.

Squad Leader L. C. LeClear was the first to respond to the call. But he was downtown, miles away, headed for the police gas pumps on Smith Street, and couldn't come until he got fuel. Squad Leader Tommy Dennis was near the coliseum in the southwestern section of the city, nearly eight miles distant, and he radioed that he was on his way.

Soon afterward, officers close to the apartment called on their hand radios that Fritz and Susie were loading things into Fritz's Blazer. They saw Fritz carrying what appeared to be military weapons to the vehicle, while

Susie ferried duffel bags. Then they saw something that startled and unsettled all of them.

John and Jim emerged from the apartment dressed in camouflage fatigues.

The officers had assumed that the boys were in school.

The boys climbed into the back of the Blazer with their dogs, Chowy and Maizie. Susie got into the passenger side of the vehicle, carrying books and papers. Fritz was last to leave the apartment and clamber into the Blazer. He backed it out of the parking space and headed away from the watching detectives down winding Hunt Club Road toward the apartment complex's main entrance on Friendly Avenue.

Police cars began to scramble.

Fritz had turned his black K-5 Blazer into an ominous-looking machine, a gunship designed for combat and survival under harsh conditions. Short and stumpy, it sat high on ballooning tires that could deliver it over almost any terrain. The front bumper was made of steel nearly three-quarters of an inch thick, capable of plowing through formidible obstacles. A heavy winch built into the bumper could be used to pull stumps from the ground or vehicles from tight spots. Stout roll bars protected the cab, where Fritz always carried vital spare parts as well as powerful weapons, and black-tinted windows kept prying eyes from knowing what was inside. The vehicle was equipped for nighttime operations, too. Seven headlights across the front could throw a 180-degree arc of light for a great distance. Floodlights on the back could blind pursuers.

As the Blazer rolled slowly down Hunt Club Road toward the apartment complex's entrance on Friendly Avenue, police cars moved to close in. A red Camaro driven by a young narcotics officer, Marc Fetter, had been parked behind Susie's apartment on Vinegar Hill Drive, from where Fetter and SBI agent Walt House were keeping watch. Fetter now hurried down Vinegar Hill to Quail Hollow Road, hoping to cut off Fritz before he got to the entrance. Bryant and Carden followed in a Chevrolet Impala.

As soon as Greensboro detective A. G. Travis, the driver of the command car, saw the direction Fritz was taking, he said, "We can cut him off at the entrance!" He whipped the Buick onto College Road going north and turned left onto Friendly, speeding toward the entrance.

Five minutes after Travis had put in his call for a uniformed officer, two were on the way, L. C. LeClear and Tommy Dennis, both patrol squad leaders, both coming from different directions. LeClear was several miles away on Friendly, Dennis closer, on Interstate 40.

While Fritz and Susie were loading the vehicle, Travis had radioed again to ask the whereabouts of the uniformed officer. Dennis reported he was arriving at College Road only minutes away.

"What's it in reference to?" LeClear wanted to know.

"Just tell him to come on, and I'll fill him in," Travis said. "Tell both of 'em to pull in front of the Big Star."

At 2:47, Travis called to Dennis. "Three-o-three, where are you?"

"Just passing the fire station."

A minute and a half later, Dennis reported his arrival at Big Star, but by then Travis had already gone. Dennis spotted a gray Ford that had just left the parking lot and recognized it as an SBI car. It was followed by a blue Mustang driven by another young narcotics agent, Terry Spainhour. In that car were the Kentucky detectives, Nobles and Childers, Nobles in front, Childers in back. But Dennis had no idea that these were officers, nor did he know what was going on.

Now Travis radioed again: "That uniform car, come on out Friendly. By the exit to Guilford Hills," he said, giving the wrong name of the apartment complex. "Rush it up."

The gray Ford and blue Mustang stopped in the left turn lane at the traffic light at Friendly, and Dennis, driving an unmarked dark blue Chevrolet Malibu police cruiser with a blue light on the dashboard, pulled to the right side of the SBI car and rolled down his window. He didn't recognize the three men inside.

Gentry was closest to him. Later, Gentry remembered telling Dennis that they were after a serious felony suspect. Three murders. A black Blazer. He recalled Sturgill saying, "Have you got a vest? Better get it on."

Dennis remembered both men talking, but heard only about felony warrants and a black Blazer, nothing about murders or a bullet-proof vest.

"Wait a minute and I'll let you know which way he's coming," he recalled Gentry telling him as he listened to his hand radio. "He's coming our way. Be careful."

Dennis always wore a bullet-proof vest. His wife, Sandy, made him. Two weeks earlier, he had traded an old vest for a new one designed to stop bigger and faster bullets. Dennis was a by-the-book officer who loved his work. He had been on the force thirteen years. In that time, he'd been in the news for helping to capture a stray bear, for being seriously injured during a chase on a motorcycle, and for receiving a commendation for saving the life of a wreck victim. He was about to make the news again.

"Can you give me any idea what he's got?" LeClear asked the dispatcher after hearing Travis's call to "rush it up." He said he'd have to run with lights and siren to get there.

"Nine-ninety, can you advise its nature?" the dispatcher asked Travis.

"Just have him keep coming this way," Travis said.

Patrol Captain Charles Allen interrupted. "What do they have out there?"

"I'm unable to advise," the dispatcher said. "Nine-ninety will not say."

"If it's urgent enough for us to get there," Allen said, "respond ten–thirty-nine."

LeClear turned on his blue lights and siren and speeded up.

The Blazer reached the apartment complex's entrance at the same time as the command car. Travis saw the Blazer and attempted to block it at the entrance, swerving in front as Hunt held up his badge and Davidson and Barker tried to wave Fritz down from the backseat.

The attempt to stop Fritz was instinctual. "We couldn't just let him disappear out into the world," Barker said later. "We just understood that we had to stop him somehow."

The Buick skidded to a halt, overshooting the Blazer by a few feet. Later the officers inside remembered Fritz as looking surprised but not frightened. Fritz whipped off a hat he was wearing, turned the Blazer up onto the curb, and went behind the Buick, which had stalled momentarily.

"There's the truck!" Travis radioed excitedly at 2:49. "I want him stopped! Get him! He's considered—" But he never finished that sentence. Instead, he turned his attention to getting his car started again and turning it around.

Fetter and House, followed by Bryant and Carden, were coming out of the apartment complex on Quail Hollow Road and reached the entrance in time to see Fritz pull behind the command car and turn right onto Friendly. Both cars came out behind him. Fritz was not speeding away. He drove slowly and deliberately as always.

"Nine-ninety, give a description," the dispatcher pleaded. She got no answer. "Four-forty-one and three-o-three, we have a truck that nine-ninety wants stopped. I have no description."

Dennis was now heading west on Friendly after pulling ahead of the SBI car. He saw the Blazer coming toward him, followed by other cars. He did not know that two of those cars contained police officers. Dennis flicked on his blue light and began to make a U-turn to get behind the Blazer and attempt a standard felony stop, something he'd practiced many times in training but rarely had an opportunity to use. He hoped to stop the car before it got to Francis King Street, a narrow side street about a hundred yards from the major intersection at College Road from which he'd just come.

At that moment, Debbie Blanton was headed east on Friendly in her 1970 red Mustang. She was on her way back to work after lunch. She saw the police car coming toward her. Then, in her rearview mirror, she saw it begin a U-turn.

"Oh, no," she thought. "What have I done?" She slowed for the traffic light ahead, just up a slight rise.

Dennis was in the middle of his U-turn when he heard Travis's excited command to stop the truck. Before he could finish his turn, the Camaro driven by Fetter pulled out from behind another car and started to pass Fritz. Dennis had to swerve to avoid hitting Fetter's car. Fetter pulled directly across Fritz's path at Francis King Street, but Fritz simply maneuvered to the left and went around him.

Debbie Blanton had stopped at the light in the center eastbound lane of Friendly. In the left-turn lane, beside and to the back of her, was a gray car driven by a woman with a young child. The gray car had stopped short of the light. Its front bumper was aligned with Blanton's rear wheel.

The SBI car driven by Sturgill and the blue Mustang driven by Spainhour had followed Dennis onto Friendly, and both also made U-turns. Suddenly, Spainhour pulled out to try to overtake Fritz, causing Dennis to evade again, sending him into a skid. Dennis realized that he was skidding at an angle into the left side of the Blazer, his windshield facing Fritz's door. He saw Fritz with his left arm propped in the open window. The next few moments passed in slow motion for Dennis.

He saw the arm in the window lowering, then realized that it was holding a gun, an Uzi 9-millimeter submachine gun, the same type weapon the Israeli army used. His training told him not to sit still. He reached for his pistol at the same time he began squirming high in his seat to protect his head. He saw the first flash from the muzzle but not the others.

Five bullets hit his car in quick succession. The first three struck the car's body. The last two came through the lower right side of his windshield. The first of the latter two hit him in the upper right chest, passing through a notepad in his pocket. He felt as if he'd been hit with a sledgehammer, he said later. He didn't feel the second shot. It hit the buckle of his utility belt and deflected into the leather.

Dennis's car stopped only inches from the Blazer. Fritz halted behind Blanton's car. With tires squealing, the blue Mustang driven by Spainhour slid past the front of the gray car in the lane next to Blanton and slammed into Blanton's door. In the backseat, Nobles could see Fritz swinging his upper body out of the door of the Blazer.

"He's got a gun!" Nobles shouted. "Get down!"

But before Nobles finished his warning, Fritz turned the Uzi on them and fired another blast. A spray of glass went up as at least eight bullets struck the car.

Debbie Blanton dived into her seat. So did Childers and Nobles in Spainhour's Mustang. Both officers had their guns drawn. Spainhour jumped out, pistol in hand, to return fire, leaving the Mustang in gear and pushing against Blanton's car. She could see Spainhour through her windshield. She thought he was a madman and that he was going to kill her.

As Nobles tried to get down in the backseat, a bullet struck the 9-millimeter Smith & Wesson pistol he was bringing across his chest. The bullet broke in two, and both pieces hit Nobles under the pit of his right arm. In the excitement, he didn't realize he'd been hit. He looked up and saw Susie's face in the windshield of the Blazer. He would remember her as having a blank, unconcerned look. He drew a bead on her but stopped himself from pulling the trigger.

"I could've taken her right out," he said later.

In the front seat, Childers's left arm was bleeding where it had been sprayed with broken glass. With his other arm, he used the butt of his pistol to break out the rest of his window. He could see Fritz, and he got off one quick shot toward the windshield, but it struck low, missing its target.

In his cruiser, Dennis was telling himself not to panic. His siren was driving him crazy. He reached to cut it off, trying to compose his thoughts.

"I've been hurt," he was trying to tell himself, but it came out over the radio, faintly, almost a cry.

"Ten-nine?" the dispatcher said, asking him to repeat.

"I've been shot," Dennis said.

"All units, three-o-three has been shot," the dispatcher said immediately. "Two-forty-one, two-sixty, two-sixty-one, and one-sixty, assist out in Friendly Hills area."

When the bullets began to fly at the busy intersection, people all around ducked for cover. A woman pumping gas at the Wilco station crouched behind her car after a bullet hit her windshield. A woman mowing on the Guilford College campus dived off her tractor and clung to the ground. In the Wachovia branch bank on the corner, tellers rushed to the door when they heard the shots. When they saw Spainhour standing in the road with a gun, they locked the door and scrambled out of sight, thinking that a robbery attempt might be in progress.

Fritz had been almost boxed in. Travis and Sturgill had come up behind him. Dennis was beside him. Blanton, the gray car, and Spainhour were in front of him. But Fritz backed up and, banging fenders, maneuvered out of the trap and turned left onto New Garden Road by the campus of Guilford College. As he pulled away, Spainhour fired toward the rear of the Blazer with his 9-millimeter pistol.

The command car made its way through the wreckage and took off after Fritz, followed by Sturgill in the SBI car and Fetter in the Camaro. Spainhour jumped into the blue Mustang and started to back away from Blanton's car, but in his excitement he put the bullet-riddled Mustang into the wrong gear and slammed again into Blantons fender before wheeling around and rejoining the chase.

"I think I took a hit," Nobles said from the backseat.

"How bad is it?" Spainhour asked.

"I don't know. I've never been shot before. It's burning."

"Take that shirt off and let me have a look," Childers said.

Nobles worked his way painfully out of the shirt and turned his shoulder to Childers.

"I don't see any exit wounds," Childers said.

"I'm all right," Nobles said, dabbing angrily at the blood with his shirt. "Let's go get the son of a bitch."

All the cars in the chase sped away, leaving the wounded Dennis in his car. A volunteer firefighter who had stopped at the intersection was the first to run to him.

"Just give me a minute," Dennis said. "I want to compose myself."

"Three-o-three, an ambulance is en route," the dispatcher radioed at 2:51.

Thirty-eight seconds later, LeClear pulled alongside Dennis's car and jumped out.

Greensboro police who had been summoned to the scene knew nothing about what had happened and had no idea who the assailant might be.

"As soon as somebody can, will they give me a little

information, please," Patrol Captain Allen radioed impatiently.

The first report the Greensboro police dispatcher got was that the shots had come from a red car, and she put that alert on the air. Nobody informed her that the assailant was being chased by five law enforcement cars and observed by an SBI airplane.

In the command car, Dan Davidson was worried. He had seen the Mustang in which Childers and Nobles were riding get hit by a spray of bullets, and he had heard over the car radio that an officer was shot. He thought one of his men was hit.

"I said, 'Oh, Lord, I've brought one of these boys down here and got him killed,' " he recalled later.

He kept looking back. Only when he saw the blue Mustang coming was he able to concentrate on the matters at hand. Then he asked if anybody had extra ammo for a .357 Magnum. He had only six shots with him.

Just past Guilford College, New Garden Road, on which Fritz was traveling, runs into Fleming Road, and New Garden juts to the right. Travis saw Fritz taking the right turn, and he led the procession of police cars in pursuit. A few hundred yards beyond that intersection, New Garden curves sharply left. Travis was starting into the curve when he saw something that caused him to slam on the brakes and skid off the road.

The Blazer was stopped sideways in the road, straddling the center line, and Fritz was standing outside, Uzi in hand. He opened fire as Travis hit his brakes.

All of the police cars slid to a halt on the right side of the road, and the officers began bailing out. Ed Hunt dived from the command car and rolled over on the ground, getting off three quick shots, as Travis crouched behind his car door.

Fetter came out of the Camaro firing an AR15 assault rifle, causing Fritz to get back into the Blazer.

"I think Fetter saved our lives," Barker said later.

He and Davidson had been trapped in the backseat of the vulnerable command car, which had only two doors, and as they were still trying to get out, Fritz took off again. Travis and Hunt climbed back into the car and resumed pursuit, but Fetter got the jump on them and took the lead.

"He stopped right in the middle of the road and returned fire!" Travis radioed.

Just four minutes had passed since Dennis had been shot.

"Damn," Hunt said, feeling his back pocket. "I lost my wallet."

Fritz drove leisurely, rarely topping thirty-five miles per hour, and the police cars kept their distance, staying several hundred yards behind.

"When a man's firing on you with a machine gun, you don't run up his tail pipe," one officer later observed.

Several times Fritz stopped again on blind curves and at the bottom of hills, but the airplane warned the pursuing officers in time for them to stop.

Greensboro police, meanwhile, were in confusion. First reports from the scene sent them after a red Camaro and a Mustang—the officers' cars. One Greensboro officer called in that a black Blazer was involved and he was behind it. But he was on the opposite end of New Garden Road. Several cars rushed to stop the Blazer after it turned south on U.S. 220, the officers ordering the hapless and innocent motorist from the vehicle at gunpoint.

At 2:55, Travis radioed again. "This is a black Bronco. The occupant is Fred Klenner, white male, thirty-two."

But his transmission was weak and hard to understand.

"Ten-four," the dispatcher said. "It's a white male, thirty-two, name of Red Fleming. It's a black what kind of vehicle?"

"Going to be a black Mustang," another officer radioed, adding to the confusion.

At 2:56, a Greensboro officer called impatiently from the intersection where Dennis was shot. "I want to know if we've got an ambulance for the officer."

Dennis was conscious but in great pain. His vest had stopped the bullet, fired from less than ten feet away, but his chest and shoulder looked like raw meat, and he was in shock.

Three minutes later, another officer at the intersection radioed a signal fifty—everything under control. "He's still with us," he said of Dennis.

The highway patrol had been alerted about the shooting and also was sending cars to join the chase. Sturgill radioed that he was in pursuit on New Garden Road, heading for 220. Sturgill's was the third car in the line of police vehicles.

"Can you get some Greensboro units out that way?" he asked.

"We have several units en route," said the highway patrol dispatcher. "Are you behind the Blazer?"

"We're pursuing him at a distance. He's stopping and returning fire. He has an automatic weapon."

"What's the license number on it?"

"It's a black Blazer occupied by a white male, white female, and two small children."

This was not only the first mention of an automatic weapon, it was also the first time that children were said to be in the vehicle. The transmission went only to the highway patrol dispatcher.

Travis's transmissions to the Greensboro dispatcher were now breaking up and inaudible, and the only information the dispatcher got came from the highway patrol.

Fritz reached U.S. 220 and turned north, firing back at the pursuing cars as he turned.

"Any possibility of getting an HP roadblock on 220 north?" Sturgill asked.

Two highway patrol cars were headed south on 220 from Rockingham County, but they were still many miles away. Other cars coming from U.S. 29 to the east were even more distant.

Several Guilford County sheriff's cars in the area were responding to alerts from their dispatcher, who had phoned the highway patrol for information. Corporal Hubert Jackson was going west on N.C. 150 toward 220, only a few miles away, when he radioed his position. He turned onto Strawberry Road, which intersects with 220. Warrant deputies John Patzsch and Ronald Scott were in an unmarked car in Summerfield, a community just a few miles to the north. They drove to the parking lot of a bank at the intersection of 220 and 150 and waited there. Deputy David Thacker was coming south on 220 near Summerfield. These deputies knew only that an officer had been shot and that the suspect vehicle was headed north on 220. They had been told nothing of a machine gun—or of children in the vehicle.

As Fritz continued northward well under the speed limit, holding back traffic, drivers of some civilian cars, unaware that a chase was going on, began passing police cars at the back of the pack. Sturgill moved into the center of the highway to hold back the befuddled drivers.

Gentry had not realized that Spainhour was still in pursuit with two wounded Kentucky deputies in his car. When he found out, he angrily ordered Spainhour to drop out and head for a hospital. On the way, Spainhour was stopped by Greensboro police, who thought his Mustang was the suspect vehicle.

Sturgill, meanwhile, was giving regular reports to the highway patrol.

The procession was at Lake Brandt. At Strawberry Road.

At one point Sturgill radioed that Fritz had a farm in Rockingham County and likely was headed there.

Guilford County deputy Thacker was just south of 150 when he saw the Blazer coming toward him. He pulled into the parking lot of a Food Lion supermarket to turn around as Fritz passed. Jackson was waiting in that parking lot. Fritz saw both deputies and gave them a big smile. Thacker turned on his blue lights and siren and came out behind the Blazer, followed by Jackson.

Fritz turned right at 150, and Deputy Patzsch pulled out behind him, ahead of Thacker and Jackson.

"He's not stopping," Patzsch radioed at 3:05.

"Did you advise westbound?" another, more distant deputy asked the dispatcher.

Fritz opened fire again, sending Patzsch off the road. Suddenly Patzsch came back on the air, his voice filled with alarm. "He's got an automatic weapon!" he called to Thacker, who'd moved in to fill his position behind the Blazer. "He's got it pointed at you."

"Ten-four," Thacker acknowledged, sounding remarkably calm. "Subject will have an automatic weapon, firing at this time."

His mind was not nearly so calm, though. The first thing that popped into it when he heard the submachine gun was something his wife, Robin, had asked him: "David, why don't you get a normal job?"

Fritz veered into the left lane as he fired, going head-on toward an approaching Volkswagen van. The van swerved right into the eastbound lane to avoid a collision, then back into the westbound lane and off the road, where it stopped, the driver thoroughly rattled.

Sturgill had radioed the highway patrol dispatcher that Fritz had turned onto 150, and shortly afterward the dispatcher notified him that a roadblock was being set up at the Guilford–Rockingham County line just a few miles ahead.

Fritz, meanwhile, continued at his slow pace, the Guilford County cars only a few hundred feet behind him. Thacker reported that he was at Bronco Lane. Soon after passing that road, Fritz slowed almost to a crawl. Both Thacker and Jackson, who was close behind Thacker, reported later that they heard sounds come from the Blazer, two distinct sounds in quick succession.

Clack. Clack.

Through the tinted windows, both officers saw frantic movement in the front seats of the Blazer.

Then the brake lights came on.

A school bus just had passed down Highway 150. It stopped at Strader Road, and Kerry Loggins and Crystal Jessie, neighbors, both thirteen, got off and started for their homes by the side of the highway. Kerry's dog, Benji, raced to meet him, tail wagging, and Kerry stopped in the yard to play with him.

Crystal was on her front porch, about to go into the house, when she heard the sirens coming and stopped to see what was going on. Benji began barking wildly at the sirens and ran toward the road with Kerry chasing, trying to stop him. Kerry saw a black Blazer coming, moving slowly, pursued by sheriff's cars. The Blazer seemed about to stop by the sign for Sunburst Farm, just down the road, where Susan Stout was at a nearby barn saddling a horse.

When Deputy David Thacker saw the brake lights on the Blazer, he hit his own brakes and went off the right side of the road. He thought Fritz was about to come out firing and would cut him to pieces with his submachine gun.

Before Thacker could jump from his car, he saw fire spurt from beneath the Blazer. A tremendous blast rocked his car. He sat, stunned, watching the Blazer belch a cloud of grayish white smoke as it rose from the pavement, pieces of it flying in every direction. It went nearly as high as the telephone lines, then slammed back to earth, obscured by a hovering smoke cloud.

Debris rained about him, and Thacker came out of his car and crouched behind the door, clutching his .357 Magnum. Behind him, Jackson hunkered with a shotgun.

Thacker was so scared and excited that he wasn't sure he had breath enough to speak, but he reached for his microphone to answer a call from his dispatcher.

"Ten-four, it appears it's going to be a ten-fifty," he said, using police radio lingo for a traffic accident. "Possible explosion at one-five-o, just east of Bronco Lane."

The time was 3:07.

"He just blew the whole thing up!" Travis radioed excitedly. "Get an ambulance out here!"

Kerry Loggins watched the explosion, which sent his startled dog fleeing in fear, then turned away, not wanting to see the aftermath. Crystal Jessie came off her porch and started toward the road to see what had happened. Susan Stout was trying to control her horse, which had been frightened by the tremendous blast. She couldn't imagine what had happened.

The line of unmarked cars came to a halt behind the sheriff's cars, and officers were piling out with weapons ready, some taking cover behind cars, others in the ditch. Nobody was certain whether Fritz might have jumped from the Blazer before the explosion and was waiting in ambush.

But even before the smoke began to clear, Fetter leaped from the lead car with his AR15 and began running toward the wreckage. So did Gentry, carrying a shotgun, and House with a pistol. Gentry could see Crystal Jessie coming toward the wreckage, and he was fearful that other bombs might go off.

"Get back inside!" he yelled as he ran, waving the shotgun in the air.

Other officers began moving cautiously toward the scene, stepping gingerly through the widely scattered debris. Yards of primer cord lay in the road, indicating that their fears of other explosives might be well founded. But Gentry knew that they need not fear ambush, for he already had spotted Fritz's and Susie's bodies.

Fritz lay facedown, straddling a drainage ditch on the east side of a driveway culvert on the north side of the road, about a hundred feet from the small crater in the pavement where the blast occurred. He was wearing tan corduroy pants, a checkered shirt in autumnal colors, and low-cut, blue hiking boots. He was remarkably unmarked by the blast, and even more surprising to the officers, he was still breathing.

Davidson hurried to his side and bent over him, touching his shoulder, saying, "Fritz. Fritz. Can you hear me? Can you hear me?" He was hoping for a last-minute confession.

Susie lay crumpled on the other side of the culvert with parts of the Blazer's red seat imbedded in her. She wore blue jeans and a long-sleeve shirt, mustard color with pink and green stripes. Blood seeped from her nose, mouth, and ears. Her jeans were shredded, and the back of her body was pulp from the waist down. Her right leg ended at the knee, her left at mid-shin. A seat spring protruded from her vagina. She was dead without doubt, and it was obvious that she had been sitting atop the bomb.

When the officers turned Fritz over, they heard sounds from his body, as if bones were scraping. Gurgles came from his chest, and his breathing faded and slowly stopped as he drowned in his own blood.

What was left of the Blazer had gone down a slight embankment on the other side of the road and flattened a section of barbed wire fence around a horse pasture. The frame of the vehicle was bowed in the middle. The top and sides were gone, but the roll bars remained in place. The hood and front fenders looked as if they had been peeled forward, angling slightly toward the driver's side, but the engine was relatively undamaged. The driver's seat remained intact, a throne to destruction. The driver's door hung askew. The passenger door was gone, and where the passenger seat had been was a gaping three-foot hole. Jim's pale head sagged into the hole.

John lay behind the driver's seat. Both boys were dead, their frail, camouflage-clad limbs entwined with the bodies of their big dogs.

Davidson walked over and took a quick glimpse of the remains of the Blazer. He saw what he feared he would see and turned away. Later, he would call that the worst moment in his long career in law enforcement, a vision he never would be able to shake from his mind. "I saw those two little children lying there dead and that just broke my heart."

For a few minutes he had to walk off alone and compose himself.

Debris from the explosion was scattered for more than a hundred yards around. The Blazer's passenger door was lodged fifty feet up in a pine tree. A small arsenal lay scattered. The Uzi was found yards from the blast site with a shell jammed in its chamber. A cocked 9-millimeter pistol, with a shell in the chamber and two other shells missing from the magazine, was propped upside down against the base of a utility pole. Two Ithaca lightweight automatic shotguns were gathered from the debris, along with a .45-caliber semi-automatic pistol, a 308 assault rifle with bipod, and a flare gun. Ammunition was everywhere, including KTW armor-piercing shells.

There were gas masks, tarps, tools, a big wood-cutting saw, extra boots, C-rations, climbing ropes, several kinds of knives, a machete, brass knuckles, handcuffs, choke wires, martial arts weapons, holsters, bandoleers, smoke grenades, flares, waterproof matches, a portable water treatment unit, and *The Pocket Black Book*, a guide to survival.

A plastic sandwich bag containing a thin stack of hundred-dollar bills was concealed in a pack. In the woods was a duffel bag stuffed with vitamins. Loose vitamin tablets were strewn hither and yon.

Amid all of this were classical music tapes, including Haydn's "Mass in Time of War," parts of a syllabus from a business course, some of Susie's homewok, and a children's book with an ironic title: *No Monsters in the Closet*.

Fritz's Rolex watch was stopped at 3:08. He had a knife on his belt and Susie's .25-caliber Browning pistol in his right hip pocket. On his right hand he wore a gold ring in the shape of a horseshoe with a lightning bolt across it, on his left hand a gold wedding band. Around his neck was a gold chain with a religious medallion. AGLA was the inscription on one side, IVA IANA AOY JEVA on the other. In his right front pocket were rosary beads and a cross on a gold chain.

Susie wore a Rolex watch and a gold ring with three small red stones on her left hand. Around her neck was a gold chain with a cross. She also wore around her neck a scapular, a string with two small cloth patches bearing prayers. On one of the patches was a pledge of salvation, on the other a plea for a release from purgatory. The boys also wore these scapulars, and all three were carrying rosary beads.

Near Fritz's and Susie's bodies were laminated cards bearing prayers to St. Joseph, the patron saint of departing souls, that clearly had been ineffective: "Whoever shall read this prayer or hear it or keep it about themselves shall never die a sudden death or be drowned, nor shall poison take effect on them," the cards said. "Neither shall they fall into the hands of the enemy, or shall be burned in any fire or shall be overpowered in any battle."

As soon as Gentry had assessed the situation, he went to Crystal Jessie's house and called his boss, Sheriff Preston Oldham. "It's all come down," he said. "We got him. It didn't go quite like we thought it would."

He went on to tell about the shoot-out, the explosion, the deaths of Fritz and Susie and the boys. He would remember the sheriff as sounding very subdued. "I'll call the families," the sheriff said.

Next, Gentry called his wife, Lu Ann, who was about to get off work at the telephone office in Greensboro.

"I just wanted to let you know I'm all right before you got to the car and heard the news on the radio," he said.

She could not remember him ever sounding so wound-up

and hyper as he was when he told her what had just happened.

This had been a blisteringly hot and sunny day for early June, and within twenty minutes of the explosion, the weather changed. The sky to the north and west turned dark and angry. Thunder rumbled ominously. The churning clouds were the blackest some officers could remember.

The storm came quickly and with an intense ferocity. Wind bent the trees. Lightning struck close enough to be smelled. Some officers took refuge in their cars. Gentry and Sturgill went to Crystal Jessie's house. Davidson found shelter in Susan Stout's barn. A dog that had been wandering amid the wreckage tried to shoulder into a police car, then scampered off with a whimper.

Hail the size of marbles beat down on the bodies of Fritz, Susie, and the boys. Torrents of rain washed away the blood and the acrid, lingering odor of explosives.

"It was like the Lord was mad," Davidson said later. "Like He was *real* mad. I mean really pissed off."

When the storm had passed and the officers emerged into the cooled and freshened air, steam rose from the melting hailstones and clung to the awesome scene of death and destruction, lending it an element of surrealism.

"It made it almost like a dream," Gentry recalled.

PART SIX

THE AFTERMATH

43

Tom Lynch had just returned to his dental clinic from lunch when the phone call came from North Carolina.

The caller identified herself as a reporter. She asked Tom for a description of his former wife, Susie.

"Why do you want to know?" he said.

"Something has happened."

"What?"

"I'm not at liberty to say."

"What the hell has happened?" he demanded.

"I can't—"

He slammed down the receiver.

Earlier that day, Tom had tried to call Dan Davidson to find out if there had been any developments in the investigations. Two weeks had passed since he'd called to tell police of his suspicions about Susie and Fritz, and he had heard nothing. He had been growing more anxious by the day.

"We could feel the pressure building up without information," he said. "It was like the silence was making the pressure go up."

He had hoped to relieve some of that pressure with his morning call to Kentucky State Police Post Five, but the information it brought only increased his anxiety. Davidson, he learned, was in North Carolina with the other detectives investigating the murders of his mother and sister.

"We don't have any word yet," he was told, "but we understand something's going to happen today."

Tom took that to mean an arrest.

473

Now he was certain that something had happened. Had Susie been arrested? He dialed Rob's number i Greensboro.

Rob had reached a heavy decision that day. While th police were chasing Fritz and Susie, Rob was at Southsid Hardware buying a ten-shot .44 Magnum carbine. H was going to use it to kill his cousin—"der Fritzer," h called him.

From the time his parents' and grandmother's bodie were found, Rob had feared that Fritz might kill him an his family. "I figured he was going to come through thos doors pretty soon," he said later.

He had decided not to wait for Fritz to make a move He had been thinking about killing him for two weeks although he had kept it to himself. It was the mai reason he didn't tell police of his suspicions about Frit when he was first questioned, he said later. He didn' want them to get Fritz before he had a chance to settl scores himself.

"I was going to invite him over and kill him," h explained. "I was just going to plug the boy."

He was buying the carbine to make sure that he did th job properly. "I'm no hand with a pistol," he said, "bu I'm a very good rifle shot, and I figured that one woul be a real stopper."

He felt a certain peace after reaching the decision an had no qualms about it.

"I wanted to kill him," he said, "and I don't think was the only one. I think people were standing in line t blow him away. The guy was a monster, just a complet monster."

Despite his moral upbringing, his brilliance, his lon studies in theology, philosophy, and law, in the end hi decision had been elemental. His justification was simpl and basic and he summed it up in a single short sentenc that might have graced the cover of a supermarket tab loid: "He hacked my mama to pieces."

While Rob was paying for the powerful weapon, as fierce thunderstorm beat on the store's awning, the cler mentioned hearing over a police scanner that a shoot-ou had taken place with "some terrorist" at Guilford Col lege. Could the police have already done his work fo him? When the rain subsided, Rob dashed to his car, locked the gun in his trunk, and drove to his office. Jean Cook, the office records manager, rushed out to meet him.

"You have to go home," she said without explanation, "and I'm going to ride with you."

Rob knew that something terrible had happened, and Alice tearfully broke the news of the explosion to him when he got home. Friends arrived quickly as word spread, just as they had two weeks before. Among them was Wally Harrelson, the public defender, who began making calls seeking information.

"We couldn't get any information from anybody," Rob remembered.

Word finally came that Susie and Fritz were dead, but there still was no news about the boys.

When Susie's death was confirmed, Alice called Tom's home number and Kathy answered. The two women had never met. Alice told Kathy what had happened, and Kathy's first question was about John and Jim.

"We don't know," Alice said, crying. "We can't find the boys."

"What do you mean you can't find the boys?" Kathy said, but Alice was sobbing and handed the phone to a neighbor, Dr. John Chandler, who told Kathy that the boys' whereabouts were unknown.

As soon as Dr. Chandler hung up, the phone rang and Tom was on the line, wanting to talk to Rob.

"There's been an explosion," Rob told him. "Susie and Fritz are dead."

"Where are the boys?" Tom asked.

"We don't know yet," Rob said. "We haven't heard anything about the boys."

"I'm looking at my watch," Tom recalled later. It was a little after 1:30 in Albuquerque, two hours later in Greensboro. "I'm thinking, 'The kids are in school, I'm all right.' "

Later, Tom told Bart Ripp of the *Albuquerque Tribune* of his reaction to Susie's death: "I was glad. I thought, 'I'm rid of her, and the boys will be out here tomorrow.' "

Later still, he explained his reaction: "She had thrown

up so many obstacles and been so cold and so overtly evil that there was no remorse at all that she was gone."

Rob and Alice learned of the boys' deaths from a neighbor who worked at Cone Hospital and had gotten the news from police. Soon afterward, Rob called Tom at his office. Tom knew from the tone of Rob's voice that he didn't want to hear his message.

"We've got word that the boys were with Susie and Fritz when the bomb went off," Rob said. "It hasn't been confirmed."

Tom hung up and frantically called Greensboro police, only to hear that he could be told nothing until he was officially notified. His heart dropped. He knew what that meant.

Nothing ever hit him like that. Later, he was unable to find words sufficient to describe his pain, his anger, his feeling of helplessness.

Dr. Chandler called Kathy to tell her the boys were dead, and crying, she called Tom.

"Let me come and get you," she pleaded. "Let me have somebody come and get you."

"No," he said, and hung up.

He picked up a single item from his desk. On his way out, he told the office receptionist that he didn't know when he'd be back. He drove home and walked inside without saying anything. He was carrying a small photograph he had taken from his desk. The snapshot had been made at a friend's house at Christmas 1983. In it, he, Kathy, and the boys were smiling broadly. At the heavy wood dining room table where they all had shared many happy meals he paused. Suddenly, he slammed the picture facedown onto the tabletop, shattering the glass frame to match his dreams for his sons.

District Attorney Don Tisdale was halfway through another afternoon in his controversial murder-rape trial when somebody tapped him on the shoulder, and he looked up to see Sheriff Preston Oldham motioning to him from the courtroom door. Oldham looked shaken. Tisdale had never seen him like that.

They stepped into the hallway, and Oldham told Tisdale

about the shoot-out and explosion. The sheriff clearly was upset about the boys' deaths.

Tisdale had a curious verbal quirk, a phrase that popped automatically to his lips whenever he faced something that couldn't be changed.

"Well, good," he said, realizing as it came out how inappropriate it was.

"What do we do now?" Tisdale remembered the sheriff asking.

"Well, as tragic as it is, there's not much you can do. You didn't do anything wrong. You couldn't dictate what happened. He dictated who his victims were going to be."

Later, Tisdale admitted to another regret about the way things turned out.

"I felt sort of cheated, because I would've loved to have tried the case. It would have been the trial of the century."

The bomb blast site teemed with police, emergency workers, reporters, and photographers. A truck with a high extension arm was brought in so that a highway patrol cameraman could get an overview for a videotape of the scene. A bomb squad moved through the debris, making sure no explosives had been thrown from the vehicle. When the bomb squad finished, grids were laid out, and evidence technicians swept through, noting and marking every piece of debris.

The boys' bodies remained in the Blazer for several hours. Fearing that the Blazer might be booby-trapped or contain other explosives, the bomb experts treated it gingerly. Ropes were attached to the bodies and they were pulled slowly from the wreckage from a great distance.

Officers who got close-up looks at the boys before they were lifted into oversized body bags saw something that they kept to themselves, something that reporters would be two days in learning.

After the boys' bodies were taken away to be sent to North Carolina Memorial Hospital in Chapel Hill for autopsy, officers borrowed a shovel and buried Chowy and Maizie in the horse pasture.

* * *

The three officers hurt in the shoot-out all were treated at Moses Cone Hospital on Tuesday afternoon and released.

Dennis, the Greensboro patrolman, was most seriously injured, with muscle, nerve, and lung damage. He was upset that he had been called into such a dangerous situation without adequate information. Some Greensboro patrol officers thought that Dennis had been made a sitting duck by the detectives, brought in to take the gunfire for them, and they were angry. Angriest of all was Dennis's wife, Sandy, who that night loudly confronted some of the officers involved in the shoot-out.

The injured Kentucky detectives, Childers and Nobles, were taken to the explosion site after treatment and rejoined their commander, Dan Davidson.

Davidson had suffered two blows that afternoon, the first being the deaths of the boys. The second came when he called his post commander to tell him about the shoot-out and explosion. Then he learned that his own son had been seriously hurt that day when the wall of a coal mine collapsed.

Later, Davidson, Childers, and Nobles checked into the Comfort Inn in Greensboro, and after calling to check on his son, Davidson did what he'd been dreading for hours. He called Tom Lynch.

"Doc, I'm real sorry," he began.

"What happened, Dan?"

Davidson gave a capsule description of the day's events.

"He just blew the truck up and killed everybody," he concluded.

"I'll be there tomorrow," Tom told him.

"I just felt terrible," Davidson recalled later. "I don't ever remember feeling that bad over anything."

Following the explosion, Greensboro police evacuated Susie's apartment building and several others near it. The entire area was roped off, and nobody was allowed enter for fear that other bombs might be in the apartment, timed to go off. A SWAT team arrived. Sharpshooters took up positions in nearby apartments in case armed confederates might be in the apartment. A special bomb-removal truck pulled up to the apartment.

Near dusk, Gentry and Sturgill left the blast site and went to the Greensboro Police Department, where Sturgill drew up a search warrant for Susie's apartment and Blazer. Darkness was falling before police moved warily on the apartment.

A bomb squad used small charges to blow open the doors of Susie's Blazer, but no explosives were found inside. Squad members broke the kitchen window of the apartment and entered cautiously. They disconnected the tear gas cannister above the door and began a thorough search. Not until nearly 11 P.M. was the apartment declared free of explosives and residents of nearby apartments allowed to return to their homes.

Davidson, Childers, and Nobles had joined Gentry, Sturgill, and other detectives outside Susie's apartment. When they were allowed to enter, their attention was first drawn to four sheets of white stationery, near an open edition of that day's *New York Times*, on the cluttered kitchen table. The stationery bore the letterhead of Dr. Frederick R. Klenner of Reidsville, but his name and address had been scratched through. Each sheet bore a separate handwritten note that looked hurriedly scribbled.

This is to certify that my friend Ian Perkins was in no way involved in any wrongdoings of any kind. He was with me on a camping trip to Peaks of Otter on the weekend of May 18th and to the best of his certain knowledge in training for a possible career in covert operations.

Fred R. Klenner Jr.

The firearms in this apartment and in the Blazer were the property of Fred. R. Klenner Sr. and are the property of Annie Sharp Klenner, as are the computer, TV, electronics equipment, weight machines and camping gear.

Fred R. Klenner Jr.

I have in my life never physically harmed anyone as in taking human life. I am innocent of any accusations that have come to my attention and fear an elaborate frame. I have spent my life in the service of my God, my country and my family.

Fred R. Klenner Jr.

Mother,
I love you now and always.

Your Fritz

Whatever else Gentry and Sturgill could say about Fritz, they had to say one thing: he was consistent. He played out his games to the end.

44

The explosion on Highway 150 was the biggest news in Greensboro since a band of homegrown Nazis and Ku Klux Klansmen opened fire on anti-Klan demonstrators in a black neighborhood in November of 1979, killing five members of the Communist Workers Party, an event that pleased Fritz, who gloated when all of the Klansmen and Nazis charged in the case were acquitted, even though the killings had been recorded by TV cameras and seen throughout the world. Ironically, a civil rights suit brought by survivors of the attack was being tried in federal court in Winston-Salem as police began closing in on Fritz; but in the coming days, that trial would be greatly overshadowed in the news by repercussions from Fritz's own violent acts.

As reporters dug deeper into the story on Tuesday, Tom and Kathy were flying to Greensboro. Tom had but one purpose: to bring home his boys. He would not allow them to be buried in North Carolina.

At first Tom and Kathy had not been able to believe what had happened. "This is just a mistake," they kept telling themselves. "They're going to call us back and say the boys are all right and we're going to get them."

But the truth had sunk in as they sat up grieving all night, and Tom's anger and disbelief had become weighted with guilt. He blamed himself for not doing something to prevent his sons' deaths.

Why hadn't he realized earlier that Susie might have been behind killing his mother and sister? Why hadn't he told the police to check her long before the Newsoms were murdered? The thought had crossed his mind, to be sure, but just as he hadn't been able to believe that she could abuse the children, neither could he believe she could have a hand in murder. Why hadn't the strange things he'd heard about Fritz prompted him to realize his potential danger? And why, most of all, hadn't he just gone back to North Carolina as soon as he heard about the Newsom murders and snatched his kids from school? Why had he depended on lawyers and courts and patience and civilities to save his boys? Why hadn't he just grabbed them and run and hid, hang the consequences?

He had been concerned about the boys from the moment he heard about the Newsom murders. His first thought was to go to North Carolina for the funerals, not only to pay respects to the Newsoms, whom he'd always liked, but also to be available to the boys in such a traumatic time. He consulted a child psychologist, who told him that it would be good for the boys to have him there, but when he called Louise to find out what effect his appearance might have, she told him that Susie didn't want him to come. Rather than cause a scene and create more difficulty for the family, he didn't go.

Instead, he and Kathy tried to get the boys away from their morbid situation. Their hope was to find a way to begin the summer visit early and bring the boys to Albuquerque.

Over and over, they tried to reach the boys by telephone but couldn't. They called Rob, Louise, and others, but the boys were not available.

On the day after the funerals, Tom called Guilford Middle School and asked the principal to get John and Jim out of class.

"Why are you calling us at school?" Jim asked.

"I haven't been able to get a hold of you anywhere, Jim," Tom said. "I wanted to make sure you guys were all right. How are you feeling?"

"We're all right," Jim said.

John sounded sad and scared and had little to say.

"Well, I just wanted to find out how you were and let you know that we're okay," Tom told him. "We'll see you soon, okay?"

When he had been unable to reach the boys earlier, Tom had called his lawyer, Bill Horsley, in Reidsville.

He wanted to express his concern and to see if Horsley could get an earlier visit.

"I told him I was worried about the boys emotionally, mentally, and physically, right up to and including their safety," Tom said later.

Horsley talked with Susie's lawyer, Sandy Sands, to see if he could work out something, but Sands told Horsley that he was having trouble reaching Susie, Horsley said later. After Sands did talk with her, Horsley said he had trouble getting Sands to agree to a convenient time for rescheduling the visitation hearing.

"It was like everything was in slow motion," Kathy recalled later. "It was so frustrating being so far away, waiting for the phone to ring with some news and hearing nothing. We were so desperate to do something, and nobody else seemed concerned."

As they grew more fearful, Tom tried calling John and Jim again. He found them at home on Wednesday night, May 29.

"I tried to be as normal as I could," he said later. "They didn't say much. I told John I was trying to arrange for them to come out early. It was pretty obvious that somebody was standing over him. John was monosyllabic. The last thing I told him was, 'Don't worry. We'll work something out.' "

Two days later, when they still had heard nothing, Kathy called Horsley in an emotional state.

"I said, 'This is ridiculous! We're afraid for their safety! Go directly to the judge!' "

"We had a real problem," Horsley recalled later. "The law enforcement people weren't favoring us with the results of their investigation. It was almost as if they were making a decided effort to keep us from thinking Fritz and Susie were involved. The only person Tom could think of who might have done it was this guy Fritz. He was very uneasy about Fritz, but there wasn't anything we could put a finger on. We couldn't go to a judge and say, This looks funny. You've got to have some grounds. Tom had a hard time accepting that. I think he felt something should be done."

Soon after the Newsom funerals, Horsley had been interviewed by an SBI agent. "The way he was questioning me was that they looked at it as a breaking-and-entering that went wrong. It was almost like he was apologizing for taking up my time. They had this list of people they were supposed to talk to, and they were just checking me off. I don't recall that he asked me anything of a substantive nature. I asked him if we should be concerned about anybody's safety, and he said, 'Nah.' He was real flip. My feeling is very strong that the SBI intentionally misled me to keep us from going into court and blowing their investigation."

Horsley prepared a motion for a new hearing to have the boys' summer visitation begin early, and he had been trying without success to get the judge to hear it out of session. He probably would see the judge at church Sunday, he told Tom and Kathy on their last call, and he would ask him about it then. That was indeed what had happened, and the judge had told him he would hear the motion during the coming week. But Tom and Kathy didn't know that, and the next day the boys were dead.

Now, as they flew toward North Carolina, both Tom and Kathy kept hearing John crying and pleading not to have to go back home at the end of their Disneyland trip just two months earlier. The burden of guilt was almost unbearable.

"Both Tom and I feel like we let the boys down," Kathy said later.

"I told them everything would be all right," Tom said, "and it wasn't."

Allen Gentry and Tom Sturgill spent Tuesday rummaging through Susie's apartment in search of evidence. The clutter was even more amazing than they had imagined from their earlier visit.

Boxes of clothing, toys (including two plastic submachine guns), books, and papers littered the dirty gold carpet in the living room. The two wicker chairs and a folding table were piled with newspapers, magazines, schoolwork, and books. Among the papers on the folding table was a Dear Abby column that told how to prevent child-snatching. A sturdy pine corner cupboard built by Paw-Paw was covered with bric-a-brac from Susie's marriage. On the floor in front of it was a doll cradle Paw-

Paw had made for one of her childhood Christmases. A wooden bookcase held volumes ranging from *Iacocca* to *Crossroads of Modern Warfare* and *Having It All* by Helen Gurley Brown. A thirteen-inch color TV sat on a small table, a cheap computer atop a wooden desk. The walls were decorated with Chinese scrolls Susie had brought back from Taiwan.

The small dining room, which had been shrouded by a screen on Gentry and Sturgill's earlier visit, resembled a military supply dump. Piled on the floor around a Gympac 1000 exercise machine were loaded packs, ammunition clips, ammunition boxes, water cans, sleeping bags, military uniforms, camouflage folding chairs, filled canteens, field toilet paper, gasoline lanterns, and other field gear. Stacks of plastic milk crates, each carefully labeled in Fritz's hand, held food and emergency medical supplies—one marked "Extras for long trip." On the only piece of furniture in the room, a small desk, stood a framed color portrait of Susie's Aunt Su-Su. Beside it lay a small snapshot of Dr. Klenner and Annie Hill.

John's and Jim's bikes were parked in the hallway, where each boy had his own wall displaying artwork and records of achievement. Jim's wall included drawings of airplanes, a sunset, Columbus's three ships. John's had drawings of sea creatures and a big red ax, plus his honor roll certificate and another paper making him the adoptive parent of a white azalea at his school.

On the door to the boys' room, next to a drawing by Jim of a barn in a snowstorm, a picture he had entitled "Winter Days, Winter Nights," was a poster from the Rhodesian police showing the sihouette of a man with a rifle. YOUR MIND IS YOUR PRIMARY WEAPON, the poster said.

Inside the room, on a wall near a small picture of a Madonna and child and next to a Garfield poster, was another Rhodesian police warning, offering guerrilla war survival tips: IF ALONE BE EXTRA ALERT. USE A BACKUP WHERE POSSIBLE. AVOID SNIPER AREAS AND ALWAYS LOOK FOR COVER. CHANGE YOUR FIRING POSITION. REMEMBER SHAPE, SHINE, SHADOW, SILHOUETTE, SMELL AND MOVEMENT. CASUALTIES HELP THE ENEMY.

Filled canteens and scabbarded knives on field belts

were draped from the posts of the boys' bunk beds. The night before, the officers had found two loaded Ruger .22 rifles, made to look like assault rifles, on an *Empire Strikes Back* blanket on the top bunk. On the closet door were two targets peppered with small bullet holes, most near the bull's-eye. Shells for the rifles were scattered around on the floor, where lay two military packs filled with schoolbooks. A toy rifle was propped against one wall. A kite hung from the ceiling. An inflatable R2D2 robot stood in a chair. Bible stories and *Robinson Crusoe* were on a small bookcase.

The windows in the other bedroom were covered with a camouflage blanket. The stout double bed, also made by Paw-Paw, was piled high with clutter. Above the bed was a framed tapestry of a horse and colt. On another wall was a picture of Susie with Paw-Paw at her wedding and a quote from Henry Van Dyke decoupaged by Nanna: "Be glad of life because it gives you the chance to love and to work and to play and to look up at the stars." On another wall were big maps of the Soviet Union and the world.

In the mound of clutter on the bed was a recent transcript of Susie's grades—all A's. There, too, was a scrapbook containing her achievement certificates from grammar school, a picture of her as a tiny child with her mother and her aunts Susie and Annie Hill, other pictures of her as the Queen of the May at age five and as a college sweetheart. Also in the clutter, next to a cross-stitch pillow done by Nanna that said "Home—the place where we grumble the most and are treated the best," was a plastic bag containing the boys' two stuffed travel toys with their throats slit.

On a bedside table were over-the-counter antihistamines and birth control pills with a current prescription bearing Susie's name. On the floor were sleeping bags, more military gear, a wicked-looking, machetelike knife, combat survival kits, a military first aid kit, a book on emergency war surgery, and the *Army Special Forces Medical Handbook*.

In the bathroom, off the hallway, the rechargeable electric razor Fritz had used to shave off his beard after the Newsom murders lay beside the sink. A colorful

Folies Bergère poster adorned the wall over the commode. The reading material at hand was a book by Gayle Rivers: *The Specialist, Revelations of a Counter Terrorist.*

In every room were crucifixes, and above the windows were small palm crosses like the ones found arranged in the hallway of the Lynch house two days after the discovery of Delores's and Janie's bodies. Over the front door was a small card, hand-lettered by Fritz:

I

NIR

I

Sanctitus Spiritus

I

NIR

I

All this be guarded here in time and there in eternity

Amen

Later, when Alice took down the card, she turned it over and found written on the back, also in Fritz's hand: "I know that my Redeemer liveth. He will call me from the grave."

The kitchen table was too cluttered to allow room for eating. Two tropical fish swam sluggishly in a small aquarium on a countertop. Garfield cartoons clipped from Sunday comic sections decorated the walls, along with a Kitchen Prayer. The refrigerator, freezer, and cabinets looked as if Fritz and Susie had been stockpiling against famine. They were jammed with supplies, much of them convenience foods. A large cache of liquor and wine filled the cabinet under the kitchen sink. One cabinet was crammed with vitamins and medicines. Eventually, the officers would find enough vitamins and prescription drugs in the apartment to fill five large cardboard boxes. The heavy aroma of B vitamins permeated the air.

The night before, officers had assembled a small arsenal of weapons from the apartment, including the rifles Fritz had bought for the boys, an M6 survival weapon that would fire .22-caliber bullets and .410 shotgun shells, a .20-gauge shotgun, a .22 revolver, a .25-caliber automatic pistol, two .45-caliber pistols, a 5.56-millimeter assault rifle, spare barrels, thousands of rounds of ammunition, a big assortment of knives and exotic martial arts weapons, Mace, gas masks, bullet-proof vests, bullet-proof diapers, a police scanner, and a parabolic microphone used for collecting sounds from great distances.

In Susie's bedroom they found military ammo boxes that turned out to be treasure chests, each filled with gold and silver jewelry, hundreds of rings, bracelets, necklaces, brooches, many adorned with pearls and precious stones. They suspected some of the jewelry to be booty from burglaries, but they never would be able to prove it. Also found in ammo boxes were $1,219 in cash, a Presidential Rolex watch valued at nearly $9,000, a 100-ounce silver bar, 118 one-ounce silver bars, 3 one-ounce South African Krugerrand gold coins, 6 half-ounce, 10 quarter-ounce, and 20 tenth-ounce Krugerrands, plus numerous other gold and silver coins.

Gentry and Sturgill spent most of the day cataloging all of the items being seized as possible evidence. Among the weapons they would overlook was one that Rob found later atop the frame of the front door, just under the card with the strange religious references. It looked like a ballpoint pen, but when Rob picked it up and touched the button on the side, a stiletto leaped out.

Forsyth County Sheriff Preston Oldham held a press conference at his office on Tuesday morning and gave the first official account of the investigation that led to the shoot-out and explosion.

On Saturday night, May 18, Fritz had caught a ride to Winston-Salem with a friend from Greensboro, who let him out near the Newsom house, he said. He declined to identify the friend, but described him as "clean," saying that he had known nothing of the events that were about to take place.

"Klenner made his way to the residence through a footpath behind the house," Oldham said, although detectives had determined no such thing. "Upon his arrival, we believe that because Klenner was known, he was let in"—another matter about which there was dispute among investigators.

He told how Klenner left the house in Nanna's gold Plymouth Voláre after the killings and was stopped by a

Winston-Salem policeman who had no reason to suspect him of crimes and let him go. He returned to the house in the same car and left it, Oldham said without explaining why. At that time he dropped a set of keys belonging to Florence beside the car and left Nanna's keys in the back door.

"Upon arriving at the house, Klenner went in again to the residence. This time he picked up the empty casings in the residence. There were only two left on the scene.

"It is unclear at this time how Klenner left the area."

He said that Fritz had become a suspect five days earlier and that an "infiltrator" had helped get information that confirmed Fritz was the killer.

"He indicated through his statements things we knew," Oldham said of Fritz. "There are certain key facts we know only the killer would know."

Questioned later, Oldham did not say what those facts were, nor would he identify the infiltrator.

The decision to arrest Fritz came after officers determined that he might be preparing to leave to kill people who had information about the killings, Oldham said, apparently referring to the officers' theory that Fritz might have been planning to kill Tom or other family members.

"At our last infiltration Monday, it was indicated that Klenner posed a danger to the witnesses," he said without amplification.

Quizzed about motive, Oldham said that child custody and large inheritances were possibilities, and he mentioned the upcoming visitation hearing.

"Almost everyone who died was going to testify in that custody case," he said, although Bob, in fact, was the only one. "But the questions may never be answered. There are a multitude of things that could have prompted it. An exact, hard-core motive will never be known. It could have been revenge. It could have been greed. It could have been personal problems. It could have been child custody. Now we'll never know.

"There are a number of questions that can never be answered. If it had gone to court we might have answered them."

Was Susie a suspect?

"She was in loose terms a suspect. It was a natural

process that she could be considered a suspect because of that relationship, but there is no hard-core evidence that she was involved."

Would there be further investigation?

"The case is closed. Based on our district attorney's opinion, the physical evidence and Klenner's own statements that link everything together . . . the Newsom case is resolved. This whole case, including the Kentucky murders and ours, it's unreal how it was played out, almost like a dime-store novel with so many twists and turns. We have no doubt that he was the killer."

Even as Oldham spoke, more strange twists and turns were about to surface.

At North Carolina Memorial Hospital in Chapel Hill, Assistant Medical Examiner Dr. John D. Butts began his autopsy of Jim's body by noting the obvious. Jim had been shot through the left eye, clearly at close range. Stippling surrounded the wound, indicating that the weapon had been held no more than a foot away. The bullet traveled upward and slightly to the right, exiting from the back of his head, clearly a fatal wound. He had a few minor lacerations on his thighs and some scratches and scrapes around his neck, but no blatant injuries from the bomb blast.

When Dr. Butts sliced into Jim's body, he got a surprise. A familiar bittersweet, almond-chlorine odor rose to meet him. He recognized it immediately as cyanide.

Dr. Robert L. Thompson, who was performing the autopsy on John's body, was recording similar findings. Like Jim, John had few injuries from the bomb blast, a minor cut on his cheek, abrasions on his left thigh. But like Jim, John also had been shot. Black powder in his hair indicated the weapon had been held no more than two feet away. The bullet entered the back of his head near the base of the skull and traveled upward, exiting above the left ear. Dr. Thompson found a fragment from a 9-millimeter copper-jacketed bullet in John's brain. He also found cyanide in John's stomach.

Cyanide, the poison used in gas chamber executions, is also commonly used by jewelers for processing metal and is easily available in powder or pellet form from chemical supply companies. Ingested or inhaled in sufficient quantity, it brings unconsciousness, convulsions, and death within a matter of minutes. An average lethal amount in the blood is 1.2 milligrams per 100 milliliters of blood for an adult. As little as .6 milligrams has been known to kill. Blood tests showed that John had 1.7 milligrams in his blood. Jim, Susie's favored son, had a whopping 18 milligrams, indicating that he probably had been given the cyanide first, allowing more time for it to get into his bloodstream.

Both doctors agreed that Jim and John had been shot soon after taking the poison. The doctors believed the boys' hearts were beating but both children were unconscious when shot.

Autopsies also were performed on the bodies of Susie and Fritz that day. The results showed that neither had ingested cyanide, nor had they been shot. Both died from blast injuries, and both appeared to have been conscious when the bomb went off. Fritz had bruises, scrapes, and lacerations. A rivet had been driven into his liver. Several ribs were fractured. But internal hemorrhaging had killed him. A quart of blood had collected in his right chest cavity, a pint in his left.

Susie's was the only mangled body, her most blatant injuries from the waist down. She suffered multiple fractures and massive blunt-force trauma throughout her body. In her stomach was a partly dissolved capsule containing pink, white, and red particles that the doctors removed and turned over to the SBI for analysis. Her injuries made it clear that the bomb had been underneath her seat when it exploded.

The autopsy findings were powerful, and they were summed up in a note on the boys' reports: "The two brothers were apparently killed by their mother and her cousin prior to the vehicle being destroyed by a bomb contained within it."

The reports brought relief to the police, who had realized at the scene that the boys had been shot and feared that the wounds had come from police guns.

At three Tuesday afternoon, the big bomb-disposal truck that had been parked in front of Susie's apartment the night before pulled up to 1205 Huntsdale Road in Reidsville, and soon afterward, with Annie Hill's permission, a group of officers began a search through the clutter of the Klenner house. In addition to vast amounts of prescription drugs and vitamins, they found large stores of military gear and survivalist supplies, plus a case and a half of dynamite, blasting caps, safety caps, fuses, twenty-eight pounds of black powder, fifteen tear gas grenades, two claymore mines stolen from the army, more than thirty thousand rounds of varied ammunition, another Uzi submachine gun, seven handguns, five semiautomatic military rifles, and six shotguns.

The dynamite, grenades, and other explosives were loaded into the disposal truck and taken to the Reidsville city dump to be detonated.

After the search, Reidsville Police Chief James Festerman told reporters that some of the discoveries had come as a surprise to Annie Hill.

"She was not aware of the entire contents of the house, but she may have known of the dynamite," he said.

No charges would be brought against her for possession of illegal weapons, explosives, or stolen U.S. government property.

45

The murders and explosion continued to dominate the news in North Carolina and would for nearly a week.

Much of Wednesday's newspaper coverage centered on Fritz and Susie. Officials made clear that they had no doubt about Fritz's guilt in the five murders. Susie's possible involvement was another matter. Tisdale was quoted as calling her "an ostensibly innocent person." Sheriff Oldham said his detectives had compiled no "hardcore evidence" against her.

In another story, *Greensboro News & Record* reporters Jim Brady and Mike Vogel quoted unnamed family friends as saying that Susie had been fearful after the Lynch murders, that she had recently received anonymous threatening calls, and that the throats of two of the boys' toy animals had been slit.

They quoted Susie Sharp as saying, "She loved those boys and she loved her grandmother. I can't believe that she would knowingly hurt them."

Of her nephew, Judge Sharp said: "Fritz is bound to have been insane. I just can't conceive of any sane person doing what he did."

Several news stories reported that Rockingham Sheriff Bobby Vernon had granted Fritz fifty-one permits to buy handguns in recent years, noting that no permits were required for other weapons that he owned. Vernon, calling Fritz a "clean-cut and intelligent" gun collector, said he couldn't deny the permits.

"He was crazy about guns," Louise Sharp was quoted as saying of her nephew.

Other newspapers were still reporting that Fritz had attended Duke Medical School, but Brady and Vogel revealed in the *News & Record* that it all had been a hoax, that he'd never been enrolled nor received any formal training as a physician, although many people still thought him a doctor.

The *News & Record* also devoted a story to John and Jim, written by Sharon Bond. Several children from the apartment complex where the boys lived were quoted. They said the boys often wore military clothes, never went to the pool, rarely played outside.

"The only time they came out was when they walked the dogs," said Charlene Tatum, a neighbor, who was fourteen. "They didn't say anything. They just kept to themselves. They always stuck real close together. It was just those two little boys. When you saw one, you saw the other."

"They didn't have many friends," said Robbie Dunham, another neighbor, also fourteen.

Jim's teacher at Guilford Middle School, Judy Glascow, described the reaction to Jim's death of his classmates: "They took it hard. I don't think there was a dry eye in the class. It was just sobbing openly."

She asked her students to express their feelings in words and pictures, and one drew a picture of Jim at Disneyland. At show and tell, Jim had happily told about his trip to California with his daddy and Kathy.

Another Wednesday story in the *News & Record* told of Susie's Monday call to Bob Connolly, her UNC-G professor, to reschedule a test.

Connolly had talked at length with Susie about the strain she had been under since the murders.

"She appeared to be greatly concerned about her kids," Connolly said. "She talked about how she snatched the newspapers, tried to keep news reports of what had happened to their grandparents away from them. She talked about how they snuck the children into the church for the funeral and kept them away from the gravesite to keep them from being photographed. That seemed a little obsessive to me, but I didn't know at the time how affluent these people were."

Connolly said news reports belied everything he'd

learned about Susie's personality in the three weeks she had been in his class. He called her quiet and one of the most attentive students he'd ever had. He said other faculty members had told him that "the Susie Lynch in the paper was not the Susie Lynch they knew."

"I used to be in your business—a reporter—and after five years of interviewing and seven years as a teacher, I think I have a pretty good sense for people," Connolly said. "She either fooled me completely or the things in the paper are wrong. She was as nice a person as I've run into in this business. Cool, calm, and collected.

"I still can't get over how this woman sat here, extra calm and collected, and said these things. Of course, you never can tell about some people. Some, that's just the way they are. Others, it's a defense mechanism, and still others are dissembling. The whole thing about her and him and what happened reminds me of the Patty Hearst story."

Tom Lynch read Wednesday morning's news stories with growing anger. He had become convinced that Susie was involved in all the murders, and talk of her innocence grated. He was determined not to allow her to be portrayed as a Patty Hearst figure, a duped and brainwashed innocent, but other things had to be attended to first.

Tom and Kathy had arrived the day before; they were met at the airport by his old college friend, Bob Brenner, who took them into his home in High Point and made a car available for their use. On Tuesday night, they went to Greensboro to meet Dan Davidson, who was deeply distressed about the boys' deaths and dreaded facing Tom. For two hours, Davidson, Childers, and Nobles went over the events of the past few days. Tom talked about what a raw deal he'd gotten from North Carolina courts. If only he'd been given fair visitation to begin with, Tom said, none of this might have happened. But he didn't blame Davidson.

"I knew he would feel real bad," Tom said. "I knew it wasn't their fault. They'd done everything they could."

But Tom knew, too, that somebody had failed to ensure his sons' safety, and he wanted to know why.

"I just couldn't understand why it happened like this,"

he said, "why they couldn't have taken Fritz when he was alone."

He'd gotten no good answers to that question when he talked to SBI agents on Tuesday, and on Wednesday morning, when he received a call asking him to come to the SBI office in Greensboro, he thought he might get a better explanation.

He and Kathy were greeted by Tom Sturgill and Ed Hunt, the district supervisor, who ushered them into the conference room where, two weeks earlier, Sturgill and Gentry had interviewed Fritz. Hunt told them that other revelations were forthcoming and that he wanted them to know in advance. The boys, he said, had been given cyanide and shot in the head at close range before the explosion.

The news not only confirmed Tom's suspicions that Susie had a hand in destroying the boys, it convinced him that she had shot them herself. Two words described his feelings, and he uttered them to himself: "That monster."

The new revelations prompted Tom to an immediate decision. He would make himself available to the press.

"I couldn't let her get away with this," he explained later. "This was outrageous, more than just outrageous. As far as I was concerned, this was motherhood's worst moment. There had never been anything worse than this. Not only that, but to have a hand in killing your parents and your grandmother, too. This was a monstrosity. It's the equivalent of the Holocaust, of turning your family in to the Nazis and having them gassed. I just could not *not* do something about it."

On Wednesday afternoon a press conference was held at the Greensboro Police Department. Present were Greensboro Police Chief Conrad Wade, Ed Hunt, Allen Gentry, Reidsville Police Chief James Festerman, and Guilford County Sheriff Jim Proffitt. Hunt disclosed the autopsy findings to the surprised reporters. He revealed that a fragment of a 9-millimeter bullet had been taken from John's brain and that the bullet was believed to have been fired from a pistol found at the scene.

"In our opinion, it came from that vehicle," he said of the pistol. "It was found cocked and loaded, lying beside a telephone pole to the left of where the explosion took place."

Asked whether Susie or Fritz had shot the boys, Hunt said, "We're not drawing any conclusions until we see the final autopsy reports."

Chief Wade disclosed that a Forsyth deputy and a Kentucky officer had fired six shots when Fritz first opened fire at the intersection, and that a Forsyth deputy and an SBI agent had returned four more shots in the second exchange of fire a few minutes later. Hunt, who had been one of those firing, declined to identify any of the officers. Hunt also said that he knew of no hits by the officers.

"As best we can tell, the holes were from the inside out," he said. Later examination, however, would show at least one incoming bullet hole in the Blazer's rear panel.

Hunt also disclosed that the SBI was interviewing a "possible accomplice" in the Newsom murders but would neither identify him nor reveal what role he might have played.

Questioned about the nature of the bomb, Hunt replied, "I don't have a report on that at this time. There could be several possibilities. It may be some time before we get all the results on that."

Had problems in arresting Fritz been foreseen?

"Based on our information, we thought that there possibly could be problems," Hunt said. "The nature of the crimes we were going to arrest him for would indicate that."

Gentry told the reporters that Fritz had become a suspect "early on."

"A couple of family members had expressed a little concern over the relationship as well as over his background," he said. "He obviously had the interest and the capabilities. We had no idea just how capable he was until all this happened."

Chief Festerman revealed that large amounts of prescription drugs and vitamins had been found at the Klenner home and office, but that was not unusual for Dr. Klenner, he said.

"Dr. Klenner was a proponent of vitamin C and there

were large amounts of vitamin C in his office and his residence in boxes and cases," he went on.

Was Fritz selling drugs?

"During our investigation, we at no time found any indication that he was involved in selling narcotics," responded Gentry.

Was cyanide found at Susie's apartment or the Klenner house?

"Not to my knowledge," said Gentry.

While the officers were talking to reporters on Wednesday afternoon, Tom was doing the same. In the next thirty-six hours, he granted several interviews, but the first was with Jim Schlosser of the *Greensboro News & Record,* whom he told he wouldn't be surprised if proof emerged that Susie had shot the boys.

"I kind of assumed that she might have fired the shots because Fritz was busy driving," he said.

He labeled as "ridiculous" claims that Susie might not have been aware of Fritz's involvement in the murders.

"She may have been the mastermind-manipulator," he said.

He said officers had told him that Susie might have gone to Kentucky with Fritz to point out his mother's house, which would be difficult to locate otherwise. He thought Susie wanted his mother dead because she believed Delores was paying for his court fight.

"I wasn't attempting to make Susie look bad," he said, "only to make increased visitation look good."

Tom quoted Susie's father as calling her "headstrong, stubborn, and pathological in her paranoia about her children."

"She wrapped herself in a world with those boys," Tom said. "It was them against everyone else. She just thought everyone was trying to get her kids away from her.

"Fritz was her protector. They fed off each other's paranoia. She reinforced him. He reinforced her. You talk of spiraling insanity, this is the worst I have ever hard of."

Tom told of his own fear after the Newsom murders ("I had the guns loaded and the windows locked") and of his and Kathy's frantic efforts to try to get the boys from Susie and Fritz after the murders.

"They wouldn't have let them go," he said dejectedly. "They were not going to let the kids live if they were caught. The boys were doomed."

Tom summed up his feelings with two sentences: "I don't know what I think about this at this time. I'm just so angry."

On Wednesday morning, a group of officers and the Greensboro Police Department bomb squad showed up at the Mountain, the Klenner farm a mile east of Eden on Chumley Road. Reporters were not allowed onto the rugged, wooded property bordering the Dan River, and while the officers searched, reporters talked to neighbors. Frank Underwood, a sixty-three-year-old man who lived nearby, told them that once when his brother, George, was walking near the property, Fritz appeared from the woods, pulled a .44 Magnum, and ordered him never to come near the land again. S. B. Gilley, a sixty-eight-year-old farmer who had looked after the land for two years, told them: "In my book, they are fine people. I've never met the boy, but Mr. and Mrs. Klenner, when he was living, were as nice a people as I've ever known."

When the search was completed, Wednesday afternoon, Rockingham County Sheriff Bobby Vernon revealed that the officers had found some empty casings for a .223 rifle, three reinforced foxhole bunkers, two of which appeared recently dug, several campsites, twenty-five well-tended marijuana plants, and twenty-five pounds of ammonium nitrate, a fertilizer that, when mixed with fuel oil, creates an explosive. No weapons were found.

On Wednesday at 7 P.M., a memorial service was held for John and Jim at St. Andrew's Episcopal Church in Greensboro. The boys' bodies were not present. Tom had gone earlier to a funeral home to see them and make arrangements to have them flown to Albuquerque.

"They didn't look dead," he sorrowfully told a reporter later. "They looked asleep. They didn't look mangled or anything."

Nearly one hundred people, including some of John's

and Jim's classmates, attended the service. Tom, Kathy, and other family members filed into the church behind the priest.

"And anyone who has life, and has committed himself to me in faith shall not die forever," the priest intoned during the ten-minute service, as he asked God to "take James and John into your kingdom of heaven."

After the service, Tom and Kathy received callers at the Newsom home in Greensboro. When Susie Sharp said to Tom, "I just can't believe Susie would have had anything to do with killing those boys," Kathy became so angry that Tom had to lead her into another room to calm down.

YOUTHS POISONED, SHOT BEFORE BLAST, read the front-page headline in Thursday morning's *Greensboro News & Record.*

The shocking news was the first strong public evidence that Susie might have been something more than an innocent bystander in the bizarre series of events. But Susie's family simply could not accept that she had taken part in killing her children.

"She wouldn't have allowed that," Susie Sharp told the *News & Record.* "Maybe she was dead and sitting up in the seat before they were killed. The possibilities are limitless. I just can't imagine even a crazy person being so deranged."

Louise blamed Fritz completely. "She was under his power," she said.

The *Winston-Salem Journal* quoted District Attorney Tisdale as saying an undercover person had provided information that Fritz might choose suicide over arrest.

"We had an insight into him that he wouldn't be taken alive," he said. "They were trying to handle him with kid gloves, but this man couldn't be handled with kid gloves.

"To be quite honest with you, if they weren't going to have the children, nobody was."

On Thursday morning, an unannounced graveside service with only family members and close friends in attendance was held for Fritz at Greenview Cemetery in Reidsville. He was buried beside his father. The footstone on Dr.

Klenner's grave read, BELOVED PHYSICIAN. The stone that would be placed at Fritz's grave would read, DEVOTED SON.

Thursday afternoon's *Reidsville Review* carried a story in which Louise responded to Tom's charge that Susie might have accompanied Fritz to Kentucky to kill Delores and Janie.

"I don't believe it," she said. "I don't believe one word of it."

Neither could she accept that Susie might have been involved in any of the other killings.

"We feel that she was afraid of an unknown killer," she said.

Susie Sharp was quoted as calling Susie "a most devoted mother, almost overprotective of the children." She said that her niece had become withdrawn and very fearful in the past year.

She said of Fritz: "I've come to the conclusion he was evidently a paranoid schizophrenic."

Louise called Fritz "obsessed and insane." She said Dr. Klenner was very possessive of his son and wouldn't let him see his aunts.

"I didn't have any affection for him," she said of Fritz. "He was taught to have little affection for his aunts. His daddy seemed to feel we wouldn't mold the child the way he wanted him to be molded."

One thing Louise didn't mention was that, a year earlier, the Sharp family home had been broken into and her jewelry and the family silver stolen. She and her sister Susie had been certain that Fritz had done it. Fritz never visited his aunts, but one day the previous summer he had shown up at the house and told Louise he wanted to inspect her locks because he was concerned about her security. She had let him in, and after a tour of the house, he had pronounced her locks woefully insufficient. A week later, while Louise was out of town, the house was broken into and the jewelry and silver were taken. But Louise and Susie had not been able to bring themselves to tell the police about their suspicions of Fritz. He was family, after all, and they didn't want to risk hurting their sister Annie Hill and creating a family scandal. The police had never solved the crime.

The Sharp and Newsom families gathered for a memorial service for Susie at 2 P.M. on Thursday in the same sanctuary where the service for the boys had been held the night before. Her body had been cremated, and her ashes were interred in the church columbarium.

After his sister's service, Rob granted his first interview to two reporters from the *News & Record.* He described Susie, whom he'd seen only infrequently in the past twenty years, as "bright, hard-working, very reliable, very dependable, always carried through." He told of her estrangement from her family, of her family's fear that she was growing inward and too dependent on Fritz.

"We felt she was becoming very, very isolated, very withdrawn, that she wasn't sharing her feelings or her plans with anyone but her cousin," he said.

His parents thought that an "unhealthy relationship," he said.

He told of his November meeting with Susie, during which she had expressed her fears of losing her children and being murdered. He revealed that she had been seeing a psychiatrist and had attended three group therapy sessions to try to learn to detach from her children.

Several months earlier, he said, he had arranged another meeting with his sister and Fritz to try to get a reading on how things were going. They met for lunch at Stamey's Barbecue and had "the most normal conversation you can imagine," mostly about his work as an alcoholism counselor.

He last saw his sister on the Saturday before her death, he said, when she came to his house and spent nearly an hour talking about their parents' estate.

"She did not seem any more distant or different than she had for the past several years."

Rob said he couldn't believe that Susie had any part in the murders. "Nothing that has been disclosed to me by any police agency would lead me to believe that she was a participant," he said, noting that he realized that Tom felt otherwise. "I certainly do understand why he thinks to the contrary. We have made it clear we are going to respect one another's feelings."

The blame, Rob felt, lay completely on Fritz. "I believe that Fritz came to see himself as my sister's and her children's protector and defender and anyone who irritated her or seemed to be causing her difficulty in her life, he set out to eliminate them. In his illness, that's how he saw reality. Maybe in his illness he thought if he killed my sister and the boys before he went, it was like protecting them. I don't think he had any more control over his own destiny and his own behavior than my sister did. I think their lives were just out of control and completely unmanageable."

At the same time Rob was talking to reporters, Annie Hill Klenner and her two daughters were granting an interview to Jack Scism, of the *News & Record,* whose mother once had been a patient of Dr. Klenner. Annie Hill's main purpose in giving the interview was to clarify what she said were inaccuracies about the weapons and explosives that had been found at her house.

Most of the guns taken by police had belonged to her gun-collecting husband, Annie Hill explained.

"It was Doctor's hobby before Fritz was ever born. I could not tell you offhand the date of purchases, but I know there have always been guns around here and some are collector's items. It's not something Fritz started."

She was particularly concerned about a .12-gauge cannon listed as being seized. It was just a "toy" replica of a Civil War cannon that fired a shotgun shell, she said, but it had caused great apprehension and misunderstanding in Reidsville.

"People drive by and slow down and you know they're looking for the gun emplacement," her daughter Gertrude said.

The dynamite found at the house had been bought by Doctor to remove stumps and boulders at the farm, Annie Hill said. She noted that she had been unaware of the land mines and submachine gun.

She could offer only one explanation for her son's recent actions: he had multiple sclerosis, diagnosed by his father in 1977, which had gone untreated since Doctor's death.

"When his father was alive, he gave him treatment for it. Since then, there's been no one to give him that, and he's had some difficulty. Sometimes he had to use a cane, and he's had eye problems.

"In his right mind, he would not harm a flea. If he has done something like that, it certainly was out of keeping with his character, and the only explanation I have is that he was sick and had all he could take."

Both of Fritz's sisters pointed out that he loved children, and Mary Ann called him "a very, very caring person."

Annie Hill acknowledged that Fritz had pretended to go to medical school to please his father, who, she said, was ill with heart problems and always had dreamed that Fritz would succeed him.

"Fritz told me he started it as a charade, but it built up so big he did not know how to stop it."

Fritz's relationship with Susie, she said, was simply one of consoling and helping, and she had joined in it.

"I went to Susie's apartment; they came here. I cooked for them, mended, ironed, did anything they needed, and I loved them both the same way."

As Annie Hill spoke, officers were completing the two-day cleanup job of removing drugs and vitamins from Dr. Klenner's clinic in downtown Reidsville. All told, four dump truck loads were hauled away to be destroyed.

The main story in Friday's *News & Record* quoted Ed Hunt, the SBI district supervisor, as saying Fritz had left a note naming an accomplice in the Newsom murders.

"It was not a confession," Hunt said. "I really don't want to address the specifics of it. It might bear on another case."

Hunt wouldn't name the accomplice, who, he said, drove Fritz to Winston-Salem on the night of the murders but didn't take part in the killing.

Fritz's note, Hunt said, contained statements "about some of the crimes he thought he was accused of. He knew he was a suspect. I'm not sure about the Kentucky cases, but I'm sure he knew he was suspected in the Winston-Salem crimes."

Hunt said the note wasn't a suicide note, didn't imply that Fritz wouldn't be taken alive, and didn't indicate whether Susie knew about Fritz's involvement in the murders.

Despite Hunt's claim that a case might be developed against an accomplice, the *Winston-Salem Journal* was reporting that District Attorney Tisdale had called the case closed and said that "no charges would be brought against an unnamed man who gave Klenner a ride to Old Town." The paper quoted Captain Ron Barker of the Forsyth County Sheriff's Department as saying the accomplice "didn't know what Klenner planned to do."

Friday's *Journal* also offered quotes from John S. Shumaker of Rural Hall, near Winston-Salem, who said he had been Fritz's friend and patient for three years. Fritz had confided to him that he had been in Special Forces and was a member of the Delta Team. Shumaker had been impressed when Fritz predicted certain Russian moves in Afghanistan. He called Fritz a patriot and a staunch anti-Communist, and said that he never seemed violent.

"He was reasonable and sane," Shumaker said.

Shumaker said Fritz confided in him that he and Susie lived together without sex.

"He said they just shared an apartment and he had taken up with the kids."

Shumaker said Fritz had treated him for low blood pressure and a dislocated shoulder as recently as November 1984, six months after Dr. Klenner's death.

"As far as I know, he was a doctor," he said.

The story that attracted the most attention on Friday was the one in which Annie Hill placed the blame for Fritz's actions on his supposed multiple sclerosis. It provoked outrage from MS patients and the National MS Society.

Saturday's *News & Record* quoted Stephen Reingold, the National MS Society's vice president of research and development, as saying: "I think the newspaper and this woman are doing an enormous disservice to the 250,000 persons with multiple sclerosis in the country by attributing such pathological social behavior to this disease when there is absolutely no evidence that this is the case."

The story quoted Dr. John Butts, the medical examiner who had performed the autopsy on Fritz, as saying that he saw no signs that Fritz suffered from MS, although he couldn't be absolutely certain that Fritz didn' have it.

"It's not always obvious," Butts said. "It is a disease with progressive stages and early stages. There may be very little to see."

The story went on to note that Dr. Klenner was not a neurologist and that doctors with neurological backgrounds often disagreed with his diagnoses.

"As far as I know," Dr. Butts said about MS, "i doesn't induce people to collect guns and kill other people."

Of Fritz, he said, "If he had severe multiple sclerosis he couldn't have been able to be running around shooting people."

Both the *Greensboro News & Record* and the *Winston Salem Journal* offered recaps of the week's events in their Sunday editions. The *Journal*, which had lagged in coverage all week, used the occasion to catch up. Written by Tom Sieg, the paper's experienced columnist, the story filled half the front page and two inside pages.

It offered further evidence that even close family members hadn't been told that Fritz had never gone to medical school.

"He was very devoted to his father," said Bill Palmer a Mississippi lawyer married to Fritz's sister Mary Ann "He felt his father wanted him to be a doctor and anything his father wanted to do, Fritz would do it. . . . When his father died, he was supposedly finishing up hi internship at Chapel Hill under some sort of special program. . . . After his father died . . . it all seemed too much for him to take."

Sandy Sands, Susie's lawyer, pegged the beginning of Susie's fears on Tom's attempt to have custody decide in New Mexico. "She was always convinced that there was something funny going on because of the first judge not releasing jurisdiction. . . . Susie was very, very concerned—and rightly so—that there was so much trouble. . . . One of the basic fears she had was that if the children got out to New Mexico . . . Tom would start it all over again. . . . This was a fear that was with her from 1981 until she died."

Susie's fears had convinced Sands that she had no role in the murders. "There is no doubt in my mind that she felt the deaths in Kentucky were a result of some gangland hit, and she was afraid that it was the result of some tie-in Tom had."

Sands said he was also convinced that when the police closed in the previous Monday, Susie thought they were actually killers who had come for her and the boys.

But Susie's aunt Frances and cousin Nancy were quoted as saying they believed Susie accompanied Fritz to Kentucky to kill Delores and Janie and that the evidence would be forthcoming.

Asked about Susie's possible complicity in the murders of her parents and grandmother, Frances said, "I'm having real difficulty with that question. When I think about it, I wonder how an intelligent person—and Susie was very intelligent, she was very smart—how an intelligent person could be exposed to all these guns and all this stuff and not put two and two together."

Tom also was quoted about Susie. "I don't want people to think she was a poor little Patty Hearst under the influence of some lunatic," he said. "I believe . . . that she knew what was going on."

Albuquerque is a city set in a vast raw landscape of desert grays and reds, spotted with scrub growth, unmercifully beaten by the sun. Rainfall is scant, and those who desire the comforts of green growth must water it faithfully.

One of the city's largest expanses of grass and trees is called Sunset Memorial Park. Shortly before noon on Monday, June 10, with the help of friends, Tom carried the small coffins bearing the bodies of his sons across that green oasis to their final resting places beneath a spreading cedar.

In the weeks to come, he would return to this spot nearly every day to stand looking at the tiny graves with temporary markers bearing the names of John and Jim.

On one of those occasions, a Sunday morning brittle with heat, he brought with him a visitor. At the gravesite, he stood for long moments, saying nothing as birds sang in nearby trees. Finally he spoke, his voice breaking.

"I wanted you to see it," he said, "so you could tell the people back in North Carolina that I got them a shady spot."

And he began to cry.

46

Early on the Monday morning that John and Jim were to be buried in Albuquerque, the detectives in the Newsom murder case met at the Forsyth County Sheriff's Department with Sheriff Preston Oldham and District Attorney Don Tisdale. The subject was Ian Perkins.

The officers didn't want Ian to be charged. They thought that he had been genuinely duped by Fritz, that he had displayed courage by helping them, and that he had made amends by risking his life. They felt an obligation to Ian, and argued his case with Tisdale.

Caught between the pressures of the officers and those of Newsom family members who wanted Ian prosecuted, Tisdale decided he had to seek an indictment.

"In my way of thinking, it would have been unconscionable not to have an accountability there," he explained later.

No matter what he had done to make amends, Ian had knowingly set out to kill somebody, even though he thought he was acting in behalf of his country, Tisdale noted.

"You can't condone that kind of conduct. It's dangerous no matter whose name it is in, God or country or creed. People who kill in the name of God and country are probably more dangerous than people who kill for greed. You don't know where these clowns are coming from."

Tisdale placated the officers by agreeing to charge Ian only with accessory after the fact of murder, a far less serious charge than accessory before the fact.

After the meeting, Oldham held a press conference to announce that an indictment would be sought. The name of the person would be revealed, he said, "when the indictment is handed down and the person is charged."

That would not be for two weeks, when the grand jury next met.

"Our opinion is that an indictment can be handed down and probably will be," he said.

Oldham went on to tantalize the reporters a little.

"This is the type of case that'll drive you crazy," he said. "It's had more surprises than any case I can remember. It's a unique case. It's got all kinds of twists and bends. You talk about bizarre. It's got twists and turns you wouldn't believe. The twists I know, I can't reveal."

When would they be revealed? That would depend on whether there was an indictment and when it came to trial, Oldham said.

And if there was no indictment?

Then the information wouldn't be released, Oldham said with a small grin of satisfaction.

Ian was indicted June 24 on three counts of accessory after the fact of murder. Allen Gentry appeared before the grand jury for about an hour, and the indictments were issued before noon. At 2 P.M., Ian arrived at the Hall of Justice to turn himself in, accompanied by his attorney, Jim Medford. Reporters, TV camera crews, and photographers swarmed around the pair as they were ushered into Gentry's office. Ian looked pale and frightened. A short, neat young man with darting dark eyes and a military haircut, he wore a blue blazer, a striped tie, khaki pants, and moccasin-type loafers. After preliminary processing, Ian and Medford went upstairs to Tisdale's office, where they were joined by Ian's mother and stepfather.

Medford wanted Tisdale to drop charges, or failing that, to agree to a plea bargain that would grant Ian a probationary sentence. A tall, hulking man with a round Irish face and a poet's soul, Medford was a member of one of the state's largest and most prestigious law firms, a North Carolina native, a cum laude graduate of Harvard Law School, a Fulbright scholar. He knew that he was not in a good bargaining position. His client had admitted guilt without seeing an attorney and had already done all that he could to help the police.

Tisdale was firm. He would not drop the charges or make any deals. But he indicated that he would not fight for an active sentence.

After the meeting, Ian, visibly trembling, his eyes red from crying, was taken before Superior Court Judge William H. Freeman, Jr., for a bond hearing. Medford pointed out Ian's cooperation with the authorities, and Tisdale noted that he was "probably responsible for making" the case against Fritz.

"I have no reason to believe he will not show up," Tisdale told the judge.

Freeman set a $25,000 unsecured bond, and Ian left with his mother and stepfather.

Quoting the district attorney, the next morning's *Journal* described Tisdale as sounding "as much like a defense attorney as a prosecutor."

"I wouldn't guarantee him probation," Tisdale said. "I would leave that to a judge. I wouldn't oppose it. . . ."

He also said this about Ian: "He's extremely patriotic. He was playing war games at a time when he should have been doing something else. . . . This is probably a prime example of too much television and too many *Rambo* movies."

Tisdale acknowledged that Ian had made three tapes with Fritz, and said that he would play them at the trial. The tapes, he said, would show Ian's limited role in the murders.

Ian was scheduled for arraignment on July 9, but did not appear in court. Instead, Medford waived the proceeding, and trial was set for July 29. But Medford maneuvered to have the trial delayed two days so that Ian would come before Judge Edward Washington.

A tall, rawboned man, Washington had played football at the University of North Carolina with Charlie "Choo-Choo" Justice. Elected district judge in 1968, he was appointed chief judge for the 18th district by Susie Sharp in 1976. Two years later, he moved up to superior court. Now sixty-two, and a year from retirement, Washington was a kind, sincere man, a favorite of defense attorneys, who called him decent and fair. Prosecutors tended to think him too easy. Tisdale, who liked Washington ("He's easy but he's very honest and serious"), didn't resist the move.

"Are you in fact guilty?" Washington asked in a rumbling voice as Ian stood before him on July 31.

"Yes," Ian said in a gush of tears.

Gentry took the stand to sketch in details of the case, to tell of interviewing Ian and of Ian's agreeing to help. He read the note Fritz had left exonerating Ian. Gentry was followed by SBI agent J. W. Bryant, who told of wiring Ian and gave details of the three taping sessions. Bryant played the tapes of the first two sessions for the judge. When he left the stand without playing the third tape, a stir went up among reporters. Why wasn't the tape being played? Was something on it that the SBI didn't want known?

Rob was next on the stand, speaking slowly and thoughtfully in behalf of the family.

"I wanted the court to know most of all that the people who died that night weren't just special to us," he said, "that Hattie Carter Newsom was easily the most beloved person in her community, and that my mother and father had been active in civic affairs in this city and in Greensboro, and that in addition to the emotional impact on the family that there are two communities which are going to miss them very, very much. Certainly I miss their wise counsel and advice and gentle ways and the rest of the family does too.

"I think the feeling that the family would like to convey to the court about the emotional impact of all this is that it's rather like being a survivor of the Holocaust. We've lost four generations of people. Aunt and cousin are the closest kin I have left aside from my children. Others have suffered similarly.

"We simply cannot foresee what all the consequences of this are going to be. I have an eight-year-old son who every once in a while wants to know where children can get bullet-proof vests.

"I don't think that we'll see life in quite the same way that we did before.

"The other thing that the family would like to express is just the impact it's had on things like the homeplace itself. The residence on Valley Road was the family homeplace, and it was so full of good memories . . . and for economic reasons and emotional ones, we simply won't have that place anymore.

"The family feels that what we've lost is an awful lot to lose. At least at this point, we can't foresee a time when we'll be free of all this."

Medford called Ian to the stand and led him gently through his association with Fritz and his involvement in the murders.

"That Saturday night in Winston-Salem, did you believe that you were on a mission for the United States government?" Medford asked.

"I did."

"Was there any doubt in your mind about it?"

"There was no doubt at that time."

Ian went on to explain that doubt did not surface until Gentry and Sturgill came to Lexington to ask about his activities that night. He had been uncomfortable having to lie, he said, because of his school's honor code, but thought he had to for national security reasons. But when the officers began pointing out discrepancies, he realized that he could not stick with his story.

"It struck me that something was just very wrong," he said. "It didn't make a lot of sense. I figured the best thing I could do was tell them the truth and do whatever they wanted me to do."

He told of assisting the officers in trying to find evidence the following day, of their asking him to come to Winston-Salem to try to trap Fritz.

"Were you willing to do so?" Medford asked.

"Yes, I was."

"Why?"

Ian took a long pause. "Because," he said, beginning to sob, "I had realized that something was terribly wrong, and I wanted to attempt to right that wrong as much as I could."

"Were you frightened to get in the car with Fritz?"

"Yes, I was."

"Now, Ian, sitting there right now, do you have any regrets for having cooperated with the police?"

"No," Ian said, crying again. "I have no regrets at all. I was glad to be able to help."

Tisdale evoked laughter when he asked Ian about his grades. Ian said he got a D on the final exam with which Fritz had helped him. The course was medical ethics.

Tisdale asked only a few questions. Among them was this: "Going back to May of this year, did you think it was legal for somebody to be killed even by the CIA?"

"That was a point I had to wrestle with," Ian said. "It is an odious thing, but I figured if by my actions that I could prevent even an iota of suffering from those who might possibly become hooked on drugs as a result of what I believed to be the situation that Fritz told me about, then I thought and I sincerely believe that it was worth the stain upon myself."

The answer left the impression that Ian still believed his actions were right, causing Medford to wince. When Tisdale passed the witness, Medford sought to clarify the point.

"In response to the district attorney's question about whether you thought killing a drug dealer was legal, let me ask you, you replied as you saw it, you felt it was. Was that because you felt you were working for the United States government?"

"Yes, I would not have attempted to do that on my own."

Medford submitted the results of a polygraph test showing that Ian was telling the truth about his role in the murders, and his associate Jack Floyd, who had also worked on the case, called Norwood Robinson as a character witness.

Robinson, a prominent Reidsville lawyer, lived next door to Ian's family on Huntsdale Road. He had known the family for thirty years and had first met Ian when Ian came to visit his grandmother as a small child. When he first came to Reidsville, Robinson worked with James Sharp, and he knew all the Sharps. Later, he worked with Sandy Sands, Susie's attorney. He was a friend of Bob and Florence Newsom and was well acquainted with the Klenners. He had known Fritz from babyhood.

He was shocked, he said, when Ian's father told him that Ian was involved in the murders and wanted to talk to him. Ian's father wanted him to defend Ian, but he could not because of his associations with the families involved. Nevertheless, he offered Ian his counsel on "two or three" occasions.

"Ian cried about it," he said. "In fact, he told me at one point that when the enormity of the situation hit him that if he'd had the .45 he would have killed himself, he would have committed suicide, and he broke down and cried, said it just absolutely got to him.

"I was concerned that he might even try to do that at that time. He was very much upset about it. I told his stepfather about what he did tell me, but Ian assured me he was not going to do anything like that. I talked to him and told him that would not solve anything."

"Do you know Ian Perkins's reputation for character in the community?" Floyd asked.

"Yes, sir."

"What is that?"

"It's good."

"Yeah," somebody cracked in the press room, "just don't let him mistake you for a drug dealer."

"What you've heard here today," Medford said in his closing arguments, "is an absolute tragedy from all aspects of it. In all of this bizarre happening, it's clear that the person behind it was Fritz Klenner, the person who sucked Ian Perkins into believing through all sorts of subtle means that he, Fritz Klenner, was working for the CIA, was doing a job for his government, and when he found out about Ian Perkins's background, it looks like to me that he laid a trap for him starting in November and going on into May.

"There is no excuse for the absolute utter naïveté of this young man, but I think when he accompanied Fritz to Winston-Salem, he thought he was not doing anything wrong. . . . He thought he was doing something for his country.

"Your honor, I confess to you, when I heard the initial outline of the story, I said, This just can't be right. The more I heard and the more I got to understand Ian, the more I came to see how something that on its surface is totally bizarre, how Ian could believe it.

"Your honor, I realize that this is a very difficult

decision, but I want to emphasize from the bottom of my heart, I do not think that an active sentence for this young man would serve any useful purpose."

Jack Floyd spoke of punishment in his closing remarks. "Insofar as we can be punished in this world, I submit to you that this young man has undergone it. He's suffering as he sits here now.

"He put his life on the line; he sat on a bomb to try to help the authorities get evidence to bring Fritz Klenner to justice. He will continue to suffer no matter what your honor may adjudge today.

"He has demonstrated throughout his life that he is committed to his God and his country. He thought he was serving his country when he got pulled into this thing. He was set up beautifully to do as Fritz Klenner wanted him to do. He is probably as vulnerable as they come. Active time, your honor, may complete the ruin of this young man that Klenner started."

"Insofar as Mr. Perkins is concerned," intoned the judge, "I cannot believe, nor can the law be construed to allow any individual to share in a plan where a person is to be executed without trial, without an opportunity to defend himself, or herself, without a determination of that person's guilt."

He went on to quote a North Carolina Supreme Court decision in another case. " 'If we take our eyes from the law and give our attention only to consequences, or if we stop to consider who is morally right or wrong without regard to right or wrong as judicially ascertained, we will soon have a government not of law but without law, and the lawlessness which is sought to be avoided will follow as an inevitable result.' "

The judge noted Ian's immaturity. "But ignorance of the law has been described as no excuse. Does then naïveté or gullibility present a mitigating factor? There is no evidence of threat. There is no evidence of duress. There is evidence that the role of this person was a minor role. . . ."

Ian had risked his life to assist the officers, Washington pointed out. "From that standpoint then it could be said that he voluntarily acknowledged his wrong at an early stage of the criminal investigation. . . .

"Mr. Perkins, stand up, please, sir."

Ian rose, trembling.

"This court and the law give to you the right to make the last statement to the court before judgment is pronounced. Do you have anything else you'd like to say?"

"Your honor," Ian said, struggling to hold back tears as he spoke with hesitation, "I can't take away the pain that the Newsoms suffer, nor do I blame them for what they feel. They have every right." He paused, sniffling. "Nor can I expect myself to not share some of the pain that they suffer. But my only desire is"—his voice broke—"to see justice done."

He dabbed at his tears.

"Take your time," the judge said.

"That's all, your honor."

With that, Washington sentenced Ian to six years, suspended on grounds that he serve a four-month active sentence, remain on probation five years, and pay a $3,000 fine. Medford asked for a five-day delay in having Ian report to jail, and it was granted.

Ian's family was surprised that he got an active sentence, although his attorneys were not unhappy with it. Members of the Newsom family, however, thought the sentence too lenient.

"He was kind of pitiful," Frances Miller said much later of Ian. "He was a nerd to be that gullible. People have to be responsible for their own actions, though. I just didn't feel it was enough punishment."

Before the year was out, noted Nancy Dunn, Frances's daughter, Ian would be free to start his life anew.

"We'd like to start new lives, too, but we can't," she said. "Why should he?"

47

At the close of Ian's trial, reporters swarmed around the district attorney, asking why the third tape hadn't been played. On that tape Ian asked Fritz whether he'd murdered the Newsoms and Fritz claimed he was being set up. Fritz hinted at suicide and told Ian that he had things to do and wouldn't see him again. But only the police and attorneys knew what was on the tape, and none had made any of the contents public. Was there something that the police wanted to keep hidden? Nothing that he knew about, Tisdale responded. He had not played the third tape, he said, for the simple reason that after listening to two tapes, the judge indicated that he didn't care to hear the third.

Tisdale said he wanted the tape made public, and told reporters to call SBI agent J. W. Bryant, who would play it for them. But Bryant said no on orders from SBI Deputy Director Harold Elliott, who said the tape would not be released without a court order. Apprised of this, Tisdale said he would get the tape and play it for reporters, but the SBI denied it even to him.

The following day, the *Greensboro News & Record* filed a motion seeking a court order releasing the tape, but later dropped it after the SBI's feisty director, Robert Morgan, told the paper's editors that he would fight to the Supreme Court if necessary and the paper's lawyers advised that the SBI likely would win.

North Carolina law required the SBI to keep all investigative records secret, but custom allowed top officials to release as much information as they deemed appropriate.

Usually any information that made the agency look good was released. All else was kept secret.

Because some information deemed inappropriate for public purview had been leaked to reporters and unfriendly politicians, the SBI had become almost obsessed with secrecy.

Although primarily an assistance agency for local police, the SBI wouldn't even provide copies of investigative reports to those it assisted. In some instances, it was resentful of supplying documents to district attorneys. Agents who slipped copies of reports to fellow law enforcement officers knew that they did so in the face of certain dismissal and criminal charges. Agents knew, too, that they spoke to reporters at the risk of their careers, prompting most to remain mum.

Critics suspected that the real reasons for the strict secrecy were to allow the SBI to cover ineptitude and inaction and to use its considerable power against political enemies of the director and attorney general as well as perceived enemies of the state and big business (the SBI had been criticized, for example, for infiltrating and monitoring peaceful anti-nuclear-power groups while bothering little to keep tabs on heavily armed and violent racist and right-wing commando groups). The SBI was susceptible to political use because it answered only to the elected attorney general and was without review from the governor or effective legislative control. The press found penetrating the SBI's operations difficult and rarely attempted it with succes.

Started in 1938 with only a dozen agents, the SBI had remained small until Robert Morgan was elected attorney general in 1968. A former state senator who entered statewide politics as campaign manager for a segregationist candidate for governor, Morgan transformed the SBI from an agency with only 70 employees and a budget of less than $700,000 into one with 270 employees and a $4 million budget. He reveled in being called the "father of the modern SBI" and presided over it for six years before being elected to the U.S. Senate.

Although his single term in Washington was without notable achievement, Morgan seemed a likely candidate for reelection in 1980. His opponent was an obscure, right-wing, wheelchair-bound college professor, John East, the candidate of the National Congressional Club, which raised millions to finance the campaigns of North Carolina's radical Senator Jesse Helms and other arch conservatives. Morgan had been declared the most conservative Democrat in the Senate by the American Conservative Union, and Ralph Nader had labeled him a "corporate tout," but with the Congressional Club's help, East mounted a campaign of deceptive TV commercials that painted Morgan liberal and led to his defeat.

"They were saying things like 'Morgan's for killing babies' or 'Morgan's soft on Commies,'" Morgan later complained to a reporter. "It left me with bitter feelings."

Morgan practiced law and lobbied the legislature after his loss. He was considering a return to politics when Lacy Thornburg was elected attorney general in 1984. Thornburg succeeded Rufus Edmisten, who gave up the attorney general's office in an unsuccessful bid for the governorship. During his tenure, Edmisten, who gained fame as Sam Ervin's assistant in the Watergate hearings, had made brazen political use of the SBI. By the time Thornburg was elected, the SBI had burgeoned into a powerful bureaucracy of more than 500 employees with a budget of more than $16 million, and Thornburg, a former legislator and superior court judge, took office promising to free the agency from politics. To do that, he appointed an old friend, Robert Morgan, as SBI director.

That a politician should be charged with eliminating politics from the state police seemed high irony, especially a politician of Morgan's disposition. A short, banty-rooster-like man, Morgan harbored a peevish temper that was almost legendary. As a state senator, he once threatened to punch a fellow legislator who joked about his stature. As a U.S. senator, he angrily disputed constituents who disagreed with him.

"If somebody says no to him, he's going to stand up and scream and stomp his feet," a friend once told a reporter.

"If he gets peeved at you, he's a real mean person," an aide said.

"There will be no personal or partisan political roles in the SBI so long as I am associated with it," Morgan said at his swearing-in ceremony. "I come to this assignment, to this opportunity, with but one thought in mind, and that is to give the people of North Carolina the most effective law enforcement possible."

Now reporters wondered if politics might be the reason the SBI was keeping the Newsom murder investigation so secret. From the beginning, the SBI had released only the results of the autopsies, which were public records anyway. What had been done to determine whether Susie had anything to do with the murders of her parents and grandmother? Why wasn't the attempt to arrest Fritz made before he got back to the apartment? Had any effort been made to find out whether Fritz or Susie had poisoned and shot the children? Did hand wipings taken from Fritz and Susie by the medical examiners reveal whether Susie had fired a weapon? What kind of bomb had been in the Blazer? All these questions and many more went unanswered. What purpose was served by keeping such information secret when the case was effectively closed and no trial could be jeopardized by release of the information? The SBI wouldn't say.

Reports circulated that both Morgan and Thornburg had taken an unusual interest in the investigation, with Morgan closely monitoring events on the day of the shootout and explosion. Added to this, the SBI's refusal to allow the third tape to be heard publicly raised several questions. Was the SBI trying to hide something? Was somebody trying to protect former Chief Justice Sharp and her family from embarrassment? Was the SBI trying to cover a bungled operation? Had the agent in charge acted with proper caution in trying to arrest Fritz, considering that the boys in the Blazer were essentially hostages? Should officers have fired at the Blazer knowing the boys were inside? Was the SBI fearful of a lawsuit from Tom Lynch?

Six days after Ian's trial, the *Greensboro News & Record* revealed that the SBI had been warned that Fritz would not be taken alive and that methods used by some officers to stop him—"John Wayne tactics," veteran officers called them—endangered police and bystanders.

More significantly, the paper reported that the SBI had an earlier file on Fritz, that Sam Phillips and John Forrest had told an SBI agent four years earlier that Fritz was "a dangerous psychopath," who was practicing medicine without a license, but nothing had been done about it.

Surely, even a perfunctory investigation would have revealed that Fritz was posing as a doctor, treating patients and passing out prescription drugs. The unasked question in the story was clear: Had the SBI declined to act against Fritz because it learned that he was the nephew of the recently retired chief justice of the state supreme court, a greatly admired figure in state political circles?

"It was never brought to my attention," said Rufus Edmisten, attorney general at the time the report was made. "I wish it had been."

Justice Sharp said she'd never been told that her nephew had been reported to the SBI.

"If the SBI knew that and didn't do anything about it, I think that was reprehensible," she said.

Robert Morgan reacted angrily to the story, calling it "Monday morning quarterbacking." Of the attempt to arrest Fritz, he said: "I can think of a hundred scenarios of how it might have been handled differently, but I'm not sure the results would have been different. We did the best we could under the circumstances."

He called his agents' handling of the case "commendable."

Morgan acknowledged that Fritz had been reported to the SBI four years earlier. Ignoring that the point of the report was that Fritz was practicing medicine without a license, he noted that the SBI regularly gets allegations about dangerous people and that being a "dangerous psychopath" is no grounds for arrest.

"Apparently a lot of people in the Greensboro area who knew him didn't think he was a psychopath," Morgan said. "There were a lot of people who thought he was all right."

Despite Morgan's close involvement in the investigation and his strongly stated opinions about it, Attorney General Thornburg appointed him to conduct an inquiry into his agency's handling of the case.

Morgan's report was ready ten days later, on August 15, and he and Thornburg appeared at a press conference at SBI headquarters in Raleigh to reveal it. Thornburg spoke first, but only briefly. He said he was satisfied that the case had been handled in a "competent and commendable manner." He went on to especially commend Ed Hunt, the SBI district supervisor who had commanded the operation to arrest Fritz. Hunt was then recovering from wounds he had suffered a few weeks earlier, when he was shot through the neck in a police standoff with a man who had killed his employer.

Morgan, who was himself recovering from a recent operation to repair nerve damage from tumor surgery, took the podium to offer his twenty-three-page report. He was flanked by huge charts showing the position of police vehicles at different points in the chase as well as a huge montage of aerial photographs showing the 12.1-mile route from Susie's apartment to the spot where the Blazer exploded.

Acknowledging that he had been closely involved in the investigation from the beginning, including almost hourly briefings on June 3, the day of the arrest attempt, Morgan gave a version of events that at some points varied widely with descriptions offered by officers and eyewitnesses.

Fritz had been under surveillance "throughout all of Monday," he said, when it fact it had begun only shortly before noon; otherwise, officers would not have been surprised when the boys appeared, for they thought the boys were in school. He emphatically denied that the SBI had been warned in advance that Fritz wouldn't be taken alive and would "come out shooting," although District Attorney Tisdale said so in print, and both Sam Phillips and John Forrest claimed they had told the same thing to SBI agents who called them beforehand.

Morgan further denied that "John Wayne tactics" had been used to stop Fritz. At the intersection where the first shooting erupted, he placed the blue Mustang driven by Officer Spainhour alongside the Blazer instead of blocking it from the front, where officers in the car and eyewitnesses placed it. The chart Morgan used to show the placement of cars at the intersection didn't show the civilian cars that had played a crucial part in the situation.

The actions of officers at the intersection were "reasonable," Morgan concluded.

"Knowing what is now known, and after reflecting on what did occur, one might speculate that some other approach should have been made," he said. "But that was a judgmental decision that had to be made under extreme time constraints and very tense conditions. The several officers involved had no opportunity to call 'time out' and plan another strategy."

That officer Dennis was left shot at the scene was "not accurate," Morgan said, although all cars involved in the operation sped off in pursuit of Fritz, according to Dennis and other witnesses. Questioned later, Morgan acknowledged that he had not talked to Dennis during his investigation.

In summary, Morgan found the actions of the officers not only faultless but laudable, although he did recognize that a problem in communications existed, which under later questioning he acknowledged "could have been disastrous."

Asked why the officers tried to stop Fritz knowing that the children were in the Blazer, Morgan said that they had information that Fritz cared very much for the boys and "would do nothing" to hurt them.

About the file on Fritz, Morgan said that it had been kept in the intelligence files of the Bureau's Special Operations Division. The file was submitted by agent Mike Kelly on July 13, 1981, Morgan said, which was two and a half months after Sam Phillips had told Kelly about Fritz.

Referring to Phillips as a "confidential informant," Morgan called him a member of a "survivalist group" to which he said Fritz also belonged. He said that Fritz had talked the informant's wife into leaving him. "The informant's wife had left him and taken the children, and they all were living with Klenner in his apartment at that time," Morgan said, although in fact Cynthia Phillips never left her home and at no time did Fritz live there.

Morgan went on to list the contents of the bag of medical paraphernalia and prescription drugs that Sam Phillips had turned over to Kelly. The drugs included an antibiotic, a muscle relaxant, plus Darvon and Dexamyl, both controlled substances.

"The possession of six Darvon and one Dexamyl tablet

was not sufficient to indicate that an individual was selling drugs," Morgan said.

Kelly, he said, supported by Assistant Director Cuyler Windham and Drug Supervisor Charlie Overton, determined that the contents of the bag were not a "drug dealer stash."

While Morgan was making it appear that Phillips reported Fritz for dealing drugs, the intelligence report submitted by Kelly, which Morgan refused to release, made it clear that Phillips only wanted Fritz investigated for practicing medicine without a license.

"Klenner was introduced to everyone in the group as a medical student at Duke University," Kelly wrote. "From that point, Klenner began treating group members for various medical problems. The CI [confidential informant] subsequently learned that Klenner's father was in fact a practicing physician in Reidsville, N.C., who mailed checks to his son for large amounts. Klenner, Jr. was supposed to be paying for his education with the money from his father.

"The CI advised that Klenner, Jr. had treated his two sons and his wife, including giving them oral medication and an injection on occasion. It was believed that Klenner was getting the medicine from his father with his dad's knowledge. Group members eventually found out that Klenner was not in medical school, and in fact did not work or go to any school. Most of the money from his father was being used to buy weapons, which most group members possessed several of.

"The CI said Klenner was a very paranoid person, and usually carried several weapons with him along with his black medical bag. He also said he had a bag of various drugs obtained form [*sic*] Klenner that he would give to Writer if it would help in an investigation of Klenner."

Morgan said that Kelly had investigated the matter by making routine checks of the apartment complex where Fritz lived, by checking with the Durham police vice squad, which said it had no information on him, and by asking agent Fred Tucker in the Greensboro office to check around Reidsville for information that might be helpful about Fritz or his father.

"Tucker reported back that there was nothing unusual about Dr. Klenner or his son," Morgan said.

Morgan went on to say that in his own investigation following the newspaper report, he had gone to Rockingham County and talked with Sheriff Bobby Vernon about the Klenners. "He said that he knew that the family was a prominent family in the area and that to his knowledge, neither Klenner or anyone in the family had ever been involved in any kind of illegal or suspicious activities and that they all enjoyed the finest reputation."

Morgan's conclusions were that the report about Fritz had been handled appropriately and that "the possession of the six Darvon and one Dexamyl did not indicate a 'drug dealer stash' or give cause for further proceedings."

Questioned persistently about details of the case after finishing his report, Morgan grew angry and abruptly shut down the press conference.

He got angry again the following day, when he read the *Winston-Salem Journal*'s report of his findings. The story noted that Morgan still declined to release the tape of the third conversation between Fritz and Ian. It quoted District Attorney Tisdale as saying that even he still had been unable to get a copy of the tape. "I've been getting the runaround," Tisdale said.

In a fit of pique, Morgan fired off a letter to Tisdale.

He quoted law and said that the attorney general as well as himself had decided that the tape shouldn't be released and that Tisdale's stand was "a specific affront" to both that also eroded public confidence in law enforcement. Nevertheless, he would provide the tape if Tisdale demanded it, he said, adding that if Tisdale played it for reporters, "I think you will have violated the law."

In all of his years as a prosecutor, Tisdale had never known an SBI director to get involved in an individual case, and he wondered why Morgan was so wrapped up in this one. He also wondered why Morgan had come to Winston-Salem during his investigation and not bothered to call him. Now he wondered who Morgan thought he was.

He composed a three-page letter to the attorney general to tell him that he didn't appreciate Morgan's letter or his attitude.

"It is not appropriate for the director, who is, after all, a police officer, to instruct me as to what the law is," Tisdale wrote. "I believe the director is way out of line both in the tone of his letter and in issuing a subtle threat to me."

He requested the tape and said he intended to play it for reporters unless Thornburg asked that he not.

Thornburg responded with a conciliatory letter saying that he hadn't taken affront at Tisdale's actions and that he hadn't seen Morgan's letter before it was mailed, nor had Morgan discussed it with him. He made it clear, however, that he didn't want the tape made public.

"Our concern goes to the much broader problem of protecting sensitive information in a variety of cases. The tape, in this instance, could be considered innocuous. The release, though, could add to the difficulties we are already experiencing."

Tisdale dropped his request for the tape, although he still thought it should be made public.

"I would have pushed the thing further," he said later, "except for my relationship with Ed Hunt. I wasn't going to put him in the middle."

The contents of the tape were never made public by the SBI, nor did the agency reveal any more information about the Newsom murder investigation. Letting the public know whether Susie played any role in the murders of her parents and grandmother, or whether she took a hand in the killing of her children, clearly was of no interest to North Carolina's top police organization.

48

Dan Davidson blamed himself for not becoming more suspicious of Susie early in his investigation. Yet, he had to ask, what did he have to go on? Gossip from Delores's friends that she and Susie didn't get along well? That was about it. Hell, half the mothers-in-law and daughters-in-law he'd ever encountered didn't get along, but that was no reason for murder. Not even Tom had thought Susie capable of the murders when Davidson asked about the possibility, and if anybody should have been suspicious, surely it was Tom.

"Who's going to think some damn daughter-in-law over children?" Davidson grumbled to fellow detectives.

Too, it was not as if he had let Susie escape investigation. On the day of Delores's and Janie's funeral, when suspicion was still directed toward Tom, Detective Tom Swinney had been assigned to call Susie and interview her. She told him she had no idea who might want to kill Delores and Janie. Swinney reported back to Davidson that she said Tom was very close to his mother and sister and she thought him incapable of killing them. She described Delores as "overbearing" and "very demanding of her family."

In August, Davidson had run an intelligence check on Susie with North Carolina authorities, which produced nothing to arouse suspicions toward her.

Later, after Tom had been eliminated as a suspect, Davidson had included reinterviewing Susie on a list of things that needed to be done, but not until two days after Christmas did Detective Sherman Childers call the Greensboro Police Department and ask if a detective could question Susie. Sergeant Furman Melton was assigned the task, and Childers filled him in about the case. Two hours later, Melton called back.

"Sgt. Melton advised he interviewed Susan Sharp, the ex-wife of Thomas Lynch," Childers wrote in his report. "Sgt. Melton stated she didn't know anything about the murders or have any idea who would commit such a crime. Sgt. Melton advised he doesn't believe Susan Sharp had anything to do with the homicide and she does have a good reputation in the community."

Now Davidson knew that, months before this interview, Susie had been telling family and friends that Tom had had his mother and sister killed by the Mafia so he could inherit money to pay off gambling debts. Yet when two detectives showed up to question her about the murders, she made no mention of any of that.

This was just one more reason to make Davidson think that Susie had directed the executions of Delores and Janie. And as soon as he and his two wounded detectives had returned to Kentucky after the distressing events of June 3, Davidson set out to do what North Carolina authorities had failed to accomplish and now showed no interest in doing: proving that Susie had had a hand in murder.

That Susie could have plotted or committed murder was something that her brother, her aunts Susie and Louise, her lawyers and close friends could not fathom and refused to believe. Fritz had gone to so much trouble to fool Susie about being a doctor and a CIA agent, as well as so many other things, that they were convinced that he had fooled her about the murders, too. He had killed Delores and Janie, they figured, not only to stop Delores from encouraging Tom's visitation and custody notions but also to instill fear in Susie, to give him control over her and make her dependent on him for protection. The Mafia story was solely the product of Fritz's troubled mind, they were certain, and Susie's irrational actions were evidence of the effectiveness of it. Those who knew her best had no doubt that Susie sincerely believed the Mafia had killed Delores and Janie, just as they had no doubt of the authenticity of her fear that the Mafia was after her and the boys.

Sandy Sands, who had seen that fear close up when Susie brought the boys' toy animals to show him how their throats had been slit, could not accept that she had been pretending. Later, it was clear to him that it was Fritz who had slit the toys' throats (the slits were almost identical to the one he inflicted on Florence) and made the "two down and two to go" call that had so frightened and intimidated Susie. Why would he have done that except to build her fear and allow him to continue to manipulate her?

The fake bombs that Fritz had planted and other supposed attempts on his and Susie's lives were, to Susie's defenders, further evidence of Fritz's determination to control her with fear. The slayings of Bob, Florence, and Nanna had been carried out by Fritz, they thought, for several reasons: to stop the visitation hearing, to punish Florence for her opposition to Susie's relationship with Fritz, to wreak retribution on Bob for being a "traitor" to his daughter by agreeing to testify for Tom, to further convince Susie that the Mafia was closing in on her, and perhaps to make Susie the beneficiary of her considerable inheritance.

Some of Susie's defenders thought that with Susie nearing completion of her degree and talking of starting a career in some faroff place, Fritz feared losing her and the boys and that only by pulling her deeper and deeper into his deadly games could he hold onto her.

"Fritz created a lot of self-fulfilling prophecies for Susie," Rob said. " 'Tom will have his family wiped out. Tom will have your parents killed.' Everything Fritz was telling her was coming true."

Susie's aunt Frances and cousin Nancy were among those who did not subscribe to the theory that Susie was an innocent, duped and manipulated by her devious cousin. She was too intelligent for that, they thought. If she hadn't been involved, they were sure that she was smart enough to become suspicious of Fritz and begin asking questions. Her irrational behavior of recent years, her lack of grief about the deaths of her parents and grand-

mother, her strange actions after the murders, all pointed
to her involvement.

"Anybody who could take their children away from
their grandparents and not let them see them must've
hated them so bad that she could've had something to do
with it," Nancy recalled thinking.

"I'm not totally, absolutely sure of how deeply she was
involved in the killing," Frances said. "I think she was
deeply involved in this game they played."

Frances and Nancy searched for reasons to believe
Susie was not a participant but kept coming up with
evidence that indicated otherwise. Why had she lied to
the SBI agent who called to ask Fritz to come for an
interview on the last day of their lives if not to protect
Fritz? Surely after the police had come back to interview Fritz, and after Ian's frantic calls to the apartment,
she had to realize that the police were now suspicious of
Fritz. Had Fritz told her nothing about his interview and
his meetings with Ian? Was her curiosity not aroused
enough to ask?

At Ian's trial, Frances and Nancy heard something
during the playing of the tapes that led them to think
Fritz must have told Susie at least some of what went on
in his meetings with Ian. On the Sunday of Fritz's and
Ian's second meeting, Ian had told Fritz about the police
taking him to Nanna's house, where he saw the car Fritz
was driving on the night of the murders. Fritz had asked
how many cars were at the house. Ian said two. "Unless
Rob has picked the car up, there should have been three
cars," Fritz said. Actually, Rob had gone to Winston-
Salem the day before and driven his father's car back
home, but neither Susie nor Fritz knew that.

At 5:30 P.M. that Sunday, Susie had driven past her
parents' house after Rob and Alice had walked to the
home of a neighbor for supper. Chris Hunt, Annette's
son, saw Susie and waved her to a stop. He had locked
himself out of the house, and he talked to her about his
problem. Frances and Nancy had wondered why Susie
would come by the house with no apparent intention to
stop. Now they saw a reason. Fritz must have sent her to
see if Bob's car was at the house so he would know

whether Ian had been telling the truth. If Fritz had done so, wouldn't he have had to explain why to Susie?

Frances and Nancy also had many unanswered questions about the events leading up to the deaths of Fritz, Susie, and the boys. Was Susie aware of the notes Fritz left behind? Was it for Susie's benefit that Fritz wrote the note in which he denied killing anybody and pictured himself a victim of a frame-up? Or was it for his mother's sake? For both? Fritz had been last to leave the apartment. Did he secretly write the notes and leave them without Susie's knowledge? Clearly, the notes, which were neither released by authorities nor made available to the families, showed that Fritz knew that he would never be returning to the apartment. Did Susie know that? Why had she kept the boys out of school that day if she were not anticipating that they might have to flee forever? But if she thought they were never to return, would she have taken her schoolwork? Where could they have been headed when they left the apartment so hurriedly, apparently unaware that it was surrounded by police?

Susie's defenders thought that Fritz had convinced Susie that the Mafia was closing in on them when they fled. They thought Susie believed that the police officers who first tried to stop them were hit men sent by Tom. After all, the officers were in unmarked cars and plain clothes.

But once Susie saw a uniformed officer and watched Fritz shoot him, didn't she know better? Why didn't she do something then to stop Fritz? If she had killed him, she could have claimed she'd been duped all along and nobody would have been able to prove otherwise. She would have emerged a hero. Yet, she remained at his side as he continued on his disastrous course, and she stayed in the Blazer when he stopped in the middle of the road and got out to fire at officers. Couldn't she have made some effort to flee with the boys at one of those moments? Couldn't she have picked up one of the many weapons in the Blazer and shot Fritz or forced him to surrender? That she didn't indicated complicity.

Even if Susie were completely innocent, did she realize when the shooting began that her mere association with Fritz would cause her to lose the boys, that the courts surely would take custody from her, and did she then decide that without the boys, life was not worth living? Or was she so deeply involved in the murders that she had made a suicide pact with Fritz that included the boys should the arrest of either her or Fritz become imminent? Were the notes left by Fritz proof of their suicidal intentions? Did the scapulars Susie and the boys were wearing add to that proof?

The autopsy showed that Susie had been alive and conscious when the bomb went off, which meant that she had to be aware of the killing of her children. Did she participate in it? Did Fritz do it against her wishes, as her defenders wanted to believe? Did he get the boys to take the cyanide by telling them it was something else, vitamins perhaps? Were her children shot so that Susie didn't have to watch the violent death throes produced by the poison? Did she shoot them, or did Fritz? Could Fritz have performed the contortions necessary to shoot the boys in the back of the Blazer while driving and firing out the window at the sheriff's deputies who had pulled in behind him with their blue lights flashing and their sirens wailing? If so, did Susie just sit calmly and watch?

Was Susie indeed a modern Medea, or just another innocent duped by Fritz?

With the SBI declining further investigation and refusing to make known any information it might have, that question seemed likely to go unanswered. But Frances and Nancy didn't stop searching for the truth, and neither did Dan Davidson.

Like all other police officers involved in investigating the murders, Davidson believed that Susie had been a full participant from the beginning. He was certain that she had talked Fritz into killing Delores and had gone to Kentucky with him to do it. He believed she had directed Fritz to murder her parents, too. Janie and Nanna, he figured, were victims who just happened to be in the wrong place at the wrong time. Davidson was also certain that Susie had killed her children to keep Tom from getting them. But he had no proof of that. In fact, he still had no solid evidence connecting either Fritz or Susie to the murders of Delores and Janie.

With his chief suspects dead, Davidson could have closed the books on the case, confident of their guilt. That was the usual procedure, but he didn't want that. Neither did Bruce Hamilton, the commonwealth attorney for the 12th Judicial District of Kentucky.

Bruce Hamilton had been a prosecutor for twenty-five years, and he loved his work. At fifty-five, a shambling man whose suits always seemed too big and whose shirt-tail always seemed to be peeking from the back of his trousers, Hamilton had passions for guns and Harry Truman, whose portrait dominated his office. In some ways he had modeled himself after Truman. He was tough and outspoken and never shied from trouble or profanity.

"I'm a hard-nosed son of a bitch," he liked to say, "and I don't back up from nobody."

Hamilton considered himself "a knight in shining armor" standing up for decent citizens. He particularly disliked slick, big-city defense lawyers who thought they could thwart justice by coming into his rural, small-town district to "run over the local police and the prosecutors and the victims," and he took pride in sending them back with a message for others of their ilk: "They're going to hit a concrete wall. We're going to fight."

Like most prosecutors, his sympathies lay with the police and victims, but that did not stop him from disagreeing with the officers who had to make his cases for him, nor did it keep them from sometimes feeling the sting of his invective.

Dan Davidson, whose area of jurisdiction included Hamilton's district, sometimes disagreed with Hamilton about details of crimes and how to solve them, and now and then they found themselves locked in irresolvable dispute. Hamilton liked to involve himself in investigations of big cases, and Davidson dreaded his intrusion and quietly resented it. Hamilton had done that in the Lynch case, and he and Davidson had argued about the order of the shots and from where they had come.

But on one important point Hamilton and Davidson agreed. Hamilton was also convinced that Susie was behind the Lynch murders—"She was the link, the cause, and the motive," he said later. "She had to be conjected. Why would Klenner do it if not for Susie?"—and a week after the shoot-out and bomb blast in North Carolina, he was speaking out to reporters about it. He called Susie "the brains of the outfit."

"She used Klenner like you would a broom—to sweep things out," Hamilton declared, going on to say that he planned to take the case before a grand jury.

Davidson had called Hamilton several days earlier to tell him that he planned to continue the investigation and to ask if Hamilton could take the unusual step of taking the case to the grand jury when he had accumulated enough evidence.

Davidson wanted a grand jury declaration not only to assure the public that the murders had been solved and no killers were still at large but also to get a public record of Susie's guilt, which he hoped to prove. Hamilton concurred. He usually took all homicides to a grand jury, and it made no difference that in this case the suspects could never be brought to trial. A grand jury could make a finding of responsibility and allow a clean closing of the case. But there was another reason that Hamilton agreed.

"PMA," he later said with a little grin. "It protects my ass."

Davidson began his renewed investigation by making a seven-state check of traffic records to see if Fritz or Susie had by chance received a ticket on their way to or from Kentucky in July of 1984. They hadn't. He also sent officers to check the registration records of all motels and campgrounds in the Louisville area and along major highways leading to Oldham County from North Carolina. Officers took the names and addresses of anybody who had registered with a North Carolina address on the weekend of the murders and checked them out to make sure Fritz or Susie had not registered under a false name. The extensive check produced nothing.

When he returned from North Carolina, Davidson had brought with him the telephone records for the summer of 1984 for Susie's apartment, Annie Hill Klenner's house, and Dr. Klenner's office. These offered more promise.

Long-distance calls were made from Susie's phone nearly every day, and they were made in great numbers. David-

son and his officers began calling every number and
questioning whomever answered about Fritz and Susie.
Many of the calls were to manufacturers and distributors
of exotic weaponry who reported orders placed by Fritz.
A call to a business named Military World in Tucker,
Georgia, an Atlanta suburb, provided the information
that Fritz had been there half a dozen times, that he
bought lots of equipment—including flak jackets, bullet-
proof diapers, and gas masks—always paid with hundred-
dollar bills, and tore up the receipts, saying he didn't
want his wife to know how much he was spending.

A call to Mebane, North Carolina, about twenty-five
miles east of Greensboro, brought to the phone Everett
Smith at Arrowhead Gulf station, who said he'd known
Fritz for ten years, that Fritz had prescribed medicine for
him, treated his mother, and confided to him that he was
a CIA agent. Fritz had never mentioned Tom or the
Newsoms, Smith said, but in the summer of 1984 Smith
had put four new tires on Fritz's Blazer. Fritz told him he
was going on a long trip for the CIA.

A frequently called number in Winston-Salem produced the most intriguing results for Davidson. The number turned out to be that of McHargue's Guns and Coins,
where Fritz had told many secrets and bought and traded
so many weapons over the years that the McHargues
wouldn't even attempt a guess at the number. Mike
McHargue told Davidson of Fritz buying rifles for the
boys and telling him that Tom was going to have all of
them killed. He'd last seen Fritz four days before he was
killed, when Fritz came in and bought a 308 automatic
rifle. Davidson suspected that Fritz might have bought
from the McHargues the military assault rifle that had
been used to kill Delores and Janie. He had the bullet
that had passed through Janie's head, and it was in good
enough condition that ballistics tests could prove from
which weapon it had been fired. Davidson filed a request
with the Federal Bureau of Alcohol, Tobacco, and Firearms for a record of all the weapons transactions between
McHargue's and Fritz.

Surprisingly, Davidson found two calls to the Oldham
County Police Department on the night of July 24, the

day Delores's and Janie's bodies were found, and he retrieved the tapes of those calls.

The first had occurred at 10:06 P.M.

"This is Mrs. Lynch," Susie said. "I'm calling from out of state. I'm trying to get some information on Delores Lynch and Janie Lynch. Do you have any information on what might have happened to them in the last few days?"

"Okay, what is your name?" asked the dispatcher.

"Susie Lynch. L-y-n-c-h. I was given information through the family that they have been murdered and wanted to find somebody who could give me some confirmation."

"Okay. Hold on a minute, okay?"

Silence ensued until the dispatcher's voice returned. "Yes, that is true. That did happen."

"It is?" Susie said incredulously. "It is for real? Both of them?"

"Yes, ma'am, I'm sorry. Could I have your phone number and I'll have an officer give you a call back."

"God, yes, please. I'd appreciate it."

She gave her phone number.

"What is your address?"

"Greensboro, North Carolina. 28-L Hunt Club Road. My name is Susie Lynch. This happened today?"

"It happened today."

Susie let out a heavy breath. "Okay, thank you very much."

The second call came an hour and a half later. Susie identified herself, said she'd called earlier, and asked if an officer was available to give her more information. The dispatcher switched the call to another number where conversations were not automatically recorded, indicating that Susie had spoken with an officer. But nobody in the department recalled talking with her. Davidson thought there were two reasons for these calls: to get information on what the police knew and were thinking about the murders, and to make Susie appear unaware and innocent. He also thought it significant that Susie had asked about what had happened to Delores and Janie "in the last few days." At that time, Tom, who'd called to tell Susie of the murders, knew only that the bodies had been found that day and had no idea that the murders had occurred two days earlier.

A call to Raleigh turned out to be to the North Carolina Board of Medical Examiners, the organization that licenses physicians, but the board had no record of the call and nobody there remembered talking to Fritz or Susie. Davidson had no particular interest in the call, but it did raise some interesting questions. Although Susie's Aunt Su-Su and her parents had decided to keep from her their discovery that Fritz had never been to Duke, Susie was aware that Fritz did not have his license to practice medicine. At one point, concerned about Fritz's doctoring on the boys, Su-Su had cautioned Susie about it, indicating that Fritz might not be fully qualified for that. "The only thing standing between him and his degree at Duke is a dissertation," Susie said indignantly. Later, Susie indicated that she believed Fritz had received his degree. Two months before her death, she had dropped by her parents' house with the boys and was chatting with Alice about classes. "Fritz has a degree from Duke," Susie said out of the blue, for Alice would never dare bring up his name with Susie, "but there's a problem with the computer. It'll be straightened out." Had Fritz convinced her that he had finished his dissertation and gotten his degree but couldn't get his license because of a computer mix-up? Had he placed that call to try to make Susie believe that he was trying to straighten out the problem and obtain his license? Or had Susie made the call herself? If so, what had provoked it? Had she become suspicious of Fritz's stories? Was she wondering about the closing of his father's clinic? If she had indeed harbored suspicions about Fritz, why hadn't they led her to take the next step and check with Duke about his degree? The call would remain another intriguing mystery among many.

To Davidson, the most interesting thing about Susie's phone records was a lack of calls over one three-day stretch in July 1984. Normally, long-distance calls were made from the phone every day, but on those three days covering the weekend that Delores and Janie were killed no calls were made. That indicated to Davidson that neither Susie nor Fritz was at her apartment that weekend, and he was sure that he knew where both had been.

At 12:03 P.M. on Friday, July 20, a call was made to a

company in California that manufactures combat pistols. The next call was not made until 11:47 P.M. on Monday, July 23, the day after the murders. Interestingly, that call was to Tom Lynch in Albuquerque, where the boys were at the time.

Tom remembered the call. He had thought it unusual because it came so late, nearly 10 P.M. Albuquerque time. Usually, when Susie called to talk to the boys, she called at dinnertime, about 6 P.M. They would have just sat down to eat and the phone would ring. Kathy would have to keep the boys' meals warm while they talked to their mother. Susie had never called so late before, and Tom wondered why this call had come when it did. He also remembered another unusual thing about the call that he mentioned to Davidson. Susie had sounded surprised when he answered. But not for nearly two more years would Tom remember exactly what she said. It came to him one night when a movie, *The Invasion of the Body Snatchers*, came on TV. Then he remembered clearly. He and the boys had been watching that movie when Susie called, and the boys were upset about missing the ending. When he answered the phone, Tom recalled, Susie said, "Oh, you're there."

Susie talked to the boys for ten minutes, and three minutes after she hung up, a call was made from her number to the Klenner house in Reidsville. That call lasted nineteen minutes.

Davidson was convinced that Susie was concerned because she and Fritz had heard no news about the murders. She had called the boys, Davidson thought, to try to get a reading on what was going on and had expected to find that Tom was in Kentucky. He was sure that Fritz was at his mother's house and Susie had called him immediately to let him know that the bodies apparently hadn't been found.

Another set of calls on the following day confirmed this in Davidson's mind. At 7:20 P.M. in Albuquerque, 9:20 in Greensboro, Tom called Susie to tell her about the murders. Their conversation lasted eight minutes. Four minutes after it ended, a call was made from Susie's phone to the Klenner house. Surely, Davidson thought,

Susie was calling Fritz to tell him the bodies had been found.

After the last call to the Oldham County Police Department on the night the bodies were found, another call was made from Susie's phone to the Klenner house.

To Davidson, this series of calls was strong circumstantial evidence that Susie was a participant in the murders and was seeking information about the investigation to feed to Fritz.

On July 7, Davidson and Lennie Nobles returned to North Carolina in search of more evidence. They visited Susie's apartment, from which they took a brochure for the La Quinta Motor Inn in Lexington, Kentucky, which was found in Fritz's briefcase, plus a map of eastern states with a plastic overlay on which lines had been drawn to various cities, including Lexington. Davidson thought the map might be part of Fritz's CIA fantasies and preparation for the trip to kill Delores, but in fact Susie had prepared it for a report she had written for one of her business classes on distribution patterns from the port of Wilmington. He also wanted to poke around to see if a turquoise cross might have been overlooked in the clutter. Earlier, local authorities had sent Davidson photos of such a cross that had been found in Fritz's treasure chests of jewelry, but Helen Stewart, Delores's former maid, said it wasn't the one Delores frequently wore, the only item known to be missing from the murder scene.

During their three-day stay, Davidson and Nobles questioned Rob, Ian, Annie Hill, Annette Hunt, members of the McHargue family, and Greensboro Police Detective Furman Melton, who had interviewed Susie six months earlier at the request of Sherman Childers.

Melton had made no written report of his interview and remembered few details. He did recall that Fritz had been at the apartment but went into the bedroom and closed the door while Melton and another detective talked with Susie. He added one curious memory. He thought he heard a noise, which could have been a rifle bolt closing, in the bedroom.

Davidson quizzed Annie Hill carefully about Fritz's

whereabouts the previous July, but she professed to remember little.

"You'll have to remember my husband had just died," she said. "I was under quite a bit of strain at that time."

She thought that Fritz might have gone to Pennsylvania during that month. "The only time he told me he was going anywhere was on the twenty-ninth, when he went to Atlanta." She had marked that on her calendar, she discovered.

Did she know of any travels by Susie during the month?

"I know she went to Atlanta with Fritz."

Davidson brought up the phone calls from Susie's apartment to her house on the nights of July 23 and 24. Did she answer the phone and talk with Susie or Fritz? Or was Fritz there to take the calls and talk to Susie?

"I have no notation about it and I do not remember."

Had she ever heard Susie say anything against Delores?

Only that Delores had alcohol problems, Annie Hill said, and Fritz had told her that at the visitation hearing in Wentworth, Delores had stalked out.

Did Fritz say anything about Delores?

"I don't think he even knew her."

Davidson asked what Fritz and Susie had told her about the Lynch murders. She said she'd heard that the murders appeared to be a gangland execution and that if Tom hadn't had it done, some Mafia connections had done it unbeknownst to him so that he would get money to pay off gambling debts.

"As far as Susie and Fritz were concerned, there was never any connection," Annie Hill said.

Davidson went on to quiz her about Susie's and Fritz's actions after the Newsom killings.

"Susie was in a state of shock, very, very concerned," she said. "Susie was very much upset. When I did see Fritz, he didn't make any great statements one way or another." She described Fritz as being "like someone shocked and trying to console Susie."

Did Susie say anything about who might have done this?

"She had no idea. None of us could understand why Hattie Newsom, who was such a dear person . . . it just didn't seem logical to anybody except she just happened to be there."

Annie Hill said that she never suspected that Susie or Fritz were involved in any of the killings.

"I do not think they had anything to do with the Lynches," she said. "It is hard for me to believe that Fritz killed my sister. If he did, I do not believe that Susie knew it. The fact that he could come here and he was so natural that I did not suspect anything . . . and I'm not sure that Susie and Fritz were all that close. They helped each other out, but Fritz sort of would come and go. Be here till one, two, three in the morning and he would call Susie when he left. . . ."

Davidson could see that he was going to get nothing useful here and gave up the interview.

From Ian, Annette, and Rob, he got only helpful tidbits.

Ian told him of Susie firing weapons at the farm and of the attempts Fritz claimed had been made on his and Susie's lives. He told how Fritz preached thoroughness—a body shot to bring a person down, a head shot for insurance, and never leave casings. That was the pattern of the Lynch murders, and it was sure to interest a grand jury.

Annette told him how Susie felt that Tom didn't want custody but was being pushed to get it by Delores, who was paying the lawyers. That established motive.

Rob said Susie had told him that she was in Atlanta on the weekend of the Lynch murders but he had been unable to find anybody who could place her there, including their cousin Debbie Parham, who lived there, and to whom Davidson later talked.

When he had asked Susie if she thought there was any connection between the Lynch murders and the killing of their parents and grandmother, Rob told Davidson, Susie replied, "Obviously, somebody wants my children to be very rich."

"What do you mean?" Rob said he had asked.

"What do you think I mean?" she said.

He took it to mean that whoever had killed the Lynches also had killed their parents and grandmother—and for the same motive, so that Tom would eventually get money. He thought Susie figured that if Susie got her share of her grandmother's and parents' estates and then she and the boys were killed, that money would go to Tom, just as had the money from the estates of his parents and sister.

It was from Mike McHargue at the Winston-Salem gun shop that Davidson got some of the most helpful information from his trip. McHargue said that Fritz had told him that if he ever was killed, the government would cover up the circumstances of his death. That had now taken place, McHargue believed. He didn't think that Fritz had anything to do with killing the boys or exploding a bomb. Police gunfire had set off dynamite Fritz had in the Blazer, he said. He further believed that the police had shot the boys and the medical examiner had added cyanide to their blood.

In answer to a question, McHargue said he had no doubt that Fritz would kill anybody who messed with him or Susie and the kids. That was a help to Davidson's case because he knew that Fritz and Susie thought Delores was behind an effort to take away the boys.

Asked about cyanide, McHargue said he knew that Fritz carried it and would take it if he was captured by enemies or if nuclear war or some other catastrophe occurred. Susie carried it, too, he said, and she had told him and other members of his family that she and the boys would take it if anything ever happened to Fritz.

"You don't have to do that," McHargue said he'd told her. "If anything happens to Fritz, we'll take care of you and the boys."

That Susie carried cyanide and had told the McHargues that she and the boys would take it made Davidson all the more certain that she had poisoned John and Jim, then shot them for the sake of thoroughness before joining Fritz in the dramatic suicide that he had been fantasizing for so long.

Five days after returning from North Carolina, Davidson finally got a report from the Alcohol, Tobacco, and Firearms Bureau detailing all of the weapons transactions between Fritz and the McHargues. From August 1983 until the week before his death, Fritz had bought 119 long guns from the McHargues. Many of those he had traded back, including more than twenty .223 military assault rifles, but one of those weapons fairly leaped from the report as Davidson read through it. A Colt AR15 .223, serial number SP 202537. Fritz had bought it in July of 1984 and traded it back on July 23, the day after the murders in Kentucky. Davidson immediately requested that the ATF trace and find the weapon. Later, Davidson called Mike McHargue to ask him about the gun.

Yes, McHargue said, he remembered it because it was unusual. It had a nickel finish and Fritz didn't like it. Fritz complained that he couldn't find interchangeable barrels for it because they were so rare. Did he remember what time Fritz brought the gun in? Davidson asked McHargue. Sometime in the afternoon. Was he alone? No, said McHargue, Susie was with him.

That was more evidence for the case Davidson was making against Susie. Winston-Salem is west of Greensboro on Interstate 40, the fastest and most direct route to Kentucky from central North Carolina. Surely, Fritz had stopped on his way back from Kentucky to trade in the weapon. That Susie was with him was significant. It was highly unlikely that he would have driven on twenty-five miles to Greensboro and picked up Susie merely to double back to Winston-Salem and trade the gun. Common sense told Davidson that Susie clearly had accompanied Fritz on his murder mission to Kentucky.

Davidson figured that it was now just a matter of time until the ATF traced the rifle to its present owner, and he would finally have the solid evidence he needed to show who had killed Delores and Janie. He was right. The owner was found in Fayetteville, and Tom Sturgill drove there to pick up the rifle and take it back to Raleigh where it was test fired and the bullets forwarded to the Kentucky State Police ballistics lab.

On August 19, Davidson was on his way back to Post Five from Standiford Field, the Louisville airport, where he had gone to check some records on another case. Suddenly, his car radio crackled to life.

"Fifty-one?" said the dispatcher.

"Fifty-one," answered Davidson.

"Unit thirty advises that in case five, dash, eight, four, dash, five, four, three, ballistics tests are positive."

Davidson never violated the rules about unnecessary radio chatter, but in this instance he couldn't help himself. He wanted to let out a whoop.

"Ten-four," he said instead. "That's the best news I've heard in a long, long time."

"I was tickled to death," he said later. "That's probably the damned happiest ride I've ever had up an interstate highway."

The joy that Davidson felt for finally having a solution to the most vexing case of his career was not deeply satisfying because it also brought a grave confirmation that things might have been otherwise, for he knew that at least three of the deaths inflicted by Fritz's hand should not have been allowed to happen.

In August of 1984, when Davidson requested an intelligence check on Susie from the North Carolina SBI, it had come back with a bit of information that caught Davidson's eye. It said that a camping trailer was jointly registered to Susie and Frederick R. Klenner, Jr., of Reidsville, "a doctor." Curious about who Klenner might be, Davidson asked for intelligence on him. He got back nothing more than the basic data—date of birth, address, social security and driver's license numbers, plus the information that Fritz had no criminal record and was a physician.

After the Newsom murders, when his detectives went to Winston-Salem and called back the information that Fritz was the primary suspect, Davidson again asked for an intelligence check with the SBI. He got back a notation that a check had been made the previous summer and the status was unchanged.

He was furious when he later learned that all along the SBI had in its files a memorandum saying that Fritz was a survivalist, that he was masquerading as a doctor, that he was paranoid and spent all of his money on exotic military weapons that he carried wherever he went.

"That's intelligence information," Davidson said angrily. "It should have been in intelligence. Records don't mean shit to me. I'm wanting to know what kind of feller we're dealing with. I want to know what his friends and neighbors say about him. I should have had that."

If he'd been supplied that information, as the SBI was obligated to do as a member of a private network designed for trading intelligence, the Law Enforcement Intelligence Unit, Davidson knew that his suspicions would have been immediately directed to Fritz and Susie. He would have requested their telephone records, which would have led him to McHargue's, which would have led him to the weapon, and he would have moved on Fritz long before Fritz had a chance to murder Bob and Florence and Nanna. Perhaps Fritz could have been taken in a situation that would have allowed the boys to survive.

Davidson thought he had not received the information because for some reason it had not been in the SBI's intelligence files, and he was furious when he learned that Robert Morgan had acknowledged at his August 15 press conference that the memorandum was indeed in the intelligence files.

Why had Davidson not received that information and instead been supplied with the falsehood that Fritz was a doctor and a reputable citizen? Was it ineptitude? Was it because of the SBI's obsession with secrecy? Or was it for political reasons?

Davidson would not know, because the SBI would not tell (SBI officials declined to be interviewed about that or any other aspect of the Newsom murder case for this book), but he tended to believe it was for the latter reason. He thought that the SBI was either influenced by Susie Sharp or acting without her knowledge to protect her from embarrassment.

Susie Sharp was appalled at that notion. A woman of utmost integrity, she had never spoken with anybody at the SBI or the attorney general's office about Fritz or Susie or the Newsom murder case, she said, and she was doubtful that the SBI had acted in her behalf. "I can't imagine Robert Morgan trying to cover up for me," she said. "Robert Morgan has never been a friend of mine."

Bruce Hamilton still thought politics the likely reason that Davidson had not received the information that would have drawn his attention to Fritz immediately after the

Lynch murders, and privately he spoke bluntly of a cover-up by the SBI.

"If we'd had that information, we'd have been there the next day," Hamilton said. "We'd have been on Klenner like a flea on a hound dog."

Hamilton's suspicions about a cover-up were reinforced when his August 14 letter to Robert Morgan requesting SBI records to assist him in presenting his case to the grand jury was never even acknowledged.

In Davidson's mind, the SBI would forever bear a heavy portion of responsibility, not only for the murders of the Newsoms but also for the deaths that still bothered him most, those of John and Jim.

The Oldham County courthouse occupies a verdant square in the center of La Grange. It faces Main Street, which has a railroad track running down the middle of it along which freight trains occasionally rumble. The courthouse is old and quaint, two stories high, built of red brick, with a cupola on top and a small, unsightly jail wing off to one side in the back. The spacious lawn is decorated with a gazebo and a huge tire rim that once served as a bell to summon the town's volunteer firemen. It is shaded by stately oaks that in summer offer refuge to old-timers who come to escape the heat and while away the hours on benches provided by the county. On a sultry Thursday, September 5, 1985, the old-timers on the benches outside were unaware that in an annex of a second-floor courtroom a tale most bizarre was unfolding before a group of their fellow citizens serving as a grand jury.

Directed by Bruce Hamilton, the jury members began hearing the story at 9:30 A.M. from Dan Davidson. After a break for lunch, they moved a block away from the courthouse to the District Court Building, which occupied a former skating rink on Jefferson Street, where Davidson picked up the story. Allen Gentry and Tom Sturgill had driven from North Carolina to testify, bringing with them the AR15 that Fritz used to kill Janie. It lay on the courtroom floor in an olive-colored carrying case. Warren Mitchell, a ballistics expert for the Kentucky State Police, also was present, carrying in his pocket the bullet that had passed through Janie's head.

After giving his testimony, Davidson chatted with newspaper reporters and left no doubt of his feelings about Susie and how gently she had been treated by North Carolina authorities.

"Susie is not the least bit innocent," he said, "and I don't mind saying it because I'm not afraid of Big Susie down there in Raleigh."

As each officer was called into the closed anteroom to tell his part of the story, the others sat around a large table in the courtroom, laughing and talking. Stacks of grisly color photographs from the two murder scenes lay on the table, and court workers occasionally ambled in to thumb through them, shaking their heads in fascinated revulsion. Among the officers, the conversation kept returning to Fritz and Susie and the many angles and remaining mysteries of these combined cases, which had so consumed their energies and imaginations.

Late in the afternoon, TV news crews arrived and set up their cameras, but after learning that the grand jury would not be making its report as expected this day, because Circuit Court Judge Dennis Fritz, who was to receive it, had fallen ill and gone home, the reporters asked Dan Davidson a few questions on camera and left.

Not until 6:40 P.M., after more than eight hours of testimony, did Bruce Hamilton and the grand jury members finally emerge, the jurors still talking in wonder of all that they had heard.

Later, the jury foreman, Rick Lucas, who was thirty-three, a Baptist minister from Westport, the father of two young children, observed, "It was one of those kind of fantastic stories you expect to see on TV and not in real life."

The detectives gathered up their reports and evidence and made ready to leave. Their work on these cases was now, finally, behind them, but Susie and Fritz had forged a bond of comradeship among them that would not end. They all knew that their work was unlikely ever again to lead them to anything so big, so complex, so utterly unbelievable as the strange story they had just told the grand jury. But they knew that the jurors had believed it, and joined by Lennie Nobles, they went out to the nightspots of Louisville to celebrate.

* * *

On the same day that the grand jury in Kentucky was hearing evidence against Fritz and Susie, the *Greensboro News & Record* was preparing a story that would deal a serious blow to the theories of Susie's defenders who thought her incapable of having anything to do with the deaths of her children.

The newspaper learned of an SBI report that said Susie likely fired a weapon shortly before the explosion that took her life.

Normally, hand wipings taken during autopsies to determine if a person has fired a weapon are evaluated within a matter of days. But the hand wipings taken from Fritz and Susie and turned over to the SBI on June 4 were not even submitted to the lab until July 18. Not until August 21 was a report finally made by lab technician M. L. Creasy.

When a weapon is fired, sprayed residue forms a cloud that settles on the hand of the person who fired it. The residue contains three elements, barium and antimony from the primer of the shell and lead from the bullet itself. The presence of those elements on the hand is strong evidence that the hand held a weapon that was fired.

"Both subjects had significant concentrations of barium, antimony and lead, three trace elements, on backs of both hands and very high concentrations on palms of both hands," said the SBI report.

"These results indicate both subjects could have fired or handled guns which had been fired."

That the elements were found on the backs of Susie's hands indicated that she had done more than just handle a gun.

The SBI would not release the report or officially acknowledge it, but the newspaper quoted an unnamed "high-ranking SBI source" as saying, "We aren't saying she killed one or both children, but that she most likely fired a shot."

The implication of this powerful new evidence was plain. Susie obviously fired a weapon, but at what or whom had she shot? Neither she nor Fritz suffered bullet wounds, so she hadn't shot herself or him. No officer ever saw her leave the Blazer to fire at anybody, nor did any see her shoot out of the window during the pursuit. Unless she was just shooting willy-nilly into the roof of the Blazer, that left only two objects at which Susie might have fired: the heads of her sons. That Jim, who was behind Susie's seat, suffered a wound from a bullet fired very close to his head, while John, who was behind Fritz's seat, was shot from as much as two feet away, added weight to the evidence that it was Susie who had destroyed her sons.

On Thursday morning, September 12, Dan Davidson went to the District Court Building in La Grange where he joined Bruce Hamilton. They sat at the prosecutor's table in the court room and listened while Rick Lucas fulfilled his duties as grand jury foreman by reading the jury's four-page report on the Lynch murder case to Judge Dennis Fritz. The report called Susie "Susan" throughout, misspelled Fritz as "Fritts," and added an *e* to the end of the Newsom family name, but it linked the Lynch and Newsom murders and found that either Fritz or Susie had killed the boys. The last paragraph was the one for which Davidson was waiting.

"It is therefore the recommendation of the Oldham County Grand Jury at this session that the murder cases now open by the Kentucky State Police and the office of the Commonwealth Attorney and the Oldham County Police Department be closed and show that Frederick 'Fritts' Klenner and Susan Sharp Newsome Lynch were and are the persons responsible for the deaths of Jane Lynch and Delores Lynch at the residence of Delores Lynch in Oldham County, Kentucky, on or about July 22, 1984, which were discovered July 24, 1984, and that said cases be closed by all Departments with this report."

The judge accepted the report, thanked the jurors, commended their work, and dismissed them. Reporters crowded around Davidson and Hamilton for comments. A short time later, Davidson went to his desk at Post Five, where he talked to several more reporters by telephone.

"The right two people have been blamed for the deaths

up here," he told Jim Schlosser of the *Greensboro News & Record*. "I'm going to close the case now."

Davidson was elated that the case had come to a successful conclusion and even more delighted that he finally had an official record of Susie's guilt. Yet, alone at his desk with no more reporters calling and no last little bit of evidence to track down, he was struck by a feeling of emptiness, a letdown unlike any he'd ever experienced.

Instinct told him just how to deal with such an awkward and unfamiliar mix of emotions.

He got into his cruiser, drove to the Kentucky State Reformatory Lake, and went fishing.

EPILOGUE

Dan Davidson had difficulty letting go of the Lynch case. Even after the grand jury released its report implicating Susie, he wasn't satisfied. He thought that Susie might have played more than a passive role in the murders. Certain that she had directed Fritz and accompanied him to Kentucky, he suspected that Susie had killed Delores herself.

"I think she would have wanted her to know," he said.

To prove his theory, Davidson again questioned the bicyclist who had heard the shots, getting him to repeat time and again the sequence of two rapid shots followed soon after by a third. Davidson timed the bicyclist's memory of the shots, seeking an average of the time that elapsed between the second and third shots. He then tried to reenact the crime within that time frame, he and his detectives pretending to fire the first two shots from the spot where angles determined they most likely had emanated, then dashing for the back steps to get off a third shot from a spot that would match the trajectory of the bullet that struck Janie in the back, passing through her and the gutter drain.

"I didn't even make the first step," Davidson remembered.

Neither did anybody else.

"If he heard the shot sequence right, it's impossible for one guy to do that," Davidson said. "Hell, there's no way. I believe that Susie shot Delores and Fritz shot Janie. I'll believe it until I go in the grave."

Susie's role wasn't the only thing that continued to bother Davidson about the case. He was sometimes jolted awake by dreams in which he saw the pale, life-

ss, camouflage-clad bodies of John and Jim entwined
with their dead dogs in the wreckage of the Blazer.
Whenever that happened, sleep was usually ruined for the
est of the night. On one such night more than a year after
he boys' deaths, he got up and began to write a long
allad of the whole tragic story. It ended with these lines:

Nine people are dead and I wonder why,
Especially why those two little boys had to die.

On May 31, 1987, Dan Davidson retired from the
Kentucky State Police after thirty years of service.

"The Lynch case had a lot to do with it," he said
fterward. "Seemed like after that, everything was down-
ill. Nothing was interesting to me anymore."

As for other officers involved in the Lynch and Newsom
murder cases:

In the spring of 1987, Kentucky State Police Detective
herman Childers, Dan Davidson's close friend, was cited
or bravery by the state police for returning fire after
eing struck by flying glass from Fritz's bullets in the
Greensboro shoot-out. He was one of only two state
olicemen honored for bravery that year.

Lennie Nobles, the young Oldham County detective,
ecovered quickly from his gunshot wounds and returned
o duty, confident that he had learned much from his first
omicide investigation.

Ron Barker, captain of detectives for the Forsyth County
heriff's Department, ran against his boss in the primary
lection in the spring of 1986, citing his work on the
Newsom case as one reason he should be elected. He was
efeated by Sheriff Preston Oldham, who went on to win
he general election in November. After the primary,
Oldham demoted Barker to dispatcher, reducing his sal-
ry by half. Barker resigned and went to work selling
ecurity systems. Oldham promoted his old partner from
ndercover drug days, E. B. Hiatt, to captain of detectives.

Allen Gentry, the detective sergeant who directed the
Newsom murder investigation, was promoted to lieuten-
nt and made deputy commander of the Criminal Investi-
ation Division. On July 12, 1987, Gentry's wife, Lu
Ann, gave birth to their first child, a daughter, Stephanie
Nicole.

Tommy Dennis, the Greensboro squad leader whose bullet-proof vest and heavy leather gear stopped two slugs from Fritz's Uzi, was slow in recovering from his injuries. He developed pneumonia, sustained permanent lung and nerve damage, and was out of work for two months. After returning to patrol duty and facing two more unnerving situations in the span of a year, he resigned from the police force in December 1986, for the sake of his wife and three-year-old daughter. He became a jeweler.

Ian Perkins appeared at the Forsyth County Jail as scheduled on August 5, 1985, to begin serving his four-month sentence. He was sent to the Polk Youth Center in Raleigh for processing, and on October 1, he was transferred to the McLeansville Prison Unit near Greensboro where he was approved for work release. A week later he was moved to a minimum-custody unit at Sandy Ridge west of Greensboro, where he was released during daytime hours to work as a laborer for a Greensboro insulation company, a job arranged by his lawyer. He continued to work for the company after his release on parole.

"He's doing very well," his mother told a reporter a year after he helped police gather evidence on Fritz. "He's working and planning to go back to school."

Beyond that, she did not want to talk about her son's experience, and he declined to be interviewed.

"It's a difficult thing for us to talk about," his mother explained.

In the summer of 1987, Ian still worked for the company that had hired him in prison. He had enrolled again in college, this time at the University of North Carolina at Greensboro, the college from which Florence Newsom graduated.

"He's trying to rebuild his life," said a family friend.

After granting two brief interviews following her son's death, Annie Hill Klenner declined to be interviewed further and retreated to the solace offered by family, friends, and former patients of her husband. She broke her public silence on the anniversary of Fritz's death after vandals cracked the footstone on his grave and splattered it with red paint.

"Whoever did it, the only person they hurt was me," she told a reporter.

Of Fritz, she said this: "He was just as dear and thoughtful to me as anyone can possibly be. He was just not himself. . . . It was just unfortunate that he and my niece got together. They were two lost souls helping each other."

A few weeks later, hundreds of antique dealers, collectors and curiosity seekers gathered in a sweltering tobacco warehouse in Mebane, a small textile-mill town about twenty-five miles east of Greensboro, to get a glimpse of some of the clutter that had filled the Klenner house and office. Many of the personal belongings of Dr. Klenner and his notorious son had been hauled in on flatbed trucks covered with tarpaulins and spread over a huge area of the warehouse, all to be sold at public auction. The auctioneers, rotating in shifts, all wearing western hats and string ties and calling one another Colonel in twangy country voices, mopped sweat from their brows as they cajoled the crowd to spirited bidding for hours on end.

The sale continued over two weekends, and Dr. Klenner's packrat instincts proved profitable. His large collections of cut glass, German beer steins, clocks, miniature wagons, Lionel trains, and toys still in original boxes turned out to be sound investments, all fetching handsome prices.

Scattered through the mounds of material offered for sale were many personal items belonging to Fritz—his childhood Roy Rogers lunchbox (which brought thirty-five dollars); a ceramic crèche made for him by his favorite aunt, Marie; some of his grammar school homework; a scrapbook about the Civil War that he made in school; a postcard he sent home from a weekend jaunt to the beach at Panama City, Florida, while he was finishing high school in Atlanta ("Dear Mom, Dad. The waters wet and suns hot and I wish you all where [sic] here and I was there. Love Fritz"); his diploma from Woodward Academy, his only symbol of genuine success. But the objects that drew the most comment from the hundreds of people who came to the sale were the toy guns, hundreds of them—so many that they were sold by the box and barrel—all well used, Fritz's vast childhood arsenal that later was replaced by a real arsenal nearly as big and far more deadly (the real arsenal, returned to Annie Hill Klenner by the police, was not offered at the auction, for it had already been sold to the Reidsville police chief).

Tucked into one of those boxes of toy guns was a large cardboard poster handlettered in Fritz's childish scrawl. "Guns. Guards. NOW!" it said, then added, "Please come to my fort"—a plaintive plea from a lonely and frightened child who found comfort only in guns and bunkers.

In the clutter of Susie's apartment, her friend Annette Hunt found a copy of a book *When Bad Things Happen to Good People* by Rabbi Harold Kushner. Susie had written her name inside it and dated it 1982, the year she began to draw close to Fritz. Throughout the book, passages had been underlined.

In the last chapter, Kushner wrote of a survivor of the Holocaust who had suffered unbearable personal tragedy, yet he chose to focus on the future, not the past, refusing to search for villains, deciding that "accusing other people of being responsible for your misery only makes a lonely person lonelier. Life," he concluded, "has to be lived for something, not just against something." Susie had underlined the last sentence.

A few pages later, Susie had underlined this: "You're a good person, and you deserve better. Let me come and sit with you so that you'll know that you are not alone."

On the front flyleaf, Susie had written: "What each of us makes of our loneliness is the individual stamp of our destiny."

"It's almost like an epitaph," Annette said.

Ironically, in the weeks following Susie's death, her namesake aunt, Judge Susie Sharp, was reading her own copy of that book, given to her by a friend, although she was finding little comfort in it.

"I don't know that I'll ever have any more peace on this earth," she said.

Frequently, she was awakened in the night to the sound of Susie and her boys crying.

"It's just unbelievable," she said. "Those sweet little boys."

Susie had been her favorite niece, and although in the time of her greatest need Susie had turned to Annie Hill, not her, Judge Sharp still held her close in her heart.

"All my special things were going to Susie," she said. "I don't know what to do with them now."

Two years later, as her eightieth birthday neared, Judge Sharp still hadn't decided what to do with her special things. Seven months earlier, she had been struck by a car while taking her morning walk and was seriously injured. The effects of her injuries made it impossible for her to take long walks anymore and difficult even to stand at her desk for work.

Two years and many revelations had not diminished her belief that Susie was completely under the control of Fritz.

"I don't believe Susie killed anybody. I don't believe Fritz wanted her to. I believe he wanted to do that himself."

Suddenly, Judge Sharp was struck by a memory of Susie as a little girl. An Easter. Back when Bob and Florence were newly married and living in the little rented house in Winston-Salem, before Bob got his big promotion at R. J. Reynolds, at a time when they had little money. She smiled as she recalled it.

"Florence didn't have a new hat or a new dress, but she dressed up Susie. She had a new dress and new shoes and little white gloves. 'Isn't she cute?' Florence said. She was, and I loved her dearly, too."

Clearly, time had not diminished the pain of all that had happened. Asked about the emotional damage she had suffered, Judge Sharp replied, "Oh, dear, I wouldn't try to describe it. It's just a constant source of grief. There's no way anybody could come to terms with it. You keep wondering if there was anything you could have done. But none of us had the full information. There just won't be an end of it. It'll haunt us until we die."

*　　*　　*

Soon after the Newsom murders, Frances Miller and her daughters, Nancy Dunn and Debbie Parham, filled out victim impact statements for Allen Gentry.

Debbie called her experience "unbearable emotional devastation." She told of newly imposed fears, suspicions, depression. "My life will never, ever be the same," she wrote. "It seems as if the hurt will never go away."

"Unbearable," wrote Nancy. "Life cannot be normal again. My torment for my mother . . . cannot be expressed."

Wrote Frances: "I've lost all my family members other than my children, and because of these deaths, our homeplace, the well from which I and my children draw so much love, peace and spiritual support. I'm devastated that my beloved mother, who taught so many others to live and love in peace, died violently and had to witness as she died the brutal murder of her loved ones. Grief and rage will be with me the rest of my life."

On a rainy Sunday in August, three months after the murders, Frances sat at the scene of the violence in the living room of the big house on Valley Road that had been the family homeplace for nearly half a century. She had come to make the house ready for market.

"This was the most nonviolent place on earth," she said. "It's where everybody came for spiritual renewal. It was so peaceful, and the lesson of love was always here. To think that kind of violence had to happen here and destroy that for everybody forever. It's like a family has been raped."

The house did not sell for nearly a year and a half, until the end of 1986. On Easter weekend of 1987, Frances, her daughter Nancy and son, David, drove to Winston-Salem to participate in the ritualistic scrubbing of family headstones at God's Acre, the Moravian cemetery at Old Salem. Nanna had always done that in preparation for the Easter sunrise service, and they were intent on continuing the tradition.

Afterward, they drove by the family homeplace without stopping. The new owners had removed Paw-Paw's little fence in front and drastically pruned back the huge boxwoods that Paw-Paw and Nanna had allowed to overtake the sidewalk leading to the front door.

"Looks nice, huh, Mom?" said Nancy.

"I guess it's better to have somebody living there," Frances responded.

At Forsyth Memorial Gardens, a couple of miles from the house, the family arranged fresh flowers over the graves of Paw-Paw and Nanna, Bob and Florence. As Frances stood silently in a cold drizzle, looking at her mother's grave, she began crying softly, and her son and daughter moved to comfort her at each side. They stood for several minutes, arms locked, before Nancy and David led their mother back to her car.

"It never gets any easier," Frances said, dabbing at her tears with a tissue.

Those who knew Rob Newsom marveled at the strength with which he faced the loss of his parents, his grandmother, his sister, and nephews. He credited his ability to deal with his problems to family, friends, neighbors, his church, and fellow members of Alcoholics Anonymous, who rallied to his and his family's support.

"This has been an uplifting experience in a peculiar sort of way," he said soon after the deaths. "My wife and I have found that with all the love and care and concern that we have been richly blessed."

Shortly before his parents' murders, he had been declared cured of organic brain syndrome, the condition that came in the aftermath of his heavy drinking and caused the short-term memory loss that led to surrendering his law license, and he was strong in his resolve not to risk his gains by turning again to alcohol.

Soon after his sister's death, Rob gave up his job as an alcoholism counselor for Guilford County to attend to his family's affairs. He hired a lawyer and a private investigator and took other steps to protect his parents' and his sister's estates.

He and his family chose to remain in his parents' house in Greensboro, and they began remodeling it to suit their own needs. The renovation was done by Christmas 1985, and over the mantel of the living room fireplace was hung the framed antique needlepoint quotation from Joshua that had been on the wall in Nanna's living room, where his parents and grandmother had died: "As for me and my house, we will serve the Lord."

In May of 1986, Rob regained his law license, and when the reason for its surrender was announced, he spoke publicly about his alcoholism for the first time. A few weeks later, on the first anniversary of the explosion that took his sister's life, he spoke, too, about the effects of the previous year's events on himself and his family.

"I think everybody has one thing or another that's hardest for them to accept," he told Tom Sieg of the *Winston-Salem Journal*. "But everybody's back to activities and to doing things and working and earning their living and getting on with life.

"I think people are doing pretty well. I don't see any signs of anyone in the family just falling into deep depression and being unable to function. I think that's what you have to avoid."

Despite his upbeat mood, Rob told Jim Schlosser of the *Greensboro News & Record* that he still had difficult days.

"You think the grief is behind you, then Daddy's roses bloom at the house and it reminds you. Or something exciting will happen and I'll say to myself, 'I can't wait to tell Dad,' and you realize you can't."

Rob opened a law office in a shopping mall not far from his home and returned to practice, but he closed the office in the summer of 1987, when he was appointed an assistant public defender. As he was about to be sworn in, he said later, a wish came to mind: that his mother and father could see the ceremony.

"My parents had awaited that day when I would be well enough to go back to practicing law and do something that I would enjoy doing," he said.

The violence and destruction wrought by his cousin Fritz still haunted him, still produced occasional fits of depression and wakeful nights.

"I have had a recurring nightmare ever since this happened," he said. "I dream that I'm running down a road, just an asphalt road, and that humongous Blazer of his is coming up behind me, and I'm realizing I'm not going to make it. I'm running toward something, someplace where

I have a gun or something, and I'm realizing that I'm not going to make it."

His cousin's actions also gave him a different perspective on crime and the role of police in preventing and dealing with it.

"I have really come to believe that this whole establishment here is a joke," he said, as he sat in his small office in the county court building of Greensboro's governmental center. He motioned toward the nearby police department. "This whole fiction that the people over there in the lower floors of the municipal building protect us is a sick joke. They don't do doodly squat. They can't.

"Anglo-Saxon jurisprudence just was not designed to handle massive violations of criminal law. It was not designed to handle sociopaths with automatic weapons. The police cannot and do not protect us. They avenge us sometimes, but they don't prevent anything.

"That may be why the cops are still agitated over this case, one reason Dr. Lynch is so agitated, is that it is an incidence of utter police failure. I'm not blaming the individual officer. In my personal opinion, they all did their duty. But the job description is all wrong if what you want to do is prevent something like this. They can't."

In the wake of his parents' murders, Rob sought permission to view the police photographs of their bodies. "I don't know why I did it," he said. "I just had to." Those images were indelibly seared in his brain, and along with his cousin's actions and his new perspective on the police, served to create a permanent sense of fear and distrust.

"My doors still stay double-bolted," he said. "I'm always going to have a barking dog and there's always going to be buckshot for my shotgun. I do not intend for anybody to find me lying on the floor the way my daddy was. Or for my children to see my wife looking the way my mother looked. Not ever."

By the fall of 1987, Rob had come to have a different perspective on his sister's role in those brutal deaths. He still was convinced, he said, that she wasn't present at any of the murders and that she hadn't conspired with Fritz to commit them. "I'm also convinced she could have suspected he had done it and silently approved," he said. "I think what it comes down to is she didn't want to know the truth and she never would have confronted him about it. I think she had to have noticed that people who were causing her problems were dying. It's conceivable to me that she could've announced to Fritz that Mother and Daddy were helping Tom with the suspicion that Daddy was going to end up dead before he got to court. I think at most my sister suspected and just didn't do anything because it seemed to her that problems were being solved."

Several months after his sons' deaths, Tom Lynch appeared before a committee of the New Mexico legislature to testify in behalf of new child custody laws that would give equal consideration to both parents. Although he was asked to become active in fathers' rights and antigun groups, he declined; he was no activist and knew that he never could be. He and Kathy tried to resume normal activities. He continued his dental practice. Kathy enrolled again at the University of New Mexico to complete a degree in speech pathology.

They made a concerted effort to keep busy, especially on weekends. They spent many weekends skiing in the nearby mountains, others prowling the desert in the beat-up, four-wheel-drive pickup truck that Tom bought. Realizing that they needed things to look forward to, they planned trips. They flew to Hawaii. They spent two weeks learning to sail in the Virgin Islands. But memories always tagged along.

"We always say, 'The boys would have so much fun here,'" Kathy said.

Nothing seemed to offer more than momentary relief for their sorrow, pain, anger—and guilt.

"Nobody will ever know what we've been through," Kathy said nearly two years after the boys' deaths. "Just the feeling of helplessness, the sense of loss and emptiness.

"Why? Why? Why? Why us? Why the boys? Why not save the boys? At least one of the boys. My attitude about religion has totally just gone down the toilet. Life isn't fair, but it ought to be just a little bit fair. If we had just saved the boys. . . .

"People tell us, 'What you're feeling is normal.' That's

reassuring, but it doesn't make you feel any better. There are some days when you just don't even want to get out of bed. It's hard sometimes just to do everyday tasks. I'll get days when all I want to do is cry. Nights, I'll sit up with Tom sometimes until two or three in the morning and he just sits and cries. He gets so angry, and he'll throw things, and then he'll just sit and cry.

"Everybody says, 'time, time, time.' But neither of us can go through a day without thinking about it, and I don't think we ever will. There'll be some little thing that will trigger it."

Seeking relief from daily reminders, Tom and Kathy took down the boys' bunk beds and put their bikes and other belongings in storage with Delores's and Janie's things. But other things still caused the pain to surge to the surface. Something as simple as the song "Hotel California" coming from a radio would do it. Jim had loved that song and had gone around singing it throughout one of his summer visits.

Tom struggled to understand why his life had come to such a point.

"It's hard to explain," he said. "I'm not a goody-two-shoes guy. You know, I've done things in my life that aren't nice, but I have always lived pretty much by what's right and wrong and by the laws and everything has always worked out for me. I wanted to play basketball in college and it worked out. I had a couple of bad breaks and I didn't play much but that was all right; I got to play. I wanted to be a doctor and I got to be a doctor. I wanted to do certain things and I always worked hard for them and when I was patient and worked at it, it always happened. We were being patient and working at this and doing exactly the right thing, and we were within just minutes of having everything come out. To have it end like that was . . . I don't know. You know, it's hard to describe. You have got to this point in your life, and you had a couple of sons, and you're going to pass a little heritage on and teach them things to make things easier for them, and now I had a bunch of money and I could leave them with some money, too, and it's just . . . I mean, it's . . . so sad."

In his grief and anger, Tom wanted to strike back, to

do something, as he put it, "for the boys," and he retained a North Carolina lawyer to investigate suing the SBI for not taking proper precautions to protect John and Jim in the attempt to arrest Fritz. When the lawyer had not made satisfactory progress after nearly a year, Tom retained a Greensboro law firm. In April of 1987, that firm filed the first actions on Tom's behalf: suits against the estates of Susie, Bob and Florence, and Nanna. The suits maintained that Susie was involved in the murders of her parents and her grandmother and either killed or was "culpably negligent in the deaths of her children." Susie's inheritance from her parents and grandmother, estimated at perhaps $500,000, rightfully belonged to the boys' estates, the suits claimed.

Rob Newsom expressed surprise about the lawsuits. Despite their differing views about Susie's involvement in the murders, Tom and Rob had agreed to respect one another's feelings and had maintained cordial relations. On Thanksgiving of 1985, Tom and Kathy had flown to North Carolina and spent a weekend at the beach with Rob and Alice and their children. Rob had visited Tom and Kathy in Albuquerque.

"There is no vendetta against the Newsoms," Tom told a reporter when the suits were filed. "It's just a matter of going after some information to see if anything was coming to the boys."

"We feel bad about this," Kathy said. "We're just doing what our attorneys are advising."

Soon after the suits were filed, Rob flew to Albuquerque to attempt to reach a settlement with Tom, but they came to no agreement. In January 1988, a judge dismissed the suits, but Tom's lawyers appealed and the case seemed headed for court.

Twelve days before the second anniversary of the boys' deaths, Tom's lawyers filed suit against the SBI, the Forsyth County Sheriff's Department, the Greensboro Police Department, and most of the officers involved in the attempt to arrest Fritz. The suit charged "deliberate indifference and recklessness" for the boys' lives and "gross negligence" that would "shock the conscience." "Little, if any, rational planning" was used in the arrest attempt, according to the suit, and once Fritz started shooting, the officers "abandoned reason and their duty of care for innocent persons and became consumed with taking Klenner at any and all costs, including innocent life."

The decision to sue the law enforcement agencies—it was primarily the SBI that was the target—had not been easy for Tom. He'd been warned that it would be a hard and painful fight, but he felt he had to do it for John and Jim. The suit was dismissed by a judge in September 1987, but Tom's lawyers appealed the decision.

"I'm resolved," Tom said. "I won't be beaten down. My demons chase me around every night and I beat them down and I get up the next morning and go on."

More than two years after the deaths of the boys, Tom and Kathy were thinking of selling their house on La Mancha. It held too many memories.

"We really want to move," Kathy said. "I just think we need to start over."

They were looking at land, considering house plans—and thinking of having children.

"We're just going to kind of let it happen," Kathy said of having children. "If it happens, that's fine."

"If we ever do have kids," Tom added, "they'll be the luckiest kids in the world. There won't be any kids who will get any more attention or any more love."

AFTERWORD

I set out to write this book with two major goals: to learn to my own satisfaction what had happened in this immense family tragedy, and, more important, to understand why.

I failed at both.

I knew that I never would know exactly what happened. Some details simply could not be known because all the people who knew them were dead. I knew, too, that some people who could shed light on what had happened would choose not to talk with me, and that was indeed the case. Still, I hoped to learn enough to convince myself with sufficient certainty at least where the major guilt lay. But after more than two years of searching and talking with hundreds of people, I still lacked that certainty.

I had no doubt of Fritz's guilt in the murders, but of Susie's I could not be sure. If Susie and the boys had not died, she probably never would have faced charges for her parents' and grandmother's murders, for the police simply had no evidence against her. And although she surely would have been indicted in Kentucky, the chances of convincing a jury of her guilt beyond reasonable doubt seemed slight.

The murders of her children were another matter, however. If she didn't kill them herself—and I was convinced that she did—neither did she make any apparent effort to save them. Were their murders evidence of her complicity in the other slayings or merely the outgrowth of a desperate and deranged woman caught in a hopeless situation?

Was she indeed, as the police and Tom thought, the mastermind manipulator, or was she, as some of her family members still believed, the manipulated victim? When two manipulators come together, as Fritz and Susie did, who ends up manipulated? I never could be sure.

What bothered me most, however, was that I couldn't understand why Susie had come to so horrible a fate. What in her past had led her there?

Early in my work on this book, I wrote to Dr. Donald T. Lunde, a forensic psychiatrist and professor in the Stanford University Law School. Dr. Lunde, the author of *Murder and Madness*, is reputed to be one of America's foremost experts on multiple murder. He was involved in two of the nation's most sensational serial murder cases—the unsolved Zodiac killings of northern California, and the Hillside stranglings in the Los Angeles area. I sent Dr. Lunde an extensive series of newspaper articles that I wrote about the Lynch and Newsom murders, including lengthy articles on the backgrounds of both Fritz and Susie. I knew that he could not analyze the motivations of dead people from perceptions in newspaper articles, but I hoped that he might offer some impressions and insights that would lead to understanding.

"It is difficult to say what motivated Fritz Klenner," he wrote in reply. "It would seem to me that he was not suffering from one of the classical mental disorders sometimes associated with this kind of behavior (e.g., paranoid schizophrenia). I would wonder if he was using drugs which are frequently associated with paranoia (e.g., amphetamines or cocaine). Susie Lynch is even more mysterious, but my impression is that she came under the domination of Fritz with regard to his paranoid ideas."

While I had uncovered no evidence that Fritz had used cocaine, it was known that he always carried amphetamines, and he certainly had access to whatever prescription drugs he desired. But drugs alone could not account for his paranoia, I thought, and it seemed unlikely that they played a large role in the murders. Drug-induced killings come in a sudden burst of rage. Fritz's murders were coldly calculated and savored.

Although I make no claim to special knowledge of psychology or psychiatry, I felt that I understood what had led Fritz to murder. The blame seemed clearly to lie with his father. The kindly doctor that patients saw at the office was a tyrant at home, and while Fritz loved him and sought desperately to please him, he also feared and resented him. Fritz never wanted to be a doctor. From childhood, he dreamed secretly of being a soldier or a spy, yet he never could bring himself to stand up to his father and seize his own life—and he hated him for it.

While he appeared to seek to please his father, Fritz's actions all seemed designed, perhaps subconsciously, eventually to bring his father pain. How else to explain his failure to finish college for lack of a single course—and that course German, the tongue of the beloved homeland of his father's family? Surely, Fritz had to know that his father would someday find out that he had never been to medical school and that it would bring him great grief. (There are indications, incidentally, that Fritz's parents were told as early as 1979 that he was simply posing as a medical student but they refused to believe it; that was two years before Fritz's wife and former mistress joined to make certain that they knew.)

My suspicion is that Fritz wanted to kill his father, then take his own life. I thought the stories he made up of attacks on his father were his own secret desires. But just as he was never able to stand up to this all-powerful presence in his life, neither could he bring himself to destroy it. After his father's death, when he could hurt him no more, the tumultuous mix of emotions and long-simmering rage within Fritz had to erupt, and the murders and grandly dramatic suicide that resulted seemed aimed at his father. It was no coincidence, I thought, that the Newsom murders fell on the same weekend that Dr. Klenner had died a year earlier, just as I felt sure that it was no simple mistake that Fritz would involve in the murders somebody so vulnerable and certain to betray him as Ian Perkins. I suspected that deep inside Fritz wanted the police to know he had done it, needed them to give him the courage to go out in his vision of glory, and the ultimate purpose was to disgrace his father's name and destroy the reputation that Fritz knew he never could live up to.

But how, finally, to explain Susie's role in all of this?

year and a half after Dr. Lunde told me that he found
er mysterious, so, too, did I, despite months of addi-
onal research into her background.

As I was nearing the end of my work on this book,
usie's aunt Frances Miller asked me how I felt about it.
told her that I was troubled, particularly about my
omprehension of Susie's role.

"I just don't understand why," I said.

"Neither does any of us," she said.

Several weeks later, on a stormy July afternoon, I told
he same thing to Rob Newsom.

"To me," he said, "the simplest part is my sister."

How so?

"Why would somebody have this incredible psychotic
utburst over extended visitation rights? Because we're
ot talking about custody here. Dr. Lynch wasn't asking
or custody of his children. He was asking for a couple of
ore weeks to visit in the summer. What triggers a
igantic psychotic outburst over two more weeks of visi-
ation? What single mother doesn't want her husband to
ave two more weeks of visitation? Say, please, you
now, six weeks of freedom instead of four.

"My theory is that my sister's problem essentially was
hat she wanted to believe the fantasies that Fritz Klenner
oun for her about the danger she was in, about the evil
f her ex-husband, about the reality of the threat he
osed to her and her children, that she wanted to believe
hat.

"Why would she want to believe it? I think it has to do
ith a seriously flawed character, flawed in this respect,
hat my sister believed that once a person did something
rong, there was no forgiveness for it.

"My sister despised the parable of the prodigal son.
he thought it was unjust, unfair, and she didn't believe
esus said it, that it was made up. So in my sister's mind,
ou always had to be right because the consequences of
eing wrong were awesome. So when her marriage failed,
had to be Tom Lynch's fault. She had not been back in
orth Carolina a month after their separation when she
old me how furious she was with Mother. I said, 'Why?'
ecause Mother had dared to suggest that maybe Susie
ould have done something different to save their mar-

riage. Mother and Daddy were suggesting already at tha
early stage that she not be bitter, that she try to hav
amicable relationships with Tom for the sake of the chi
dren, that she examine herself and her own motives an
see where maybe she had contributed to the failure
her marriage, and this made her furious.

"I don't know anything to call that but a sort of spiri
tual sickness. I think my sister's sense of self-worth wa
derived from a sense of being right. If she was wrong, sh
was worthless. If she was right, she was worthy. I thin
that's how she saw the world and her place in it. That i
sick thinking, and you can see the price she paid for i
and lots of other people, too.

"How she got it, I don't know. I've pondered and
have no earthly idea. I know she didn't hear it in St
Paul's Episcopal Church. That's not the message preache
there. I know she never heard it from my mother an
father. My grandfather Newsom was a Calvinist, and tha
was part of his religious thought. Now understand, h
didn't live that way, though. He didn't live a hard an
unforgiving life. He was one of the most forgiving peopl
I know. But he talked it. I remember him once saying h
never apologized in his life because he didn't have any
thing to apologize for. Maybe things like that leave a
impression on a little kid's mind, I don't know. Mayb
my sister began to think that way because she did sens
she was very different from the children around her a
school. I'm not sure where it came from exactly. Th
only person who could tell us, I guess, maybe she coul
have found it someday, you know, after two or thre
years of hard analysis, is Susie, but she's not here to d
it."

Wasn't it true, though, I asked, that Susie was neve
one to see her own faults?

"That's right. If you ever read Scott Peck's books, i
his book *People Who Lie*, that's his definition of an ev
person, is a person who refuses to look within, refuses t
see the plank in their eye, refuses self-analysis and i
always scapegoating other people, places, and things fo
their own dilemmas."

Was that Susie?

"I agree it was my sister. I think there was a very rea

sense in which my sister was an evil person. I don't think it's the sense in which Dr. Lynch believes it."

With the subject of evil broached, I asked how he viewed it.

"I think there are different kinds. I'm coming more and more to subscribe to John Steinbeck's theory. Steinbeck believed that there were some creatures on the face of the earth that looked like human beings, they had human parents, but they were really monsters. The mother in *East of Eden*, Cathy, was one such character, and I've come to buy that a little bit."

Perhaps not so strangely, a few weeks earlier, when I was talking with Rob's aunt Frances, she had touched on a similar theory.

"You can talk about all kinds and aspects of mental illness," she said, "but I don't think that explains some people. I sometimes think there are people in the world who are just by nature mean. It's almost like a touch of autism, where the rest of the world doesn't matter. We'll never understand that kind of mind."

She had been talking about her niece, and I wondered now if Rob, too, thought the Steinbeck vision of evil applied to Susie.

"I don't think that's true of my sister, because she didn't show all the propensities that people like that show. I think it's true of Fritz. I think Fritz was a monster. I think an examination of the photographs of my mother's body is all that's needed to show that. I feel pretty strongly that only a monster would have done that to my mother."

More than two years after his parents' murders, Rob had hired a lawyer, investigators, and a forensics expert from California to dig deeper into Fritz's background. Part of the reason was to help defend his sister's estate, but there was more to it.

"I really feel like I understand my sister," he said. "I may be wrong, but I think that what I've described is the way that her brain worked. I'm not sure that I understand Fritz. I've got some questions myself that just interest me personally. I want to know more about Fritz. I think it's important to know what fuels these incredible sociopaths. It's probably important for, you know, like serial killers, it's probably important not to execute them. I mean, they're a national resource. If we can learn enough about them, we may be able to stop them, and I just feel like knowing about Fritz is important. If anything is important in all of this, it's how do we create a Mr. Hyde like that, number one, and number two, how do we keep ourselves from being victims of people like that?"

Rob thought that he understood some of Fritz's motivations.

"I think there was a pile of pent-up hatred. I think that Fritz felt that the rest of the family felt that Dr. Klenner, Annie Hill, him, and everybody in the Klenner household was eccentric, superstitious, and laughable. And I think that he hated us for it. I think he misjudged that a little bit. I think people felt that Dr. Klenner was in many ways eccentric, that his political views were laughable, but I never heard anybody in my family question Dr. Klenner's brilliance or his creativity."

This brought up a theory I had been mulling. Did Rob think it possible that the Klenners might have set out to alienate Susie from her family, to claim and conquer her as the prize fruit on the Sharp family tree, the one bearing the name of the resented family matriarch and most successful member? Was it a means of striking back at the family for its failure to fully accept Dr. Klenner?

"Susie was always drawn to the Klenners," he said. "She always liked them, even as a little girl, and Fred was especially fond of Susie. And when Susie got back to North Carolina after her separation, and my mother and father were telling her to do things like examine yourself and see where you might be at fault, all she had to do was ride up the road to the Klenner household where everybody was saying, 'You were perfect. It was that son of a bitch that caused all of this.' It wasn't healthy, but it was what she wanted to hear. I think the Klenners did take a certain perverse pleasure to my sister being closer to them than to her own parents, in preferring their advice to her own parents' advice, no question in my mind about that. And for some of the same reasons that you mentioned. They're saying, 'Aha, you high and mighty Sharps, one of your own has to turn to us.'"

Weren't Susie's spiteful acts toward her family and Tom a form of violence? I asked.

"Well, they express feelings of vengeance and hatred, yeah. You know, the difference between the way I look at my sister and the wrongness of Fritz goes beyond the way she acts out or chose to act out. There's a big difference between spitefulness and meanness and scapegoating and a refusal to do any honest self-examination, on the one hand, and being a cold, calculating, premeditated life taker. There are orders of magnitude to wrongness and evil, and to my mind Fritz Klenner hit the platinum-label level."

So did he believe that Susie was a victim of evil that she built herself, one spiteful and unforgiving act upon another, until it was out of control, while Fritz was simply born evil, or possessed with it at such an early age that it merely took a catalyst for it to assume command?

"Yes, I do. And they happened to come together."

TRUE CRIME AT ITS BEST

MY LIFE IN THE NYPD
    by James Wagner with Patrick Picciarell

James "Jimmy the Wags" Wagner takes readers behind
the badge and into the daily drama of working New
York City's toughest job in New York City's toughest
precinct. It's the NYPD as no one has ever seen it
before—from a street cop who walked the walk
through the turbulent 1960s, the violent 1970s, and the
drug-fueled 1980s.

FATAL VISION
    by Joe McGinniss

The writer Joe McGinniss went to visit Dr. Jeffery
MacDonald, with the intent of writing a book that
would help clear his name. But after extensive
interviews and painstaking research, a very different
picture emerged. This is the electrifying story of a
Princeton-educated Green Beret convicted of slaying
his wife and children.

"A haunting story told in detail." –*Newsweek*